# PATTERN FOR PEACE

# PATTERN FOR PEACE

*Catholic Statements on*
*International Order*

Edited by
Harry W. Flannery

N/P
## THE NEWMAN PRESS
Westminster, Maryland
1962

*Nihil Obstat:* Edward A. Cerny, S.S.,
    *Censor Librorum*

*Imprimatur:* Francis P. Keough, D.D.
    *Archbishop of Baltimore*
November 6, 1961

IN MEMORY OF MY MOTHER
*Who Gave Me a Pattern for Life*

# Preface

FOR the last twenty years, my lectures and talks have always included an exhortation to my audience to read, study, and form discussion groups for a better understanding of the international encyclicals. For it is my belief that if the Catholic people had understood more fully the statements of recent pontiffs on international problems, there might have been no World War II at all, and there would have been certainly a more effective United Nations.

Within these encyclicals can be found wise statements on such vital issues as international organizations, juridical institutions, disarmament, an international police force, the rights of minorities, and the responsibilities of colonial powers. Within recent years, Pope Pius XII had even discussed the problems of nuclear power and space explorations. Readers of these documents will come to a realization, I trust, of the depth, scope and significance of the study and wisdom of the Holy Fathers of recent times. May this anthology also inspire a greater desire in the readers to unite with all men of good will in calling upon our leaders to build that type of world, which, as it is firmly based on principles, gives the best hope for peace.

Recently I discovered how difficult it is for most people to obtain copies of the encyclicals and other statements on international affairs. Copies of these major papal statements were necessary for a seminar to be held for the chaplains of the Christian Family Movement and the Young Christian Workers Movement at which I was to participate. Copies were unavailable in parish and retreat-house pamphlet racks, religious book stores, and appeals to publishers and to the National Catholic Welfare Conference offices disclosed that many of these principal statements were now out of print. The necessity and usefulness of a volume that would include the major encyclicals and statements on international topics from the time of Pope Leo XIII to the present seemed more than evident. The result is here presented in *Pattern for Peace*.

May I at this point extend my appreciation and gratitude to the Right Reverend Monsignor George Higgins, director of the National Catholic Welfare Conference Department of Social Action, to the Right Reverend Monsignor Harry C. Koenig, S.T.D., editor of *Principles for Peace* (published in 1943 in behalf of the Bishops' Committee on the Pope's Peace Points), to Alba Zizzamia of the National Catholic Welfare Conference office for United Nations Affairs, who has written many excellent articles on international affairs, and to Eleanor Waters, Secretary of the Catholic Association for International Peace, for their assistance and suggestions as well as their generous gift of valuable hours.

In the preparation of this volume, I have followed the pattern set by *Principles for Peace* which included statements of the Holy Fathers and Vatican officials on these topics up to the time of its publication in 1943. I have omitted a number of documents, which in the opinion of others might have been included, because of my previous decision to limit my selections to statements on international order with the consequent omission of many significant writings on the social order. This, however, by no means, indicates that international order is possible without social justice; rather the limitations of space demand the exclusion of these many valuable documents. For instance, much can be said in favor of the inclusion of *Quadragesimo Anno*, but if that were included, logic would suggest that *Rerum Novarum* and other major social encyclicals should not be passed by.

*Divini Redemptoris* (on atheistic communism) has been included in part for obvious reasons, although it is considered a social encyclical. My first impulse was to include as well the excellent address to the World Congress of the Lay Apostolate by Pope Pius XII, but much the same argument was presented to me for its omission as on the social encyclicals. Pope Pius X's address on "The Teaching Authority of the Church" appealed to me because of the importance of the subject, but I was persuaded to content myself with some remarks on this matter that are made later in this preface. Some statements on European Union and on the Food and Agriculture Organization were omitted because there were so many of them and in some cases repetitious of the ones included. I hope that I have selected the best and most useful on each topic.

The statements on international order made by the bishops of the United States have been included because these excellent documents aid materially in understanding and applying the papal statements. "The Pattern for Peace," written and subscribed to by Catholic, Protestant and Jewish leaders prior to the San Francisco conference establishing the United Nations has been added to remind us that the moral principles for realization of international peace, as enunciated by the popes, are basic principles, on which all who believe in God can agree.

Pius XII told us that world peace can be realized if "Catholics and non-Catholics will labor together in the task." He appealed to "those who, while not belonging in the Church, feel themselves united with us in this hour of perhaps irrevocable decisions."

Catholics have a responsibility to be familiar with and to try to apply the principles set forth in the encyclicals. Theologians have made it plain that although the pope does not speak *ex cathedra* in encyclicals, the Holy Father has the right and duty to draw upon "the treasury of right reason and Divine Revelation," and "urge in season and out of season the entire moral law." The popes themselves have referred to this factor, and the Catholic bishops of the United States took up the subject in their 1940 statement. The question arose then about the application of the social encyclicals, which are fortunately now fairly well known and applied, but the principle is the same for other encyclicals. "Because these are moral principles and spiritual truths, jurisdiction in expounding their full scope and obligation belongs to the Church which Christ established as the teacher of men in this world," stated the bishops.

"We ardently desire that more and more attention be given to the study of this (social) doctrine," Pope John XXIII said in *Mater et Magistra*. "While we note with satisfaction that in some schools it has been taught with success for years, We strongly urge that it be included as an item in the required curriculum in Catholic schools of every kind, particularly in seminaries. It should be part of the religious instruction programs of parishes and of associations of the lay apostolate. It should be publicized by every modern means of mass communication—daily newspapers and periodicals, publications of both a scientific and a popular nature, radio and television.

"In this task of communication, Our beloved sons of the laity can make a great contribution. They can do this by making their actions conform to it and by zealously striving to make others understand its significance. They should realize that the truth and efficacy of this teaching can most easily be demonstrated when they show that it offers an effective solution for present-day difficulties. . . . It is not enough merely to publicize a social doctrine; it must be translated into action. This is particularly true of Christian social doctrine, whose light is truth, whose objective is justice and whose driving force is love."

To again quote Pius XII, "We nourish the hope that all our sons and daughters scattered over the earth may have a lively consciousness of their collective and individual responsibility for the setting up of a public order conformable to the fundamental exigencies of the human and Christian conscience." May this volume help them to know the principles for peace, and "not to be satisfied with good intentions and fine projects, but to proceed courageously to put them into practice. Neither should they hesitate to join forces with those who, remaining outside our ranks, are none the less in agreement with the social teaching of the Catholic Church and are disposed to follow the road that she has marked out."

September 10, 1961                                              HWF
Washington, D. C.

# Table of Contents

Preface . . . . . . . . . . . . . vii

### LEO XIII
The Bonds of Peace . . . . . . . . . . . 1
The Might of Law . . . . . . . . . . 2
An Institution of Mediation . . . . . . . . 4
Nationalistic Rivalry . . . . . . . . . . 5

### PIUS X
Organizations for Peace . . . . . . . . . . 7

### BENEDICT XV
Respect for the Rights of Others . . . . . . . 9
The Role of Catholics . . . . . . . . . 10
Proposals for Peace . . . . . . . . . . 10
The Means to Disarmament . . . . . . . . 11
The Effects of War . . . . . . . . . . 12
Brotherly Love . . . . . . . . . . . 13
Justice and Charity . . . . . . . . . . 13
A Lasting Treaty . . . . . . . . . . . 18
The Fount of True Peace . . . . . . . . 19

### PIUS XI
Mutual Confidence . . . . . . . . . . 21
The Peace of Christ . . . . . . . . . . 22
Reparations . . . . . . . . . . . 29
Interpretation of Letter on Reparations . . . . . 30
The Holy See and the League of Nations . . . . . 32
Relief Aid to the Russian People . . . . . . . 33
The Holy See and National Disputes . . . . . . 34
True Peace . . . . . . . . . . . . 34
Selfish Nationalism . . . . . . . . . . 36
The Common International Welfare . . . . . . 36
Nazi Germany and the Church . . . . . . . . 38

Atheistic Communism . . . . . . . . . . 45
Exaggerated Nationalism . . . . . . . . 71
The State and the Individual . . . . . . . 71

## PIUS XII

How Can There Be Peace? . . . . . . . . . 73
A Plea for Peace . . . . . . . . . . . 74
A Plea to Belligerents . . . . . . . . . 76
Function of the State in the Modern World . . . . 77
The Cult of Might Against Right . . . . . . . 98
Fundamental Points for a Just and Honorable Peace . . 99
Necessary Premises for a New Order . . . . . . 102
Essential Conditions for a Just and Lasting Peace . . 104
The Internal Order of States . . . . . . . 108
Future Peace . . . . . . . . . . . . 115
The Problem of Democracy . . . . . . . . 118
Nazism and Peace . . . . . . . . . . 131
Moral Prerequisites for a Free and Lasting Peace . . . 141
Points for the Attainment of Peace . . . . . . 145
The World Is Far From Peace . . . . . . . 153
Pray for Peace . . . . . . . . . . . 163
For a United Europe . . . . . . . . . . 164
The Christian Will for Peace . . . . . . . 167
Barriers to Peace . . . . . . . . . . . 172
World Federal Government . . . . . . . . 178
Contribution of the Church to Peace . . . . . . 181
"Blessed Be the Peacemaker" . . . . . . . 192
International Penal Law . . . . . . . . . 196
The International Community . . . . . . . 212
Modern Technology and Peace . . . . . . . 222
The Threat of ABC Warfare . . . . . . . 234
War and Peace . . . . . . . . . . . 236
Coexistence: Its Meaning and Its Future . . . . 240
International Reconciliation . . . . . . . . 253
Food, Agriculture, and Human Society . . . . 265
Nuclear Weapons and Armament Control . . . . 269
No Peace in Materialism . . . . . . . . . 274
Faith, Peace, and the Atom . . . . . . . . 276
An Appeal for Peace . . . . . . . . . . 278
The Contradiction of Our Age . . . . . . . 282
The Peaceful Use of Nuclear Energy . . . . . 286
The Christian and the World Community . . . . 287
European Unity . . . . . . . . . . . 291
The Problem of Peace . . . . . . . . . 295

## JOHN XXIII

The Plight of the Refugees . . . . . . . . . 297
At the Chair of Peter . . . . . . . . . . 299
Peace on Earth . . . . . . . . . . .. . . 301
The Campaign Against Hunger . . . . . . . 305
Self-Determination . . . . . . . . . . . 308
New Aspects on Modern International Crises . . . . 308
All Is Lost by War . . . . . . . . . . . 322

## STATEMENTS BY THE BISHOPS OF THE
## UNITED STATES OF AMERICA

The Crisis of Christianity . . . . . . . . . 329
International Order . . . . . . . . . . . 335
Organizing World Peace . . . . . . . . . 341
Between War and Peace . . . . . . . . . . 346
Man and the Peace . . . . . . . . . . . 351
Discrimination and the Christian Conscience . . . . 358
The Dignity of Man . . . . . . . . . . . 364
Peter's Chains . . . . . . . . . . . . . 372
The Hope of Mankind . . . . . . . . . . 375
World Refugee Year and Migration . . . . . . 379
Freedom and Peace . . . . . . . . . . . 384
Personal Responsibility . . . . . . . . . . 391

## APPENDIX

Pattern for Peace: Catholic, Jewish, and Protestant Declaration on World Peace . . . . . . . . . 393

Index . . . . . . . . . . . . . . . 401

# PATTERN FOR PEACE

# Leo XIII

## The Bonds of Peace*

(*Allocution* NOSTIS ERROREM *to the College of Cardinals, February 11, 1889*)

THERE is . . . nothing of more importance than to remove from Europe the danger of war, and all that is done for that purpose deserves to be considered as a contribution to the public safety.

But the wish does not do much to render peace assured, and the mere desire for peace is not a sufficient guarantee. A vast number of soldiers and stupendous armaments may for a while prevent an enemy attacking, but they can never secure a sure and lasting peace. Moreover, armaments which are a menace are more likely to hasten than to retard a conflict; they fill the mind with disquietude for the future, and among other drawbacks, impose such burdens upon nations that it is doubtful if war would not be more bearable.

Wherefore We must seek for peace some basis more sound and more in accordance with nature; for if nature does not forbid one to defend one's rights by force, she does not permit that force should become the efficient cause of right. Since peace is based upon good order, it follows that, for empires as well as for individuals, concord should have her principal foundation in justice and charity.

To commit no wrong against another, to respect the sanctity of another's rights, to practice mutual trust and good will, these are indeed the unchanging and most lasting bonds of

* Translation from *Principles for Peace*, edited by Rev. Harry W. Koenig (Milwaukee: Bruce Publishing Company).

peace, whose virtue is such that she stifles even the germs of hatred and jealousy.

God has made His Church guardian and mother of the two virtues of which We speak; on this account she has had and will have nothing dearer to her heart than to uphold, spread, and protect the laws of justice and charity. For this purpose the Church has overrun all parts of the earth; and all the world knows that she tamed the barbarian races by inspiring them with love of justice and led them from the ferocity of their warlike habits to the practice of the arts of peace and civilization. To the great and the small, to those who obey and those who command, she imposes alike the duty of observing justice and of attacking no one unjustly. It is the Church who, in spite of distances and in spite of the differences of race, has joined together all peoples by friendship and brotherly charity. Mindful always of the law and example of her Divine Founder, Who desired to be called the Prince of Peace and Whose birth was even announced in heavenly canticles of peace, the Church wishes men to rest in the beauty of peace and ceases not her prayers to God that He will preserve the lives and fortunes of the nations from war. As often as was necessary and the circumstances permitted, the Church has labored with all her heart, by interposing her authority, to re-establish concord and peace among nations.

# The Might of Law*

(*First Diplomatic Note of Cardinal Rampolla, Secretary of State, to Count Mouraviev, Secretary of Foreign Affairs for Russia, September 15, 1898*)

THE Pope holds that peace cannot possibly be established if it does not rest on the foundation of Christian public law, from which comes the concord of princes among themselves and of peoples with their rulers.

---

* Translation from *Principles for Peace*.

In order that mutual mistrust and the reciprocal motives of offense and defense, which have led the nations of our day to develop armaments, should cease, and in order that a spirit of peace, spreading throughout the universe should bring nations to regard one another as brothers, Christian justice must have full vigor in the world; the maxims of the Gospel must again be held in honor and the difficult art of governing peoples must have as its principal element that fear of God which is the beginning of wisdom.

Men have wished to regulate the relations among nations by a new law founded on utilitarian interests, the predominance of force, the success of accomplished coups, and on other theories which negate the eternal and immutable principles of justice. This is the capital error which has brought Europe to a state of disaster.

Against such a baneful system, the Holy See has not ceased to raise its voice to arouse the attention of princes and peoples. Throughout the Middle Ages, by means of the happy union of Christendom, the voice of the Roman pontiffs found everywhere easy access, and succeeded by the force of its authority alone to conciliate princes and nations, to put an end to quarrels by words of arbitration, to defend the weak against the unjust oppression of the strong, to prevent war, and to save Christian civilization.

Today once more, although conditions in the world have changed, the Pope does not cease to use his moral power with a constant solicitude in order to fill the mind of people with the Christian idea of justice and love, to recall nations to reciprocal obligations of brotherhood, to inculcate respect for the authority established by God for the good of all people, and to oppose to the law of might the might of the law in conformity with the principles of the Gospel. . . .

# An Institution of Mediation*

*(Second Diplomatic Note of Cardinal Rampolla, Secretary of State, to Count Mouraviev, Secretary of Foreign Affairs for Russia, February 10, 1899)*

THERE is lacking in the international consortium of nations a system of legal and moral means to determine and guarantee the rights of each. Only an immediate recourse to force remains. Rivalry among nations and the development of their military power are the results of these policies.

. . . In view of such an unfortunate state of things, the institution of mediation and arbitration appears to be the most opportune remedy; it corresponds in all respects to the aspirations of the Holy See. Perhaps—and this will be better brought out in the discussions of the conference—perhaps We can hope that arbitration, obligatory by its very nature, can become in all circumstances the object of unanimous acceptance and assent. An institution of mediation, invested with authority and clothed with all the necessary moral prestige, if fortified with the indispensable guarantees of competence and impartiality and in no way restricting the liberty of the litigating powers, would be less exposed to meet obstacles.

. . . At the same time, the Holy See expresses a most ardent wish that in the councils of these powers the principle of mediation and arbitration may find favorable welcome and be applied as widely as possible. We give Our keenest sympathy to such a proposal and declare that We are always disposed to cooperate most willingly in order that such a proposal may have a favorable outcome. For We are convinced that, if an effective international accord could be realized, the latter would have a most happy effect in the interests of civilization.

---

* Translation from *Principles for Peace*.

4

# Nationalistic Rivalry*

(*Papal letter* PERVENUTI, *March 19, 1902*)

As a result of the repudiation of those Christian principles which have contributed so efficaciously to the unity of nations in the bonds of brotherhood and have brought all humanity into one great family, there has gradually arisen in the international order a system of jealous egoism. Nations, consequently, now watch each other, if not with hate, at least with the suspicion of rivals. Hence, in their great undertakings, losing sight of the lofty principles of morality and justice, they forget the protection which the feeble and oppressed have a right to demand.

Actuated solely by the desire to increase their national riches, these nations regard only the opportunity afforded by present circumstances, the advantages of successful enterprises and the tempting bait of an accomplished fact, in the certainty that no one will trouble them in the name of right or respect due to rights and justice. Such are the fatal principles which have consecrated material power as the supreme law of the world; on these principles rests the blame for the limitless increase of military establishments and an armed peace in many respects equivalent to a disastrous war. This lamentable confusion in the realm of ideas has produced restlessness, outbreaks, and a general spirit of rebellion among the people. From these have arisen the frequent and popular agitations and disorders of our times which can only be preludes of a much more terrible chaos in the future.

---

* Translation from *Principles for Peace*.

# *Pius  X*

---

## Organizations for Peace*

(*Letter* POLONIAE POPULUM *to the Bishops of Russian Po-land, December 3, 1905*)

. . . IN order that Catholics may not only love and pray most ardently for this tranquility of peace, but also, as is their duty, hasten to bring it into realization, and when it has been obtained preserve it in safety, it is absolutely necessary that following the example of the turbulent they enter into societies and unions wherein with united plans and efforts they may fight efficaciously for their religion and country. . . .

* Translation from *Principles for Peace.*

# Benedict XV

## Respect for Rights of Others*

*(Exhortation* ALLORCHÈ FUMMO *to the Belligerent Peoples and to Their Leaders, July 28, 1915)*

. . . NOR let it be said that the immense conflict cannot be settled without the violence of war. Lay aside your mutual purpose of destruction; remember that nations do not die; humbled and oppressed, they chafe under the yoke imposed upon them, preparing a renewal of the combat, and passing down from generation to generation a mournful heritage of hatred and revenge.

Why not from this moment weigh with serene mind the rights and lawful aspirations of the peoples? Why not initiate with a good will an exchange of views, directly or indirectly, with the purpose of respecting those rights and aspirations within the limits of possibility, and thus succeed in putting an end to the monstrous struggle, as has been done under other similar circumstances? Blessed be he who will first raise the olive branch and hold out his right hand to the enemy with an offer of reasonable terms of peace. The equilibrium of the world and the prosperity and assured tranquility of nations rest upon mutual benevolence and respect for the rights and dignities of others, much more than upon hosts of armed men and a ring of formidable fortresses. . . .

* Translation from *Principles for Peace.*

# The Role of Catholics*

*(Papal letter* FULDAE *to Cardinal van Hartmann, Archbishop of Cologne, September 6, 1915)*

. . . WE should very much wish that these desires should seek among all men a royal road which lies open to peace: of patient and benign charity; from this road they would indeed wander far, who deem it permissible in their writings and speeches to find such fault with the Catholics of another nation that, by mutual provocation (as the Apostle says, *envying one another*) they add new fuel to those feelings of wrath whose flames they are obligated to extinguish with kindness of judgment and gentleness of mind.

Wherefore, while We desire peace with great longing—a peace indeed such as is required by justice and consonant with the dignity of all nations—We exhort Catholics to do nothing through a spirit of contention but to devote themselves to the restoration of peace with a Christian spirit of brotherly love.

# Proposals for Peace*

*(Exhortation* DES LE DEBUT *to the belligerent peoples and their leaders, August 1, 1917)*

As We may no longer limit Ourselves to general statements, which circumstances made advisable in the past, We desire now to put forward more concrete and practical propositions. We invite the governments of the belligerents to come to some agreement on the following points, which seem to offer the basis for a just and lasting peace, although We leave to these nations the task of their final adjustment and completion.

First of all, a fundamental point must be stressed: moral force of right must be substituted for the material force of arms; subsequently, there must follow a just agreement for

---

* Translation from *Principles for Peace.*

the simultaneous and reciprocal diminution of armaments, in accordance with rules and guarantees to be established hereafter and in a measure sufficient and necessary for the maintenance of public order in each state; next, as a substitute for armies, the institution of arbitration with its lofty role of peace-making and subject to predetermined and previously agreed-upon regulations and sanctions against the state, which should refuse either to submit to an international arbitration of disputes or to accept the decisions of this international arbiter.

Once the supremacy of right is thus established, let all obstacles to the free intercourse of people be swept aside and assure, by means of rules adopted in the same way, the true freedom and common rights of all on the high seas. This, on the one hand, would eliminate numerous causes of conflict, and on the other, open to all new sources of prosperity and progress.

With regard to reparations for damages and the cost of war, no other solution appears to Us evident but to lay down, as a general principle, a total and reciprocal pardon. This is justified, furthermore, by the immense benefits that will accrue from disarmament—the more so since the continuance of such carnage solely for economic reasons is inconceivable. If particular problems arise in certain cases for special reasons, let them be weighed justly and with equity. . . .

# The Means to Disarmament*

*(Letter of Cardinal Gasparri, Secretary of State to Lloyd George, Prime Minister of England, September 28, 1917)*

WITH regard to a reciprocal and simultaneous disarmament, universally sought for as a true symbol of peace and prosperity, the Holy Father, with deference to the belligerent powers, did not intend to specify the means to accomplish and main-

---

* Translation from *Principles for Peace.*

tain this in His letter, but preferred to leave the determination of these means for disarmament to the Powers themselves. Still, He considers that the only practical and easy method to bring this about is as follows: a pact among civilized nations, including non-belligerents, that requires the simultaneous and reciprocal suppression of all compulsory military service; the institution of a tribunal of arbitration to decide international controversies; the imposition of a general boycott in sanction against any nation that might attempt to re-establish obligatory military service or refuse to submit to international arbitration any grave question or finally to refuse to accept the decisions of such body on the issue in question.

# The Effects of War*

(*Allocution* E LA QUINTA VOLTA *to the College of Cardinals, December 24, 1918*)

THE dreadful tempest which has passed over the earth has left behind many sad traces of its havoc. It is even more to be feared that it has left in the hearts of men distressing vestiges of ancient rancors, the unwholesome germs of discord, revenge, and selfish reprisals. The very ardors of war and the burning desire—noble in origin—of defending one's fatherland, inflame the soul with an indignation, which however just it may have been in its beginnings, yet in its final consequences can too easily lead to excess by failing to stifle or even strengthening with new life the ancient seeds of social discord which it ought to desire to see remedied by justice.

* Translation from *Principles for Peace*.

# Brotherly Love*

*(Papal Letter* DIUTURNI *to the Bishops of Germany, July 15, 1919)*

IT is especially necessary to eliminate every feeling of hatred, either toward foreigners with whom the nation was at war or toward fellow-citizens of opposite parties. In place of hatred put that brotherly love of Christ's which knows no barrier, limit, or class-struggle. We repeat here the hope We expressed at the last Consistory, that "men and nations may be again united in Christian charity, for if that is lacking, every treaty of peace will be in vain."

# Justice and Charity*

*(Encyclical Letter* PACEM DEI MUNUS PULCHERRIMUM *on Peace and Reconciliation, May 23, 1920)*

. . . THE germs of former enmities remain; and you well know, Venerable Brethren, that there can be no stable peace or lasting treaties even though they have been duly signed after long and difficult negotiation, unless there be a return to mutual charity in order to appease hatreds and banish enmities.

There is no need from Us of lengthy proof to show that society would incur the risk of grave loss if, while peace is signed, latent hostility and enmity were to continue among the nations. There is no need to mention the loss of all that maintains and fosters civil life, such as commerce and industry, art and literature. These flourish only when the nations are at peace. But even more important, grave harm would accrue to the form and essence of Christian life, which consists essentially in charity and the preaching of what is called the Gospel of peace.

---

* Translation from *Principles for Peace.*

You know well, and We have many times reminded you of the fact, that nothing was so frequently and carefully inculcated on His disciples by Jesus Christ as this precept of mutual charity, which contains all other commands. Christ called it a new commandment, His very own; He desired that it should be the sign of Christians by which they might be distinguished from all others; on the eve of His death His last testament to His disciples was to love one another and thus imitate the ineffable unity of the three Divine Persons in the Trinity. *That they may be one as we also are one . . . that they may be made perfect in one.*

The Apostles, following in the steps of the Divine Master and conforming to His word and commands, were unceasing in their exhortation to the faithful: *Before all things have a constant mutual charity among yourselves. But above all things have charity which is the bond of perfection. Dearly beloved, let us love one another, for charity is of God.* Our brethren of the first Christian ages faithfully observed these commands of Jesus Christ and the Apostles. They belonged to different and rival nations, yet they willingly forgot their causes of quarrel and lived in perfect concord; such union of hearts was in striking contrast to the deadly enmities which at that time consumed society.

### Forgive and Love Our Enemies

The emphasis placed on the virtue of charity applies as well to the inculcation of forgiveness of injuries—a point no less solemnly commanded by the Lord: *But I say to you, love your enemies; do good to them that hate you; pray for those who persecute and calumniate you, that you may be the children of your Father Who is in heaven, Who maketh His sun to rise upon the good and the bad.* Hence, that terribly severe warning of the Apostle, St. John: *Whosoever hateth his brother is a murderer. And you know that no murderer hath eternal life abiding in himself.*

Our Lord Jesus Christ, when He taught us how to pray told us to seek for pardon as we forgive others: *Forgive us our trespasses as we forgive them that trespass against us.* If the observance of this law is sometimes hard and difficult,

14

we have not only the timely assurance of the grace of Our Divine Redeemer, but also His example to help us to overcome the difficulty. For as He hung on the Cross, He thus excused those who so unjustly and wickedly tortured Him: *Father, forgive them, for they know not what they do.* We then, who should be the first to imitate the pity and loving kindness of Jesus Christ, Whose Vicar, without any merit of Our own, We are, with all Our Heart and following His example, forgive all Our enemies who knowingly or unknowingly have and are still heaping on Our person and Our work vituperation of every kind; We embrace all in Our charity and benevolence and We neglect no opportunity to do them all the good in Our power. That is, indeed, what Christians worthy of the name ought to do toward those who during the war wronged them.

Christian charity ought not to be content with not hating our enemies and loving them as brothers; it also demands that we treat them with kindness, following the example of the Divine Master who *went about doing good and healing all that were oppressed by the devil,* and who finished His mortal life, marked throughout by good deeds, by shedding His blood for them. So said St. John: *In this we have known the charity of God, because He has laid down His life for us, and we ought to lay down our lives for the brethren. He that hath the wealth of this world and shall see his brother in need and shall shut up his bowels from him: how does the charity of God abide in him? My little children, let us not love in word nor by tongue but in deed and in truth.*

### Never Was Charity More Needed

Never indeed was there a time when we should "stretch the bounds of charity" more than in these days of universal suffering and sorrow; never perhaps as today has humanity so needed the universal beneficence which springs from the love of others and is full of sacrifice and zeal. For if we look around where the fury of the war has been let loose, we see immense regions utterly desolate, uncultivated, and abandoned; multitudes reduced to want of food, clothing and shelter; innumerable widows and orphans deprived of all possessions, and an incredible number of enfeebled persons, particularly children and young people, who carry on their bodies the ravages of this atrocious war.

When one regards all these miseries by which the human race is stricken one inevitably thinks of the traveler in the Gospel, who, going down from Jerusalem to Jericho, fell among thieves, who robbed him, covered him with wounds, and left him half dead. The two cases are very similar; and as to the traveler there came the good Samaritan, full of compassion, who bound up his wounds, pouring in oil and wine, took him to an inn, and undertook all care for him, so, too, is it necessary that Jesus, of Whom the Samaritan was the figure, should lay His Hands upon the wounds of society.

. . . Venerable Brethren, We beg and exhort you in the mercy and charity of Jesus Christ to strive with all zeal and diligence not only to urge the faithful entrusted to your care to abandon hatred and pardon offenses, but—what is more immediately practical—to promote all those works of Christian benevolence which bring aid to the needy, comfort to the afflicted, and protection to the weak, and to give opportune and appropriate assistance to all who have suffered from the war. It is Our special wish that you exhort your priests, as ministers of peace, to be assiduous in promoting this love of one's neighbor, even of enemies, which is the essence of the Christian life. By *being all things to all men* and giving an example to others, let them wage war everywhere on enmity and hatred—a thing most agreeable to the loving Heart of Jesus and to him who, however unworthy, holds His place on earth. In this connection Catholic writers and journalists should be invited to clothe themselves as elect of God, holy and beloved, with pity and kindness. Let them show this charity in their writings by abstaining not only from false and groundless accusations but also from all intemperate, violent language which is contrary to the law of Christ and reopens sores as yet unhealed, because any slight touch is a serious irritant to a heart recently wounded.

### To Nations as Well as Individuals

Whatever We have said here to individuals about the duty of charity, We wish to say to nations as well who have been delivered from the burden of a long war, in order that, after the roots of disagreement have been removed as far as possible, and without prejudice to the rights of justice, they may resume friendly relations among each other. The Gospel has not one law of charity for individuals and another for states and nations, for these are but collections of individuals. Since the war is over now, a general reconciliation is demanded not only for reasons of charity, but also of necessity; nations are drawn together by a natural interdependence founded on necessity and the bonds of mutual good-will which today are strengthened by the developments of civilization and the marvelous progress of communication.

Once the restoration of the order of justice and charity and the reconciliation of nations has been accomplished, it is much to be desired, Venerable Brethren, that all states, putting aside mutual suspicion, should maintain their own independence and safeguard the order of human society by a union into one league or rather a sort of family of nations. One specific reason among others demands such an association of nations: the generally recognized necessity of every effort being made to abolish or reduce the enormous burden of military expenditures which nations can no longer bear, so that disastrous wars, or at least the danger of war, be removed as much as possible. In that way, would be assured for each nation not only its independence but also the integrity of its territory within its just frontiers and boundaries.

The Church will certainly not refuse her zealous aid to a union of nations under Christian law in any of their undertakings inspired by justice and charity, inasmuch as she is herself the more perfect type of universal society. She possesses in her organization and institutions a wonderful instrument for accomplishing this brotherhood among men, not only for their eternal salvation but also for their material well-being in this world; she leads them from temporal welfare to the certainty of the acquisition of an eternal felicity. History teaches us that, when the spirit of the Church pervaded the ancient, barbarous nations of Europe, the great variety of differences among them were diminished and the quarrels that divided them were extinguished. In time, they formed a homogeneous society, which gave birth to Christian Europe and under the guidance and auspices of the Church, preserved the diversity of nations while tending to a unity that favored its prosperity and glory. On this point Saint Augustine speaks well:

This celestial city, in its life here on earth, calls to itself citizens of every nation, and forms from all peoples one varied society; it is not harassed by differences in customs, laws, and institutions, which hinder the attainment or maintenance of peace on earth; it neither rends nor destroys anything, but rather guards all and adapts itself to all; no matter how many differences may exist among nations, they are all directed to the same end of peace on earth, as long as they do not hinder the exercise of religion, which teaches the worship of the true Supreme God.

And the same holy Doctor thus addresses the Church: "Citizens, peoples, and all men, recalling your common origin, you shall not only unite among yourselves, but shall make of each other brothers."

To come back to what We said at the beginning, We turn affectionately to all Our children and urge them in the name of Our Lord Jesus Christ to forget mutual differences and grievances and unite in the bonds of Christian charity which excludes none as a stranger. We fervently exhort all nations under the inspiration of Christian benevolence to establish true peace and to join in an alliance of all nations, which is just and, therefore, a lasting covenant.

# A Lasting Treaty*

(*Encyclical Letter* SACRA PROPEDIEM *on the Seventh Centenary of the Third Order of Saint Francis, January 6, 1921*)

. . . A MAN-MADE treaty, whether of states or classes of men, can neither endure nor possess any value for real peace, unless it rests upon a peaceful disposition; but the latter can exist only where duty, as it were, puts the bridle on passions, for these

---

* Translation from *Principles for Peace.*

are the sources of discord of whatsoever nature at all. *From whence*, asks the Apostle, *are wars and contentions among you? Are they not hence, from your concupiscences, which are in your members?* Now it is Christ, Who has power to harmonize all that is in man and make of him, not a slave but a ruler of his desires, obedient and submissive always to the Will of God; this harmony is the foundation of all true peace.

# The Fount of True Peace*

(*Allocution* GRATUM VEHEMENTER *to the College of Cardinals, March* 7, *1921*)

NEVER before has the need for the exercise of self-sacrifice and brotherly love summoned a poor human race, first scourged by war and now thrown into disorder by a lust for material goods and by political passions; never has the necessity of a beginning by individuals of conversion along Christian paths been so great, to check effectively a paganism truly infiltrating every manifestation of public and private life. It is true, indeed, that the actual state of war has ceased; still a certain and lasting peace has not yet arrived to bring consolation to the world; much less has there returned to families and groups of societies and nations the tranquility of order which comes from the spirit of brotherhood and Christian solidarity. We see today the miserable spectacle of fratricidal strife between citizens of the same nations; people, born and reared on the same land, now fighting hand to hand for it, raising up barriers of hatred and enmity among themselves. We see, too, ancient, latent differences between nations rise again through displays of violence which are utterly at variance with the rules of humanity and morality and which We must deplore regardless of their origins. By now it is evident to all that the rules of peace, so laboriously elaborated by the most experienced politicians, are truly written on treaties; but they never can

---

* Translation from *Principles for Peace.*

19

become living agreements nor have strength nor power nor penetrate human consciences, unless, first of all, they are based on the main principles of justice and equity, and secondly, there arise again in the minds and hearts of men those principles which transformed the world from pagan to Christian and in the day of Saint Francis of Assisi healed a society full of disorder and corruption by their restoration. Only from the control of one's passion comes that interior order in the individual man, which is the basis of social order; only by the Christian practice of brotherly love will come again among social classes and nations that mutual trust which is the fount of true and lasting peace. . . .

# Pius XI

## Mutual Confidence*

(*Papal Letter* CON VIVO PIACERE *to Archbishop Signori of Genoa, April 7, 1922*)

IF, in the very clatter and shock of arms, according to the beautiful insignia of the Red Cross—*Inter arma caritas*—Christian charity ought to reign, this motto should influence men with even stronger motives when the weapons have been laid aside and the treaties of peace signed; all the more so, since international enmities, the sad heritage of wars, are prejudicial to the victorious nations as well and preludes to future difficulties for all.

It should not be forgotten that the best guarantee of peace is not a forest of bayonets, but mutual confidence and friendship. If the conference should exclude from discussion, not only existing treaties but also reparations, this need not prevent further exchanges of views which might help the conquered to a speedier fulfillment of their obligations and work to the advantage of the victors.

* Translation from *Principles for Peace*.

# The Peace of Christ*

*(Encyclical* UBI ARCANO DEI *on the Kingdom of Christ, December 23, 1922)*

ONE thing today is certain: since the close of the Great War individuals, different classes of society, the nations of the earth have not yet found true peace. They do not enjoy, therefore, that active and fruitful tranquility which is the aspiration and need of mankind. This sad truth forces itself upon us from every side. For anyone, who desires to study profoundly and apply successfully the means necessary to overcome such evils, as We do, it is all-important to recognize both the fact and gravity of this state of affairs and seek to find its causes first of all. This duty is imposed on Us in commanding fashion by the very consciousness which We have of Our Apostolic Office. We cannot but resolve to fulfill that which is so clearly Our duty. We shall do this now by Our first Encyclical, and later with all solicitude in the course of Our Sacred ministry.

Since the selfsame sad conditions continue to exist in the world today which were the object of constant and almost heartbreaking preoccupation on the part of Our respected Predecessor, Benedict XV, during the whole period of his Pontificate, naturally We have come to make his thoughts and his solutions of these problems Our own. May they become, too, the thoughts and ideals of everyone, as they are Our thoughts, and if this should happen we would certainly see, with the help of God and the cooperation of all men of good will, the most wonderful effects come to pass through a true and lasting reconciliation of men one with another.

The inspired words of the Prophets seem to have been written expressly for our own times: *We looked for peace and no good came: for a time of healing, and behold fear, for the time of healing, and behold trouble. We looked for light, and behold darkness . . . we have looked for judgment, and there is none: for salvation, and it is far from us.*

---

* Translation from *Principles for Peace.*

22

## All Nations Suffer

. . . Public life is so enveloped, even at the present hour, by the dense fog of mutual hatreds and grievances that it is almost impossible for the common people so much as freely to breathe therein. If the defeated nations continue to suffer most terribly, no less serious are the evils which will afflict their conquerers. Small nations complain that they are being oppressed and exploited by great nations. The great Powers, on their side, contend that they are being judged wrongly and circumvented by the smaller. All nations, great and small, suffer acutely from the sad effects of the late war. Neither can those nations which were neutral contend that they have escaped altogether the tremendous sufferings of the war or failed to experience its evil results almost equally with the actual belligerents. These evil results grow in volume from day to day because of the utter impossibility of finding anything like a safe remedy to cure the ills of society, and this in spite of all the efforts of politicians and statesmen whose work has come to naught, if it has not unfortunately tended to aggravate the very evils they tried to overcome. Conditions have become increasingly worse because the fears of the people are being constantly played upon by the ever-present menace of new wars, likely to be more frightful and destructive than any which have preceded them. Whence it is that the nations of today live in a state of armed peace which is scarcely better than war itself, a condition which tends to exhaust national finances, to waste the flower of youth, to muddy and poison the very fountainheads of life, physical, intellectual, religious and moral.

## Peace in Words Only

. . . Peace indeed was signed in solemn conclave between the belligerents of the late war. This peace, however, was only written into treaties. It was not received into the hearts of men, who still cherish the desire to fight one another and to continue to menace in a most serious manner the quiet and stability of civil society. Unfortunately, the law of violence has held sway so long that it has weakened and almost obliterated

23

all traces of those natural feelings of love and mercy which the law of Christian charity has done so much to encourage. Nor has this illusory peace, written only on paper, served as yet to awaken noble sentiments in the souls of men. On the contrary, there has been born a spirit of violence and of hatred which, because it has been indulged in for so long, has become almost second nature in many men. There has followed the blind rule of the inferior parts of the soul over the superior, that rule of the lower elements *fighting against the law of the mind*, which St. Paul grieved over.

Men today do not act as Christians, as brothers, but as strangers, and even enemies. The sense of man's personal dignity and of the value of human life has been lost in the brutal domination begotten of might and mere superiority in numbers. Many are intent on exploiting their neighbors solely for the purpose of enjoying more fully and on a larger scale the goods of this world. But they err grievously who have turned to the acquisition of material and temporal possessions and are forgetful of eternal and spiritual things, to the possession of which Jesus, Our Redeemer, by means of the Church, His living interpreter, calls mankind.

. . . The same effects which result from these evils among individuals may likewise be expected among nations. *From whence are wars and contentions among you?* asks the Apostle St. James. *Are they not hence, from your concupiscences, which are in your members?* The inordinate desire for pleasure, *concupiscence of the flesh*, sows the fatal seeds of division not only among families but likewise among States; the inordinate desire for possessions, *concupiscence of the eyes*, inevitably turns into class warfare and into social egotism; the inordinate desire to rule or domineer over others, *pride of life*, soon becomes mere party or factional rivalries, manifesting itself in constant displays of conflicting ambitions and ending in open rebellion, in the crime of *lése majesté*, and even in national parricide.

These unsuppressed desires, this inordinate love of the things of the world, are precisely the source of all international misunderstandings and rivalries, despite the fact that oftentimes men dare to maintain that acts prompted by such motives are excusable and even justifiable because, perhaps, they were performed for reasons of State or public welfare, or love for one's country. Patriotism—the stimulus of so many virtues and of so many noble acts of heroism when kept within the bounds of the law of Christ—becomes merely an occasion, an added incentive to grave injustice when true love of country is debased to the condition of an extreme nationalism; when we forget that all men are our brothers and members of the same great human family, that other nations have a right equal to ours to life and to prosperity, that it is never lawful nor even wise, to disassociate morality from the affairs of practical life, that, in the last analysis, it is *justice which exalts a nation: but sin makes nations miserable.*

Perhaps the advantages to one's family, city or nation obtained in some such way as this may well appear to be a wonderful and great victory (this thought has been already expressed by St. Augustine), but in the end it turns out to be a very shallow victory, one rather to inspire us with the most fearful apprehensions of approaching ruin. *It is a happiness which appears beautiful, but is brittle as glass. We must ever be on guard lest with horror we see it broken into a thousand pieces at the first touch.*

## The Lord Forsaken

There is, over and above the absence of peace and the evils attendant on this absence, another deeper and more profound cause for present-day conditions. This cause was beginning to show its head before the war. The terrible calamities consequent on that cataclysm should have provided a remedy for them if mankind had only taken the trouble to understand the real meaning of those terrible events. In the Holy Scripture we read: *They that have forsaken the Lord shall be consumed.* No less well-known are the words of the Divine Teacher, Jesus Christ, Who said: *Without Me you can do nothing*, and again, *He that gathereth not with Me, scattereth.*

These words of the Holy Bible have been fulfilled and are now at this very moment being fulfilled before our very eyes. Because men have forsaken God and Jesus Christ, they have sunk to the depths of evil. They waste their energies and consume their time and efforts in vain sterile attempts to find a remedy for these ills, but without even being successful in saving what little remains from the existing ruins. It was a quite general desire that both our laws and our governments should exist *without recognizing God* or Jesus Christ, on the theory that all authority comes from men, not from God. Because of such an assumption, these theorists fell quite short of the ability to bestow upon law not only those sanctions which it must possess but also that secure basis for the supreme criterion of justice which even a pagan philosopher like Cicero saw clearly could not be derived except from the divine law. Authority itself lost its hold upon mankind, for it had lost that sound and unquestionable justification for its right to command on one hand and to be obeyed on the other. Society, quite logically and inevitably, was shaken to its very depths and threatened with destruction, since there was left to it no longer a stable foundation; everything has been reduced to a series of conflicts, to the domination by the majority, or to the supremacy of special interests.

. . . Is it to be wondered at, then, that with the widespread refusal to accept the principles of true Christian wisdom, the seeds of discord sown everywhere should find a kindly soil in which to grow and bear fruit in that most tremendous struggle, the Great War, which unfortunately did not serve to lessen but increase, by its acts of violence and bloodshed, the international and social animosities which already existed?

### The Path to Peace

We have analyzed briefly the causes of the ills which afflict present-day society; the recital of these causes, however, Venerable Brethren, should not bring us to lose hope of finding their appropriate remedy, since the evils themselves seem to suggest a way out of these difficulties.

The first and most important need, for mankind today is spiritual peace. We do not need a peace that will consist merely in acts of external or formal courtesy, but a peace which will penetrate the souls of men and unite, heal and reopen their hearts to a mutual affection born of brotherly love. The Peace of Christ is the only peace answering this description: *Let the Peace of Christ rejoice in your hearts.* Nor is there any other peace possible than that which Christ gave to

26

His disciples for since He is God, He *beholdeth the heart* and in our hearts His kingdom is set up. Again, Jesus Christ is perfectly justified when He calls this peace of soul His own, for He was the first Who said to all men, *All you are brethren.* He gave likewise to us, sealing it with His own life's Blood, the law of brotherly love, of mutual forbearance—*This is My commandment, that you love one another, as I have loved you. Bear ye one another's burden, and so you shall fulfill the law of Christ.*

From this follows, as an immediate consequence, that the Peace of Christ can only be the peace of justice according to the words of the prophet, *the work of justice shall be peace,* for He is God *Who judges justice.* But peace does not consist merely in severe, inflexible justice. It must be made acceptable and easy through the mixture equally of charity and the sincere desire for reconciliation. Such peace was acquired for us and the whole world by Jesus Christ, a peace which the Apostle, in a most expressive manner, makes incarnate in the very Person of Christ Himself when he speaks of Him: *He is our Peace,* for it was He Who satisfied completely divine justice by His death on the Cross, destroying thus in His own flesh all enmities toward others and making peace and reconciliation with God possible for all mankind. Therefore, the Apostle beholds in the work of Redemption, which is a work of justice, at one and the same time a divine work of reconciliation and of love. *God indeed was in Christ, reconciling the world to Himself. God so loved the world, as to give His only begotten Son.*

Thomas Aquinas, the Angelic Doctor, also discovered in this fact the formula and essence of our belief, for he writes that a true and lasting peace is more a question of love than of justice. The reason for his statement is that it is the function of justice merely to do away with obstacles to peace; for example, the injury done or the damage caused. Peace itself, however, is an act which arises only from love.

. . . For the Church teaches (she alone has been given by God the mandate and the right to teach with authority) that not only our acts as individuals but also as groups and nations must conform to the eternal law of God. In fact, it is much more important that the acts of a nation follow God's law, because on the nation rests a far greater responsibility for the consequences of its acts than on the individual.

## The Way to Faith in Each Other

When, therefore, governments and nations follow in all their activities, whether they be national or international, the dictates of conscience grounded on the teachings, precepts, and example of Jesus Christ, binding on each and every individual, then only can we have faith in one another's word and trust in the peaceful solution of the difficulties and controversies which may arise from differences of viewpoint or clashes of interests. An attempt in this direction has already been made and is being carried on now; its results, however, are practically negligible, particularly with respect to any effects on the major questions which seriously divide nations and pit them one against the other. No merely human institution of today can successfully devise a set of international laws which can bring in harmony world conditions as well as the Middle Ages which was in truth a League of Nations: Christianity. It cannot be denied that in the Middle Ages this law was often violated; still it always existed as an ideal, according to which one might judge the acts of nations, as well as a beacon light guiding the wanderers and the lost back to the road of safety.

. . . We pray most fervently and ask others likewise to pray for this much-desired peace among nations, especially at this hour, when after twenty centuries, the day and hour approach when all over the world men will celebrate the humble and meek coming among us of the sweet Prince of Peace, at whose birth the heavenly hosts sang: *Glory to God in the highest, and on earth peace to men of good will.*

# Reparations*

*(Papal Letter* QUANDO NEL PRINCIPIO *to Cardinal Gasparri,
Secretary of State, June 24, 1923)*

. . . Since among the governments of the Powers most closely
concerned in the past war new diplomatic conversations are
in view to discuss fresh proposals for a friendly solution to
the questions still troubling Central Europe with their inevitable effects on all nations, We believe it is Our duty to raise
again Our voice of disinterested, impartial good-will toward
all, as the voice of the Common Father must be. A consideration of the grave responsibility incumbent upon us and those
who hold in their hands the destinies of the nations, We exhort them once again to examine the different questions, particularly that of reparations, in a Christian spirit which sets
no dividing line between justice and social charity on which
the perfection of civil society is based. If and when the debtor,
with the intention of paying reparations for the serious damage
suffered by populations and places once so prosperous and
flourishing, gives proof of his serious will to reach a fair and
definite agreement and asks for an impartial judgment on the
limits of his own capacity to pay or seeks to entrust to judges
all forms of true and exact control, then justice and social charity, as well as the interests of the creditors and of all nations,
weary of war and longing for peace, seem to demand that no
claims shall be made of the debtor which he cannot meet without entirely exhausting his own resources and capacity for
production, with consequent irreparable damage to himself
and his creditors, with the danger of social disturbances that
would be the ruin of Europe, and with resentments that would
be a perpetual threat to new and worse conflagrations.

In equal measure it is just that the creditors shall have
guarantees in proportion to the dues, that insure the payments
of vital interest and dependence for them. We leave to them,
however, the consideration whether for that purpose it is
necessary to maintain in every case territorial occupations
which impose heavy sacrifices on the occupied and the

---

* Translation from *Principles for Peace.*

occupiers or whether it might not be better to substitute, possibly by degrees, other guarantees equally effective and certainly less painful.

If these foundations of peace be mutually agreed upon with the consequent result that bitterness brought about by territorial occupations may be gradually reduced until it disappears entirely, then will it be possible to show that a true state of peace among nations is also a necessary condition for the economic restoration which all keenly desire. A state of peace and restoration are of such great benefit to all nations, conquerors and conquered, that no sacrifice which is seen to be necessary should appear too great to obtain these benefits.

# Reparations*

*(Official interpretation by Cardinal Gasparri, Secretary of State, of the Papal Letter* QUANDO NEL PRINCIPIO, *June 29, 1923)*

WITH an awareness of the heavy responsibility which weighs upon him at the present hour, as well as upon those who hold the destinies of nations in their hands, the Holy Father implores them once again to examine the various questions, especially that of reparations, in that Christian spirit which does not separate the demands of justice from those of social charity. With a view to dissipating future misunderstandings, let us see what the demands of justice and social charity are according to the papal document; let us give a brief commentary on the text, but let us scrupulously respect the sense of the letter.

Following the rule laid down in the letter of the Pope, Germany, the debtor nation—in its request for impartial judgment on the limits of its own ability to pay, pledges to submit the entire matter before judges, who are honestly in

---

* Translation from *Principles for Peace.*

possession of the facts, and to furnish them with every means of exercising a genuine and exact control—admits its obligation to make reparation to the extent possible for the damages inflicted on populations and regions once prosperous and flourishing.

At the same time, on their side, the creditors—the Powers of the Entente, above all France and Belgium, who are more directly interested—certainly have the right to demand of the debtor reparations for the damage suffered but not beyond the limits of its ability to pay. In other words, they cannot demand of Germany what it would not be able to pay without exhausting its own resources and productive capacity. Such a demand would be contrary to justice and social charity, as well as the interests not only of the debtor but of the creditors themselves. It would entail the danger of grave social upheavals and a bitterness which would constitute a continual threat to new and more disastrous conflagrations.

As a matter of fact, the creditors do not make such demands, but they deny the sincerity of Germany's new proposals and are of the opinion that the reparations now demanded, after the successive reductions already made, do not exceed the solvency of Germany, without any need of proof of their contention through estimates and check-ups as the Germans demand. These are questions which must be the subject of diplomatic conversations in the near future.

The Holy See neither can nor wishes to interfere here; it is sufficient for her to have recalled the principles of justice and charity whose conservation and spread God has entrusted to her care.

### Thoughts of Peace and Not of Affliction

There is reason to hope that in a friendly way by means of an expert appraisal and check-up requested by Germany, the Powers will arrive at the fixation of the amount which Germany can and must pay as reparations. They will succeed in this if they are animated by *thoughts of peace and not of affliction,* to use the Bibical expression quoted in the Pope's letter.

The pontifical document treats of another point, equally as important as that which we have just mentioned; it is the question of guarantees. The Holy Father recognizes the right of creditors to acquire proportionate guarantees which would assure the payment of the amount of credit. This payment involves interests that are equally vital for the creditors. In reality, territorial occupation is the guarantee or pledge of payment. The Holy Father leaves to creditors the duty of deciding whether the maintenance of territorial occupations which impose heavy sacrifices on the populations of occupied lands and on the conquerors themselves, or whether it would be preferable to substitute by degrees even, other, equally efficacious but less odious to the subjugated peoples, means of guarantee of repayments.

If the Powers would accept the suggestions of the Holy Father, the occupations would gradually lose some of their rigor; they would be more easily borne by the people and progressively reduced until totally diminished. Then, but only then, one could arrive at last at the sincere peace among nations which is also a necessary condition of the economic restoration so ardently desired by all. . . .

# The Holy See and the League of Nations*

(Letter of Cardinal Gasparri, Secretary of State, to Mr. John Eppstein, an Officer of the League of Nations Union, August 11, 1923)

. . . THE project can be accepted only in the sense that the Holy See would be at the disposal of the League for matters within its own competence: that is to say, the elucidation of questions of principle in morality and public international law; assistance to the League's relief works, where its aid would be of value to suffering peoples. On this occasion I feel I must tell you how much the Holy Father appreciates

---

* Translation from Principles for Peace.

the zeal with which, as an Officer of the League of Nations, you uphold Catholic principles in all circumstances. . . .

# Relief Aid to the Russian People*

(*Allocution* NOSTIS QUA PRAECIPUE *to the College of Cardinals, December 18, 1924*)

. . . ON Our part We have decided, as far as it is possible to do so, to continue, as We have in the past, to help the Russians, both those who are living in Russia and those exiles who are afflicted with a heavier cross. To more than one, We may seem in some way, by this charity toward the Russian people whom We have mentioned, to have helped a form of government which is so far from meriting Our approval. In spite of the fact that We have striven, with might and main, for so long a time, to alleviate the many and great evils which exist in Russia, We consider it part of the duty of Universal Fatherhood committed to Us by God, to admonish and earnestly to beseech all in the Lord, but especially the rulers of nations, as lovers of prosperity and peace and promoters of the sanctity of the family and human dignity, to make a united and serious effort to protect themselves and their people from the very grave and certain dangers and losses arising from Socialism and Communism, as they are called, while they make use, at the same time, of the necessary means and diligence to better the lot of workingmen and, in general, of all men in humble condition. . . .

---

* Translation from *Principles for Peace.*

# The Holy See and National Disputes*

*(The Lateran Treaty between the Holy See and the Italian Government, February 11, 1929)*

. . . With regard to the sovereignty pertaining to it in the field of international relations, the Holy See declared that it wishes to remain, and will remain extraneous to all temporal disputes between nations, and to international congresses for the settlement of such disputes unless the contending parties make a joint appeal to its mission of peace; nevertheless, it reserves the right to exercise its moral and spiritual power in every case. In consequence of this declaration the State of the Vatican will always and in every case be considered neutral and inviolable territory. . . .

# True Peace*

*(Allocution* BENEDETTO IL NATALE *to the College of Cardinals, December 24, 1930)*

. . . We wish you the "Peace of Christ," not a sentimental, confused and unwise pacificism, for that only true peace is that which comes from God. It bears the essential and indispensable marks and priceless fruits of true peace. The Church, incomparable teacher, called this to mind a few days ago in enclosing within the sacredness of the Divine Sacrifice those beautiful and profound words of the Apostle of the Gentiles: *And the Peace of God, which surpasseth all understanding, keep your hearts and minds in Jesus Christ.*

The Peace of Christ transcends, therefore, the senses. It is a grave error to think that true and lasting peace can rule among men and nations so long as they turn first and foremost with avid searching for sensible, material and earthly goods. For

---

* Translation from *Principles for Peace.*

34

these are limited and satisfy all men with difficulty, even in the event no one should desire the lion's share (which is hard to imagine). These are necessarily unsatisfying, for the greater the number of sharers, the smaller the share of each; wherefore, almost inevitably they are source of strife and discord as well as of greed and envy. The contrary is true of spiritual treasures—truth, goodness, virtue—for the more widely they are shared, the more they abound and give fruit to the advantage of each and of all.

Another error, against which the Apostolic Word, divinely inspired, wishes to fortify us, is that of supposing that true external peace can reign between men and peoples where there is not internal peace; where, that is to say, the spirit of peace does not possess the intellects and hearts, or better, the souls of men—the intelligence so that it recognizes and respects the claims of justice, the heart so that charity may be joined to and prevail over justice. For if peace, according to the prophet, must be the work and fruit of justice, it belongs, as St. Thomas luminously teaches (and this is true, by the very nature of things) more to charity than to justice.

It is, however, difficult for the internal peace of minds and hearts to rule for long among citizens and social classes, if a strong sense of contrast arises and is maintained among them by an unequal distribution and proportion of benefits and burdens, of rights and duties, of the contribution made by capital, management, and labor and of the participation in those fruits which can be produced only by their friendly collaboration.

Even more difficult—not to say impossible—is it for peace to last among peoples and States, if in place of true and genuine love of country, there rules and abounds a hard and selfish nationalism, which is the same as hatred and envy; in place of mutual desire for the good, distrust and suspicion; in place of the confidence of brothers, competition and struggle; in place of willing cooperation, ambition for control and mastery; in place of respect and care for the rights of all, pride.

# Selfish Nationalism*

(*Encyclical* CARITATE CHRISTI COMPULSI *May 3, 1932*)

. . . THE right order of Christian charity does not disapprove of lawful love of country and sentiments of justifiable nationalism; on the contrary, it controls, sanctifies, and enlivens them. If, however, egoism, abusing this love of country and exaggerating this sentiment of nationalism, insinuates itself into the relations between people and people, there is no excess that will not seem justified; and that which between individuals would be judged blameworthy by all, is now considered lawful and praiseworthy if it is done in the name of this exaggerated nationalism. Instead of the great law of love and human brotherhood, which embraces and holds in a single family all nations and peoples with one Father Who is in heaven, there enters hatred, driving all to destruction. In public life sacred principles, the guide of all social intercourse, are trampled upon; the solid foundations of right and honesty, on which the State should rest, are undermined; polluted and closed are the sources of those ancient traditions which, based on faith in God and fidelity to His law, secured the true progress of nations. . . .

# The Common International Welfare*

(*Letter of Cardinal Pacelli, Secretary of State, to M. Eugene Duthoit, President of the* SEMAINE SOCIALE *at Lille, France, June 28, 1932*)

. . . IT will be of great benefit that the lessons of this Social Week be proclaimed in an environment so well designed to guarantee a wide publicity, for they will be animated—your program assures this—by a marshalling of the capital truths

---

* Translation from *Principles for Peace.*

36

which must constitute the spiritual bulwark of a sound international economy.

The first of these truths is the fundamental unity of the great human family which, as Christ taught, has one Father in heaven; from this truth, follows the duty binding on the members of the different nations to effect a generous overflow upon other nations of the love which they first must entertain for their own country. It is likewise a duty for every nation to take into account the legitimate interests of other peoples; hence, there arises also for all nations the mutual obligation of justice and charity. Above all, the various political entities collectively are obliged to promote and serve the common international welfare, just as the citizens and the governing class of each individual state are bound to promote and serve the common welfare which affects them more intimately and is more limited in its extent. By the same token, it is necessary for all peoples to keep in view their interdependence, and to work into the various types of national solidarity corresponding forms of collaboration with those of other nationalities. Granted the necessity of a general build-up of national economic strength, this must not be accomplished by a systematic isolation behind economic barriers that grow evermore impassable; rather by a renewal of the time-honored practices of those austere virtues recommended by His Holiness Pius XI in His last Encyclical. This Encyclical, *Caritate Christi Compulsi* as well as *Quadragesimo Anno* have furnished you . . . with precious lights to discover the method of reconstruction that must be effected. . . .

# Nazi Germany and the Church*

*(Encyclical letter,* MIT BRENNENDER SORGE, *to the arch-bishops and bishops of Germany, March 14, 1937)*

IT is with deep anxiety and growing surprise that We have long been following the painful trials of the Church and the increasing vexations which afflict those who have remained loyal in heart and action in the midst of a people that once received from St. Boniface the bright message and the Gospel of Christ and God's Kingdom. . . .

When, in 1933, We consented, Venerable Brethren, to open negotiations for a concordat, which the Reich Government proposed on the basis of a scheme of several years' standing; and when, to your unanimous satisfaction, We concluded the negotiations by a solemn treaty, We were prompted by the desire, as it behooved Us, to secure for Germany the freedom of the Church's beneficent mission and the salvation of the souls in her care, as well as by the sincere wish to render the German people a service essential for its peaceful development and prosperity. Hence, despite many and grave misgivings, We then decided not to withhold Our consent, for We wished to spare the Faithful of Germany, as far as it was humanly possible, the trials and difficulties they would have had to face, given the circumstances, had the negotiations fallen through. It was by acts that We wished to make it plain, Christ's interests being Our sole object, that the pacific and maternal hand of the Church would be extended to anyone who did not actually refuse it.

While we tried to sow the seeds of a sincere peace, other men—"the enemy" of Holy Scripture—oversowed the cockle of distrust, unrest, hatred, defamation, of a determined hostility, overt or veiled, fed from many sources and wielding many tools, against Christ and His Church. They, and they alone, with their accomplices, silent or vociferous, are today responsible, should the storm of religious war, instead of the rainbow of peace, blacken the German skies.

* Translation from National Catholic Welfare Conference pamphlet.

## Who Kept the Peace and Who Broke It

We have never ceased, Venerable Brethren, to represent to the responsible rulers of your country's destiny, the consequences which would inevitably follow the protection, and even the favor, extended to such a policy. We have done everything in Our power to defend the sacred pledge of the given word of honor against theories and practices, which, if officially endorsed, would wreck every faith in treaties and make every signature worthless. Should the day ever come when We should place before the world the record of Our efforts, all right-minded persons will know who kept the peace and who broke it. All who seek the truth and who have a feeling for justice, will realize that in the grievous and eventful years after the Concordat was signed, every one of Our words, every one of Our acts, has been inspired by the binding law of treaties. At the same time, anyone must acknowledge, not without surprise and reprobation, how the other contracting party emasculated the terms of the treaty, distorted their meaning, and eventually considered its more or less official violation as a normal policy. The moderation We showed in spite of all this was not inspired by motives of worldly interest, still less by unwarranted weakness, but merely by Our anxiety not to draw out the wheat with the cockle; not to pronounce open judgment, before the public was ready to see its force; not to impeach other people's honesty, before the evidence of events should have torn the mask off the systematic hostility leveled at the Church. Even now that a campaign against the confessional schools, which are guaranteed by the Concordat, and the destruction of free election, where Catholics have a right to their children's Catholic education, afford evidence, in a matter so essential to the life of the Church, of the extreme gravity of the situation and the anxiety of every Christian conscience; even now Our responsibility for Christian souls induces Us not to overlook the last possibilities, however slight, of a return to fidelity to treaties, and to any arrangement that may be acceptable to the episcopate. We shall continue without failing, to stand before the rulers of your people as the defender of violated rights, and in obedience to Our Conscience and Our pastoral mission, whether We be successful or not, to oppose the policy which seeks, by open or secret means, to strangle rights guaranteed by a treaty. . . .

### True Use of God's Name

Take care, Venerable Brethren, that first of all belief in God, the primary and irreplaceable foundation of all religion, be preserved true and unadulterated in German lands. He is not a believer in God who uses the word of God rhetorically but he who associates with the sacred word the true and worthy idea of God.

He who, in pantheistic vagueness, equates God with the universe, and identifies God with the world and the world with God does not belong to believers in God.

He who replaces a personal God with a weird impersonal Fate supposedly according to ancient pre-Christian German concepts denies the wisdom and providence of God, that *reacheth from end to end mightily and ordereth all things sweetly* and directs everything for the best. Such a one cannot claim to be numbered among those who believe in God.

He who takes the race, or the people, or the State, or the form of Government, the bearers of the power of the State or other fundamental elements of human society—which in the temporal order of things have an essential and honorable place—out of the system of their earthly valuation, and makes them the ultimate norm of all, even of religious, values, and deifies them with an idolatrous worship, perverts and falsifies the order of things created and commanded by God. Such a one is far from true belief in God and a conception of life corresponding to true belief.

Beware, Venerable Brethren, of the growing abuse in speech and writing, of using the thrice holy name of God as a meaningless label for a more or less capricious form of human search and longing. Use your influence on the Faithful, that they refuse to yield to this aberration. Our God is the Personal God, supernatural, omnipotent, infinitely perfect, one in the Trinity of Persons, tri-personal in the unity of divine essence, the Creator of all existence, Lord, King and ultimate Consummator of the history of the world, Who will not, and cannot, tolerate a rival god by His side.

This God, this Sovereign Master, has issued commandments whose value is independent of time and space, of country and race. As God's sun shines on every human face, so His law knows neither privilege nor exception. Rulers and subjects, crowned and uncrowned, rich and poor are equally subject to His word. From the fulness of the Creator's right there naturally arises the fulness of His right to be obeyed by individuals and communities, whoever they are. This obedience permeates all branches of activity in which moral values claim harmony with the law of God, and pervades all integration of the ever-changing laws of man into the immutable laws of God.

None but superficial minds could stumble into concepts of a national God, of a national religion; or attempt to lock within the frontiers of a single people, within the narrow limits of a single race, God, the Creator of the universe, King and Legislator of all nations before whose immensity they are *as a drop in a bucket.*

We thank you, Venerable Brethren, your priests and Faithful, who have persisted in their Christian duty and in the defense of God's rights in the teeth of an aggressive paganism. Our gratitude, warmer still and admiring, goes out to those who, in fulfilment of their duty, have been deemed worthy of sacrifice and suffering for the love of God. . . .

### The Myth of Race and Blood

The peak of the Revelation as reached in the Gospel of Christ is final and permanent. It knows no retouches by human hand; it admits no substitutes or arbitrary alternatives such as certain leaders pretend to draw from the so-called myth of race and blood. Since Christ, the Lord's Anointed, finished the task of Redemption, and by breaking up the reign of sin deserved for us the grace of being the children of God, since that day *no other name under heaven has been given to men, whereby we must be saved.* No man, were every science, power and worldly strength incarnated in him, can lay any other foundation but that which is laid: which is Christ Jesus. Should any man dare, in sacrilegious disregard of the essential differences between God and His creature, between the God-man and the children of man, to place a mortal, were he the greatest of all times, by the side of, or over, or against, Christ, he would deserve to be called a prophet of nothingness, to whom the terrifying words of Scripture would be applicable: *He that dwelleth in heaven shall laugh at them.*

## Morality and Moral Order

It is on the faith in God, preserved pure and stainless, that man's morality is based. All efforts to remove from under morality and the moral order the granite foundation of faith and to substitute for it the shifting sands of human regulations, sooner or later lead these individuals or societies to moral degradation. The fool who has said in his heart *there is no God* goes straight to moral corruption, and the number of these fools who today are out to sever morality from religion, is legion. They either do not see or refuse to see that the banishment of confessional Christianity, *i. e.*, the clear and precise notion of Christianity, from teaching and education, from the organization of social and political life, spells spiritual spoliation and degradation. No coercive power of the State, no purely human ideal, however noble and lofty it be, will ever be able to make shift for the supreme and decisive impulses generated by faith in God and in Christ.

If a man, who is called to the hard sacrifice of his own ego to the common good, loses the support of the eternal and the divine, that comforting and consoling faith in a God who rewards all good and punishes all evil, then the result for the majority will be, not the acceptance, but the refusal of their duty. The conscientious observation of the Ten Commandments of God and the precepts of the Church (which are nothing but practical specifications of the rules of the Gospels) is for every one an unrivaled school of personal discipline, moral education and formation of character, a school that is exacting, but not to excess. A merciful God, who as Legislator, says—Thou must!—also gives by His grace the power to will and to do. To let forces of moral formation of such efficacy lie fallow, or to exclude them positively from public education, would spell religious under-feeding of a nation. To hand over the moral law to man's subjective opinion, which changes with the times, instead of anchoring it in the holy will of the eternal God and His commandments, is to open wide every door to the forces of destruction. The resulting dereliction of the eternal principles of an objective morality, which educates conscience and ennobles every department and organization of life, is a sin against the destiny of a nation, a sin whose bitter fruit will poison future generations.

## *Recognition of the Natural Law*

It is part of the trend of the day to sever more and more not only morality but also the foundation of law and jurisprudence, from true belief in God and from His revealed commandments. Here We have in mind particularly the so-called natural law that is written by the finger of the Creator Himself in the tables of the hearts of men and which can be read on these tables by sound reason not darkened by sin and passion. Every positive law, from whatever lawgiver it may come, can be examined as to its moral implications, and consequently as to its moral authority to bind in conscience, in the light of the commandments of the natural law. The laws of man that are in direct contradiction with the natural law bear an initial defect that no violent means, no outward display of power can remedy. By this standard must we judge the principle: "What helps the people is right." A right meaning may be given to this sentence if understood as expressing that what is morally illicit can never serve the true interests of the people. But even ancient paganism recognized that the sentence, to be perfectly accurate, should be inverted and read: "Never is anything useful, if it is not at the same time morally good" (Cicero, *De Off.* ii. 30). Emancipated from this moral rule, the principle would in international law carry a perpetual state of war between nations; for it ignores in national life, by confusing right and utility, the basic fact that man as a person possesses rights he holds from God, and which any collectivity must protect against denial, suppression or neglect. To overlook this truth is to forget that the real common good ultimately takes its measure from man's nature, which balances personal rights and social obligations, and from the purpose of society, established for the benefit of human nature. Society was intended by the Creator for the full development of individual possibilities, and for the social benefits, which by a

43

give and take process, everyone can claim for his own sake
and that of others. Higher and more general values, which collectivity alone can provide, also derive from the Creator for
the good of man, and for the full development, natural and
supernatural, and the realization of his perfection. To neglect
this order is to shake the pillars on which society rests, and to
compromise social tranquility, security and existence.

The believer has an absolute right to profess his Faith and
live according to its dictates. Laws which impede this profession and practice of Faith are against natural law.

Parents who are earnest and conscious of their educative
duties, have a primary right to the education of the children
God has given them in the spirit of their Faith, and according
to its prescriptions. Laws and measures which in school questions fail to respect this freedom of the parents go against
natural law, and are immoral. The Church, whose mission it
is to preserve and explain the natural law, as it is divine in its
origin, cannot but declare that the recent enrollment into
schools organized without a semblance of freedom, is the result of unjust pressure, and is a violation of every common
right. . . .

### To the Youth

No one would think of preventing young Germans from
establishing a true ethnical community in a noble love of
freedom and loyalty to their country. What We object to is the
voluntary and systematic antagonism raised between national
education and religious duty. That is why We tell the young:
Sing your hymns to freedom, but do not forget the freedom of
the children of God. Do not drag the nobility of that freedom
in the mud of sin and sensuality. He who sings hymns of
loyalty to his terrestrial country should not, for that reason,
become unfaithful to God and His Church, or a deserter and
traitor to His heavenly country. You are often told about
heroic greatness, in lying opposition to evangelical humility
and patience. Why conceal the fact that there are heroisms in
moral life? That the preservation of baptismal innocence is an
act of heroism which deserves credit? You are often told about
the human deficiencies which mar the history of the Church:
why ignore the exploits which fill her history, the saints she

begot, the blessing that came upon Western civilization from the union between that Church and your people?

You are told about sports. Indulged in with moderation, physical education is a boon for youth. But so much time is now devoted to sporting activities, that the harmonious development of body and mind is disregarded, that duties to one's family, and the observation of the Lord's Day are neglected. With an indifference bordering on contempt the day of the Lord is divested of its sacred character, against the best of German traditions. But We expect the Catholic youth, in the more favorable organizations of the State, to uphold its right to a Christian sanctification of the Sunday, not to exercise the body at the expense of the immortal soul, not to be overcome by evil, but to aim at the triumph of good over evil as its highest achievement will be the gaining of the crown in the stadium of eternal life.

He who searches the hearts and reins is Our witness that We have no greater desire than to see in Germany the restoration of a true peace between Church and State. But if, without any fault of Ours, this peace is not to come, then the Church of God will defend her rights and her freedom in the name of the Almighty whose arm has not shortened. Trusting in Him, *We cease not to pray and to beg* for you, children of the Church, that the days of tribulation may end and that you may be found faithful in the day of judgment; for the persecutors and oppressors; that the Father of light and mercy may enlighten them as He enlightened Saul on the Road of Damascus.

# Atheistic Communism*

(*Encyclical* DIVINI REDEMPTORIS, *March 19, 1937*)

. . . THIS modern revolution, it may be said, has actually broken out or threatens everywhere, and it exceeds in amplitude and violence anything yet experienced in the preceding persecutions launched against the Church. Entire peoples find

* Translation from National Catholic Welfare Conference pamphlet.

45

themselves in danger of falling back into a barbarism worse than that which oppressed the greater part of the world at the coming of the Redeemer. . . .

. . . We wish to expose once more in a brief synthesis the principles of atheistic communism as they are manifested chiefly in Bolshevism. We wish also to indicate its method of action and to contrast with its false principles the clear doctrine of the Church in order to inculcate once more and with greater insistence the means by which the Christian civilization, the true *civitas humana*, can be saved from the satanic scourge, and be better developed for the well-being of human society.

## *I*

## COMMUNISM IN THEORY AND PRACTICE

The Communism of today, more emphatically than similar movements in the past, conceals in itself a false messianic idea. A psuedo-ideal of justice, of equality and fraternity in labor impregnates all its doctrine and activity with a deceptive mysticism, which communicates a zealous and contagious enthusiasm to the multitudes entrapped by delusive promises. This is especially true in an age like ours, when unusual misery has resulted from the unequal distribution of the goods of this world. This pseudo-ideal is even boastfully advanced as if it were responsible for a certain economic progress. As a matter of fact, when such progress is at all real, its true causes are quite different, as for instance the intensification of industrialism in countries which were formerly almost without it, the exploitation of immense natural resources, and the use of the most brutal methods to insure the achievement of gigantic projects with a minimum of expense.

The doctrine of modern Communism, which is often concealed under the most seductive trappings, is in substance based on the principles of dialectical and historical materialism previously advocated by Marx, of which the theoricians of Bolshevism claim to have the only genuine interpretation. According to this doctrine there is in the world only one reality, matter, whose blind forces evolve into plant, animal and man. Even human society is nothing but a phenomenon and form of matter, evolving in the same way. By a law of inexorable necessity and through a perpetual conflict of forces, matter moves towards the final synthesis of a classless society. In such a doctrine, as is evident, there is no room for the idea of God; there is no difference between matter and spirit, between soul and body; there is neither survival of the soul after death nor any hope in a future life. Insisting on the dialectical aspect of their materialism, the Communists claim that the conflict which carries the world towards its final synthesis can be accelerated by man. Hence they endeavor to sharpen the antagonisms which arise between the various classes of society. Thus the class-struggle with its consequent violent hate and destruction takes on the aspect of a crusade for the progress of humanity. On the other hand, all other forces whatever, as long as they resist such systematic violence, must be annihilated as hostile to the human race.

*Man and the Family Under Communism*

Communism moreover, strips man of his liberty, robs human personality of all its dignity, and removes all the moral restraints that check the eruptions of blind impulse. There is no recognition of any right of the individual in his relations to the collectivity; no natural right is accorded to human personality, which is a mere cogwheel in the Communist system. In man's relations with other individuals, besides, Communists hold the principle of absolute equality, rejecting all hierarchy and divinely-constituted authority, including the authority of parents. What men call authority and subordination is derived from the community as its first and only font. Nor is the individual granted any property rights over material goods or the means of production, for inasmuch as these are the source of further wealth, their possession would give one man power over another. Precisely on this score, all forms of private property must be eradicated, for they are at the origin of all economic enslavement.

Refusing to human life any sacred or spiritual character, such a doctrine logically makes of marriage and the family a purely artificial and civil institution, the outcome of a specific economic system. There exists no matrimonial bond of a juridicomoral nature that is not subject to the whim of the individ-

47

ual or of the collectivity. Naturally, therefore, the notion of an indissoluble marriage-tie is scouted. Communism is particularly characterized by the rejection of any link that binds woman to the family and the home, and her emancipation is proclaimed as a basic principle. She is withdrawn from the family and the care of her children, to be thrust instead into public life and collective production under the same conditions as man. The care of home and children then devolves upon the collectivity. Finally, the right of education is denied to parents, for it is conceived as the exclusive prerogative of the community, in whose name and by whose mandate alone parents may exercise this right.

### "A Humanity Without God"

What would be the condition of a human society based on such materialistic tenets? It would be a collectivity with no other hierarchy than that of the economic system. It would have only one mission: the production of material things by means of collective labor, so that the goods of this world might be enjoyed in a paradise where each would "give according to his powers" and would "receive according to his needs." Communism recognizes in the collectivity the right, or rather, unlimited discretion, to draft individuals for the labor of the collectivity with no regard for their personal welfare; so that even violence could be legitimately exercised to dragoon the recalcitrant against their wills. In the Communistic commonwealth morality and law would be nothing but a derivation of the existing economic order, purely earthly in origin and unstable in character. In a word, the Communists claim to inaugurate a new era and a new civilization which is the result of blind evolutionary forces culminating in a humanity without God.

When all men have finally acquired the collectivist mentality in this Utopia of a really classless society, the political State, which is now conceived by Communists merely as the instrument by which the proletariat is oppressed by the capitalists, will have lost all reason for its existence and will "wither away." However, until that happy consummation is realized, the State and the powers of the State furnish Communism with

48

the most efficacious and most extensive means for the achievement of its goal.

Such, Venerable Brethren, is the new gospel which bolshevistic and atheistic Communism offers the world as the glad tidings of deliverance and salvation! It is a system full of errors and sophisms. It is in opposition both to reason and to Divine Revelation. It subverts the social order, because it means the destruction of its foundations; because it ignores the true origin and purpose of the State; because it denies the rights, dignity and liberty of human personality.

## Spread of Communism Explained

How is it possible that such a system, long since rejected scientifically and now proved erroneous by experience, how is it, We ask, that such a system could spread so rapidly in all parts of the world? The explanation lies in the fact that too few have been able to grasp the nature of Communism. The majority instead succumb to its deception, skillfully concealed by the most extravagant promises. By pretending to desire only the betterment of the condition of the working-classes, by urging the removal of the very real abuses chargeable to the liberalistic economic order, and by demanding a more equitable distribution of this world's goods (objects entirely and undoubtedly legitimate), the Communist takes advantage of the present world-wide economic crisis to draw into the sphere of his influence even those sections of the populace which on principle reject all forms of materialism and terrorism. And as every error contains its element of truth, the partial truths to which we have referred are astutely presented according to the needs of time and place, to conceal, when convenient, the repulsive crudity and inhumanity of Communistic principles and tactics. Thus the Communist ideal wins over many of the better-minded members of the community. These in turn become the apostles of the movement among the younger intelligentsia who are still too immature to recognize the intrinsic errors of the system. The preachers of Communism are also proficient in exploiting racial antagonisms and political divisions and oppositions. They take advantage of the lack of orientation characteristic of modern agnostic science in order to burrow into the universities where they bolster up the principles of their doctrine with pseudo-scientific arguments. . . .

There is another explanation for the rapid diffusion of the Communistic ideas now seeping into every nation, great and small, advanced and backward, so that no corner of the earth is free from them. This explanation is to be found in a propaganda so truly diabolical that the world has perhaps never witnessed its like before. It is directed from one common center. It is shrewdly adapted to the varying conditions of diverse peoples. It has at its disposal great financial resources, gigantic organizations, international congresses, and countless trained workers. It makes use of pamphlets and reviews, of cinema, theater and radio, of schools and even universities. Little by little it penetrates into all classes of the people and even reaches the better-minded groups of the community, with the result that few are aware of the poison which increasingly pervades their minds and hearts. . . .

### Communism Anti-Religious

For the first time in history we are witnessing a struggle, cold-blooded in purpose and mapped out to the least detail, between man and "all that is called God." Communism is by its nature anti-religious. It considers religion as "the opiate of the people" because the principles of religion which speak of a life beyond the grave dissuade the proletariat from the dream of a Soviet paradise which is of this world.

But the law of nature and its Author cannot be flouted with impunity. Communism has not been able, and will not be able, to achieve its objectives even in the merely economic sphere. It is true that in Russia it has been a contributing factor in rousing men and materials from the inertia of centuries, and in obtaining by all manner of means, often without scruple, some measure of material success. Nevertheless We know from reliable and even very recent testimony that not even there, in spite of slavery imposed on millions of men, has Communism reached its promised goal. After all, even the sphere of economics needs some morality, some moral sense of responsibility, which can find no place in a system so thoroughly materialistic as Communism. Terrorism is the only possible substitute, and it is terrorism that reigns today in Russia, where former comrades in revolution are exterminating each other. Terrorism, having failed despite all to stem the tide of moral corruption, cannot even prevent the dissolution of society itself.

In making these observations it is no part of Our intention to condemn *en masse* the peoples of the Soviet Union. For them We cherish the warmest paternal affection. We are well aware that not a few of them groan beneath the yoke imposed on them by men who in very large part are strangers to the real interests of the country. We recognize that many others were deceived by fallacious hopes. We blame only the system, with its authors and abettors who considered Russia the best-prepared field for experimenting with a plan elaborated decades ago, and who from there continue to spread it from one end of the world to the other.

## II

## *DOCTRINE OF THE CHURCH IN CONTRAST*

We have exposed the errors and the violent, deceptive tactics of Bolshevistic and Atheistic Communism. It is now time, Venerable Brethren, to contrast with it the true notion, already familiar to you, of the *"civitas humana"* or human society, as taught by reason and Revelation through the mouth of the Church, *"Magistra gentium."*

Above all other reality there exists one supreme Being: God, the omnipotent Creator of all things, the all-wise and just Judge of all men. This supreme reality, God, is the absolute condemnation of the impudent falsehoods of Communism. In truth, it is not because men believe in God that He exists; rather because He exists do all men whose eyes are not deliberately closed to the truth believe in Him and pray to Him.

In the Encyclical on Christian Education We explained the fundamental doctrine concerning man as it may be gathered from reason and Faith. Man has a spiritual and immortal soul. He is a person, marvelously endowed by his Creator with gifts of body and mind. He is a true "microcosm," as the ancients said, a world in miniature, with a value far surpassing that of the vast inanimate cosmos. God alone is his last end, in this life and the next. By sanctifying grace he is raised to the dignity of a son of God, and incorporated into the Kingdom of God in the Mystical Body of Christ. In consequence he has been endowed by God with many and varied prerogatives: the right to life, to bodily integrity, to the necessary means of existence; the right to tend toward his ultimate goal in the path marked out for him by God; the right of association and the right to possess and use property.

Just as matrimony and the right to its natural use are of divine origin, so likewise are the constitution and fundamental prerogatives of the family fixed and determined by the Creator. . . .

## Society Is for Man

But God has likewise destined man for civil society according to the dictates of his very nature. In the plan of the Creator, society is a natural means which man can and must use to reach his destined end. Society is for man and not vice versa. This must not be understood in the sense of liberalistic individualism, which subordinates society to the selfish use of the individual; but only in the sense that by means of an organic union with society and by mutual collaboration the attainment of earthly happiness is placed within the reach of all. In a further sense, it is society which affords the opportunities for the development of all the individual and social gifts bestowed on human nature. These natural gifts have a value surpassing the immediate interests of the moment, for in society they reflect the divine perfection, which would not be true were man to live alone. But on final analysis, even in this latter function, society is made for man, that he may recognize this reflection of God's perfection, and refer it in praise and adoration to the Creator. Only man, the human person, and not society in any form is endowed with reason and a morally free will.

Man cannot be exempted from his divinely-imposed obligations toward civil society, and the representatives of authority have the right to coerce him when he refuses without reason to do his duty. Society, on the other hand, cannot defraud man of his God-granted rights. Nor can society systematically void these rights by making their use impossible. It is therefore according to the dictates of reason that ultimately all material things should be ordained to man as a person, that through his mediation they may find their way to the Creator. In this wise we can apply to man, the human person, the words of the Apostle of the Gentiles, who writes to the Corinthians on the Christian economy of salvation: *All things are yours, and you are Christ's, and Christ is God's.* While Communism impoverishes human personality by inverting the terms of the relation of man to society, to what lofty heights is man not elevated by reason and Revelation! . . .

With good reason outstanding statesmen have asserted that, after a study of various social systems, they have found nothing sounder than the principles expounded in the Encyclicals *Rerum Novarum* and *Quadragesimo Anno.* In non-Catholic, even in non-Christian countries, men recognize the great value to society of the social doctrine of the Church. Thus, scarcely a month ago, an eminent political figure of the Far East, a non-Christian, did not hesitate to affirm publicly that the Church, with her doctrine of peace and Christian brotherhood, is rendering a signal contribution to the difficult task of establishing and maintaining peace among the nations. Finally, We know from reliable information that flows into this Center of Christendom from all parts of the world, that the Communists themselves, where they are not utterly depraved, recognize the superiority of the social doctrine of the Church, when once explained to them, over the doctrines of their leaders and their teachers. Only those blinded by passion and hatred close their eyes to the light of truth and obstinately struggle against it . . .

. . . Christianity first affirmed the real and universal brotherhood of all men of whatever race and condition. This doctrine she proclaimed by a method, and with an amplitude and conviction, unknown to preceding centuries; and with it she potently contributed to the abolition of slavery. Not bloody revolution, but the inner force of her teaching made the proud Roman matron see in her slave a sister in Christ. It is Christianity that adores the Son of God, made Man for love of man, and become not only the "Son of a carpenter" but Himself a "Carpenter"; it was Christianity that raised manual labor to its true dignity. . . .

53

Faithful to these principles, the Church has given new life to human society. Under her influence arose prodigious charitable organizations, great guilds of artisans and workingmen of every type. These guilds, ridiculed as "medieval" by the liberalism of the last century, are today claiming the admiration of our contemporaries in many countries who are endeavoring to revive them in some modern form. And when other systems hindered her work and raised obstacles to the salutary influence of the Church, she was never done warning them of their error. We need but recall with what constant firmness and energy Our Predecessor, Leo XIII, vindicated for the workingman the right to organize, which the dominant liberalism of the more powerful States relentlessly denied him. Even today the authority of this Church doctrine is greater than it seems; for the influence of ideas in the realm of facts, though invisible and not easily measured, is surely of predominant importance. . . . There would be today neither Socialism nor Communism if the rulers of the nations had not scorned the teachings and material warnings of the Church.

## III

## URGENT NEED FOR ACTION

The most urgent need of the present day is the energetic and timely application of remedies which will effectively ward off the catastrophe that daily grows more threatening. We cherish the firm hope that the fanaticism with which the sons of darkness work day and night at their materialistic and atheistic propaganda will at least serve the holy purpose of stimulating the sons of light to a like and even greater zeal for the honor of the Divine Majesty.

What then must be done, what remedies must be employed to defend Christ and Christian civilization from this pernicious enemy? As a father in the midst of his family, We should like to speak quite intimately of those duties which the great struggle of our day imposes on all the children of the Church; and We would address Our paternal admonition even to those sons who have strayed far from her.

54

## Fundamental Remedy

As in all the stormy periods of the history of the Church, the fundamental remedy today lies in a sincere renewal of private and public life according to the principles of the Gospel by all those who belong to the Fold of Christ, that they may be in truth the salt of the earth to preserve human society from total corruption.

We cannot deny that there is still much to be done in the way of spiritual renovation. Even in Catholic countries there are still too many who are Catholics hardly more than in name. There are too many who fulfill more or less faithfully the more essential obligations of the religion they boast of professing, but have no desire of knowing it better, of deepening their inward conviction, and still less of bringing into conformity with the external gloss the inner splendor of a right and unsullied conscience, that recognizes and performs all its duties under the eye of God. We know how much Our Divine Saviour detested this empty pharisaic show, He Who wished that all should adore the Father *in spirit and in truth*. The Catholic who does not live really and sincerely according to the Faith he professes will not long be master of himself in these days when the winds of strife and persecution blow so fiercely, but will be swept away defenseless in this new deluge which threatens the world. And thus, while he is preparing his own ruin, he is exposing to ridicule the very name of Christian.

And here We wish, Venerable Brethren, to insist more particularly on two teachings of Our Lord which have a special bearing on the present condition of the human race: detachment from earthly goods and the precept of charity. *Blessed are the poor in spirit* were the first words that fell from the lips of the Divine Master in His sermon on the mount. This lesson is more than ever necessary in these days of materialism athirst for the goods and pleasures of this earth. All Christians, rich or poor, must keep their eye fixed on heaven, remembering that *we have not here a lasting city, but we seek one that is to come*. The rich should not place their happiness in things of earth nor spend their best efforts in the acquisition of them. Rather, considering themselves only as stewards of their earthly goods, let them be mindful of the account they must render of them to their Lord and Master, and value them as precious means that God has put into their hands for doing good; let them not fail, besides, to distribute of their abundance to the poor, according to the evangelical precept. Otherwise there shall be verified of them and their riches the harsh condemnation of St. James the Apostle: *Go to now, ye rich men; weep and howl in your miseries which shall come upon you. Your riches are corrupted, and your garments are moth-eaten; your gold and silver is cankered; and the rust of them shall be for a testimony against you and shall eat your flesh like fire. You have stored up to yourselves wrath against the last days. . . .*

But the poor, too, in their turn, while engaged, according to the laws of charity and justice in acquiring the necessities of life and also in bettering their condition, should always remain *poor in spirit*, and hold spiritual goods in higher esteem than earthly property and pleasures. Let them remember that the world will never be able to rid itself of misery, sorrow and tribulation, which are the portion even of those who seem most prosperous. Patience, therefore, is the need of all, that Christian patience which comforts the heart with the divine assurance of eternal happiness. *Be patient, therefore, brethren,* We repeat with St. James *until the coming of the Lord. Behold the husbandman waiteth for the precious fruit of the earth, patiently bearing until he receive the early and the later rain. Be you therefore also patient and strengthen your hearts, for the coming of the Lord is at hand.* Only thus will be fulfilled the consoling promise of the Lord: *Blessed are the poor!* These words are no vain consolation, a promise as empty as those of the Communists. They are the words of life, pregnant with a sovereign reality. They are fully verified here on earth, as well as in eternity. Indeed, how many of the poor, in anticipation of the Kingdom of Heaven already proclaimed their own: *for yours is the Kingdom of Heaven*, find in these words a happiness which so many of the wealthy, uneasy with their riches and ever thirsting for more, look for in vain!

### Necessity of Charity

Still more important as a remedy for the evil we are considering, or certainly more directly calculated to cure it, is the precept of charity. We have in mind that Christian charity, *patient and kind,* which avoids all semblance of demeaning paternalism, and all ostentation; that charity which from the very beginning of Christianity won to Christ the poorest of the poor, the slaves. And We are grateful to all those members of charitable associations, from the conferences of St. Vincent de Paul to the recent great relief-organizations, which are perseveringly practicing the spiritual and corporal works of mercy. The more the workingmen and the poor realize what the spirit of love animated by the virtue of Christ is doing for them, the more readily will they abandon the false persuasion that Christianity has lost its efficacy and that the Church stands on the side of the exploiters of their labor.

But when on the one hand We see thousands of the needy, victims of real misery for various reasons beyond their control, and on the other so many round about them who spend huge sums of money on useless things and frivolous amusement, We cannot fail to remark with sorrow not only that justice is poorly observed, but that the precept of charity also is not sufficiently appreciated, is not a vital thing in daily life. We desire, therefore, Venerable Brethren, that this divine precept, this precious mark of identification left by Christ to His true disciples, be ever more fully explained by pen and word of mouth; this precept which teaches us to see in those who suffer Christ Himself, and would have us love our brothers as Our Divine Saviour has loved us, that is, even at the sacrifice of ourselves, and, if need be, of our very life. Let all then frequently meditate on those words of the final sentence, so consoling yet so terrifying, which the Supreme Judge will pronounce on the day of the Last Judgment: *Come, ye blessed of my Father . . . for I was hungry and you gave me to eat; I was thirsty and you gave me to drink . . . Amen, I say to you, as long as you did it to one of these my least brethren you did it to me.* And the reverse: *Depart from me, you cursed, into everlasting fire . . . for I was hungry and you gave me not to eat; I was thirsty and you gave me not to drink. . . . Amen, I say to you, as long as you did it not to one of these least, neither did you do it to me.*

To be sure of eternal life, therefore, and to be able to help the poor effectively, it is imperative to return to a more moderate way of life, to renounce the joys, often sinful, which the world today holds out in such abundance; to forget self for love of the neighbor. There is a divine regenerating force in this *new precept* (as Christ called it) of Christian charity. Its faithful observance will pour into the heart an inner peace which the world knows not, and will finally cure the ills which oppress humanity.

## True Charity Includes Justice

But charity will never be true charity unless it takes justice into constant account. The Apostle teaches that *he that loveth his neighbor hath fulfilled the law* and gives the reason: For, *Thou shalt not commit adultery, Thou shalt not kill, Thou shalt not steal* . . . and if there be any other commandment, it is comprised in this word: *Thou shalt love thy neighbor as thyself.* According to the Apostle, then, all the commandments, including those which are of strict justice, as those which forbid us to kill or to steal, may be reduced to the single precept of true charity. From this it follows that a "charity" which deprives the workingman of the salary to which he has a strict title in justice, is not charity at all, but only its empty name and hollow semblance. The wage-earner is not to receive as alms what is his due in justice. And let no one attempt with trifling charitable donations to exempt himself from the great duties imposed by justice. Both justice and charity often dictate obligations touching on the same subject-matter, but under different aspects; and the very dignity of the workingman makes him justly and acutely sensitive to the duties of others in his regard.

Therefore We turn again in a special way to you, Christian employers and industrialists, whose problem is often so difficult for the reason that you are saddled with the heavy heritage of an unjust economic régime whose ruinous influence has been felt through many generations. We bid you be mindful of your responsibility. It is unfortunately true that the manner of acting in certain Catholic circles has done much to shake the faith of the working-classes in the religion of Jesus Christ. These groups have refused to understand that Christian charity demands the recognition of certain rights due to the workingman, which the Church has explicitly acknowledged. What is to be thought of the action of those Catholic employers who in one place succeeded in preventing the reading of Our Encyclical *Quadragesimo Anno,* in their local churches? Or of those Catholic industrialists who even to this day have shown themselves hostile to a labor movement that We Ourselves recommended? Is it not deplorable that the right of private property defended by the Church should so often have been used as a weapon to defraud the workingman of his just salary and his social rights?

*There Is Also Social Justice*

In reality, besides commutative justice, there is also social justice with its own set obligations, from which neither employers nor workingmen can escape. Now it is of the very essence of social justice to demand from each individual all that is necessary for the common good. But just as in the living organism it is impossible to provide for the good of the whole unless each single part and each individual member is given what it needs for the exercise of its proper functions, so it is impossible to care for the social organism and the good of society as a unit unless each single part and each individual member—that is to say, each individual man in the dignity of his human personality—is supplied with all that is necessary for the exercise of his social function. If social justice be satisfied, the result will be an intense activity in economic life as a whole, pursued in tranquility and order. This activity will be proof of the health of the social body, just as the health of the human body is recognized in the undisturbed regularity and perfect efficiency of the whole organism.

But social justice cannot be said to have been satisfied as long as workingmen are denied a salary that will enable them to secure proper sustenance for themselves and for their families; as long as they are denied the opportunity of acquiring a modest fortune and forestalling the plague of universal pauperism; as long as they cannot make suitable provision through public or private insurance for old age, for periods of illness and unemployment. In a word, to repeat what has been said in Our Encyclical *Quadragesimo Anno:*

Then only will the economic and social order be soundly established and attain its ends, when it offers, to all and to each, all those goods which the wealth and resources of nature, technical science and the corporate organization of social affairs can give. These goods should be sufficient to supply all necessities and reasonable comforts, and to uplift men to that higher standard of life which, provided it be used with prudence, is not only not a hindrance but is of singular help to virtue.

It happens all too frequently, however, under the salary system, that individual employers are helpless to ensure justice unless, with a view to its practice, they organize institutions the object of which is to prevent competition incompatible with fair treatment for the workers. Where this is true, it is the duty of contractors and employers to support and promote such necessary organizations as normal instruments enabling them to fulfill their obligations of justice. But the laborers, too, must be mindful of their duty to love and deal fairly with their employers, and persuade themselves that there is no better means of safeguarding their own interests.

If, therefore, We consider the whole structure of economic life, as We have already pointed out in Our Encyclical *Quadragesimo Anno,* the reign of mutual collaboration between justice and charity in social-economic relations can only be achieved by a body of professional and inter-professional organizations, built on solidly Christian foundations, working together to effect, under forms adapted to different places and circumstances, what has been called the Corporation.

### Social Study and Propaganda

To give to this social activity a greater efficacy, it is necessary to promote a wider study of social problems in the light of the doctrine of the Church and under the aegis of her constituted authority. If the manner of acting of some Catholics in the social-economic field has left much to be desired, this has often come about because they have not known and pondered sufficiently the teachings of the Sovereign Pontiffs on these questions. Therefore, it is of the utmost importance to foster in all classes of society an intensive program of social education adapted to the varying degrees of intellectual culture. It is necessary with all care and diligence to procure the widest possible diffusion of the teachings of the Church. The minds of men must be illuminated with the sure light of Catholic teaching, and their wills must be drawn to follow and apply it as the norm of right living in the conscientious fulfilment of their manifold social duties. Thus they will oppose that incoherence and discontinuity in Christian life which We have many times lamented. For there are some who, while exteriorly faithful to the practice of their religion, yet in the field of labor and industry, in the professions, trade and business, permit a deplorable cleavage in their conscience, and live a life too little in conformity with the clear principles of justice and Christian charity. Such lives are a scandal to the weak, and to the malicious a pretext to discredit the Church.

In this renewal the Catholic Press can play a prominent part. Its foremost duty is to foster in various attractive ways an ever better understanding of social doctrine. It should, too, supply accurate and complete information on the activity of the enemy and the means of resistance which have been found most effective in various quarters. It should offer useful suggestions and warn against the insidious deceits with which Communists endeavor, all too successfully, to attract even men of good faith.

### Distrust of Communist Tactics

In the beginning Communism showed itself for what it was in all its perversity; but very soon it realized that it was thus alienating the people. It has therefore changed its tactics, and strives to entice the multitudes by trickery of various forms, hiding its real designs behind ideas that in themselves are good and attractive. Thus, aware of the universal desire for peace, the leaders of Communism pretend to be the most zealous promoters and propagandists in the movement for world amity. Yet at the same time they stir up a class-warfare which causes rivers of blood to flow, and, realizing that their system offers no internal guarantee of peace, they have recourse to unlimited armaments. Under various names which do not suggest Communism, they establish organizations and periodicals with the sole purpose of carrying their ideas into quarters otherwise inaccessible. They try perfidiously to worm their way even into professedly Catholic and religious organizations. Again, without receding an inch from their subversive principles, they invite Catholics to collaborate with them in the realm of so-called humanitarianism and charity; and at times even make proposals that are in perfect harmony with the Christian spirit and the doctrine of the Church. Elsewhere they carry their hypocrisy so far as to encourage the belief that Communism, in countries where faith and culture are more strongly entrenched, will assume another and much milder form. It will not interfere with the practice of religion. It will respect liberty of conscience. There are some even who refer to certain changes recently introduced into soviet legislation as a proof that Communism is about to abandon its program of war against God.

See to it, Venerable Brethren, that the Faithful do not allow themselves to be deceived! Communism is intrinsically wrong, and no one who would save Christian civilization may collaborate with it in any undertaking whatsoever. Those who permit themselves to be deceived into lending their aid towards the triumph of Communism in their own country, will be the first to fall victims of their error. And the greater the antiquity and grandeur of the Christian civilization in the regions where Communism successfully penetrates, so much more devastating will be the hatred displayed by the Godless.

### Prayer and Penance

But *unless the Lord keep the city, he watcheth in vain that keepeth it*. And so, as a final and most efficacious remedy, We recommend, Venerable Brethren, that in your dioceses you use the most practical means to foster and intensify the spirit of prayer joined with Christian penance. When the Apostles asked the Saviour why they had been unable to drive the evil spirit from a demoniac, Our Lord answered: *This kind is not cast out but by prayer and fasting*. So, too, the evil which to-day torments humanity can be conquered only by a world-wide holy crusade of prayer and penance. We ask especially the contemplative Orders, men and women, to redouble their prayers and sacrifices to obtain from heaven efficacious aid for the Church in the present struggle. Let them implore also the powerful intercession of the Immaculate Virgin who, having crushed the head of the serpent of old, remains the sure protectress and invincible "Help of Christians."

## IV

## MINISTERS AND CO-WORKERS IN CATHOLIC SOCIAL ACTION

### Priests

To apply the remedies thus briefly indicated to the task of saving the world as We have traced it above, Jesus Christ, our Divine King, has chosen priests as the first-line ministers and messengers of His gospel. Theirs is the duty, assigned to them by a special vocation, under the direction of their bishops and in filial obedience to the Vicar of Christ on earth, of keeping alight in the world the torch of Faith, and of filling the hearts of the Faithful with that supernatural trust which has aided the Church to fight and win so many other battles in the name of Christ: *This is the victory which overcometh the world, our Faith.*

To priests in a special way We recommend anew the old-repeated counsel of Our Predecessor, Leo XIII, to go to the workingman. We make this advice Our own, and faithful to the teaching of Jesus Christ and His Church, We thus complete it: *Go to the workingman, especially where he is poor; and in general, go to the poor.* The poor are obviously more exposed than others to the wiles of agitators who, taking advantage of their extreme need, kindle their hearts to envy of the rich and urge them to seize by force what fortune seems to have denied them unjustly. If the priest will not go to the workingman and to the poor, to warn them or to disabuse them of prejudice and false theory, they will become an easy prey for the apostles of Communism.

Indisputably much has been done in this direction, especially after the publication of the Encyclicals *Rerum Novarum* and *Quadragesimo Anno*. We are happy to voice Our paternal approval of the zealous pastoral activity manifested by so many Bishops and priests who have with due prudence and caution been planning and applying new methods of apostolate more adapted to modern needs. But for the solution of our present problem, all this effort is still inadequate. When our country is in danger, everything not strictly necessary, everything not bearing directly on the urgent matter of unified defense, takes second place. So we must act in today's crisis. Every other enterprise, however attractive and helpful, must yield before the vital need of protecting the very foundation of the Faith and of Christian civilization. Let our parish priests, therefore, while providing of course for the normal needs of the Faithful, dedicate the better part of their endeavors and their zeal to winning back the laboring masses to Christ and to His Church. Let them work to infuse the Christian spirit into quarters where it is least at home. The willing response of the masses, and results far exceeding their expectations, will not fail to reward them for their strenuous pioneer labor. This has been and continues to be our experience in Rome and in other capitals, where zealous parish communities are being formed as new churches are built in the suburban districts, and real miracles are being worked in the conversion of people whose hostility to religion has been due solely to the fact that they did not know it.

But the most efficacious means of apostolate among the poor and lowly is the priest's example, the practice of all those sacerdotal virtues which We have described in Our Encyclical *Ad Catholici Sacerdotii.* Especially needful, however, for the present situation is the shining example of a life which is humble, poor and disinterested, in imitation of a Divine Master Who could say to the world with divine simplicity: *The foxes have holes and the birds of the air nests, but the Son of Man hath not where to lay His head.* A priest who is really poor and disinterested in the Gospel sense may work among his flock marvels recalling a St. Vincent de Paul, a Curé of Ars, a Cottolengo, a Don Bosco and so many others; while an avaricious and selfish priest, as We have noted in the above-mentioned Encyclical, even though he should not plunge with Judas to the abyss of treason, will never be more than empty "sounding brass" and useless "tinkling cymbal." Too often, indeed, he will be a hindrance rather than an instrument of grace in the midst of his people. Furthermore, where a secular priest or religious is obliged by his office to administer temporal property, let him remember that he is not only to observe scrupulously all that charity and justice prescribe, but that he has a special obligation to conduct himself in very truth as a father of the poor.

64

## Catholic Action

After this appeal to the clergy, We extend Our paternal invitation to Our beloved sons among the laity who are doing battle in the ranks of Catholic Action. On another occasion We have called this movement so dear to Our heart "a particularly providential assistance" in the work of the Church during these troublous times. Catholic Action is in effect a *social* apostolate also, inasmuch as its object is to spread the Kingdom of Jesus Christ not only among individuals, but also in families and in society. It must, therefore, make it a chief aim to train its members with special care and to prepare them to fight the battles of the Lord. This task of formation, now more urgent and indispensable than ever, which must always precede direct action in the field, will assuredly be served by study-circles, conferences, lecture courses and the various other activities undertaken with a view to making known the Christian solution of the social problem.

The militant leaders of Catholic Action, thus properly prepared and armed, will be the first and immediate apostles of their fellow workmen. They will be an invaluable aid to the priest in carrying the torch of truth, and in relieving grave spiritual and material suffering, in many sectors where inveterate anticlerical prejudice or deplorable religious indifference has proved a constant obstacle to the pastoral activity of God's ministers. In this way they will collaborate, under the direction of especially qualified priests, in that work of spiritual aid to the laboring classes on which We set so much store, because it is the means best calculated to save these, Our beloved children, from the snares of Communism.

In addition to this individual apostolate which, however useful and efficacious, often goes unheralded, Catholic Action must organize propaganda on a large scale to disseminate knowledge of the fundamental principles on which, according to the Pontifical documents, a Christian Social Order must build.

Ranged with Catholic Action are the groups which We have been happy to call its auxiliary forces. With paternal affection We exhort these valuable organizations also to dedicate themselves to the great mission of which We have been treating, a cause which today transcends all others in vital importance.

We are thinking likewise of those associations of workmen, farmers, technicians, doctors, employers, students and others of like character, groups of men and women who live in the same cultural atmosphere and share the same way of life. Precisely these groups and organizations are destined to introduce into society that order which We have envisaged in Our Encyclical *Quadragesimo Anno,* and thus to spread in the vast and various fields of culture and labor the recognition of the Kingdom of Christ.

Even where the State, because of changed social and economic conditions, has felt obliged to intervene directly in order to aid and regulate such organizations by special legislative enactments, supposing always the necessary respect for liberty and private initiative, Catholic Action may not urge the circumstance as an excuse for abandoning the field. Its members should contribute prudently and intelligently to the study of the problems of the hour in the light of Catholic doctrine. They should loyally and generously participate in the formation of the new institutions, bringing to them the Christian spirit which is the basic principle of order wherever men work together in fraternal harmony.

## Appeal to Catholic Workers

Here We should like to address a particularly affectionate word to our Catholic workingmen, young and old. They have been given, perhaps as a reward for their often heroic fidelity in these trying days, a noble and an arduous mission. Under the guidance of their Bishops and priests, they are to bring back to the Church and to God those immense multitudes of their brother-workmen who, because they were not understood or treated with the respect to which they were entitled, in bitterness have strayed far from God. Let Catholic workingmen show these their wandering brethren by word and example that the Church is a tender Mother to all those who labor and suffer, and that she has never failed, and never will fail, in her sacred maternal duty of protecting her children. If this mission, which must be fulfilled in mines, in factories, in shops, wherever they may be laboring, should at times require great sacrifices, Our workmen will remember that the Saviour of the world has given them an example not only of toil but of self-immolation.

## Need of Unity Among Catholics

To all Our children, finally, of every social rank and every nation, to every religious and lay organization in the Church, We make another and more urgent appeal for union. Many times Our paternal heart has been saddened by the divergencies—often idle in their causes, always tragic in their consequences—which array in opposing camps the sons of the same Mother Church. Thus it is that the radicals, who are not so very numerous, profiting by this discord are able to make it more acute, and end by pitting Catholics one against the other. In view of the events of the past few months, Our warning must seem superfluous. We repeat it nevertheless once more, for those who have not understood, or perhaps do not desire to understand. Those who make a practice of spreading dissension among Catholics assume a terrible responsibility before God and the Church.

But in this battle joined by the powers of darkness against the very idea of Divinity, it is Our fond hope that, besides the host which glories in the name of Christ, all those—and they comprise the overwhelming majority of mankind—who still believe in God and pay Him homage may take a decisive part. We therefore renew the invitation extended to them five years ago in Our Encyclical *Caritate Christi*, invoking their loyal and hearty collaboration "in order to ward off from mankind the great danger that threatens all alike." Since, as We then said, "belief in God is the unshakable foundation of all social order and of all responsibility on earth, it follows that all those who do not want anarchy and terrorism ought to take energetic steps to prevent the enemies of religion from attaining the goal they have so brazenly proclaimed to the world."

## Duties of the Christian State

Such is the positive task, embracing at once theory and practice, which the Church undertakes in virtue of the mission, confided to her by Christ, of constructing a Christian society, and, in our own times, of resisting unto victory the attacks of

Communism. It is the duty of the Christian State to concur actively in his spiritual enterprise of the Church, aiding her with the means at its command, which although they be external devices, have nonetheless for their prime object the good of souls.

This means that all diligence should be exercised by States to prevent within their territories the ravages of an anti-God campaign which shakes society to its very foundations. For there can be no authority on earth unless the authority of the Divine Majesty be recognized; no oath will bind which is not sworn in the Name of the Living God. We repeat what We have said with frequent insistence in the past, especially in Our Encyclical *Caritate Christi:*

> How can any contract be maintained, and what value can any treaty have, in which every guarantee of conscience is lacking? And how can there be talk of guarantees of conscience when all faith in God and all fear of God have vanished? Take away this basis, and with it all moral law falls, and there is no remedy left to stop the gradual but inevitable destruction of peoples, families, the State, civilization itself.

It must likewise be the special care of the State to create those material conditions of life without which an orderly society cannot exist. The State must take every measure necessary to supply employment, particularly for the heads of families and for the young. To achieve this end demanded by the pressing needs of the common welfare, the wealthy classes must be induced to assume those burdens without which human society cannot be saved nor they themselves remain secure. However, measures taken by the State with this end in view ought to be of such a nature that they will really affect those who actually possess more than their share of capital resources, and who continue to accumulate them to the grievous detriment of others.

The State itself, mindful of its responsibility before God and society, should be a model of prudence and sobriety in the administration of the commonwealth. Today more than ever the acute world crisis demands that those who dispose of immense funds, built up on the sweat and toil of millions, keep constantly and singly in mind the common good. State functionaries and all employees are obliged in conscience to perform their duties faithfully and unselfishly, imitating the brilliant example of distinguished men of the past and of our own day, who with unremitting labor sacrificed their all for the good of their country. In international trade-relations let all means be sedulously employed for the removal of those artificial barriers to economic life which are the effects of distrust and hatred. All must remember that the peoples of the earth form but one family in God.

### Unrestricted Freedom for the Church

At the same time the State must allow the Church full liberty to fulfill her divine and spiritual mission, and this in itself will be an effectual contribution to the rescue of nations from the dread torment of the present hour. Everywhere today there is an anxious appeal to moral and spiritual forces; and rightly so, for the evil we must combat is at its origin primarily an evil of the spiritual order. From this polluted source the monstrous emanations of the Communistic system flow with satanic logic. Now, the Catholic Church is undoubtedly preëminent among the moral and religious forces of today. Therefore the very good of humanity demands that her work be allowed to proceed unhindered.

Those who act otherwise, and at the same time fondly pretend to attain their objective with purely political or economic means, are in the grip of a dangerous error. When religion is banished from the school, from education and from public life, when the representatives of Christianity and its sacred rites are held up to ridicule, are we not really fostering the materialism which is the fertile soil of Communism? Neither force, however well organized it be, nor earthly ideals however lofty or noble, can control a movement whose roots lie in the excessive esteem for the goods of this world.

We trust that those rulers of nations, who are at all aware of the extreme danger threatening every people today, may be more and more convinced of their supreme duty not to hinder the Church in the fulfillment of her mission. This is the more imperative since, while this mission has in view man's happiness in heaven, it cannot but promote his true felicity in time.

We cannot conclude this Encyclical Letter without addressing some words to those of Our children who are more or less tainted with the Communist plague. We earnestly exhort them to hear the voice of their loving Father. We pray the Lord to enlighten them that they may abandon the slippery path which will precipitate one and all to ruin and catastrophe, and that they recognize that Jesus Christ, Our Lord, is their only Saviour: *For there is no other name under heaven given to man, whereby we must be saved.*

## CONCLUSION

### *Saint Joseph, Model and Patron*

To hasten the advent of that "peace of Christ in the kingdom of Christ" so ardently desired by all, We place the vast campaign of the Church against world Communism under the standard of St. Joseph, her mighty Protector. He belongs to the working-class and he bore the burdens of poverty for himself and the Holy Family, whose tender and vigilant head he was. To him was entrusted the Divine Child when Herod loosed his assassins against Him. In a life of faithful performance of everyday duties, he left an example for all those who must gain their bread by the toil of their hands. He won for himself the title of "The Just," serving thus as a living model of that Christian justice which should reign in social life.

With eyes lifted on high, our Faith sees the new heavens and the new earth described by Our first Predecessor, St. Peter. While the promises of the false prophets of this earth melt away in blood and tears, the great apocalyptic prophecy of the Redeemer shines forth in heavenly splendor: *Behold, I make all things new.*

# Exaggerated Nationalism\*

(*Address* LE MISSIONI E IL NAZIONALISMO *to the Students of the* COLLEGIO DE PROPAGANDA FIDE *in Rome, August 21, 1938*)

. . . BEWARE of the grave dangers of exaggerated nationalism. For there is nationalism and nationalism, which amounts to saying that there is nation and nation, personality and personality. Nations as well as nationalism are existing realities, for nations were made by God. There is, therefore, room for a fair and moderate nationalism, which is the breeding ground of many virtues, but beware of exaggerated nationalism as of a veritable curse. Unfortunately, it seems to Us that the facts justify Our terms—a veritable curse—for it breeds constant division and the threat of war. It is no less a curse of sterility where missions are concerned, for it is not along this path that the fertility of grace will be revealed, or that apostleship will flourish. . . .

# The State and the Individual\*

(*Address* VOILA UNE AUDIENCE *to a Pilgrimage of the French Christian Workers' Syndicates, September 18, 1938*)

. . . You have included among your guiding principles—We have noticed and it couldn't be otherwise with Christian workers—a denial of the doctrine, so frequently heard today, that the State is all and the individual nothing. You have done well, for the Church does not speak that way; such is not the doctrine of the Church. One might sum up this doctrine with brutal simplicity: all for the State, nothing for the individual. No, the Church does not teach such a doctrine. But neither

\* Translation from *Principles for Peace.*

71

does it teach the contrary doctine: all for the individual, nothing for the State.

. . . The Church professes and teaches a doctrine which clearly defines relations between the State and the individual. Certainly it is clearly evident that the individual, from birth until death, needs the State for his life and development, because of the necessities of daily living. But it is not true that the State is a person, an independent entity speaking in its own name. . . . Thus when one speaks of the soul of the State, it is an idiom of speech that has some foundation in reality, but is really an abstraction. The State can exercise no personal function except through the individuals who compose it. This is an evident fact, but in our day it is no longer recognized in many places. It is repeated almost everywhere in one way or another—everyone now is accustomed to hearing it—that everything belongs to the State, nothing to the individual. Oh! dear sons, what an error lies in this expression! In the first place, it is against the facts, for if the individual is really dependent upon society in some way, society without the individuals would be nothing but a pure abstraction. But there is something very grave behind this; those who say that all belongs to the State also say that the State is something divine. Then the individual is divinized, but in a new way; it is a species of social pantheism. Listen, dear sons, to the lesson which the elementary catechism taught us: it is the enemy of men who says *you will be like gods* (*eritis sicut dii*). You all know what this phrase means and how it has become the tragedy of all ages for poor, sinful humanity.

Almost everywhere it is said that everything belongs to the State, the totalitarian State, as it is called; nothing without the State, everything for the State. There is an error here so evident that it is astonishing that men, otherwise serious and talented, say it and teach it to the masses. . . .

# Pius XII

## How Can There Be Peace?*

(*Easter Homily* QUONIAM PASCHALIA SOLLEMNIA *in Saint Peter's Basilica, April 9, 1939*)

ON all sides, indeed, wherever we turn our gaze, it is a sad spectacle that meets us. For in every part of the world we can descry great numbers of men greatly disturbed, anxious as to their fate, tormented with fearful misgivings, that seem to hint at still more frightful things about to come. A fearsome anxiety possesses the souls of men, as though worse dangers yet were hanging over them in direful menace. How far removed is this unhappy state of things from that serene "tranquility of order" which is bound up with peace really worthy of its name!

And yet, how can there be real and solid peace while even men with a common nationality, heedless of their common stock or their common fatherland, are torn apart and kept asunder by intrigues and dissensions and the interests of factions? How can there be peace, We repeat, while hundreds of thousands of men, millions even, lack work? For work is not only for every man a means of decent livelihood, but it is the means through which all those manifold powers and faculties with which nature, training and art have endowed the dignity of the human personality find their necessary expression, and this with a certain natural comeliness. Who is there, then who cannot see how, in such crises of unemployment as those our own time experiences, huge multitudes of utterly wretched men are created, through this very lack of

* Translation from *Principles for Peace.*

73

work whose unhappy condition is enlarged by the bitter contrast it presents with the pleasures and luxurious living of others altogether unconcerned about these armies of the needy? Who does not see how these poor men fall an easy prey to those whose minds are deceived by a specious semblance of truth, and who spread their corrupt teaching with ensnaring attractions?

Moreover, how can there be peace, if the different nations lack mutual, equitable judgment and common agreement of minds, powers which have guided the nations of the world along the bright road of civil progress? On the contrary, when solemnly sanctioned treaties and mutually pledged agreements are stripped of the power and security that is implied and strengthened by faithful adherence to promises, when this force and security themselves are removed, then each day it becomes more difficult to diminish the growth of armaments and pacify the hearts of men, twin desires of mankind everywhere. . . . Now justice demands that lawfully constituted authority receive the respect and obedience which is due to it; that the laws enacted be in conformity with the common good; that, as a matter of conscience, all men shall render obedience to these laws. Justice requires that all men acknowledge and defend the sacrosanct rights of human freedom and human dignity, and that the distribution of the infinite wealth and resources which God has provided for the whole world be made according to right reason for the use of all His children. . . .

# A Plea for Peace*

(*A Radio Address* UN'ORA GRACE *to the Whole World and its Leaders, August 24, 1939*)

AT the present time, when the tension of hearts seems to have reached the point, where the outbreak of the terrible scourge of war appears imminent, We direct with paternal feeling, a new and more heartfelt appeal to those in power and to their

---

* Translation from *Principles for Peace.*

peoples—to the former that, laying aside accusations, threats, and reasons for mutual distrust, they may attempt to resolve their present difficulties with the only suitable means: reciprocal and trustful agreements; to the latter that, in calm tranquility and without disordered agitation, they may encourage the peaceful efforts of their rulers.

It is by force of reason, and not by force of arms, that justice makes progress, and empires which are not founded on justice are not blessed by God. Statesmanship emancipated from morality betrays those very ones who would have it so. The danger is imminent, but there is yet time. Nothing is lost with peace; all may be lost with war. Let men return to mutual understanding! Let them begin negotiations anew, conferring with good-will and with respect for reciprocal rights. Then they will find that to sincere and conscientious negotiations an honorable solution is never precluded. They will feel a sense of greatness in the true sense of the word if, by silencing the voices of passion—be it collective or private—and by leaving to reason its rightful rule, they will have spared the blood of their fellow men and saved their countries from ruin.

May the Almighty grant that the voice of this Father of the Christian family, of this Servant of Servants, who bears amongst men, unworthily indeed but nevertheless truly, the person, the voice and the authority of Jesus Christ, find in the minds and hearts of men a ready and willing reception. May the strong hear Us that they may not become weak through injustice. May the powerful hear Us if they desire that their power be not destruction, but rather protection for their peoples and a safeguard to tranquility in public order and in their labor. We beseech them by the Blood of Christ, Whose conquering force in the world was His mildness in life and in death. In beseeching them, We know and feel that We have with Us all those who are upright of heart, all those who hunger and thirst after justice, all those who already suffer every sorrow through the evils of life. We have with Us the hearts of mothers, which beat as one with Ours; of fathers, who would be obliged to abandon their families; of the lowly, who labor and do not understand; of the innocent, upon whom weighs heavily the awful threat; of the young men, generous

75

knights of purest and noblest ideals. And with Us also is the soul of this ancient Europe, which was the product of Faith and Christian genius.

With Us, all humanity seeks justice, bread, and freedom; not steel, which kills and destroys. With Us is that Christ Who has made His solemn commandment, love of one's brother, the very substance of His Religion and the promise of salvation for individuals and for nations.

# A Plea to Belligerents*

(*Reply* C'EST UNE VIVE SATISFACTION *to the Homage of the New Belgian Ambassador, Adrian Nieuwenhuys, September 14, 1939*)

. . . SINCE, despite Our unworthiness, We are the Vicar of Him Who came down to earth as the Prince of Peace, We feel Ourselves sustained furthermore by the prayers of the faithful and comforted by interior feeling of certainty of Our union with countless souls of good-will. We shall not cease to be attentively on the alert to aid them with all Our power, on any occasion that may offer itself. We shall strive above all to guide mankind, at the present time in divisive combat, toward the conclusion of an honorable peace, in conformity with the human and the Christian conscience: a peace which protects the vital rights and safeguards the security and tranquility of all nations. Finally, as long as a peaceful solution is impossible, We shall at least alleviate the wounds already received and future suffering. With this in mind, it pleases Us to recall certain declarations which, at the beginning of the conflict, the belligerents affirmed as their intention to observe, in the conduct of the war: the laws of humanity and the stipulations of international agreements. Therefore, We cling in a special manner to the hope, that civilian populations will be preserved from all direct military operations; that in the occupied territories, the life, property, honor, and religious senti-

* Translation from *Principles for Peace.*

ments of the inhabitants will be respected; that prisoners of war will be treated humanely and receive the comforts of religion without hindrance; that the use of asphyxiating gas will be excluded. . . .

# Function of the State in the Modern World*

(*Encyclical* SUMMI PONTIFICATUS, *October 20, 1939*)

. . . BEFORE all else, it is certain that the radical and ultimate cause of the evils which We deplore in modern society is the denial and the rejection of a universal norm of morality in individual and social life, as well as in international relations. We mean the disregard, so common nowadays, and the forgetfulness of the natural law itself which has its foundation in God, Almighty Creator and Father of all, Supreme and Absolute Lawgiver, All-wise and just Judge of human actions. . . .

. . . Among the many errors which flow from the poisoned source of religious and moral agnosticism, We would draw your attention, Venerable Brethren, to two in particular, which more than others render almost impossible or at least precarious and uncertain, the peaceful intercourse of people.

## Excessive Nationalism

The first of these pernicious errors, widespread today, is the forgetfulness of that law of human solidarity and charity which is dictated and imposed by our common origin, by the equality of rational nature in all men no matter to what nation they belong, and by the redemptive Sacrifice offered by Jesus Christ on the Altar of the Cross to His Heavenly Father on behalf of sinful mankind.

In fact, the first page of the Scripture, with magnificent simplicity, tells how God made man to His own Image and Likeness, as the culmination of His creative work. The same

* Translation from National Catholic Welfare Conference pamphlet.

77

Scripture tells us that He enriched man with supernatural gifts and privileges, and destined him to eternal and ineffable happiness, and shows besides, how others originated from the first parents, and in unsurpassed vividness of language recounts their division and dispersion into various parts of the Earth. When they abandoned their Creator, God did not cease to regard them as His children, who, according to His merciful plan, should one day be reunited once more in His friendship. The Apostle of the Gentiles later on makes himself the herald of this truth which associates men as brothers in one great family, when he proclaims to the Greek world that God *hath made of one, all mankind, to dwell upon the whole face of the earth, determining the appointed times and the limits of their habitations, that they should seek God.*

. . . In the light of this unity of mankind, which exists in law and in fact, individuals do not feel themselves isolated like grains of sand, but united by the very force of their nature and by their eternal destiny into an organic, harmonious mutual relationship that varies with the changing times. Nations, despite a difference of development due to diverse conditions of life and of culture, are not destined to break the unity of the human race, but rather to enrich and embellish it by the mutual sharing of their own peculiar gifts and the reciprocal interchange of goods. This can be possible and efficacious only if mutual love and a lively sense of charity unite all the sons of the same Father and all those redeemed by the same Divine Blood.

The Church of Christ, the faithful depository of the teaching of divine wisdom, cannot and does not think of depreciating or disdaining the special characteristics which each people, with jealous and intelligible pride, cherishes and retains as a precious heritage. Her aim is a supernatural union in all-embracing love, deeply felt and practiced; not the unity which is exclusively external and superficial and, by that very fact, weak. The Church hails with joy and follows with her maternal blessing every method of guidance and care which seeks a wise and orderly evolution of particular forces and tendencies which originate in the individual character of each race, provided they are not opposed to the duties incumbent on men because of their common origin and destiny.

The Church has repeatedly shown in her missionary enterprises that such a principle of action is the guiding star of her universal apostolate. Pioneer research and investigation, involving sacrifice, devotedness and love on the part of her missionaries in every age, have been undertaken in order to produce a deeper appreciative insight into the most varied civilizations and make use of their spiritual values for a living and vital preaching of the Gospel of Christ. . . . Those who enter the Church, whatever be their origin or their speech, must know that they have equal rights as children in the Lord's House, where the law and peace of Christ prevail.

In accordance with these principles of equality, the Church devotes her care to the formation of a cultured native clergy and to the gradual increase in the number of native bishops. In order to give external expression to Our intentions, We have chosen the forthcoming Feast of Christ the King to raise to the episcopal dignity at the Tomb of the Apostles twelve representatives of widely different peoples and races. In the midst of the disruptive struggles which divide the human family, may this solemn act proclaim to all Our sons, scattered over the world, that the spirit, the teaching and the work of the Church can never be other than that which the Apostle of the Gentiles preached: *putting on the new man, who is renewed unto knowledge, according to the image of Him that created Him. Where there is neither Gentile nor Jew, circumcision nor uncircumcision, Barbarian nor Scythian, bond nor free. But Christ is all, and in all.*

## Patriotism

We do not fear that the awareness of universal brotherhood, inspired by the teaching and spirit of Christianity, would contrast with the love of tradition or the glorious heritage of one's fatherland, nor that it would hinder the progress of prosperous and legitimate interests. For Christianity teaches that, in the exercise of charity, we must follow a God-given order and yield the place of honor in our affections and good-works to those who are united to us by special ties. The Divine Master, Himself, in fact, gave an example of this preference for one's own country when He wept over the coming destruction of the Holy City. But legitimate and well-ordered

79

love of our native country, however, should not make us close our eyes to the all-embracing nature of Christian charity, which calls for consideration of others and their interests in the peaceful light of love.

Such a marvelous doctrine of love and peace has been an ennobling factor in the civil and religious progress of mankind. The heralds, who have proclaimed it under the impulse of supernatural charity, not only tilled the land and cared for the sick, but above all, they reclaimed, moulded, and raised human life to divine heights, as they directed all to the summit of sanctity, where everything is viewed in the light of God. They have raised mansions and temples which show to what lofty and kindly heights the Christian ideal urges man; but above all, they have made of men, wise or ignorant, strong or weak, living temples of God and branches of the Vine which is Christ. They have handed on to future generations the treasures of ancient art and wisdom which links men as brothers by the common recognition of a supernatural ownership. Venerable Brethren, forgetfulness of the law of universal charity, which alone can consolidate peace by extinguishing hatred and softening enmities and dissensions, is the root cause of grave evils to peaceful relations.

## Totalitarianism

But there is yet another error no less destructive of the well-being of nations and the prosperity of that great human society which gathers together and embraces in its confines all races. It is the error contained in those ideas which do not hesitate to divorce civil authority from every kind of dependence upon the Supreme Being—First Cause and Absolute Master of man and society—and from every restraint of a Higher Law derived from God as its First Source. Thus, they grant to civil authority an unrestricted field of action that is at the mercy of the fickle tide of human will or of the dictates of casual historical claims and of the special interests of a privileged few.

Once the authority of God and the sway of His law are denied in this manner, civil authority inevitably results in a tendency which attributes to itself an absolute autonomy that belongs exclusively to the Supreme Maker. Appropriating for itself the place of Almighty God, it elevates the State or society into the final end of life, the supreme criterion of the moral and juridical order, and thus it forbids every appeal to the principles of natural reason and Christian conscience. We do not, of course, fail to recognize that, fortunately, false principles do not always exercise their full influence, especially when age-old Christian traditions, on which the peoples have been nurtured, remain still deeply, if unconsciously, rooted in their hearts.

Nonetheless, one must not forget that the essential insufficiency and weakness of every principle of social life, which rests upon a purely human foundation, is that it is inspired by purely earthly motives, and relies for its force on the sanction of a purely external authority. When the dependence of human right upon the divine is denied, when appeal is made only to the insecure idea of merely human authority, and when an autonomy is claimed which rests only upon utilitarian morality, then human law itself justly forfeits in its more serious undertakings the moral force which is an essential condition for the acknowledgment as well as the denial of sacrifices.

It is quite true that power, based on such weak and unsteady foundations, can attain at times, under chance circumstances, material successes apt to stir admiration in superficial observers. But the moment comes when the inevitable law triumphs, which strikes down all that has been constructed upon a hidden or open disproportion between the greatness of the material and outward success and the weakness of the inner values and moral foundations.

Such disproportion exists whenever public authority disregards or denies the dominion of the Supreme Lawgiver, Who, as He has given rulers power, has also set and marked its bounds.

Indeed, as Our great predecessor, Leo XIII, wisely taught in the Encyclical *Immortale Dei*, it was the Creator's will that civil sovereignty should regulate social life after the dictates of an order changeless in its universal principles; should facilitate the attainment in the temporal order, by individuals, of physical, intellectual and moral perfection; and should aid them to reach their supernatural end.

81

### True Function of the State

Hence, it is the noble prerogative and function of the State to control, aid and direct the private and individual activities of national life that they converge harmoniously towards the common good. That good can neither be defined according to arbitrary ideas nor can it accept for its standard primarily the material prosperity of society, but rather it should be defined according to the harmonious development and the natural perfection of man. It is for this perfection that society is designed by the Creator as a means.

To consider the State as something ultimate to which everything else should be subordinated and directed, cannot fail to harm the true and lasting prosperity of nations. This can happen either when unrestricted dominion comes to be conferred on the State as having a mandate from the nation, people, or even a social order, or when the State arrogates such dominion to itself as absolute master, despotically, without any mandate whatsoever. If, in fact, the State lays claim to and directs private enterprises, these, ruled as they are by delicate and complicated internal principles which guarantee and assure the realization of their special aims, may be damaged to the detriment of the public good, by being wrenched from their natural surroundings, that is, from responsible private action.

### Rights of the Family

Further, there would be danger lest the primary and essential cell of society, the family, with its well being and its growth, should come to be considered from the narrow standpoint of national power, and lest it be forgotten that man and the family are by nature anterior to the State, and that the Creator has given to both of them powers and rights and has assigned them a mission and a charge that correspond to undeniable natural requirements.

The education of the new generation in that case would not aim at the balanced and harmonious development of the physical powers and of all the intellectual and moral qualities, but at a one-sided formation of those civic virtues that are considered necessary for attaining political success, while the virtues which give society the fragrance of nobility, humanity and reverence would be inculcated less, for fear they should detract from the pride of the citizen.

Before Us stand out with painful clarity the dangers We fear will accrue to this and coming generations from the neglect or non-recognition, the minimizing and the gradual abolition of the rights peculiar to the family. Therefore We stand up as determined defenders of those rights in the full consciousness of the duty imposed on Us by Our Apostolic office. The stress of our times, as well external as internal, material and spiritual alike, and the manifold errors with their countless repercussions are tasted by none so bitterly as by that noble little cell, the family.

True courage and a heroism worthy in its degree of admiration and respect, are often necessary to support the hardships of life, the daily weight of misery, growing want and restrictions on a scale never before experienced, whose reason and necessity are not always apparent. Whoever has the care of souls and can search hearts knows the hidden tears of mothers, the resigned sorrow of so many fathers, the countless bitternesses of which no statistics tell or can tell. He sees with sad eyes the mass of sufferings ever on the increase; he knows how the powers of disorder and destruction stand on the alert ready to make use of all these things for their dark designs. No one of good-will and vision will think of refusing the State, in the exceptional conditions of the world of today, correspondingly wider and exceptional rights to meet the popular needs. But even in such emergencies, the moral law, established by God, demands that the lawfulness of each such measure and its real necessity be scrutinized with the greatest rigor according to the standards of the common good.

In any case, the more burdensome the material sacrifices demanded of the individual and the family by the State, the more must the rights of conscience be to it sacred and inviolable. Goods, blood it can demand; but the soul redeemed by God, never. The charge laid by God on parents to provide for the material and spiritual good of their offspring and to procure for them a suitable training saturated with the true spirit of religion, cannot be wrested from them without grave violation of their rights.

## Formation of Youth

Undoubtedly, that formation should aim as well at the preparation of youth to fulfill with intelligent understanding and pride those offices of a noble patriotism which give to one's earthly fatherland all due measure of love, self-devotion and service. But, on the other hand, a formation which forgot or, worse still, deliberately neglected to direct the eyes and hearts of youth to the heavenly country would be an injustice to youth, an injustice against the inalienable duties and rights of the Christian family and an excess to which a check must be opposed, in the interests even of the people and of the State itself.

Such an education might seem perhaps to the rulers responsible for it, a source of increased strength and vigor; it would be, in fact, the opposite, as sad experience would prove. The crime of high treason against the *King of kings and Lord of lords* perpetrated by an education that is either indifferent or opposed to Christianity, the reversal of *Suffer the little children . . . to come to me*, would bear most bitter fruits. On the contrary, the State which lifts anxiety from the bleeding and torn hearts of fathers and mothers and restores their rights, only promotes its own internal peace and lays foundations of a happy future for the country. The souls of children given to their parents by God and consecrated in Baptism with the royal character of Christ, are a sacred charge over which watches the jealous love of God. The same Christ Who pronounced the words *Suffer little children to come to me* has threatened, for all His mercy and goodness, with fearful evils, those who give scandal to those so dear to His Heart.

Now what scandal is more permanently harmful to generation after generation than a formation of youth which is misdirected towards a goal that alienates from Christ *the Way and the Truth and the Life* and leads to open or hidden apostasy from Christ? That Christ from Whom they want to alienate the youthful generations of the present day and of the future is the same Christ Who has received from His Eternal Father all power in Heaven and on earth. He holds in His omnipotent Hand the destiny of States, of peoples, and of nations. His it is to shorten or prolong life: His to grant increase,

84

prosperity and greatness. Of all that exists on the face of the earth, the soul alone has deathless life. A system of education that should not respect the sacred precincts of the Christian family, protected by God's holy law, that should attack its foundations, bar to the young the way to Christ, to the Saviour's *fountains of life and joy*, that should consider apostasy from Christ and the Church as a proof of fidelity to the people or a particular class's word: *they that depart from thee, shall be written in the earth.*

## The Rights of the State

The idea which credits the State with unlimited authority is not simply an error harmful to the internal life of nations, to their prosperity, and to the larger and well-ordered increase in their well-being, but likewise it injures the relations between peoples, for it breaks the unity of supra-national society, robs the law of nations of its foundation and vigor, leads to violation of others' rights and impedes agreement and peaceful intercourse.

A disposition, in fact, of the divinely-sanctioned natural order divides the human race into social groups, nations or States, which are mutually independent in organization and in the direction of their internal life. But for all that, the human race is bound together by reciprocal ties, moral and juridical, into a great commonwealth directed to the good of all nations and ruled by special laws which protect its unity and promote its prosperity.

Now no one can fail to see how the claim to absolute autonomy for the State stands in open opposition to this natural way that is inherent in man—nay, denies it utterly—and therefore leaves the stability of international relations at the mercy of the will of rulers, while it destroys the possibility of true union and fruitful collaboration directed to the general good.

## Respect for Rights: Fidelity to Compacts

So, Venerable Brethren, it is indispensable for the existence of harmonious and lasting contacts and of fruitful relations, that the peoples recognize and observe these principles of international natural law which regulate their normal development and activity. Such principles demand respect for corresponding rights to independence, to life and to the possibility of continuous development in the paths of civilization; they demand, further, fidelity to compacts agreed upon and sanctioned in conformity with the principles of the law of nations.

The indispensable presupposition, without doubt, of all peaceful intercourse between nations, and the very soul of the juridical relations in force among them, is mutual trust: the expectation and conviction that each party will respect its plighted word; the certainty that both sides are convinced that *Better is wisdom, than weapons of war*, and are ready to enter into discussion and to avoid recourse to force or to threats of force in case of delays, hindrances, changes or disputes, because all these things can be the result not of bad-will, but of changed circumstances and of genuine interests in conflict.

But on the other hand, to tear the law of nations from its anchor in Divine law, to base it on the autonomous will of States, is to dethrone that very law and deprive it of its noblest and strongest qualities. Thus it would stand abandoned to the fatal drive of private interest and collective selfishness exclusively intent on the assertion of its own rights and ignoring those of others.

### Treaty Obligations

Now, it is true that with the passage of time and the substantial change of circumstances, which were not and perhaps could not have been foreseen in the making of a treaty, such a treaty or some of its clauses can in fact become, or at least seem to become, unjust, impracticable or too burdensome for one of the parties. It is obvious that should such be the case, recourse should be had in good time to a frank discussion with a view to modifying the treaty or making another in its stead. But to consider treaties on principle as ephemeral and tacitly to assume the authority of rescinding them unilaterally when they are no longer to one's advantage, would be to abolish all mutual trust among States. In this way, natural order would be destroyed and there would be seen dug between different peoples and nations trenches of division impossible to refill.

Today, Venerable Brethren, all men are looking with terror

into the abyss to which they have been brought by the errors and principles which We have mentioned, and by their practical consequences. Gone are the proud illusions of limitless progress. Should any still fail to grasp this fact, the tragic situation of today would rouse them with the prophet's cry: *Hear, ye deaf, and, ye blind, behold.* What used to appear on the outside as order, was nothing but an invasion of disorder: confusion in the principles of moral life. These principles, once divorced from the majesty of the Divine law, have tainted every field of human activity.

### Peace Must Be Just

But let us leave the past and turn our eyes towards that future which, according to the promises of the powerful ones of this world, is to consist, once the bloody conflicts of today have ceased, in a new order founded on justice and on prosperity. Will that future be really different; above all, will it be better? Will treaties of peace, will the new international order at the end of this war be animated by justice and by equity towards all, by that spirit which frees and pacifies? Or will there be a lamentable repetition of ancient and of recent errors?

To hope for a decisive change exclusively from the shock of war and its final issue is idle, as experience shows. The hour of victory is an hour of external triumph for the party to whom victory falls, but it is in equal measure the hour of temptation. In this hour the angel of justice strives with the demons of violence; the heart of the victor all too easily is hardened; moderation and far-seeing wisdom appear to him weakness; the excited passions of the people, often inflamed by the sacrifices and sufferings they have borne, obscure the vision even of responsible persons and make them inattentive to the warning voice of humanity and equity, which is overwhelmed or drowned in the inhuman cry, "*Vae victis,* woe to the conquered." There is danger lest settlements and decisions born in such conditions be nothing else than injustice under the cloak of justice.

### Peace Must Come from the Spirit

No, Venerable Brethren, safety does not come to peoples from external means, from the sword, which can impose con-

87

ditions of peace but does not create peace. Forces that are to renew the face of the earth should proceed from within, from the spirit.

Once the bitterness and the cruel strifes of the present have ceased, the new order of the world, of national and international life, must rest no longer on the quicksands of changeable and ephemeral standards that depend only on the selfish interests of groups and individuals. No, they must rest on the unshakable foundation, on the solid rock of natural law and of Divine Revelation. There the human legislator must attain to that balance, that keen sense of moral responsibility, without which it is easy to mistake the boundary between the legitimate use and the abuse of power. Thus only will his decisions have internal consistency, noble dignity and religious sanction, and be immune from selfishness and passion.

### Source of Evils More Than Economic

For true though it is that the evils from which mankind suffers today come in part from economic instability and from the struggle of interests regarding a more equal distribution of the goods which God has given man as a means of sustenance and progress, it is not less true that their root is deeper and more intrinsic, belonging to the sphere of religious belief and moral convictions which have been perverted by the progressive alienation of the peoples from that unity of doctrine, faith, customs and morals which once was promoted by the tireless and beneficent work of the Church. If it is to have any effect, the re-education of mankind must be, above all things, spiritual and religious. Hence, it must proceed from Christ as from its indispensable foundation; must be actuated by justice and crowned by charity.

### The Role of the Church

The accomplishment of this task of regeneration, by adapting her means to the altered conditions of the times and to the new needs of the human race, is an essential and maternal office of the Church. Committed to her by her Divine Founder, the preaching of the Gospel, by which are inculcated to men truth, justice and charity, and the endeavor to implant its precepts solidly in mind and conscience, is the most noble and most fruitful work for peace. That mission would seem as if it ought to discourage by its very grandeur the hearts of those who make up the Church Militant. But that cooperation in the spread of the Kingdom of God which in every century is effected in different ways, with varying instruments, with manifold hard struggles, is a command incumbent on everyone who has been snatched by Divine Grace from the slavery of Satan and called in Baptism to citizenship of the Kingdom of God.

And if belonging to it, living according to its spirit, laboring for its increase and placing its benefits at the disposition of that portion of mankind also which as yet has no part in them, means in our days having to face obstacles and oppositions as vast and deep and minutely organized as never before, that does not dispense a man from the frank, bold profession of our Faith. Rather, it spurs one to stand fast in the conflict even at the price of the greatest sacrifices. Whoever lives by the spirit of Christ refuses to let himself be beaten down by the difficulties which oppose him, but on the contrary feels himself impelled to work with all his strength and with the fullest confidence in God. He does not draw back before the straits and the necessities of the moment but faces their severity ready to give aid with that love which flees no sacrifice, is stronger than death, and will not be quenched by the rushing waters of tribulation.

## Catholic Action

It gives Us, Venerable Brethren, an inward strength, a heavenly joy, for which We daily render to God Our deep and humble thanks, to see in every region of the Catholic world evident signs of a spirit which boldly faces the gigantic tasks of Our age, which with generous decision is intent on uniting in fruitful harmony the first and essential duty of individual sanctification, and apostolic activity for the spread of the Kingdom of God. From the movement of the Eucharistic Congresses, furthered with loving care by Our predecessors, and from the collaboration of the laity, formed in Catholic Action towards a deep realization of their noble mission, flow forth fountains of grace and reserves of strength, which could hardly be sufficiently prized in the present time, when threats are more numerous, needs multiply and the conflict between Christianity and anti-Christianism grows intense.

At a moment when one is forced to note with sorrow the disproportion between the number of priests and the calls upon them, when one sees that even today the words of Our Saviour apply: *The harvest indeed is great, but the laborers are few,* the collaboration of the laity in the Apostolate of the Hierarchy, a collaboration indeed given by many and animated with ardent zeal and generous self-devotion, stands out as a precious aid to the work of priests and shows possibilities of development which justify the brightest hopes. The prayer of the Church to the Lord of the Harvest that he send workers into his vineyard has been granted to a degree proportionate to the present needs, and in a manner which supplements and completes the powers, often obstructed and inadequate, of the priestly apostolate. Numbers of fervent men and women, of youth obedient to the voice of the Supreme Pastor and to the directions of their Bishops, consecrate themselves with the full ardor of their souls to the works of the apostolate in order to bring back to Christ the masses of peoples who have been separated from Him.

To them in this moment so critical for the Church and for mankind go out Our paternal greeting, Our deepfelt gratitude, Our confident hope. These have truly placed their lives and their work beneath the standard of Christ the King; and they can say with the Psalmist: *I speak my works to the king. Thy Kingdom come* is not simply the burning desire of their prayers; it is, besides, the guide of their activity.

### The Lay Apostolate

This collaboration of the laity with the priesthood in all classes, categories and groups reveals precious industry, and to the laity is entrusted a mission than which noble and loyal hearts could desire none higher nor more consoling. This apostolic work, carried out according to the mind of the Church, consecrates the layman as a kind of "Minister to Christ" in the sense which St. Augustine explains as follows: *When, Brethren, you hear Our Lord saying: where I am there too will My servant be, do not think solely of good Bishops and clerics.* You too in your way minister to Christ by a good life, by almsgiving, by preaching His Name and teaching to whom you can. Thus every father should recognize that it is under this title that he owes paternal affection to his family. Let it be for the sake of Christ and for life everlasting, that he admonishes all his household, teaches, exhorts, reproves, shows kindness, corrects; and thus in his own home he will fulfill an ecclesiastical and in a way an episcopal office ministering to Christ, that he may be for ever with Him.

In promoting this participation by the laity in the apostolate, which is so important in our times, the family has a special mission, for it is the spirit of the family that exercises the most powerful influence on that of the rising generation. As long as the sacred flame of the Faith burns on the domestic hearth, and the parents forge and fashion the lives of their children in accordance with this Faith, youth will be ever ready to acknowledge the royal prerogatives of the Redeemer, and to oppose those who wish to exclude Him from society or wrongly to usurp His rights.

When churches are closed, when the Image of the Crucified is taken from the schools, the family remains the providential and, in a certain sense, impregnable refuge of Christian life. And We give thanks to God as We see that numberless families accomplish this, their mission, with a fidelity undismayed by combat or by sacrifice. A great host of young men and women, even in those regions where faith in Christ means suffering and persecution, remain firm around the Throne of the Redeemer with a quiet, steady determination that recalls the most glorious days of the Church's struggles.

What torrents of benefits would be showered on the world; what light, order, what peace would accrue to social life; what unique and precious energies would contribute towards the betterment of mankind, if men would everywhere concede to the Church, teacher of justice and love, that liberty of action to which, in virtue of the Divine Mandate, she has a sacred and indisputable right! What calamities could be averted, what happiness and tranquillity assured, if the social and international forces working to establish peace would let themselves be permeated by the deep lessons of the Gospel of Love in their struggle against individual or collective egoism! There is no opposition between the laws that govern the life of faithful Christians and the postulates of a genuine humane humanitarianism, but rather unity and mutual support. In the interests of suffering mankind, shaken to the depth both materially and spiritually, We have no more ardent desire than this: that the present difficulties may open the eyes of many to see Our Lord Jesus Christ and the mission of His Church on this earth in their true light, and that all those who are in power may decide to allow the Church a free course to work for the formation of the rising generation according to the principles of justice and peace.

This work of pacification presupposes that obstacles are not put to the exercise of the mission which God has entrusted to His Church; that the field of this activity is not restricted, and that the masses, and especially youth, are not withdrawn from her beneficent influence.

### Appeal to Rulers

Accordingly, We, as representative on earth of Him Who was proclaimed by the Prophet *Prince of Peace*, appeal to the rulers of the peoples, and to those who can in any way influence public life, to let the Church have full liberty to fulfill her role as educator by teaching men truth, by inculcating justice, and inflaming hearts with the Divine Love of Christ.

While the Church cannot renounce the exercise of this, her mission, which has for its final end to realize here below the Divine plan and to *re-establish all things in Christ, that are in heaven and on earth,* her aid, none the less, is shown to be indispensable as never before, now that sad experience teaches that external means and human provisions and political expedients of themselves bring no efficacious healing to the ills which affect mankind.

### Need of Unity

Taught precisely by the sad failure of human expedients to stave off the tempest that threatens to sweep civilization away, many turn their gaze with renewed hope to the Church, the rock of truth and of charity, to that Chair of Peter from which, they feel, can be restored to mankind that unity of religious teaching and of the moral code which of old gave consistency to pacific international relations.

Unity, towards which so many, answerable for the destiny of nations, look with regretful yearning as they experience from day to day the vanity of the very means in which once they had placed their trust! Unity, the desired of those many legions of Our sons who daily call upon *the God of peace and of love!* Unity, the hope of so many noble minds separated from Us, who yet in their hunger and thirst for justice and peace turn their eyes to the See of Peter and from it await guidance and counsel!

These last are recognizing in the Catholic Church principles of belief and life that have stood the test of two thousand years; the strong cohesion of the Ecclesiastical Hierarchy, which in union with the Successor of Peter spends itself in enlightening minds with the teaching of the Gospel, in guiding and sanctifying men, and which is generous in its material condescension towards all, but firm when, even at the cost of torments or martyrdom, it has to say: *Non licet; it is not allowed!*

### Respect for Authority

And yet, Venerable Brethren, the teaching of Christ, which alone can furnish man with such solid bases of belief as will greatly enlarge his vision, and divinely dilate his heart and supply an efficacious remedy to the very grave difficulties of today—this and the activity of the Church in teaching and spreading that doctrine, and in forming and modeling men's minds by its precepts, are at times an object of suspicion, as if they shook the foundations of civil authority or usurped its rights.

Against such suspicions We solemnly declare with Apostolic sincerity that—without prejudice to the declarations regarding the power of Christ and of His Church made by Our predecessor, Pius XI, of venerable memory, in his Encyclical *Quas Primas* of December 11, 1925—any such aims are entirely alien to that same Church, which spreads its maternal arms towards this world not to dominate but to serve. She does not claim to take the place of other legitimate authorities in their proper spheres, but offers them her help after the example and in the spirit of her Divine Founder Who *went about doing good.*

93

The Church preaches and inculcates obedience and respect for earthly authority which derives from God its whole origin and holds to the teaching of her Divine Master Who said: *Render therefore to Caesar the things that are Caesar's;* she has no desire to usurp, and sings in the liturgy: *He takes away no earthly realms who gives us the celestial.* She does not suppress human energies but lifts them up to all that is noble and generous and forms characters which do not compromise with conscience. Nor has she who civilizes the nations ever retarded the civil progress of mankind, at which on the contrary she is pleased and glad with a mother's pride. The end of her activity was admirably expressed by the Angels over the cradle of the Word Incarnate, when they sang of glory to God and announced peace to men of good will: *Glory to God in the highest; and on earth peace to men of good will.*

This peace, which the world cannot give, has been left as a heritage to His disciples by the Divine Redeemer Himself: *Peace I leave with you, my peace I give unto you;* and thus following the sublime teaching of Christ, summed up by Himself in the two-fold precept of love of God and of the neighbor, millions of souls have reached, are reaching, and shall reach peace. History, wisely called by a great Roman "The Teacher of Life," has proved for almost two thousand years how true is the word of Scripture that he will not have peace who resists God. For Christ alone is the "corner stone" on which man and society can find stability and salvation.

On this Corner Stone the Church is built, and hence against her the adversary can never prevail: *the gates of hell shall not prevail,* nor can they ever weaken her; nay, rather, internal and external struggles tend to augment the force and multiply the laurels of her glorious victories.

On the other hand, any other building which has not been founded solidly on the teaching of Christ rests on shifting sands and is destined to perish miserably.

## Hour of Darkness

Venerable Brethren,

The hour when this Our first Encyclical reaches you is in many respects a real *Hour of Darkness,* in which the spirit of violence and of discord brings indescribable suffering on

94

mankind. Do We need to give assurance that Our paternal heart is close to all Our children in compassionate love, and especially to the afflicted, the oppressed, the persecuted? The nations swept into the tragic whirlpool of war are perhaps as yet only at the *beginnings of sorrows,* but even now there reigns in thousands of families death and desolation, lamentation and misery. The blood of countless human beings, even noncombatants, raises a piteous dirge over a nation such as Our dear Poland, which, for its fidelity to the Church, for its services in the defense of Christian civilization, written in indelible characters in the annals of history, has a right to the generous and brotherly sympathy of the whole world, while it awaits, relying on the powerful intercession of Mary, Help of Christians, the hour of a resurrection in harmony with the principles of justice and true peace.

What has already happened and is still happening was presented, as it were, in a vision before Our eyes when, while still some hope was left, We left nothing undone in the form suggested to Us by Our Apostolic office and by the means at Our disposal, to prevent recourse to arms and to keep open the way to an understanding honorable to both parties. Convinced that the use of force on one side would be answered by recourse to arms on the other, We considered it a duty inseparable from Our Apostolic office and of Christian charity to try every means to spare mankind and Christianity the horrors of a world conflagration, even at the risk of having Our intentions and Our aims misunderstood. Our advice, if heard with respect, was not, however, followed, and while Our pastoral heart looks on with sorrow and foreboding, the Image of the Good Shepherd comes up before Our gaze, and it seems as though We ought to repeat to the world in His name: *If thou . . . hadst known . . . the things that are to thy peace; but now they are hidden from thy eyes.*

### World Reconstruction

In the midst of this world which today presents such a sharp contrast to "The Peace of Christ in the Reign of Christ," the Church and her faithful are in times and in years of trial such as have rarely been known in her history of struggle and suffering. But in such times, especially, he who remains

95

firm in his faith and strong at heart knows that Christ the King is never so near as in the hour of trial, which is the hour for fidelity. With a heart torn by the sufferings and afflictions of so many of her sons, but with the courage and the stability that come from the promises of Our Lord, the Spouse of Christ goes to meet the gathering storms. This she knows, that the truth which she preaches, the charity which she teaches and practices, will be the indispensable counsellors and aids to men of good will in the reconstruction of a new world based on justice and love, when mankind, weary from its course along the way of error, has tasted the bitter fruits of hate and violence.

### Charity to War Victims

In the meantime, however, Venerable Brethren, the world and all those who are stricken by the calamity of the war must know that the obligation of Christian love, the very foundation of the Kingdom of Christ, is not an empty word, but a living reality. A vast field opens up for Christian charity in all its forms. We have full confidence that all Our sons, especially those who are not being tried by the scourge of war, will be mindful in imitation of the Divine Samaritan, of all these who, as victims of the war, have a right to compassion and help.

The "Catholic Church, the City of God, whose King is Truth, whose law love and whose measure eternity" (St. Augustine, Ep. CXXXVIII, *Ad Marcellinum, C.* 3, *N.* 17), preaching fearlessly the whole truth of Christ and toiling as the love of Christ demands with the zeal of a mother, stands as a blessed vision of peace above the storm of error and passion awaiting the moment when the all-powerful Hand of Christ the King shall quiet the tempest and banish the spirits of discord which have provoked it.

### The Hastening of Peace

Whatever We can do to hasten the day when the dove of peace may find on this earth, submerged in a deluge of discord, somewhere to alight, We shall continue to do, trusting in those statesmen who, before the outbreak of war, nobly toiled to avert such a scourge from the peoples; trusting in the millions of souls of all countries and of every sphere, who call not for justice alone but for love and mercy; above all, trusting in God

96

Almighty to Whom We daily address the prayer: *in the shadow of thy wings will I hope, until iniquity pass away.*

God can do all things. As well as the happiness and the fortunes of nations, He holds in His hands human counsels and sweetly turns them in whatever direction He wills: even the obstacles are for His Omnipotence means to mould affairs and events and to direct minds and free wills to His all-high purposes.

Pray then, Venerable Brethren, pray without ceasing; pray especially when you offer the Divine Sacrifice of Love. Do you, too, pray, you whose courageous profession of the faith entails today hard, painful and, not rarely, heroic sacrifices; pray you, suffering and agonizing members of the Church, when Jesus comes to console and to heal your pains, and do not forget with the aid of a true spirit of mortification and worthy practice of penance to make your prayers more acceptable in the eyes of Him Who *lifteth up all that fall: and setteth up all that are cast down* that He in His mercy may shorten the days of trial and that thus the words of the Psalmist may be verified: *Then they cried to the Lord in their affliction: and He delivered them out of their distresses.*

### Children's Prayers

And you, white legions of children who are so loved and dear to Jesus, when you receive in Holy Communion the Bread of Life, raise up your simple and innocent prayers and unite them with those of the Universal Church. The Heart of Jesus, Who loves you, does not resist your suppliant innocence. Pray every one, pray uninterruptedly: *Pray without ceasing.*

In this way you will put into practice the sublime precept of the Divine Master, the most sacred testament of His Heart, *That they all may be one,* that all may live in that unity of faith and of love, from which the world may know the power and efficacy of Christ's mission and of the work of His Church.

The early Church understood and practiced this Divine Precept, and expressed it in a magnificent prayer; do you associate yourselves with those sentiments which answer so well to the necessities of the present hour: "Remember, O

Lord, Thy Church, to free her from all evil and to perfect her in Thy love; and sanctify and collect her from the four winds into Thy Kingdom, which Thou hast prepared for her, because Thine is the power, and the glory for ever" (*Doctrine of the Twelve Apostles, C.* 10).

# The Cult of Might Against Right*

(*Reply* D'UNE NATION LOINTAINE *to the Homage of the New Minister of Haiti, Nicolas Leger, November 10, 1939*)

. . . THE unity of the great human family, above all of the faithful in Christ, imposes on those peoples happily preserved from war the obligation to interest themselves in those who suffer and to multiply their appeals to the mercy of God, so that His omnipotent Hand may restore order and peace to the world.

But as We have often said, the world will enjoy peace and order, which is its indispensable condition, only if men responsible for the government of peoples and their reciprocal relations renounce the cult of might employed against right; if, recognizing that morality with a purely human basis is insufficient, they accept the supreme authority of the Creator as the basis of all individual and collective morality, and if they render to the Father in heaven the homage wished by Him of fraternal concord among His children of all countries and languages. Then only will they succeed in effectuating and perfecting a stable, fruitful international organization such as is desired by men of good-will: an organization which, respecting the rights of God, will be able to assure the reciprocal independence of nations big and small, to impose fidelity to agreements mutually agreed upon, and to safeguard the sound liberty and dignity of the human person in each one's efforts toward the prosperity of all. . . .

---

* Translation from *Principles for Peace.*

# Fundamental Points for a Just and Honorable Peace*

*(Christmas Message* IN QUESTO GIORNO DI SANTA *to the College of Cardinals, December 24, 1939)*

THE unspeakable calamity of war, which Pius XI foresaw with deep misgiving, and which with all the energy of his noble spirit he strove to avert from the comity of nations, is now upon Us as a tragic reality. . . . We have been forced to witness a series of acts irreconcilable alike with the precepts of positive international law and those of the law of nature, as well as with the elementary sentiments of humanity; acts which show in what a vicious circle the juridical sense becomes involved when it is led simply by considerations of expediency. . . .

Those, who keep a watchful eye upon future consequences and calmly consider the symptoms in many parts of the world already pointing to the development of such events, will, We think, in spite of the war and its hard necessities, keep their minds open to the prospect of defining clearly, at an opportune moment and so far as it lies with them to do so, the fundamental points of a just and honorable peace; nor will they categorically refuse negotiations for such a peace in the event of a suitable occasion, with the needful guarantees and safeguards, presenting itself.

(1) A fundamental postulate of any just and honorable peace is an assurance for all nations, great or small, powerful or weak, of their right to life and independence. The will of one nation to live must never mean the death sentence passed upon another. When this equality of rights has been destroyed, attacked, or threatened, order demands that reparation shall be made, and the measure and extent of that reparation is determined, not by the sword nor by arbitrary decision of self-interest, but by the rules of justice and reciprocal equity.

(2) The order thus established, if it is to continue undis-

---

* Translation from National Catholic Welfare Conference pamphlet.

turbed and ensure true peace, requires that the nations be delivered from the slavery imposed upon them by the race for armaments, and from the danger that material force instead of serving to protect right, may become an overbearing and tyrannical master. Any peaceful settlement which fails to give fundamental importance to a mutually agreed, organic and progressive disarmament, spiritual as well as material, or which neglects to ensure the effective and loyal implementing of such an agreement, will sooner or later show itself to be lacking in coherence and vitality.

(3) The maxims of human wisdom require that in any reorganization of international life all parties should learn a lesson from the failures and deficiencies of the past. Hence, in creating or reconstructing international institutions which have so high a mission and such difficult and grave responsibilities, it is important to bear in mind the experience gained from the ineffectiveness or imperfections of previous institutions of the kind. Human frailty renders it difficult, not to say impossible, to foresee every contingency and guard against every danger at the moment in which treaties are signed; passion and bitter feeling are apt to be still rife. Hence, in order that a peace may be honorably accepted and in order to avoid arbitrary breaches and unilateral interpretations of treaties, it is of the first importance to erect some juridical institution which shall guarantee the loyal and faithful fulfillment of the conditions agreed upon, and which shall, in case of recognized need, revise and correct them.

(4) If a better European settlement is to be reached, there is one point in particular which should receive special attention: it is the real needs and the just demands of nations and populations, and of racial minorities. It may be that, in consequence of existing treaties incompatible with them, these demands are unable to establish a strictly legal right. Even so, they deserve to be examined in a friendly spirit with a view to meeting them by peaceful methods, and even, where it appears necessary, by means of an equitable and covenanted revision of the treaties themselves. If the balance between nations is thus adjusted and the foundation of mutual confidence thus laid, many incentives to violent action will be removed.

(5) But even the best and most detailed regulations will be

imperfect and foredoomed to failure unless the peoples and those who govern them submit willingly to the influence of that spirit which alone can give life, authority and binding force to the dead letter of international agreements. They must develop that sense of deep and keen responsibility which measures and weighs human statutes according to the sacred and inviolable standards of the law of God; they must cultivate that hunger and thirst after justice which is proclaimed as a beatitude in the Sermon on the Mount and which supposes as its natural foundation the moral virtue of justice; they must be guided by that universal love which is the compendium and most general expression of the Christian ideal, and which, therefore, may serve as a common ground also for those who have not the blessing of sharing the same faith with us.

We are not insensible of the grave difficulties which lie in the way of the achievement of these ends which We have described as needful for establishing and preserving a just peace between nations. But if ever there was an objective deserving the collaboration of all noble and generous minds, if there was ever a spiritual crusade which might assume with a new truth as its motto, "God wills it," then it is this high purpose, it is this crusade enlisting all unselfish and great-hearted men in an endeavor to lead the nations back from the broken cisterns of material and selfish interests to the living fountain of divine justice, which alone is able to provide that morality, nobility and stability of which the need has been so long experienced, to the great detriment of nations and of humanity. To these ideals, which are at the same time the real objectives of a true peace established in justice and love, We hope and trust that all those united with Us in the bond of faith will keep open their minds and hearts; so that when the storm of war shows signs of abating there may arise in every nation men of foresight and good-will, inspired with the courage which can suppress the base instinct of revenge and set up in its stead the grave and noble majesty of justice, sister of love and consort of true wisdom.

# Necessary Premises for a New Order*

(*Christmas Message* GRAZIE, VENERABILI FRATELLI *to the
College of Cardinals, December 24, 1940*)

. . . IT is now one year since We made some fundamental
declarations on the basic conditions of a peace built on justice,
equity, and honor, which could, therefore, be lasting. Although their realization has been put off to a later date by
events, these principles have lost nothing of their truth and
reality. . . .

Let us hope that mankind and each single nation may grow
more mature out of its present tribulations, with eyes able to
distinguish between the genuine and the fallacious, with an
ear alert for the voice of reason, be it pleasant or unpleasant,
with a mind which, open to reality, is really determined to
fulfill the demands of life and justice, not only when its own
demands are met, but also when the equitable demands of
others are heard.

Only in such a state of mind does the tempting slogan of a
new order acquire a beautiful, dignified and lasting conception
based on moral principles. Only then can the danger be
avoided that this slogan should come to be interpreted as a
liberty-destroying mechanism enforced by violence, without
sincerity, consent, joy, dignity or honor, oppressing souls.
Only then can mankind be given a new hope, an aim which
corresponds to the noble effort.

The necessary premises for such a new order are as follows:

(1) Victory over the hatred which divides the nations today and the disappearance of systems and actions which breed
this hatred. As a matter of fact, in some countries an unbridled propaganda is to be seen; it does not recoil from
methodical distortion of the truth in order to show the enemy
nations in a falsified and vilifying light. He who, however,
really wants the good of the people and wants to contribute
to the future co-operation of nations and to preserve this
co-operation from incalculable damage, will consider it as

---

* Translation from National Catholic Welfare Conference pamphlet.

his sacred duty to uphold the natural ideals of truth, justice and charity.

(2) Victory over distrust which exerts a paralyzing pressure on international law and makes all honest understanding impossible. Therefore, return to the principle of mutual trust. Return to the loyalty for treaties without which the secure co-operation of nations and especially, the living side by side of strong and weak nations, are inconceivable. The foundation of justice is loyalty, reliability and truth of the pledged word, and of the understanding which has been reached.

(3) Victory over the dismal principle that utility is the foundation and aim of law, and that might can create right. This principle is bound to upset all international relations and is inacceptable to all weaker nations. Therefore, return to honest, serious and moral international relations. This conception does not exclude the desire for the honorable improvement of conditions or the right to defend oneself if peaceful life has been attacked, or to repair the damage sustained thereby.

(4) Victory over those potential conflicts arising out of the unbalanced state of world economy. Therefore, a new economic order has to be gradually evolved which gives all nations the means to secure for their citizens an appropriate standard of life.

(5) Victory over the kind of egoism which, relying on its own power, aims at impairing the honor and sovereignty of nations, as well as the sound, just and ordered liberty of individuals. This egoism has to be replaced by a genuine Christian solidarity of a legal and economic character, and by a brotherly co-operation of the nations, the sovereignty of which has been duly secured.

# Essential Conditions for a Just and Lasting Peace*

*(Christmas Radio Message* NELL' ALBA *to the Whole World, December 24, 1941)*

. . . PREPONDERANCE of might over right, the easy opportunity for individual or collective violation of the property and life of others, as well as all the other moral devastation, are creating a mental atmosphere in which the conceptions of good and evil, of right and wrong, are losing their clear-cut issues and are in danger of being completely obliterated. . . .

Outward compulsion and domination founded purely on power seemed to prevail over the forces of order, which established the relations of law and charity in their natural and supernatural foundations as they had been laid down by God. To the detriment of human dignity and personality as well as society, the conception makes headway that it is might which creates right. . . .

In some countries, a political conception which is godless and hostile to Christ has, through its many tentacles, achieved a complete absorption of the individual, so that it can hardly be said that there is any longer any independence either in private or political life. Can anyone be surprised if this far-reaching negation of all Christian principles leads to a clash of the inward and outward tensions arising from that way of thinking, resulting in the catastrophic annihilation of human lives and goods we are witnessing today with horror? War, which is the sad result of the circumstances described, will never be able to stop this evil development. On the contrary, the war accelerates and accentuates this evolution the longer it lasts, and increases the greatness and incurability of the general collapse. . . .

Now the destruction brought about by the present war is on so vast a scale that it is imperative that there be not added to it also the further ruins of a frustrated and deluded peace. In order to avoid so great a calamity, it is fitting that in the for-

---

* Translation from National Catholic Welfare Conference pamphlet.

mulation of that peace there should be assured the co-operation, with sincerity of will and energy, with a purpose of a generous participation not only of this or that people, but of all peoples—yea, rather of all humanity. It is a universal undertaking for the common good which requires the collaboration of all Christendom in the religious and moral aspects of the new edifice which is to be constructed.

We are, therefore, making use of Our right—or, better, We are fulfilling Our duty—as to-day, on this eve of the Holy Feast of Christmas, the divine dawn of hope and of peace to the world, with all the authority of Our Apostolic Ministry and with the fervid impulse of Our heart, We direct the attention and the consideration of the entire world to the dangers which lie in wait to threaten a peace which is to be the well-prepared basis for a truly new order and which is to fulfill the expectations and desires of all people for a more tranquil future.

*A New Order Founded on the Moral Law*

Such a new order, which all people desire to see brought into being, after the trials and ruins of this war, must be founded on that immovable and unshakable rock, the moral law which the Creator Himself manifested by means of a natural order and which He has engraved with indelible character on the hearts of men: that moral law whose observance must be inculcated and fostered by the public opinion of all nations and of all States, with such a unanimity of voice and energy that no one may dare to doubt it. Like a shining beacon this moral law must direct by the light of its principles the course of action of men and of States, and they must all follow its admonishing, salutary and profitable precepts if they do not wish to abandon to the tempests and to ultimate shipwreck every labor and every effort for the establishment of a new order. Consequently, recapitulating and integrating what We have expounded on other occasions, We insist once again on certain fundamental conditions essential for an international order which will guarantee for all peoples a just and lasting peace and which will be a bountiful source of well-being and prosperity.

First: Within the limits of a new order founded on moral

principles there is no room for violation of the freedom, integrity and security of other States, no matter what may be their territorial extension or their capacity for defense. If it is inevitable that the powerful States should, by reason of their greater potentialities and their power, play leading roles in the formation of economic groups, comprising not only themselves but smaller and weaker States as well, it is nevertheless indispensable that in the interests of the common good they, and all others, respect the rights of those smaller States to political freedom, to economic development, and to the adequate protection, in the case of conflicts between nations, of that neutrality which is theirs according to the natural as well as international law. In this way, and in this way only, shall they be able to obtain a fitting share of the common good and assure the material and spiritual welfare of the peoples concerned.

Secondly: Within the limits of a new order founded on moral principles there is no place for open or secret oppression of the cultural and linguistic characteristics of national minorities, for the hindrance or restriction of their economic resources, for the limitation or abolition of their natural fertility. The more conscientiously the government of a State respects the rights of minorities, the more confidently and the more effectively can it demand from its subjects a loyal fulfillment of those civil obligations which are common to all citizens.

Thirdly: Within the limits of a new order founded on moral principles there is no place for that cold and calculating egoism which tends to hoard economic resources and materials destined for the use of all, to such an extent that the nations less favored by nature are not permitted access to them. In this regard, it is a source of great consolation to see admitted the necessity of a participation of all in the natural riches of the earth even on the part of those nations which, in the fulfillment of this principle, belong to the category of givers and not to that of receivers. It is, however, in conformity with the principles of equity that a solution to a question so vital to the world economy should be arrived at methodically, and in easy stages, with a necessary guarantee, always drawing useful lessons from the omissions and mistakes of the past. If, in the future peace, this point were not to be courageously dealt with, there would remain in the relations between people a deep and far-reaching root blossoming forth into bitter dissensions and burning jealousies, which would lead eventually to new conflicts. It must, however, be noticed how closely the satisfactory solution to this problem is connected with another fundamental point of which We shall treat next.

### *Progressive Limitation of Armaments*

Fourthly: Within the limits of a new order, founded on moral principles, once the more dangerous principles of armed conflict have been eliminated, there is no place for a total warfare or for a mad rush to armaments. The calamity of a world war, with the economic and social ruin and the moral dissolution and breakdown which follow in its train, cannot be permitted to envelop the human race for a third time. In order that mankind may be preserved from such a misfortune, it is essential to proceed with sincerity and honesty to a progressive limitation of armaments. The lack of equilibrium between the exaggerated armaments of the powerful States and the limited armaments of the weaker ones is a menace to harmony and peace among nations, and demands that a peaceful and proportionate limit be placed upon production and possession of offensive weapons.

In proportion to the degree in which disarmament is effected, means must be found which will be appropriate, honorable and efficacious in order that the principle, "pacts must be observed," may once again enjoy its vital and moral function in the juridical relations between States. Such a principle has undergone many serious crises and has suffered undeniable violations in the past, and has met with an incurable lack of trust among the various nations and among their respective rulers. To procure the re-birth of mutual trust, certain institutions must be established which will merit the respect of all, and which will dedicate themselves to the most noble office of guaranteeing the sincere observance of treaties and of promoting, in accordance with the principles of law and equity, necessary corrections and revisions of such treaties. We are well aware of the tremendous difficulties to be overcome and the almost superhuman strength and good-will required on all sides if the double task We have outlined is to be brought to a successful conclusion. But this work is so essential for a lasting peace that nothing should prevent responsible statesmen from undertaking it and cooperating in it with abundant good-will, so that, by bearing in mind the advantage to be gained in the future, they will be able to triumph over the painful remembrances of similar efforts doomed to failure in the past, and will not be daunted by the knowledge of the gigantic strength required for the accomplishment of their objective.

Fifthly: Within the limits of a new order founded on moral principles, there is no place for the persecution of religion and of the Church. From a lively faith in a personal and transcendent God there springs a sincere and unyielding moral strength which informs the whole course of life, for faith is not only a virtue, it is also the divine gift by which all the virtues enter the temple of the soul, and it is the foundation of that strong and tenacious character which does not falter before the demands of reason and justice. This fact always proves true, but it should be even more evident when there is demanded of a statesman, as of the least of citizens, the maximum of courage and moral strength for the reconstruction of a new Europe and a new world on the ruins accumulated by the violence of the world war and by the hatred and bitter disunity amongst men.

# The Internal Order of States*

(*Christmas Message* CON SEMPRE NUOVA ADUNANZA *to the Whole World December 24, 1942*)

. . . THE Church does not intend to take sides for either of the particular forms in which the several peoples and States strive to solve the gigantic problems of domestic order or international collaboration, as long as these forms conform to the

---

* Translation taken from *The Catholic Mind*.

Law of God. But, on the contrary, as the "Pillar and Ground of Truth" and guardian, by the will of God and the mandate of Christ, of the natural and supernatural order, the Church cannot renounce her right to proclaim to her sons and to the whole world the unchanging basic laws, saving them from every perversion, obfuscation, corruption, false interpretation, and error. . . .

In Our last Christmas Message, We expounded the principles which Christian thought suggests, for the establishment of an international order of friendly relations and collaboration such as to conform to the demands of God's Law; today We shall with the consent, We feel, and the interested attention of all upright men pause to consider, very carefully and with equal impartiality, the fundamental laws of the internal order of States and peoples.

International relations and internal order are intimately related. International equilibrium and harmony depend on the internal equilibrium and development of the individual states in the material, social, and intellectual spheres. A firm and steady peace policy towards other nations is, in fact, impossible without the spirit of peace within the nation which inspires trust. It is only, then, by striving for an integral peace, a peace in both fields, that people will be freed from the cruel nightmare of war; and the material and psychological causes of further discord and disorder will be diminished and gradually eliminated. . . .

We turn from the crib of the Prince of Peace, confident that His grace is diffused in all hearts, to you, beloved children, who recognize and adore in Christ your Saviour; We turn to all those who are united with Us at least by the bond of faith in God; We turn, finally, to all those who would be free of doubt and error, and who desire light and guidance; and We exhort you with suppliant, paternal insistence not only to realize fully the dreadful gravity of this hour, but also to meditate upon the vistas of good and supernatural benefit which it opens up, and to unite and collaborate towards the renewal of society in spirit and truth.

The essential aim of this necessary and holy crusade is that the star of peace, the Star of Bethlehem, may shine out again over the whole of mankind in all its brilliant splendor and reassuring consolation as a pledge and augury of a better, more fruitful and happier future.

It is true that the road from night to full day will be long; but of decisive importance are the first steps on the path, the first five milestones of which bear chiselled on them the following maxims:

### 1. Dignity and Rights of the Human Person

He who would have the star of peace shine out and stand over society should cooperate for his part in giving back to the human person the dignity given to it by God from the very beginnings; should oppose the excessive herding of men, as if they were a mass without a soul; their economic, social, political, intellectual and moral inconsistency; their dearth of solid principles and strong convictions; their surfeit of instinctive sensible excitement and their fickleness.

He should favor, by every lawful means, in every sphere of life, social institutions in which a full personal responsibility is assured and guaranteed both in the earthly and the eternal order of things.

He should uphold respect for and the practical realization of the following fundamental personal rights: the right to maintain and develop one's corporal, intellectual and moral life and especially the right to religious formation and education; the right to worship God in private and public and to carry on religious works of charity; the right to marry and to achieve the aim of married life; the right to conjugal and domestic society; the right to work as the indispensable means towards the maintenance of family life; the right to free choice of a state of life, and hence, too, of the priesthood or religious life; the right to the use of material goods, in keeping with his duties and social limitations.

### 2. Defense of Social Unity and Especially of the Family

He who would have the star of peace shine out and stand over society should reject every form of materialism which sees in the people only a herd of individuals who, divided and without any internal cohesion, are considered as a mass to be lorded over and treated arbitrarily; he should strive to understand society as an intrinsic unity, which has grown up and matured under the guidance of Providence, a unity which—within the bounds assigned to it and according to its own peculiar gifts—tends, with the collaboration of the various classes and professions, towards the eternal and ever new aims of culture and religion.

He should defend the indissolubility of matrimony; he should give to the family—that unique cell of the people—space, light and air so that it may attend to its mission of perpetuating new life, and of educating children in a spirit corresponding to its own true religious convictions, and that it may preserve, fortify and reconstitute, according to its powers, its proper economic, spiritual, moral and juridic unity.

He should take care that the material and spiritual advantages of the family be shared by the domestic servants; he should strive to secure for every family a dwelling where a materially and morally healthy family life may be seen in all its vigor and worth; he should take care that the place of work be not so separated from the home as to make the head of the family and educator of the children a virtual stranger to his own household; he should take care above all that the bond of trust and mutual help should be re-established between the family and the public school, that bond which in other times gave such happy results, but which now has been replaced by mistrust where the school, influenced and controlled by the spirit of materialism, corrupts and destroys what the parents have instilled into the minds of the children.

### 3. Dignity and Prerogatives of Labor

He who would have the star of peace shine out and stand over society should give to work the place assigned to it by God from the beginning.

As an indispensable means towards gaining over the world that mastery which God wishes, for His glory, all work has an inherent dignity and at the same time a close connection with the perfection of the person; this is the noble dignity and privilege of work which is not in any way cheapened by the fatigue and the burden, which have to be borne as the effect of original sin, in obedience and submission to the will of God.

Those who are familiar with the great Encyclicals of Our predecessors and Our Own previous messages know well that the Church does not hesitate to draw the practical conclusions which are derived from the moral nobility of work, and to give them all the support of her authority. These exigencies include, besides a just wage which covers the needs of the worker and his family, the conservation and perfection of a social order which will make possible an assured, even if modest, private property for all classes of society, which will promote higher education for the children of the working class who are especially endowed with intelligence and good will, and which will promote the care and the practice of the social spirit in one's immediate neighborhood, in the district, the province, the people and the nation—a spirit which, by smoothing over friction arising from privileges or class interests removes from the workers the sense of isolation through the assuring experience of a genuinely human, and fraternally Christian, solidarity.

The progress and the extent of urgent social reforms depend on the economic possibilities of individual nations. It is only through an intelligent and generous sharing of forces between the strong and the weak that it will be possible to effect a universal pacification in such wise as not to leave behind centers of conflagration and infection from which new disasters may come. There are evident signs which go to show that, in the ferment of all the prejudices and feelings of hate, those inevitable but lamentable offspring of the war psychosis, there is still aflame in the peoples the consciousness of their intimate mutual dependence for good or for evil, nay, that this consciousness is more alive and active.

Is it not true that deep thinkers see ever more clearly in the renunciation of egoism and national isolation the way to general salvation, ready as they are to demand of their peoples a heavy participation in the sacrifices necessary for social well-being in other peoples?

May this Christmas Message of Ours, addressed to all those who are animated by a good will and a generous heart, encourage and increase the legions of these social crusades in every nation. And may God deign to give to their peaceful cause the victory of which their noble enterprise is worthy.

## 4. *The Rehabilitation of a Juridical Order*

He who would have the star of peace shine out and stand over social life should collaborate towards a complete rehabilitation of the juridical order.

The juridic sense of today is often altered and overturned by the profession and the practice of a positivism and a utilitarianism which are subjected and bound to the service of determined groups, classes and movements, whose programs direct and determine the course of legislation and the practices of the courts.

The cure for this situation becomes feasible when we awaken again the consciousness of a juridical order resting on the supreme dominion of God, and safeguarded from all human whims; a consciousness of an order which stretches forth its arm, in protection or punishment, over the unforgettable rights of man and protects them against the attacks of every human power.

From the juridic order, as willed by God, flows man's inalienable right to juridical security, and by this very fact to a definite sphere of rights, immune from all arbitrary attack.

The relations of man to man, of the individual to society, authority, and civil duties; the relations of society and of authority to the individual, should be placed on a firm juridic footing and be guarded, when the need arises, by the authority of the courts.

This supposes (A) a tribunal and a judge who take their directions from a clearly formulated and defined right; (B) clear juridical norms which may not be overturned by unwarranted appeals to a supposed popular sentiment or by merely utilitarian considerations; (C) the recognition of the principle that even the State and the functionaries and organizations dependent on it are obliged to repair and to withdraw measures which are harmful to the liberty, property, honor, and progress of health of the individuals.

## 5. *The State According to the Christian Spirit*

He who would have the star of peace shine out and stand over human society should cooperate towards the setting up of a State in theory and practice founded on reasonable discipline, exalted kindliness, and a responsible Christian spirit.

He should help to restore the State and its power to the service of human society, to the full recognition of the respect due to the human person and his efforts to attain his eternal destiny.

He should apply and devote himself to dispelling the errors which aim at causing the State and its authority to deviate from the path of morality, at severing them from the eminently ethical bond which links them to individual and social life, and at making them deny or in practice ignore their essential dependence on the will of the Creator. He should work for the recognition and diffusion of the truth which teaches, even in matters of this world, that the deepest meaning, the ultimate moral basis and the universal validity of "reigning" lies in "serving."

## War and the Renovation of Society

Beloved children, may God grant that while you listen to Our voice your heart may be profoundly stirred and moved by the deeply felt seriousness, the loving solicitude, the unremitting insistence with which we drive home these thoughts, which are meant as an appeal to the conscience of the world, and a rallying-cry to all those who are ready to ponder and weigh the grandeur of their mission and responsibility by the vastness of this universal disaster.

A great part of mankind, and, let Us not shirk from saying it, not a few who call themselves Christians, have to some extent their share in the collective responsibility for the growth of error and for the harm and the lack of moral fibre in the society of today.

What is this world war, with all its attendant circumstances, whether they be remote or proximate causes, its progress and material, legal and moral effects? What is it but the crumbling process, not expected, perhaps, by the thoughtless but seen and deprecated by those whose gaze penetrated into the realities of a social order which—behind a deceptive exterior or the mask of conventional shibboleths—hid its mortal weakness and its unbridled lust for gain and power?

That which in peacetime lay coiled up broke loose at the outbreak of war in a sad succession of acts at variance with the human and Christian sense. International agreements to make war less inhuman by confining it to the combatants, to regulate the procedure of occupation and the imprisonment of the conquered remained in various places a dead letter. And who can see the end of this progressive demoralization of the people, who can wish to watch impotently this disastrous progress? Should they not rather, over the ruins of a social order which has given such tragic proof of its ineptitude as a factor for the good of the people, gather together the hearts of all those who are magnanimous and upright in the solemn vow not to rest until in all peoples and all nations of the earth a vast legion shall be formed of those handfuls of men who, bent on bringing back society to its center of gravity, which is the law of God, aspire to the service of the human person and of his common life ennobled in God? . . .

# Future Peace*

(*Radio Address, September 1, 1944*)

. . . CLARITY of vision, devotion, courage, inventive genius, and the sense of brotherly love in all upright and honest men will determine the measure and extent to which Christian thought will succeed in maintaining and supporting the gigantic work of restoration in social, economic and international life through a plan that does not conflict with the religious and moral content of Christian civilization.

Accordingly, to all our sons and daughters throughout the vast world, as also to those who, while not belonging to the Church, feel themselves united with us in this hour of perhaps irrevocable decision. We address an urgent appeal to weigh the extraordinary gravity of the moment and to consider that, above all beyond all such cooperation with other diverse ideological tendencies and social forces as may perhaps be suggested by purely contingent motives, fidelity to the heritage of Christian civilization and its strenuous defense against atheist and anti-Christian tendencies is never the key-

---

* Translation from National Catholic Welfare Conference pamphlet.

stone which can be sacrificed for any transitory advantage or for any shifting combination.

. . . After bitter years of want, restrictions and especially of anxious uncertainty, men expect, at the end of the war, a far-reaching and definite betterment of these unfortunate conditions.

The promises of statesmen, the many plans and proposals of experts and specialists have given rise in the victims of an unhealthy economic and social order to illusory hopes of a complete re-birth of the world and to an over-enthusiastic expectation of a millenium of universal happiness.

Such a disposition offers fertile ground for propaganda of the most radical programs, disposes men's minds to a very understandable but unreasonable and unjustified impatience, which looks for nothing from organic reforms and puts all its hopes in upheavals and violence.

Confronted with these extreme tendencies, the Christian who meditates seriously on the needs and misfortunes of his time, remains faithful, in his choice of remedies, to those standards which experience, right reason, and Christian social ethics indicate as the fundamentals of all just reforms.

. . . The Christian conscience cannot admit as a just social order which either denies in principle or renders impossible or nugatory in practice, the natural right to property whether over consumptive goods or the means of production.

## The Right to Private Property

But neither can it accept those systems which recognize the right to private property according to a completely false concept of it and which are therefore opposed to a true and healthy social order.

Accordingly where, for instance, "Capitalism" is based on such false concepts and arrogates to itself an unlimited right over property, without any subordination to the common good, the Church has condemned it as contrary to the natural law.

In fact, We see the ever increasing ranks of the workers frequently confronted with this excessive concentration of economic goods which, often hidden under anonymous titles, are successfully withdrawn from contributing, as they should, to the social order and place the worker in a situation where it is virtually impossible for him effectively to acquire private property of his own.

We see the small and medium holdings diminish and lose their value in human society, and constrained to join in a conflict ever more difficult and without hope of success.

On the one side, We see immense riches dominating public and private economic life and often even civil life; on the other, the countless number of those who, deprived of every direct or indirect security of their own livelihood, take no further interest in the true and higher values of the spirit, abandon their aspiration to genuine freedom, and throw themselves at the feet of any political party, slaves to whoever promises them in some way bread and security; and experience shows of what tyranny, under such circumstances, human nature is capable even in our times.

In defending, therefore, the principle of private property, the Church pursues a high ethico-social purpose. She does not intend to defend absolutely and simply the present state of affairs, as if she saw in it the expression of God's will, nor to defend as a matter of principle the rich and the plutocrat against the poor and the indigent. Far from it! Right from the beginning she has been the defender of the oppressed against the tyranny of the powerful, and has always sponsored the just claims of all classes of workers against every injustice. But the Church aims rather at securing that the institution of private property be such as it should be according to the designs of God's wisdom and the dispositions of nature: an element of social order, a necessary pre-supposition to human initiative, and incentive to work to the advantage of life's purpose here and hereafter, and hence of the liberty and the dignity of man, created in the likeness of God, Who, from the beginning, assigned him for his benefit domination over material things.

. . . The social and economic policy of the future, the controlling power of the State, of local bodies, of professional institutions cannot permanently secure their end, which is the genuine philosophy of social life and the normal returns on national economy, except by respecting and safeguarding the vital function of private property in its personal and social values. When the distribution of property is an obstacle to this end—which is not necessarily nor always an outcome of the extension of private inheritance—the State may, in the public interest, intervene by regulating its use or even, if it cannot equitably meet the situation in any other way, by decreeing the expropriation of property, giving a suitable indemnity.

For the same purpose small and medium holdings in agriculture, in the arts and trades, in commerce and industry should be guaranteed and promoted; cooperative unions should ensure for them the advantages of big business; where big business shows itself even today more productive, there should be given the possibility of tempering the labor contract with a contract of co-ownership. . . .

# The Problem of Democracy*

### (*Christmas Radio Message, December 24, 1944*)

. . . A STRANGE paradox this, of a war whose bitterness bids fair to reach the limits of paroxysm, and of the notable progress made in aspirations and proposals for a solid and lasting peace: undoubtedly one may well discuss the worth, the feasibility, the efficacy of this or that proposal; judgment may well be suspended in their regard, but it remains nonetheless true that the process has begun.

### The Problem of Democracy

Moreover—and this is perhaps the most important point—beneath the sinister lightning of the war that encompasses them, in the blazing heat of the furnace that imprisons them, the peoples have, as it were, awakened from a long torpor. They have assumed, in relation to the state and those who govern, a new attitude—one that questions, criticizes, distrusts.

Taught by bitter experience, they are more aggressive in opposing the concentration of dictatorial power that cannot be censured or touched, and call for a system of government

---

* Translation from National Catholic Welfare Conference pamphlet.

118

more in keeping with the dignity and liberty of the citizens. These multitudes, uneasy, stirred by the war to their inner-most depths, are today firmly convinced—at first, perhaps, in a vague and confused way, but already unyieldingly—that had there been the possibility of censuring and correcting the actions of public authority, the world would not have been dragged into the vortex of a disastrous war, and that to avoid for the future the repetition of such a catastrophe, we must vest efficient guarantees in the people itself.

In such a psychological atmosphere, is it to be wondered at if the tendency towards democracy is capturing the peoples and winning a large measure of consent and support from those who hope to play a more efficient part in the destinies of individuals and of society?

It is scarcely necessary to recall that, according to the teach-ing of the Church, "it is not forbidden to prefer temperate, popular forms of government, without prejudice, however, to Catholic teaching on the origin and use of authority," and that "the Church does not disapprove of any of the various forms of government, provided they be *per se* capable of securing the good of the citizens" (Leo XIII: Encyclical *Libertas,* June 20, 1888).

If, then, on this feast day which commemorates both the benignity of the Incarnate Word and the dignity of man (both in its personal and social aspects), We direct our atten-tion to the problem of democracy, examining the forms by which it should be directed if it is to be a true, healthy democracy answering the needs of the moment, our action shows clearly that the interest and solicitude of the Church looks not so much to its external structure and organization— which depend on the special aspirations of each people—as to the individual himself, who, so far from being the object and, as it were, a merely passive element in the social order, is in fact, and must be and continue to be, its subject, its foundation and its end.

Given that democracy, taken in the broad sense, admits of various forms, and can be realized in monarchies as well as in republics, two questions come up for our consideration: first, what characteristics should distinguish the men who live under democracy and a democratic regime? Second, what characterization should distinguish the men who hold the reins of government in a democracy?

ONE: CHARACTERISTICS PROPER TO CITIZENS IN A DEMOCRACY

To express his own views of the duties and sacrifices that are imposed on him; not compelled to obey without being heard—these are two rights of the citizen which find in democracy, as its name implies, their expression. From the solidity, harmony and good results produced between the citizens and the Government, one may decide which democracy is really healthy and well balanced, and what is its life energy and power of expansion.

If, then, we consider the extent and nature of the sacrifices demanded of all the citizens, especially in our day when the activity of the state is so vast and decisive, the democratic form of government appears to many as a postulate of nature imposed by reason itself. When, however, people call for "democracy and better democracy," such a demand cannot have any other meaning than to place the citizen ever more in the position to hold his own personal opinion, to express it, and to make it prevail in a fashion conducive to common good.

Hence follows a first conclusion with its practical consequence: the state does not contain in itself and does not mechanically bring together in a given territory a shapeless mass of individuals. It is, and should in practice be, the organic and organizing unity of a real people. The people, and a shapeless multitude (or, as it is called, "the masses") are two distinct concepts. The people lives and moves by its own life energy; the masses are inert of themselves and can only be moved from outside. The people lives by the fulness of life in the men that compose it, each of whom—at his proper place and in his own way—is a person conscious of his own responsibility and of his own views. The masses, on the contrary, wait for the impulse from outside, an easy plaything in the hands of anyone who exploits their instincts and impressions; ready to follow in turn, today this flag, tomorrow another.

From the exuberant life of a true people, an abundant rich life is diffused in the state and all its organs, instilling into them, with a vigor that is always renewing itself, the consciousness of their own responsibility, the true instinct for the common good. The elementary power of the masses, deftly managed and employed, the state also can utilize: in the ambitious hands of one or of several who have been artificially brought together for selfish aims, the state itself, with the support of the masses, reduced to the minimum status of a mere machine, can impose its whims on the better part of the real people: the common interest remains seriously, and for a long time, injured by this process, and the injury is very often hard to heal. Hence follows clearly another conclusion: the masses —as we have just defined them—are the capital enemy of true democracy and of its ideal of liberty and equality.

In a people worthy of the name, the citizen feels within him the consciousness of his personality, of his duties and rights, of his own freedom joined to respect for the freedom and dignity of others. In a people worthy of the name all inequalities based not on whim but on the nature of things, inequalities of culture, possessions, social standing—without, of course, prejudice to justice and mutual charity—do not constitute any obstacle to the existence and the prevalence of a true spirit of union and brotherhood. On the contrary, so far from impairing civil equality in any way, they give it its true meaning; namely, that, before the State, everyone has the right to live honorably his own personal life in the place and under the conditions in which the designs and dispositions of Providence have placed him.

As against this picture of the democratic ideal of liberty and equality in a people's government by honest and far-seeing men, what a spectacle is that of a democratic state left to the whims of the masses. Liberty, from being a moral duty of the individual becomes a tyrannous claim to give free rein to a man's impulses and appetites to the detriment of others. Equality degenerates to a mechanical level, a colorless uniformity; the sense of true honor, of personal activity, or respect for tradition, of dignity—in a word all that gives life its worth—gradually fades away and disappears. And the only survivors are, on the one hand, the victims deluded by the specious mirage of democracy, naively taken for the genuine spirit of democracy with its liberty and equality; and on the other, the more or less numerous exploiters, who have known how to use the power of money and of organization, in order to secure a privileged position above the others, and thus have gained power.

The democratic state, whether it be monarchical or republican, should, like any other form of government, be entrusted with the power to command with real and effective authority. The absolute order itself of beings and purposes, which shows that man is an independent person—namely the subject of inviolable duties and rights—who is the source and end of his own social life, comprises the State also as a necessary society endowed with authority, without which it could neither exist nor live. And if men, using their personal liberty, were to deny all dependence on a superior Authority possessing coercive power, they could by this very fact cut the ground from under their own dignity and liberty—by violating, that is, the absolute order of beings and purposes.

As they are established on this same foundation, the person, the State, the government, with their respective rights, are so bound together that they stand or fall together. And since that absolute order, in the light of right reason, and in particular of the Christian Faith, cannot have any other origin than in a personal God, our Creator, it follows that the dignity of man is the dignity of the moral community willed by God; the dignity of political authority is the dignity deriving from its sharing in the authority of God. No form of state can avoid taking cognizance of this intimate and indissoluble connection —least of all a democracy. Accordingly, if those in power do not see it, or more or less discount it, their own authority is shaken, as is social morality, and that specious appearance of a purely formal democracy may often serve as a mark for all that is in reality least democratic.

Only a clear appreciation of the purposes assigned by God to every human society, joined to a deep sense of the exalted duties of social activity, can put those in power in a position to fulfill their own obligations in the legislative, judicial and executive order with that objectivity, impartiality, loyalty, generosity, and integrity without which a democratic government would find it hard to command the respect and the support of the better section of the people.

The deep sense of the principles underlying a political and social order that is sound and conforms to the norms of right and justice is of special importance in those who in any kind of democratic regime have, as the people's delegates, in whole or part, the power to legislate. And since the center of gravity of a democracy normally set up resides in this popular assembly from which political currents radiate into every field of public life—for good or ill—the question of the high moral standards, practical ability and intellectual capacity of parliamentary deputies is for every people living under a democratic regime a question of life and death, of prosperity and decadence, of soundness or perpetual unrest.

To secure effective action, to win esteem and trust, every legislative body should—as experience shows beyond doubt—gather within it a group of select men, spiritually eminent and of strong character, who shall look upon themselves as the representatives of the entire people and not the mandatories of a mob, whose interests are often unfortunately made to prevail over the true needs of the common good—a select group of men not restricted to any profession or social standing but reflecting every phase of the people's life; men chosen for their solid Christian convictions, straight and steady judgment, with a sense of the practical and equitable, true to themselves in all circumstances; men of clear and sound principles, with sound and clear-cut proposals to make; men above all capable, in virtue of the authority that emanates from their untarnished consciences and radiates widely from them, to be leaders and heads especially in times when the pressing needs of the moment excite the people's impressionability unduly, and render it more liable to be led astray and get lost: men who—in periods of transition, generally stormy and disturbed by passion, by divergent opinions and opposing programs—feel themselves doubly under the obligation to send circulating through the veins of the people and of the state, burning with a thousand fevers, the spiritual antidote of clear views, kindly interest, justice equally sympathetic to all, and a bias towards national unity and concord in a sincere spirit of brotherhood.

Peoples whose spiritual and moral temperament is sufficiently sound and fecund, find in themselves and can produce the heralds and implements of democracy, who live in such dispositions and know how effectively to put them into practice. But where such men are lacking, others come to take their places in order to make politics serve their ambition, and be a quick road to profit for themselves, their caste and their class, while the race after private interests makes them lose sight of completely and jeopardize the true common good.

## State Absolutism

A sound democracy, based on the immutable principles of the natural law and revealed truth, will resolutely turn its back on such corruption as gives to the State legislature an unchecked and unlimited power, and moreover, makes of the democratic regime, notwithstanding an outward show to the contrary, purely and simply a form of absolutism.

State absolutism (not to be confused, as such, with absolute monarchy, of which we are not treating here) consists in fact in the false principle that the authority of the state is unlimited and, when it gives free rein to despotic aims beyond the confines of good and evil, there is no right of appeal against it to a higher law which binds in conscience.

A man penetrated with right ideas about the state and authority and the power that he wields as guardian of social order, will never think of derogating the majesty of the positive law within the ambit of its natural competence. But this majesty of positive law is only inviolable when it conforms— or at least is not opposed—to the absolute order set up by the Creator and placed in a new light by the revelation of the Gospel. It cannot subsist except in so far as it respects the foundation on which human personality rests, no less than the State and the Government. This is the fundamental criterion of every healthy form of government, including democracy. It is the criterion by which the moral value of every particular law should be judged.

### THREE: NATURE AND CONDITIONS OF PEACE:
### UNITY OF MANKIND AND SOCIETY

We were anxious, Beloved Sons and Daughters, to take the occasion of Christmastide to point out along what lines a democracy befitting human dignity can, in harmony with the law of nature and the designs of God as manifested in Revelation, secure happy results. Indeed, We are deeply convinced of the supreme importance of this problem for the peaceful progress of mankind. But We also realize the exalted claims that this form of government makes on the moral maturity of the individual citizen; a moral maturity to which he could never hope to attain fully and securely if the light from the Cave of Bethlehem did not illumine the dark path along which the peoples are going forward through the stormy present towards a future which they hope will be more serene.

But how far will the representatives and pioneers of democracy be inspired in their deliberations by the conviction that the absolute order of beings and purposes, of which We have repeatedly spoken, comprises also, as a moral necessity and the crowning of social development, the unity of mankind and of the family of peoples? On the recognition of this principle hangs the future of the peace. No world reform, no peace guarantee can abstract from it without being weakened and without being untrue to itself.

If, on the other hand, this same moral necessity were to find its realization in a society of peoples which succeeded in eliminating the structural defects and shortcomings of former systems, then the majesty of that order would regulate and inspire equally the deliberations of that society and the use of its instruments of sanction. For this reason, too, one understands why the authority of such a society must be real and effective over the member states, in suchwise, however, that each of them retain an equal right of its own sovereignty. Only thus will the spirit of sane democracy be able to pervade the vast and thorny ground of foreign relations.

## Against Wars of Aggression

There is a duty, besides, imposed on all, a duty which brooks no delay, no procrastination, no hesitation, no subterfuge: It is the duty to do everything to ban once and for all wars of aggression as a legitimate solution of international disputes and as a means towards realizing national aspirations.

Many attempts in this direction have been seen in the past. They all failed. And they will all fail always, until the saner section of mankind has the firm determination, the holy obstinacy, like an obligation in conscience, to fulfill the mission which past ages have not undertaken with sufficient gravity and resolution.

If ever a generation has had to appreciate in the depths of its conscience the call: "war on war," it is certainly the present generation. Having passed, as it has, through an ocean of blood and tears in a form perhaps never experienced in past ages, it has lived through the indescribable atrocities with an intensity such that the recollection of so many horrors must remain stamped in its memory, and even in the deepest recesses of its soul, like a picture of a hell against which anyone who cherishes a sense of humanity desires more than anything else to close the door forever.

### Formation of a Common Means to Maintain Peace

The decisions already published by international commissions permit one to conclude that an essential point in any future international arrangement would be the formation of an organ for the maintenance of peace, of an organ invested by common consent with supreme power to whose office it would also pertain to smother in its germinal state any threat of isolated or collective aggression.

No one could hail this development with greater joy than he who has long upheld the principle that the idea of war as an apt and proportionate means of solving international conflicts is now out of date. No one could wish success to this common effort, to be undertaken with a seriousness of purpose never before known, with greater enthusiasm, than he who has conscientiously striven to make the Christian and religious mentality reject modern war with its monstrous means of conducting hostilities.

### Chastisement of the Aggressor

Unquestionably the progress of man's inventions, which should have heralded the realization of greater well-being for all mankind, has instead been employed to destroy all that had been built up through the ages. But by that very fact the immorality of the war of aggression has been made ever more evident. And if now, to the recognition of this immorality there is to be added the threat of a judicial intervention by the nations and of chastisement inflicted on the aggressor by the society of states, so that war will always be subject to the stigma of proscription, always under surveillance and liable to preventive measures, then mankind, as it emerges from the dark night in which it has been so long submerged, will be able to hail the dawn of a new and better era of its history.

But only on one condition: namely that the peace settlement which should be strengthened and made more stable by mutual guarantees and, where necessary, economic sanctions and even armed intervention, should not give definite countenance to any injustice, does not imply any derogation of any right to the detriment of any nation (whether it be on the side of the victors, the vanquished, or the neutrals), and does not impose any perpetual burden, which can only be allowed for a time as reparation for war damages.

That any peoples, to whose Government—or perhaps even partially to themselves—the responsibility for the war is attributed, should have for a time to undergo the rigors of security measures until the bonds of mutual trust, violently broken, should be gradually welded together again, is quite understandable from a human point of view, and in practice will in all probability be inevitable. Nevertheless, even these peoples must have a well-founded hope—commensurate to their effective collaboration in the work of reconstruction—of being able, together with the other states with equal consideration and with the same rights, to be associated with the great community of nations.

To deny them that hope would be the reverse of far-seeing wisdom, it would be to assume the grave responsibility of barring the way of a general liberation from all the disastrous consequences, material, moral and political, of the gigantic cataclysm which has shaken the poor human family to its very foundations, but which, at the same time, has shown it the road to new goals.

### The Stern Lessons of Suffering

We will not renounce Our confidence that the peoples, who have all passed through the school of suffering, will be able to retain the stern lessons learned. And in this hope we are

strengthened by the words of men who have had a greater
share in the sufferings of the war and who have found generous words to express, together with the insistence on their own
need of security against any future aggression, their respect
for the vital rights of other peoples and their aversion to any
usurping of those rights.

It would be vain to expect that this sage judgment, dictated
by the experience of history and a high political sense should
be—while men's spirits are still burning white-hot—generally
accepted by public opinion, or even by the majority. Hatred
and the impossibility of mutual understanding have given rise
in peoples that have fought against each other, to a mist too
dense to hope that the hour has already come when a ray of
light may shine out to clear the tragic panorama on either
side of its dark wall.

But one thing We know: that the moment will come, perhaps sooner than the people think, when both sides realize
that, all things considered, there is only one way of getting
out of the meshes in which war and hate have wrapped the
world, namely a return to the solidarity, too long forgotten,
a solidarity not restricted to these or those peoples, but universal, founded on the intimate connection of their destiny
and rights which belong equally to both.

## The Punishment of Crimes

No one certainly thinks of disarming justice in its relations
to those who have exploited the war situation in order to commit real and proven crimes against the common law, and for
whom supposed military necessity could at most have offered a
pretext, but never a justification. But if justice presumed to
judge and punish not merely individuals but even whole
communities together, who could not see in such a procedure
a violation of the norms which guide every human trial?

### FOUR: THE CHURCH: GUARDIAN OF MAN'S TRUE
### DIGNITY AND LIBERTY

At a time when the peoples find themselves with duties such
as perhaps they have never met before in the course of their
history, they feel deeply in their tortured hearts the desire,
impatient and almost instinctive, to take the reins of their

destiny in their own hands with more independence than heretofore, hoping that thus they will find it easier to defend themselves from the periodic invasions of violence which, like a boiling lava torrent, spares nothing of all that they hold sacred and dear.

Thank God, one may believe the time has passed when the call to moral and Gospel principles to guide the life of states and peoples was disdainfully thrust aside as unreal. The events of these war years have given ample evidence to confute, in a harder way than one could ever have imagined, those who spread such doctrine. The disdain that they affected towards this supposed unreality has been changed into stark reality: brutality, iniquity, destruction, annihilation.

If the future is to belong to democracy, an essential part in its achievement will have to belong to the religion of Christ and to the Church, the messenger of our Redeemer's word which is to continue His mission of saving men. For she teaches and defends supernatural truths and communicates the supernatural helps of grace in order to actuate the divinely-established order of beings and ends which is the ultimate foundation and directive norm of every democracy. By her very existence, the Church rises before the world as a shining beacon to remind it constantly of that Divine order. Her history reflects clearly her providential mission. The struggles, which, coerced by the abuse of power, she has had to sustain in defense of the liberty given her by God, were at the same time struggles for man's true liberty.

The Church has the mission to announce to the world, which is looking for better and more perfect forms of democracy, the highest and most needed message that there can be: the dignity of man, the call to be sons of God. It is the powerful cry, which from the Manger of Bethlehem to the furthest confines of the earth resounds in the ears of men at a time when that dignity is tragically low.

The holy story of Christmas proclaims this inviolable dignity of man with a vigor and authority that cannot be gainsaid—an authority and vigor that infinitely transcends that which all possible declarations of the rights of man could achieve.

Christmas, the Great Feast of the Son of God Who appeared

in human flesh, the feast in which heaven stoops down to earth with ineffable grace and benevolence, is also the day on which Christianity and mankind, before the Crib, contemplating the *goodness and kindness of God our Saviour* become more deeply conscious of the intimate unity that God has established between them. The Birth of the Saviour of the World, of the Restorer of human dignity in all its fullness, is the moment characterized by the alliance of all men of goodwill. There to the poor world, torn by discord, divided by selfishness, poisoned by hate, love will be restored, and it will be allowed to march forward in cordial harmony, towards the common goal, to find at last the cure for its wounds in the peace of Christ.

### FIVE: CRUSADE FOR CHARITY

We do not want to close this Christmas message without addressing a word of heartfelt gratitude to all those—states, governments, Bishops and peoples—who at this time of untold misfortunes have lent Us valiant aid as We hearken to the cry of suffering which reaches Us from so many parts of the world, and give a helping hand to so many of Our beloved sons and daughters whom the misfortunes of war have reduced to extreme poverty and misery.

And in the first place it is but just to record the immense work of assistance achieved in spite of the extraordinary difficulties of transport, by the United States of America and, with regard to Italy in particular, by His Excellency the personal Representative of the President of the Union.

It is a pleasure for us to express equal praise and gratitude for the generosity of the head of the State, the Government and people of Spain, and the Governments of Ireland, Argentina, Australia, Bolivia, Brazil, Canada, Chile, Italy, Lithuania, Peru, Poland, Roumania, Slovakia, Hungary and Uruguay, who have vied with one another in noble rivalry of brotherly love and charity, the echo of which will not resound in vain through the world.

While men of goodwill are endeavoring to bridge the gulf and bring the peoples together, this purely disinterested act of charity assumes an aspect and a value of unique importance. When—as we all wish—the dissonance of hate and discord that dominates the present moment will be but a tragic memory, the good effects of this victory of active and magnanimous charity over the poison of selfishness and enmity will ripen into even a larger harvest of good.

May all who have had a share in this crusade of charity receive as an incentive and a token of gratitude our apostolic benediction and the thought that on the feast of love from numberless hearts in anguish, but not forgetful in their anguish, there rises to heaven the grateful prayer for them: Deign to reward, O Lord, all those who do good to us for Your Name's sake with eternal life!

# Nazism and Peace*

### (*Allocution to the College of Cardinals, June 2, 1945*)

TODAY, after six years, the fratricidal struggle has ended, at least in one section of this war-torn world. It is a peace—if you can call it such—as yet very fragile, which cannot endure or be consolidated except by expending on it the most assiduous care; a peace whose maintenance imposes on the whole Church, both pastors and faithful, grave and very delicate duties: patient prudence, courageous fidelity, the spirit of sacrifice.

All are called upon to devote themselves to it, each in his own office and at his own place. Nobody can bring to this task too much anxiety or zeal. Towards Us and Our apostolic ministry, We well know, Venerable Brethren, that We can safely count on your sage collaboration, your unceasing prayers, your steadfast devotion.

## I

### THE CHURCH AND NATIONAL SOCIALISM

In Europe the war is over; but what wounds has it not inflicted! Our Divine Master has said: *All that take the sword shall perish by the sword.*

Now what do you see? You see what is the result of a con-

---

* Translation taken from *The Catholic Mind*.

cept of the State reduced to practice which takes no heed of
the most sacred ideals of mankind, and overthrows the inviolable principles of the Christian Faith. The whole world today
contemplates with stupefaction the ruins that it has left behind it. These ruins We had seen when they were still in the
distant future, and few, We believe, have followed with
greater anxiety the process leading to the inevitable crash.

For over twelve years—twelve of the best years of Our
mature age—We had lived in the midst of the German people,
fulfilling the duties of the office committed to Us. During that
time, in the atmosphere of liberty which the political and
social conditions of that time allowed, We worked for con-
solidation of the status of the Catholic Church in Germany.

We thus had occasion to learn the great qualities of the people and We were personally in close contact with its most
representative men. For that reason We cherish the hope that
it can rise to a new dignity and new life when once it has laid
the satanic specter raised by National Socialism and the guilty
(as We have already at other times had occasion to expound)
have expiated the crimes they have committed.

### Germany Asked Concordat

While there was still some faint glimmer of hope that that
movement could take another and less disastrous course, either
through the disillusionment of its more moderate members or
through effective opposition from that section of German
people which opposed it, the Church did everything possible
to set up a formidable barrier to the spread of ideas at once
subversive and violent.

In the spring of 1933 the German Government asked the
Holy See to conclude a concordat with the Reich: the proposal had the approval of the Episcopate and of at least the
greater number of the German Catholics. In fact, they thought
that neither the concordats up to then negotiated with some
individual German states nor the Weimar Constitution gave
adequate guarantee or assurance of respect for their convictions, for their faith, rights or liberty of action.

In such conditions the guarantees could not be secured
except through a settlement having the solemn form of a
concordat with the Central Government of the Reich.

It should be added that, since it was the Government that made the proposal, the responsibility for all regrettable consequences would have fallen on the Holy See if it had refused the proposed concordat.

## Concordat Was Helpful

It was not that the Church for her part had any illusions built on excessive optimism or that, in concluding the concordat, She had the intention of giving any form of approval to the teachings or tendencies of National Socialism; this was expressly declared and explained at the time (Cf. *Osservatore Romano*, No. 174, July 2, 1933). It must, however, be recognized that the concordat in the years that followed brought some advantages or at least prevented worse evils.

In fact, in spite of all the violations to which it was subjected, it gave Catholics a juridical basis for their defense, a stronghold behind which to shield themselves in their opposition—as long as this was possible—to the ever growing campaign of religious persecution.

The struggle against the Church did, in fact, become ever more bitter: there was the dissolution of Catholic organizations; the gradual suppression of the flourishing Catholic schools, both public and private; the enforced weaning of youth from family and Church; the pressure brought to bear on the conscience of citizens and especially of civil servants; the systematic defamation, by means of a clever, closely organized propaganda, of the Church, the clergy, the faithful, the Church's institutions, teaching and history; the closing, dissolution and confiscation of religious houses and other ecclesiastical institutions; the complete suppression of the Catholic press and publishing houses.

To resist such attacks millions of courageous Catholics, men and women, closed their ranks around their Bishops, whose valiant and severe pronouncements never failed to resound even in these last years of war. These Catholics gathered around their priests to help them adapt their ministry to the ever changing needs and conditions. Right to the end they set up against the forces of impiety and pride their forces of faith, prayer and openly Catholic behavior and education.

In the meantime, the Holy See itself multiplied its representations and protests to governing authorities in Germany, reminding them in clear and energetic language of their duty to respect and fulfil the obligations of the natural law itself that were confirmed by the concordat.

In those critical years, joining the alert vigilance of a pastor to the long-suffering patience of a father, Our great predecessor, Pius XI, fulfilled His mission as Supreme Pontiff with intrepid courage. But when, after He had tried all means of persuasion in vain, He saw himself clearly faced with deliberate violations of a solemn pact, with a religious persecution masked or open but always rigorously organized, He proclaimed to the world on Passion Sunday, 1937, in His Encyclical *Mit Brennender Sorge*, what national socialism really was: the arrogant apostasy from Jesus Christ, the denial of His doctrine and of His work of redemption, the cult of violence, the idolatry of race and blood, the overthrow of human liberty and dignity.

### Papal Call Awoke Many

Like a clarion call that sounds the alarm, the Papal document with its vigorous terms—too vigorous, thought more than one at the time—startled the minds and hearts of men. Many— even beyond the frontiers of Germany—who up to then had closed their eyes to the incompatibility of the National Socialist viewpoint with the teachings of Christ had to recognize and confess their mistake. Many—but not all! Some even among the faithful themselves were too blinded by their prejudices or allured by political advantage.

The evidence of the facts brought forward by Our predecessor did not convince them, much less induce them to change their ways. Is it mere chance that some regions, which later suffered more from the National Socialist system were precisely those where the Encyclical *Mit Brennender Sorge* was less or not at all heeded? Would it then have been possible, by opportune and timely political action, to block once and for all the outbreak of brutal violence and to put the German people in the position to shake off the tentacles that were strangling it? Would it have been possible thus to have saved Europe and the world from this immense inundation of blood? Nobody would dare to give an unqualified judgment.

But in any case nobody could accuse the Church of not having denounced and exposed in time the true nature of the National Socialist movement and the danger to which it exposed Christian civilization.

### Nazi Hostility Summed Up

"Whoever sets up race or the people or the state or a particular form of state or the depositaries' power or any other fundamental value of the human community to be the supreme norm of all, even of religious values, and divinizes them to an idolatrous level, distorts and perverts an order of the world planned and created by God." (Cf. *Acta Apostolicae Sedis*, Vol. XXIX, 1937, pages 149 and 171.)

The radical opposition of the National Socialist State to the Catholic Church is summed up in this declaration of the Encyclical. When things had reached this point, the Church could not, withour foregoing Her mission, any longer refuse to take Her stand before the whole world.

But by doing so She became once again *a sign which shall be contradicted*, in the presence of which contrasting opinions divided off into two opposed camps.

German Catholics were, one may say, at one in recognizing that the Encyclical *Mit Brennender Sorge* had brought light, direction, consolation and comfort to all those who seriously meditated and conscientiously practiced the religion of Christ. But the reaction of those who had been inculpated was inevitable, and, in fact, that very year, 1937, was for the Catholic Church in Germany a year of indescribable bitterness and terrible outbreaks.

### Opposition Was Intensified

The important political events which marked the two following years and next the war did not bring any attenuation to the hostility of National Socialism toward the Church, a hostility which was manifest up to these last months, when National Socialists still flattered themselves with the idea that once they had secured victory in arms they could do away with the Church forever.

Authoritative and absolutely trustworthy witnesses kept Us informed of these plans—they unfolded themselves actually in the reiterated and ever more intense activity against the Church in Austria, Alsace-Lorraine and, above all, in those parts of Poland which had already been incorporated in the old Reich during the war: there everything was attacked and destroyed; that is, everything that could be reached by external violence.

Continuing the work of Our Predecessor, We ourselves have during the war, especially in Our radio messages, constantly set forth the demands and perennial laws of humanity and of the Christian Faith in contrast with the ruinous and inexorable applications of National Socialist teachings, which even went so far as to use the most exquisite scientific methods to torture or eliminate people who were often innocent.

This was for Us the most opportune—and We might even say the only—efficacious way of proclaiming before the world the immutable principles of the moral law and of confirming, in the midst of so much error and violence, the minds and hearts of German Catholics in the higher ideals of truth and justice. And Our solicitude was not without its effect. Indeed, We know that Our messages, and especially that of Christmas, 1942, despite every prohibition and obstacle, were studied in the diocesan clergy conferences in Germany and then expounded and explained to the Catholic population.

If the rulers of Germany had decided to destroy the Catholic Church even in the old Reich, Providence had decided otherwise. The tribulations inflicted on the Church by National Socialism have been brought to an end through the sudden and tragic end of the persecution! From the prisons, concentration camps and fortresses are now pouring out, together with the political prisoners, also the crowds of those, whether clergy or laymen, whose only crime was their fidelity to Christ and to the Faith of their Fathers or the dauntless fulfilment of their duties as priests.

For them, all of us have prayed and have seized every opportunity, whenever the occasion offered, to send them a word of comfort and blessing from Our paternal heart.

### Polish Priests Fared Worst

Indeed, the more the veils are drawn which up to now hid the sorrowful passion of the Church under the National Socialist regime, the more apparent becomes the strength, often steadfast unto death, of numberless Catholics and the glorious share in that noble contest which belonged to the clergy.

Although as yet not in possession of the complete statistics, We cannot refrain from recalling here, by way of example, some details from the abundant accounts which have reached us from priests and laymen who were interned in the concentration camp of Dachau and were accounted worthy to suffer reproach for the name of Jesus.

In the forefront, for the number and harshness of the treatment meted out to them, are the Polish priests. From 1940 to 1945, 2,800 Polish ecclesiastics and religious were imprisoned in that camp; among them was a Polish auxiliary bishop who died there of typhus. In April last, there were left only 816, all the others being dead except for two or three transferred to another camp.

In the summer of 1942, 480 German-speaking ministers of religion were known to be gathered there; of these, forty-five were Protestants, all the others Catholic priests. In spite of the continuous inflow of new internees, especially from some dioceses of Bavaria, the Rhineland and Westphalia, their number, as a result of the high rate of mortality, at the beginning of this year did not surpass 350.

Nor should we pass over in silence those belonging to occupied territories, Holland, Belgium, France (among whom the Bishop of Clermont), Luxemburg, Slovenia, Italy.

Many of those priests and laymen endured indescribable sufferings for their Faith and for their vocation.

In one case the hatred of the impious against Christ reached the point of parodying on the person of an interned priest, with barbed wire, the scourging and the crowning with thorns of our Redeemer.

The generous victims who during the twelve years since 1933 have in Germany sacrificed for Christ and His Church their possessions, their freedom, their lives, are raising their hands to God in expiatory sacrifice. May the just Judge accept it in reparation for the many crimes committed against mankind no less than against the present and future generation and especially against the unfortunate youth of Germany, and may He at last stay the arm of the exterminating angel!

With ever-increasing persistence National Socialism strove to denounce the Church as the enemy of the German people. The manifest injustice of the accusation would have deeply offended the sentiment of German Catholics and Our own if it had come from other lips. But on the lips of such accusers, so far from being a grievance, the accusation is the clearest and most honorable testimony to the strong, incessant opposition maintained by the Church to such disastrous doctrines and methods in the interest of true civilization and of the German people. To that people We offer the wish that, freed now from the error which plunged it into chaos, it may find again its own salvation at the pure fountains of true peace and true happiness, at the fountains of truth, humility and charity flowing with the Church from the Heart of Christ.

## II

## LOOKING TO THE FUTURE

A hard-earned lesson surely, that of these past years! God grant at least that it may have been understood and be profitable to other nations! *Receive instruction, you that judge the earth!*

That is the most ardent wish of all who sincerely love mankind. For mankind, now the victim of an impious process of exhaustion, of cynical disregard for the life and rights of men, has but one aspiration: to lead a tranquil and peaceful life in dignity and honest toil. And to this purpose it hopes that an end will be put to that insolence with which the family and the domestic hearth have been abused and profaned during the war years.

For that insolence cries to heaven and has evolved into one of the gravest perils not only for religion and morality but also for harmonious relations between men. It has, above all, created those mobs of dispossessed, disillusioned, disappointed and hopeless men who are going to swell the ranks of revolution and disorder, in the pay of a tyranny no less despotic than those for whose overthrow men planned.

The nations, and notably the medium and small nations, claim the right to take their destinies into their own hands.

They can be led to assume, with their full and willing consent, in the interest of common progress, obligations which will modify their sovereign rights.

But after having sustained their share—their large share—of suffering in order to overthrow a system of brutal violence, they are entitled to refuse to accept a new political or cultural system which is decisively rejected by the great majority of their people. They maintain, and with reason, that the primary task of the peace-framers is to put an end to the criminal war game and to safeguard vital rights and mutual obligations as between the great and small, powerful and weak.

Deep in their hearts the peoples feel that their rule would be discredited if they did not succeed in supplanting the mad folly of the rule of violence by the victory of the right.

The thought of a new peace organization is inspired—nobody could doubt it—by the most sincere and loyal good will. The whole of mankind follows the progress of this noble enterprise with anxious interest. What a bitter disillusionment it would be if it were to fail, if so many years of suffering and self-sacrifice were to be made vain, by permitting again to prevail that spirit of oppression from which the world hoped to see itself at last freed once and for all!

Poor world, to which then might be applied the words of Christ: *And the last state of that man becomes worse than the first.*

The present political and social situation suggests these words of warning to us. We have had, alas, to deplore in more than one region the murder of priests, deportations of civilians, the killing of citizens without trial or in personal vendetta. No less sad is the news that has reached us from Slovenia and Croatia.

But We will not lose heart. The speeches made by competent and responsible men in the course of the last few weeks made it clear that they are aiming at the triumph of right, not merely as a political goal, but even more as a moral duty.

Accordingly, We confidently issue an ardent appeal for prayers to Our sons and daughters of the whole world. May it reach all those who recognize in God the beloved Father of all men created to His image and likeness, to all who know that in the breast of Christ there beats a Divine Heart rich in mercy, deep and inexhaustible fountain of all good and all love, of all peace and all reconciliation.

From the cessation of hostilities to true and genuine peace, as We warned not long ago, the road will be long and arduous, too long for the pent-up aspiration of mankind starving for order and calm. But it is inevitable that it should be so.

### Calls for Peaceful Designs

It is even perhaps better thus. It is essential that the tempest of over-excited passions be first let subside: *Motos praestat componere fluctus* (Virgil, *Aeneid* 1, 135). It is essential that the hate, the diffidence, the stimuli of an extreme nationalism should give way to the growth of wise counsels, the flowering of peaceful designs, to serenity in the interchange of views and to mutual brotherly comprehension.

May the Holy Spirit, light of intellects, gentle ruler of hearts, deign to hear the prayers of His church and guide in their arduous work those who, in accordance with their mandate, are striving sincerely, despite obstacles and contradictions, to reach the goal so universally and so ardently desired: peace, a peace worthy of the name; a peace built and consolidated in sincerity and loyalty, in justice and reality; a peace of loyal and resolute force to overcome or preclude those economic and social conditions which might, as they did in the past, easily lead to new conflicts; a peace that can be approved by all right-minded men of every people and every nation; a peace which future generations may regard gratefully as the happy outcome of a sad period; a peace that may stand out in the centuries as a resolute advance in the affirmation of human dignity and of ordered liberty; a peace that may be like the Magna Charta which closed the dark age of violence; a peace that under the merciful guidance of God may let us so pass through temporal prosperity that we may not lose eternal happiness.

But before reaching this peace it still remains true that millions of men at their own fireside or in battle, in prison or in exile, must still drink their bitter chalice. How We long to see the end of their sufferings and anguish, the realization of their hopes! For them, too, and for all mankind that suffers with them and in them may Our humble and ardent prayer ascend to Almighty God.

# Moral Prerequisites for a Free and Lasting Peace*

(*Christmas Message to the College of Cardinals and Broad-cast to the World, December 24, 1945*)

. . . AT an hour like this, in which we celebrate the birth of Him Who came to reconcile men to God and to one another, We cannot let pass the opportunity of saying a word about the peace structure which the ruling classes in the State and in politics and economics have set themselves to erect. With an accumulation hitherto perhaps never achieved, of experience, goodwill, political insight and organizing talent, men have begun the preliminaries to the world peace settlement.

Never, perhaps, from the beginning of the world have statesmen found themselves faced with a task so gigantic and complex, because of the number, gravity and difficulty of the problems to be solved, so important in its effects in extent and in depth for good or for evil, as that of now restoring order, peace, and prosperity to mankind after 30 years of world war, economic crises and incalculable destitution.

Exalted, formidable is the responsibility of those who set themselves to bring such a gigantic undertaking to a successful conclusion. It is not Our intention to discuss the practical solutions that they may be able to apply to such thorny problems. We believe, however, that it belongs to Our office, in continuation of Our previous Christmas messages during the war, to indicate the fundamental moral prerequisites of a true and lasting peace which We shall reduce to three short considerations:

* Translation from National Catholic Welfare Conference pamphlet.

141

## Three Fundamental Prerequisites

(1) The present hour calls imperiously for collaboration, good will, reciprocal confidence in all peoples. The motives of hate, vengeance, rivalry, antagonism, unfair and dishonest competition must be kept out of political and economic debates and decisions.

*Who can say*, We may add, in the words of Sacred Scripture, *my heart is clean, I am pure from sin? Diverse weights and diverse measures, both are abominable before God.*

Anyone, then, who exacts the expiation of crime through the just punishment of criminals because of their misdeeds should take good care not to do himself what he denounces in others as misdeeds or crime. One who seeks reparations should base his claim on moral principles and respect for those inviolable natural rights which remain valid even for those who have surrendered unconditionally to the victor.

One who asks for security in the future should not forget that its only true guarantee lies in one's own internal force, that is, in safeguarding the family, children, and labor in fraternal charity, in the outlawing of all hate, all persecution, all unjust vexation of honest citizens, in loyal concord between State and State, between people and people.

(2) To secure this, men must everywhere forego the artificial creation, through the power of wealth, arbitrary censorship, one-sided judgments, and false assertions, of a so-called public opinion which sways the ideas and will of the electorate like reeds shaken by the wind.

Let due heed be paid to the true and overwhelming majority of men, made up of those who live honestly and peacefully by their own labor in their own family circle, and who desire to do the will of God. In their eyes disputes for more advantageous frontiers and the scramble for the treasures of the earth, even if not of necessity and *a priori* unjust in themselves, are, at least, always a dangerous venture which cannot be entered on without the risk of causing an accumulation of death and ruins.

The vast majority of good fathers and mothers of families want to protect and safeguard the future of their own children against the pretensions of every policy of brute force, against the arbitrary totalitarianism of the powerful State.

## The Tyranny of the Totalitarian State

(3) The force of the totalitarian State. The whole surface of the globe, reddened with the blood shed in these terrible years, cries aloud against the tyranny of such a State.

The fabric of peace would rest on a tottering and ever threatening base, if an end were not put to such totalitarianism, which lowers man to the state of a mere pawn in the game of politics, a cipher in economic calculations. With a stroke of the pen it changes the frontiers of states; by a peremptory decision it deprives a people's economy—always part of its life as a nation—of its natural outlets; with ill-concealed cruelty it too drives millions of men, hundreds of families, in the most squalid misery, from their homes and lands, tears them out by the roots and wrenches them from a civilization and culture which they had striven for generations to develop.

It also sets arbitrary bounds to the necessity and to the right of migration and to the desire to colonize. All this constitutes a policy contrary to the dignity and welfare of the human race.

And yet, by Divine Right it is not the will or the power of fortuitous and unstable vested interests, but man in the framework of the family and of society, who by his labor is lord of the world.

Consequently, this totalitarianism fails by what is the only measure of progress, namely the progressive creation of ever more ample and better conditions in public life to ensure that the family can evolve as an economic, juridic, moral and religious unit.

Within the confines of each particular nation as much as in the whole family of peoples, state totalitarianism is incompatible with a true and healthy democracy. Like a dangerous germ it infects the community of nations and renders it incapable of guaranteeing the security of individual peoples. It constitutes a continual menace of war.

The future peace structure aims at outlawing from the world every aggressive use of force, every war of aggression. Who could not greet such an intention enthusiastically, especially in its effective realization?

But if this is to be something more than a beautiful gesture, all oppression and all arbitrary action from within and without must be banned.

In the face of this accepted state of affairs, there remains but one solution: a return to God and to the order established by Him.

The more the veil is lifted from the origin and increase of those forces which brought about the war, the clearer it becomes that they were the heirs, the bearers and continuers of errors of which the essential element was the neglect, overthrow, denial and contempt of Christian thought and principles.

If then the root of the evil lies here, there is but one remedy: to go back to the order fixed by God also in relations between States and peoples; to go back to a real Christianity within the State and among States.

And let it not be said that this is not realism in politics. Experience should have taught all that the policy guided by eternal truths and the laws of God is the most real and tangible of policies. Realistic politicians who think otherwise pile up only ruins.

### Prisoners of War and Political Prisoners

And now, lastly, Our gaze which has wandered, if only for a moment, over the present state of the world, must pause once again on the masses, still immense, of war prisoners.

As We get ready to pass in quiet interior joy and fervent prayer the holy feast of Christmas, which reaffirms and enobles, with century-old and undiminished harmony, the bonds of the human family, and invites to the domestic hearth, as to a sacred rite, even those who habitually live long away from it, We remember with profound sorrow all those who, although the end of the war has been proclaimed, must this year again pass the beautiful season in a foreign land and feel, on the night of rejoicing and peace, the torment of their uncertain lot and of their separation from parents, wives, children, brothers, sisters—all their dear ones.

And while We wish to pay the tribute of just recognition and praise to those authorities and to those organizations and individuals who have striven to alleviate and to abbreviate their sorrowful condition, We cannot conceal the pain We felt when in addition to the sufferings inevitably accruing from the war, We heard of others which were almost on purpose inflicted on

144

prisoners and deported people; when, in some instances, We saw their captivity prolonged without reasonable cause; when the yoke of imprisonment, of itself oppressive, was aggravated by hard and unjustified labor, or when in unconscionable disregard for standards set up by international conventions and by the still more sacred standards of Christian and civil conscience, they were refused in an inhuman way the treatment due to the vanquished.

To these children, still held in prison, may Our Father's message be carried on the wings of the Christmas Angels. May they receive and be comforted by Our wish—shared by all who cherish the sense of man's brotherhood—to see them regularly and speedily restored to their anxious families and to their normal peacetime occupations.

And We are certain that We voice the sentiments of all right-thinking men when We extend that wish to include those political prisoners, men, women and youths, at times exposed to dire sufferings, against whom no accusation of crime or violation of the law can be brought, but, at most, only their past political views.

# Points for the Attainment of Peace*

*(Christmas Address to the College of Cardinals, Broadcast to the World, December 24, 1946)*

. . . HUMANITY has barely come from the horrors of a cruel war, the results of which fill her still with anguish, and she now gazes with amazement on the yawning abyss between the hopes of yesterday and the realizations of today, an abyss which the most persistent efforts can bridge only with difficulty, because man, who is capable of destruction, is not always himself capable of reconstruction.

Behold, for almost two years now, the roar of cannon is silenced. Military results in the field of battle have brought

* Translation from *The Catholic Mind.*

about an indisputable victory for one of the belligerent parties and a defeat without precedent for the other. Seldom in the history of the world has the sword traced such a clear line of division between the conquerors and the conquered.

### Peace Not in Sight

It was indeed to be feared, considering the ruinous and confused condition in which the cruel conflict left the world, that the path from the end of the war to the conclusion of the peace would be long and painful. But at present we are witnessing its continuation without being able to foresee—despite some notable progress at last made—how or when it will be terminated; and this indefinite prolonging of an abnormal state of instability and uncertainty is the clear symptom of an evil which constitutes the sad characteristic of our age.

Men were witnesses of prodigious activity in all the fields of military power, formidable in its precision and extent of preparation and organization, lightning-like in the speed and improvisation with which it was continuously adapting itself to circumstances and needs; now they see the elaboration and the drawing up of peace taking place with great slowness and amid divergencies not yet overcome in determining aims and methods.

When for the first time the Atlantic Charter was announced, the whole world listened; at last one could breathe freely. But what remains of that message and its provision? Even in some of those States which, either through free choice or under the aegis of other greater powers, love to appear to the world of today as the standard bearers of new and true progress, the "Four Freedoms," recently hailed with enthusiasm by many, now seem only a shadow or a counterfeit of what was in the mind and intentions of the most loyal of their promulgators.

We most willingly recognize the untiring efforts of outstanding statesmen who for a year or so, in a series of almost uninterrupted and toilsome conferences, have labored to bring about what honest men the world over ardently long for and desire.

But, alas, differences of opinion, mutual distrust and suspicion, the doubtful value, in fact and in justice, of not a few decisions already taken or still to be taken, have made uncertain and fragile the strength and vitality of compromises and solutions based on force or political prestige, which leave deep down in many hearts disillusion and discontent.

Instead of advancing toward a real peace, people in vast territories of the globe and in large sections especially of Europe are in a state of constant unrest from which there could arise sooner or later the flames of new conflicts.

When one sees and ponders all this, one is profoundly impressed with the gravity of the present hour and feels the need of calling on the rulers of the nations, in whose hands lies the destiny of the world and on whose deliberations depend the success and progress or the failure of the peace, and asking them to consider three points:

## A Speedy Peace

1. The first condition, in order to fulfill the expectations of the nations, to lessen and gradually to remove the internal disturbances from which they suffer, to remove the dangerous international tensions, is that all your energies and all your good will be directed to putting an end to the present intolerable state of incertitude and to hasten, as soon as possible, the coming of a definite peace among all States—and that notwithstanding difficulties which no calm consideration can fail to recognize.

During the long years of the war and post-war period, human nature, a prey to innumerable and indescribable sufferings, has given proof of incredible powers of resistance. But this power is limited!

For millions of human beings that limit has already been reached; the spring is already stretched too far; the slightest thing would cause it to snap, and its breaking could have irreparable consequences. Humanity wants to be able to hope again.

A speedy and complete conclusion of peace is of real and lively interest to all those who know that only a prompt return to normal economic, juridical and spiritual relations among nations can save the world from incalculable shocks and disorders which would only help the dark forces of evil.

Therefore, let the year that is now coming to an end be the

147

last year of vain and fruitless expectancy; let the new year see the peace a reality.

### A Just Peace

2. The year of fulfillment! This thought leads to the second appeal that every right-minded person makes to the rulers of the nations.

You rightly long to see—and how could it be otherwise?—your names written in letters of gold on the scroll of the benefactors of the human race. The mere thought that one day—even without fault on your part—they may be opprobriously listed among the authors of its ruin, fills you with horror. Apply, then, all the forces of your mind and will to give to your work of peace the seal of the true justice, of far-seeing wisdom, of a sincere service to the common interests of the entire human family.

The utter depth of misery into which the horrible war has thrown humanity calls for help and imperiously demands to be healed by means of a peace that is morally noble and irreproachable: such a peace that may teach future generations to outlaw every trace of brutal force and to restore to the idea of right the priority of place from which it was wickedly dislodged.

We justly appreciate the arduous but noble work of those statesmen who, disregarding the insidious voices of revenge and hate, have been toiling and are still toiling without respite for the fulfillment of such a high ideal. But notwithstanding their generous efforts, who could ever say that the discussions and debates of the year that is ending have resulted in a clear plan, drawn up logically in its main outlines, and calculated to reawaken in all nations confidence in a future of tranquillity and justice.

### Cooperation of All Urged

No doubt such a disastrous war, unleashed by an unjust aggression and continued beyond lawful limits when it was clear that it was irreparably lost, could not be terminated simply in a peace which did not include guarantees that similar acts of violence would not be repeated. Nevertheless, all the measures of repression and prevention should keep their character of means and hence remain subordinate to the lofty and ultimate purposes of a true peace which, while providing the necessary guarantees, contemplates the gradual cooperation of conquerors and conquered in the work of reconstruction to the advantage of the entire family of nations and as well of each of its members.

Any balanced observer will be willing to recognize that these indisputable principles have made real progress during the past year in not a few minds and that, too, as a result of the painful repercussion felt by the vital interests of the victorious States themselves. One finds some satisfaction also in noting that competent and authoritative voices in ever-increasing numbers are raised against an unlimited prolongation of the present conditions on the life and economic recovery of the defeated. Immediate contact with the indescribable misery of the post-war period in some zones has awakened in many hearts the consciousness of a common responsibility to lessen effectively, and eventually to overcome, such a great evil. This sentiment is as honorable for one as it is encouraging for the other.

Recently a new factor has arisen to stimulate the desire for peace and the determination to promote it more effectively: the might of new instruments of destruction which modern technique has developed and continues to develop to such an extent that they appear to the terrified eyes of humanity infernal creations. This factor has brought the problem of disarmament into the center of international discussions under completely new aspects, and it provides an incentive that was never felt before; thence springs hope of solving what past generations have longed for in vain.

Notwithstanding these well-founded motives of hope, in which no one can rejoice more than the Church, it seems that, in the present state of affairs, one must expect with great probability that the future peace treaties will only be an *opus imperfectum*. Many of those who write them will recognize in them the result of compromises between the policies and claims of differing political powers rather than the expression of their own personal ideas based on the true and just concepts of right and equity, of human feeling and prudence.

## Future Revisions

3. This leads naturally to the third appeal addressed to the rulers of the nations:

If you wish to give more than a superficial stability and duration to your labors for the new order and a peace that will not fail; if you wish to prevent its being violated sooner or later due to its own harshness, to the practical difficulties of putting it into effect, to its inherent defects and shortcomings, to the omissions and insufficiencies perhaps inevitable today, to its real or imagined effects in the future which cannot be calculated at the moment; then take care to leave open the way for amendments—according to a clearly determined procedure—as soon as the majority of peoples, the voice of reason and of equity, show that these amendments are opportune and desirable or even called for.

In design, a machine can appear to be of indisputable perfection for its rigorous mathematical precision, but may show itself seriously defective in a real trial when it is faced with a number of unforeseen technical difficulties. In a moral, social and political order, how much more easily can a project appear excellent on paper, the fruit of laborious discussion, but then fail in the test of time and experience, where psychological factors play an important role. Certainly everything cannot be foreseen. But it is wise to leave the door open for future revisions and eventual adjustments.

In doing this, you will show yourself faithful to the words spoken in memorable circumstances by authoritative interpreters of public opinion; you will be sure of not causing any prejudice to your best interests; you will give to the entire human family a luminous example by showing that there is no safer way toward the desired peace than that which comes from the re-education of mankind in the spirit of fraternal solidarity.

## Message from Bethlehem

When one knows one is advancing along a safe path, how beautiful a thing it is to walk in the light! The light: look at it, all of you who are united by the same Faith in the Saviour of the world! To illumine the path, it comes down from the Star that shines over Bethlehem.

If one wishes to return to the great principles of justice that lead to peace, one must go to Bethlehem. One must recall the example and the doctrine of Him Who from the cradle to the cross knew no higher mission than that of fulfilling the will of the Heavenly Father, rescuing the world from the darkness of error and mire of sin where it lay pitiably. It must be brought to acknowledge its subjection to the majesty of the Divine Law as its norm of right thinking and its measure of wholesome and conscientious conduct.

The great return to the axioms of the message of Bethlehem was never more necessary for the world than today. Indeed, rarely has the contrast between the precepts of that Divine message and the reality as we see it been made, alas, so clear to men.

Frightened by this contrast, would you wish, beloved sons and daughters, to lose courage? Would you wish to increase the number of those who, alarmed at the instability of the times, begin themselves to waver in such a way that more or less knowingly they play the part of the adversaries of Christ? No Christian has the right to show himself tired of the fight against the anti-religious surge of today. It matters little under what forms, with what methods, weapons, words—enticing or menacing—and in what disguises the enemy hides himself. No one can be excused for remaining in his presence with folded arms, bowed head and trembling knees. . . .

## Many are Still Hungry

We cannot end this Our Christmas message without recalling the suffering and the needs arising from the serious food situation and health conditions of the nations tried by the war.

Already on April 5th of this year We uttered a cry of help to the rulers and to the peoples of those countries who could come to the help of the starving populations with their reserves. And, in truth, much has been done. Moved by the tragic plight especially of the weak, the aged and the children, the civilized world did not remain insensible or slothful; and praise is due to the humane and Christian spirit of those men and nations who organized multiple relief works. Following on the sanguinary paths of the armies, they brought to the victims of the war all kinds of help. They have saved the honor of mankind which was so shamefully outraged by violence and hate.

Would to Heaven that these funds of energy and provision —charitably lavished in relieving the most needy and bringing them from utter ruin—would that they had been sufficient for the task! Alas, it is not so; therefore, We feel compelled to renew Our appeal of last spring. There looms over vast territories of Europe and the Far East the specter of the most appalling famine and starvation.

Bread—in the literal sense of the word—is needed by entire populations, who because of its lack are becoming weak, worn out, enervated, the prey of diseases and pains, and dangerously aroused by the dull goad of hopeless rancor and deep-seated social rebellion.

Such is the tremendous danger that darkens the dawn of the new year, a danger so much more serious because, from some symptoms which reveal uncertainty and weariness, the magnanimous work of human solidarity seems on the verge of deteriorating even before a remedy can be applied to the ills which it was designed to relieve.

It is but human that they upon whom fortune is smiling should be inclined to keep aloof and forget the wretchedness of others. Closing their eyes and their hearts to the misfortunes of a neighbor who is unknown and far away, they think they can justify in their own consciences the isolationism and disinterestedness in the necessities of others; their personal needs consume funds that the practice of charity would have laid aside; and their means of relief fail to provide that assistance for which charity to the neighbor would have destined them.

Therefore, We say once more to all who can lend a helping hand: let not your zeal grow cold; let your help be ever more available and generous! Away with all greedy selfishness, all mean doubts, all bitterness, all indifference, all rancor.

Let your eye see only the misery and, above all, the suffering of millions of children and young people who are perishing with hunger. In this way you, at one and the same time, give and receive the ineffable Christmas Gift: *Peace on earth to men of good will.*

Nothing is so well suited to create the indispensable spiritual requirements of peace as help liberally given by State to State, by a people to a people, without regard to national boundaries, so that nations, laying aside feelings of rivalry and of vengeance, restraining their craving for power and banishing the thought of privileged isolation, may learn from their own fortunes to understand, to tolerate, and to help one another, and thus—upon the ruins of a civilization forgetful of the teachings of the Gospel—the Christian Commonwealth may arise again, in which the law of love is supreme.

# The World Is Far from Peace*

*(Christmas Message Broadcast to the Whole World, December 24, 1947)*

WHEN last year on this same occasion We addressed Our Christmas message to the Catholic world, and to all men of good judgment and good will besides, who could have had it in his heart to predict for humanity, tired of war and hungry for peace, what has today become a cruel, undeniable reality?

Christmas bells will still ring in the feast, as from the days of old. But for many closed, embittered and tormented hearts, they ring out in the desert, where they wake no living echo any longer.

Now that another postwar year has passed, with its burden of distress and suffering, of disillusionment and privation, those who have eyes to see and ears to hear cannot but he pained and humiliated by this: Europe and the world—even to distant and tormented China—today are farther from real peace, farther from complete and definite safety, farther from a new order based firmly on agreement and justice, than ever they were before.

The champions of negation and disagreement, with the long line of profiteers in their train, are jubilant at the thought— or the illusion—that their hour is near.

Contrariwise, the friends of peace, the promoters of a lasting reconciliation between the peoples of the world, feel the

---

* Translation from National Catholic Welfare Conference pamphlet.

twinge of anguish in their hearts when they compare the moral and social wealth of Bethlehem's "good tidings" with the misery of a world that has wandered far away from Christ.

But genuine Christians, for whom the whole of life, the source of all its lights and worth, consists in "thinking with the Church," perceive and realize better than anyone else the meaning and value of times like ours; times of dense darkness, but of blinding light as well; where the enemy of Christ reaps a vast, tragic harvest of souls, but many also of the good are leading better lives; where generous hearts can scale victoriously the peak of heroism, while numbers of the tepid and the faint of heart, slaves of human respect and afraid of sacrifice, slip into mediocrity or sink into the vile depths of degradation, like these who "neither rebels proved, not yet were true to God but for themselves were only" (Dante, *Inferno*).

## Uniting in a World-wide League

In the titanic struggle between the two forces now competing for the mastery of the world, if hatred is all that is needed to marshal under the leadership of the evil-one men who would seemingly have every ground to disagree, what could love not accomplish toward uniting in a world-wide league those whose high purpose, noble instincts and community in suffering have drawn them together by ties stronger and more intimate than any difference or divergency which could keep them apart? To the millions who are disposed to become members of this world alliance, the charter of which is the message of Bethlehem and its unseen head the King and Peacemaker who lies before us in the manger, We direct at this juncture our heartfelt appeal.

The brand on the brow of one generation, and the source of its disruption and decadence, is the tendency, every day more obvious, to "insincerity," a lack of honesty, and this not merely as an occasional expedient, or of obstacles unforeseen. No. Today it amounts practically to a system. It has been raised to the distinction of a strategy, in which the lie, the garbled word or fact, and trickery have come to be an accepted weapon of offense, which some people wield with the skill of professionals, boasting even of their competence.

So clearly, as they view it, has the suppression of all sense of right and wrong come to be part and parcel of modern technique in the art of forming public opinion, of controlling it and making it serve their political ends. For they are bent on winning at any cost the battle of class-interest and theories, of ideologies and power politics.

We do not propose to describe here in detail the havoc wrought by this tournament of "insincerity" in public life. But We are in duty bound to open the eyes of Catholics all over the world—and of all others besides who share our faith in Christ and a transcendent God—to the dangers which this prevalence of falsehood presents for the Church and Christian civilization, for the entire religious and even merely human heritage which has supplied the peoples of the world with the substance of their spiritual life and of their real greatness for the past 2,000 years.

When Herod of old was plotting anxiously to slay the Babe of Bethlehem he hid his plan under a pious mask, and tried his best to make the honest men into unwitting spies. Likewise today, his modern imitators move heaven and earth to conceal their real purpose from the masses, and make them the unconscious instruments of their designs.

But once they have won power and feel the reins securely in their hands, little by little they let fall the veil, and pass by successive stages from oppression of the dignity and liberty of man to abolition of all authentic and independent religious life.

Here, then, is the question We put to all honest men: How is humanity to recover, how can any "New Order" worthy of the name emerge from the mistakes and agitation of this present hour of confusion, if the lines which mark off friend from foe, yes from no, and faith from lack of faith are to be erased and moved about?

The Church, though her heart is ever full of love and sympathy for these erring souls, cannot fail to denounce error, in loyalty to her Divine Founder's declaration: *He who is not with me, is against me.* She cannot but tear the mask from the *forgers of lies* who come forward as *wolves in sheep's clothing,* as founders and pioneers of a new golden age. She cannot but warn the faithful not to let themselves be lured from the path of rectitude, or be deluded by fallacious promises.

155

Our position between the two opposing camps is exempt from every prejudice, from any preference for this or that people, for this or that bloc of nations, as it is foreign to any sort of temporal consideration. To be with Christ or against Christ: that is the whole question.

Each of the opposing sides believes itself constrained to this mistrust, as by a duty of elementary precaution. Obviously, this very fact leads to the building of an immense wall which renders hopeless every attempt to bring to the bewildered human family the blessings of true peace.

Have we not had occasion, even during the past few weeks, to experience the tangible results of this mistrust? Have we not seen a most important conference of the great powers adjourn without having taken those essential and decisive steps along the road to peace for which the world in its anguish was waiting?

## Need for Honesty

There can be but one way out of the straits to which the cult of "insincerity" has brought the world: the return to the spirit and practice of straightforward honesty.

No one today—to whatever social or political movement or party he may belong—who wants to bring the weight of his convictions and his public acts to bear upon the present or the future destiny of nations, has any right to wear a mask, to appear to be what he is not, to avail himself of the strategy of the lie, of tension and of threats, in order to restrict the honest citizens of every land in the exercise of their just liberty and civil rights.

You will readily understand, then, how pained We are to see hostile propaganda distorting what We think and say, embittering men's hearts, hindering the peaceful exchange of ideas, and deepening the chasm which separates from Us so many souls redeemed by the Blood of the same divine and loving Saviour. At the bottom of it lies, unfailingly, the same identical duplicity, deliberately adopted and ruthlessly employed as the most incisive weapon with which to combat justice and truth, and hinder mutual understanding, reconciliation and peace.

The inevitable outcome of such a situation is the splitting

of humanity into powerful and rival groups, whose highest law of life and conduct is a basic and invincible mistrust. Here is at once the tragic paradox and the curse of our time.

That is why We would remind you, dear sons and daughters, that we celebrate tomorrow the birth of Him from Whose lips one day escaped the cry: *Veritas liberabit vos* (*John* 8:32); the truth (which is His teaching) shall make you free. Never, perhaps, has this cry re-echoed so loudly as it does today in a world hungry for peace but forced to groan beneath the oppressive yoke of falsehood.

Let all Christendom, too, make answer—to Him who was made flesh that He might be for all *way, truth and life*—in a prayerful plea that the truth may find its way back to the hearts of the rulers of nations, whose yes or no may determine the fate of the world. And with the truth may there shine out upon the earth no deceptive mirage, but Bethlehem's bright star of peace divine.

## II

Those who were absolutely determined to win the war were ready for any sacrifice, even unto death. Those who sincerely wish to win the peace must be ready for sacrifices just as generous, since nothing is more difficult for convulsed and embittered human nature than to forego reprisals and lay aside its unforgiving rancor.

The injustice and cruelty committed by those who unleashed the Second World War aroused waves of righteous indignation, but served, alas, at the same time, to develop the seeds of a natural inclination for revenge.

The saner portion of mankind—even among nations chiefly involved in the conflict—unanimously denounced the excesses and atrocities which a political system, falling into moral nihilism, not only practiced during the war which it provoked, but even dared to justify in theory. Facts and documents recently come to light have only served to confirm that those who sponsored and worked out this system are mainly responsible for the world's misery today.

Men of the post-war period could have easily confronted this degeneracy with their own moral superiority; unfortunately, in not a few instances they have let slip a golden opportunity. It must be admitted that the history of the world during the days and weeks and months immediately following the war was very far from being one of unmixed glory.

The punishment justly meted out to the chief culprits could have inspired Dante's pen with scenes for the Inferno, but the great poet would have shrunk from depicting the reprisals wrought upon the innocent.

Forced migrations and compulsory hard labor followed later, defying the most elementary laws of humanity as well as the letter and the spirit of the rights of nations. Who, then, could be surprised that the sense of justice which had been rightly shocked at the sight of such deeds perpetrated by one side should also react similarly when it sees others commit them?

Who can measure what further moral domestic and social distress, what harm to the cultural and economic stability of Europe—and not alone of Europe—will be caused by the compulsory and indiscriminate displacement of peoples, what sorrow at present, what anguish for the future? Only a broader vision, a wiser and more judicious policy on the part of those who hold the fate of the world in their hands, can provide a tolerable solution for an otherwise insoluble problem.

All honor, then, to those of every nation who shirk no privation or shun no labor to hasten the fulfilment of such a noble enterprise. Let them not be troubled at the contradictions and opposition they will have to meet and which precisely in these days seem to have grown more intense, in stimulating another war of nerves, provoking discord, reducing to naught the efforts of the champions of unity and peace. Let them be confident that the hour is at hand—as we trust and ask in our prayers—when the King of peace will grant victory to those who do battle for His cause with a right intention and with the weapons of peace.

### III

The human race, then, will be powerless to emerge from the present crisis and desolation and to go forward to a more harmonious future unless it restrain and control the forces of division and discord by means of a sincere spirit of brotherhood uniting all classes, all races and all nations with the one bond of love.

We launch such an appeal to the entire world, today, the Eve of Christmas, because We see this spirit of brotherhood in danger of being stifled and crushed: because We see selfish appetites getting the better of sound reason, and the cruel tactics of oppression and violence prevailing over loyal understanding and mutual respect, and the utter disregard for any consequent evils to the detriment of the zealous maintenance of public welfare.

The Church, whose maternal heart embraces all nations with equal affection, is following with great anxiety this new development in national and international conflicts.

When faith in God, the Father of all men, begins to grow dim, the spirit of brotherly union also loses its moral foundation and cohesive force; and when the consciousness of a society embracing all men, as wished by God, and which includes reciprocal rights and duties, determined by fixed norms, begins to die out, there arise in its place a morbid hyper-sensitiveness to what divides, a ready propensity to overstate one's rights true or imagined, and a neglect—at times thoughtless, but not for that reason less ruinous—for the essential needs of others.

At this point, the way is open for the struggle of all against all, a battle which knows no other right except that of the strongest.

Our age, alas, has provided some sad examples of fratricidal war, resulting with relentless logic from the weakening of the spirit of brotherhood.

### Loss of the Spirit of Brotherhood

Even the land which heard the hymn of the Angels announcing peace to men, which saw the Star of the Saviour shine forth, and where the Divine Redeemer died crucified for our salvation—even that Holy Land with all its memories and shrines most dear to every Christian heart, is now divided and has become the scene of blood and strife. And Europe, herself, the center of the whole great Catholic family—is she not perchance today, a warning and an example of the plight to which the loss of the spirit of brotherhood can reduce a part of the world once so beautiful and flourishing? The wounds she suffered during the late war are still unhealed, and already the sinister light of a new conflict flashes on the horizon.

Oh, if all honest men were to unite together, how quickly would the victory of the brotherhood of men be realized and along with it the rehabilitation of the world! Such people already constitute a substantial element of public opinion, and show that they possess real human instincts, with political wisdom as well.

But there are others just as numerous, whose mere word has considerable weight in hastening or impeding the peace of Europe—the necessary initial step toward world peace—and who follow a course directly opposite. Are they afraid, perhaps, that if Europe were to recover, regain her strength, and become conscious once more of her Christian mission, she would wish to rid herself of the deadly germ of atheism and revolution and live a life of her own, free from unhealthy foreign influence?

It is obvious that a Europe shivering and feverish from economic difficulties and social chaos yields more readily to the seductions and illusions of a fatuous ideal state than a healthy Europe with her vision clear.

Meanwhile, the propagators of such deceptive schemes spare no effort to make converts to their cause among the fanatics and the simple, whose aim, in turn, it will be to drag their people along the path of ruin that others have traveled before them, not from choice but because their civil and religious liberty had been systematically repressed.

Have we not had occasion to see here, on the sacred soil of the city where God has established the Chair of Peter, the emissaries of a concept of life and human society based on atheism and violence sowing cockles in the good earth of Rome, and doing their utmost to convince her sons that they have discovered and set up a new culture more worthy of man than the ancient and eternally youthful Christian civilization?

### Time to Rouse from Sleep

Since things have reached such a pass, the time has surely come for everyone who cherishes the human and spiritual heritage of his forefathers to rouse himself from sleep, take up the arms of faith and courage, and preserve the city, civilization's mother, from religious, moral and social deterioration such as might render very difficult to Our keen regret, that solemn celebration of the coming Holy Year desired by Catholics the world over.

If, however, the frank words We utter during today's celebration know no boundaries, they refer only to doctrines denying faith in God and Christ, and certainly not to the nations or groups of nations who are the victims of these doctrines. For these latter the Church ever cherishes the same constant love. Nay, the more they suffer the greater is her love for them. It is in the days of trial, rather than in untroubled hours, that men of all nations should realize that they are brothers. The real meaning, the lofty mission and the power to reconcile of this brotherhood has never been, nor shall ever be extolled with such force as it was by *the first-born among many brethren*, Who from Bethlehem to Golgotha preached by His example more than by His words that great and universal brotherhood of men.

Over this Christmas a dark cloud is gathering. As the people's anxious yearning for peace grows ever more intense, the inability of their leaders to satisfy it by merely human means is just as apparent. Do not the honest efforts of some to arrive at an equitable peace and the systematic planning of others to prevent its fulfilment bring perchance to mind the picture of a dangerous game of chance of which the stakes are fortune or ruin?

Into the meeting places of men the spirit of evil creeps unnoticed, *the angel of the Abyss;* the enemy of truth, the fomenter of hatred, the denier and destroyer of all sense of brotherhood, believing that his hour is nigh, uses everything at hand to hasten it. Nevertheless, We desire to end Our Christmas message with an irrepressible appeal for hope and confidence.

Although faith in the Divine Redeemer prompts Christians to ponder everything in the light of the truth—ever ancient, ever new—of aged Simeon's declaration concerning the Child Jesus at the presentation in the temple: *Behold this child is destined for the fall and for the rise of many. . . . and for a sign that shall be contradicted,* still We know that the number of those who do not separate themselves from Christ by unbelief, who cling to Him, who are ready to give their lives for Him and who place in Him and in the resurrection their unwavering hope—We know that the number of these is great, that it is increasing and growing strong. We see them radiating energy and influence for good in every sphere of life. We see that other men of good will are joining them.

### Your Place Is in the Vanguard

To you all, therefore, beloved sons and daughters, We say: Your hour is come.

At the assemblies of statesmen another unseen spirit presided as Sovereign Lord, the Omnipotent God to Whom nothing is secret and Who holds in His hands the thoughts and hearts of men, to bend them as He wills and when He chooses; God, all of Whose inscrutable designs are governed by His paternal love. But to fulfill these designs He wishes to make use of your cooperation. In the day of battle your place is in the vanguard, fighting at the front. The timid and those afraid to come out in the open are very close to becoming deserters and traitors. He is a deserter and a traitor who would give his material support, his services, his talents, aid or vote to parties and to forces which deny God, which put might in place of right, and threats and terror in place of liberty, which make of lying, opposition and incitement of the masses to revolt so many weapons of their policy, thus rendering national and international peace impossible.

Let us bring ourselves back 300 years, to a Europe—torn by the horrors of the Thirty Years' War. The year 1648 brought at last the message of peace, the dawn of restoration.

Pray and work to obtain from God the grace that the year 1948 may be for wounded Europe and for the nations torn by discord, a year of rebirth and of peace. So pray and work that after the rout of the spirit of darkness, the angel of the bottomless pit, the sun of justice may rise over the world: Jesus Christ our Lord, to Whom be honor and glory in time and in eternity.

And now, let Our Apostolic Blessing, a pledge of Divine grace and aid, go out to all Our beloved sons and daughters, those of this episcopal city of Ours as of the whole world. But let it extend especially to those groaning under a heavier weight of distress and pain; the sick, the poor, the unemployed; the homeless and all who are hungry and cold; for those bereft of freedom, family, country through the tragic happenings of a dreadful war, through other men's injustices or through their own past mistakes and faults and who feel the pang of discouragement and anguish all the more keenly at this holy season; to the prisoners of war not yet restored to their dear ones; to the refugees and the displaced; in a special way to those, particularly priests, suffering persecution, prison, exile, threats of torture and of death, simply because of their fidelity to God, to Christ, to the Church, and to their duty.

# Pray for Peace*

### (*Address to American Pilgrims, September 2, 1948*)

. . . THE tragic fact is that millions of human beings who were caught up in the maelstrom of a war which was declared finished more than three years ago, are still in this very Europe living in conditions that are inhuman; war still rages in other parts of the world; millions suffer under an unwanted tyranny.

To describe these conditions, which weigh so heavily on Our paternal heart, is beside our purpose here: But shortly, as you know, the Assembly of the United Nations will resume its sessions duly authorized to grapple with problems of world peace and security.

Men of learning and experience, of high character and lofty ideals, fully conscious of their momentous responsibility to civilization and culture, will put forth their best efforts for the family of nations, and, as We fondly hope, not only to save it from an unimaginable cataclysm but to put it on the road that leads to joy with justice for all, working men and employers alike, to morality in national and individual life

---

* Translation from National Catholic Welfare Conference News.

that has found its only possible basis in religious faith in God.

If ever an assembly of men, gathered at a critical crossroad in history, needed the help of prayer, it is the Assembly of the United Nations.

Hence we ask you, Venerable Brothers; you, Our cherished sons in the sacred priesthood and you, Our beloved children in Christ Jesus, to pray. Let Our voice carry beyond you to all your fellow Catholics in America, yes, to all Catholics in every country on the face of the earth. And we like to hope that you will be joined by all men of good will. . . .


# For a United Europe*

*(Address to Officials and Delegates of the Second International Congress of the European Union of Federalists, at Castel Gondolfo, November 11, 1948)*


. . . THAT the establishment of a European union presents serious difficulties no one will gainsay. At first sight the argument might be advanced that before such a union can be made psychologically acceptable to all the peoples of Europe, they must be accorded a certain period of delay to rid themselves of the memory of all that happened during the last war. Yet there is no time to lose. If it is intended that this union shall really achieve its purpose, if it is desired to make it serve to advantage the cause of European liberty and concord, the cause of economic and political peace between the continents, it is high time it were established. Some are even asking themselves whether it is not already too late.

Why, therefore, require that the memory of the war be first allowed to become blurred in distant retrospect, at a moment when contrariwise its aftermath, a painful experience, still affords encouragement for these peoples of Europe to lay by once and for all their selfish national prepossessions, the source of so many jealousies and so many hates; when the results of

---

* Translation from *The Catholic Mind.*

164

war serve them as a spur to provide for their legitimate defense against any policy of violence, open or disguised?

There is one case in point which cannot be too strongly emphasized: the abuse of a postwar political predominance with the aim of eliminating economic competition. Nothing could be better calculated to poison beyond hope of cure the work of bringing the nations together in mutual agreement.

The great nations of the Continent, with their long history freighted with memories of glory and power, may also impede the constitution of a European union, exposed as they are, if they are not careful, to measure themselves by the standards of their own past rather than by those of the realities of the present and of the foreseeable future. That is just why they are expected to disengage themselves from thoughts of their former greatness, to bring themselves into line with a higher political and economic unity. They will be the more inclined to do so if they are not forced, by an exaggerated quest for uniformity, to yield to a process of levelling. Respect for the cultural characteristics of their peoples, leading to harmony in the midst of variety, will conduce to a smoother and more stable union.

### Moral Foundation

Whatever be their value, all these considerations and many others besides yield in interest and importance to one question, to *the* fundamental question which inevitably presents itself in the matter of European reconstruction, and from which We have not the right to deflect Our attention.

No one, We believe, can refuse to subscribe to this statement: that a united Europe, if it is to maintain its equilibrium and settle disputes over its own continent—to say nothing of its influence on world security and world peace—has need to rest on an unshakable moral foundation. Where is this foundation to be found? Let history answer. There was a time when Europe formed, by virtue of her unity, one compact whole, and in the midst of all her weaknesses, despite all her human failures, this unity brought her strength; it enabled her to accomplish great things. But the soul of this unity was religion, which permeated the whole of society, to its very heart, with Christian faith.

Once culture is detached from religion, unity disintegrates. In the long run, spreading slowly but continuously like a stain of oil, irreligion has been penetrating deeper and deeper into public life. It is to irreligion above all that this continent owes its discord, its sickness, and its forebodings.

If then Europe wants to be quit of these woes, must she not put back in its place, within her own home, the bond between religion and civilization?

This will explain why We were so pleased to read, at the beginning of the resolution agreed to by the Committee on Culture, following the Hague Conference of last May, the mention of "the common heritage of Christian civilization"; yet that does not go far enough, since it falls short of the express recognition of the rights of God and of His law, at the very least of the natural law, the solid ground to which the rights of man are anchored. Isolated from religion, how can these rights and liberties insure unity, order, and peace?

## Whence the Leaders?

And can one further neglect to list among the rights of man those of the family, of parents, and children? United Europe cannot be built upon a mere abstract idea. She must needs depend for support on living men. Who will they be? Hardly the former statesmen of the old European powers. They have disappeared, or no longer wield any influence. Still less will they be the components of a mass, such as we defined it in our Christmas message of 1944: true democracy, with its ideal of wholesome freedom and equality, has no more formidable adversary.

It remains then to ask ourselves where the most insistent summons to European unity will come from? It will come from men who sincerely love peace, from men of order and tranquility, from men who—at least intentionally and of their own free will—are not "uprooted," and who find in respectable and happy home life the primary object of their thought and enjoyment. These are the people who will carry on their shoulders the edifice of united Europe. As long as no heed is paid to their appeal, nothing will be done that can endure, nothing that can measure up to the crises of our time.

But, We ask Ourselves, will the necessary comprehension

be forthcoming under present circumstances, that sympathetic understanding without which every attempt is sure to fail? Here is the great problem. It demands a solution if European union is to be achieved.

# The Christian Will for Peace*

*(Christmas Message Broadcast to the Whole World, December 23, 1948)*

. . . A CONVINCED Christian cannot confine himself within an easy and egotistical "isolationism," when he witnesses the needs and the misery of his brothers; when pleas for help come to him from those in economic distress; when he knows the aspirations of the working classes for more normal and just conditions of life; when he is aware of the abuses of an economic system which puts money above social obligations; when he is not ignorant of the aberrations of intransigent nationalism which denies or spurns the common bonds linking the separate nations together, and imposing on each one of them many and varied duties toward the great family of nations.

The Catholic doctrine on the State and civil society has always been based on the principle that, in keeping with the will of God, the nations form together a community with a common aim and common duties. Even when the proclamation of this principle and its practical consequences gave rise to violent reactions, the Church denied her assent to the erroneous concept of an absolutely autonomous sovereignty divested of all social obligations.

The Catholic Christian, persuaded that every man is his neighbor and that every nation is a member, with equal rights, of the family of nations, cooperates wholeheartedly in those generous efforts whose beginnings might be meagre and which frequently encounter strong opposition and obstacles,

* Translation from National Catholic Welfare Conference pamphlet.

but which aim at saving individual States from the narrowness of a self-centered mentality. This latter attitude of mind has been largely responsible for the conflicts of the past, and unless finally overcome or at least held in check, could lead to new conflagrations that might mean death to human civilization.

Since the cessation of hostilities, men have never been so obsessed as today by the nightmare of another war and by anxiety for the peace. They alternate between two extremes. Some adopt the ancient motto, not completely false, but which is easily misunderstood and has often been misused: *si vis pacem para bellum;* if you desire peace, prepare for war. Others think to find safety in the formula: peace at all costs!

Both parties want peace while both endanger it: on one side by arousing distrust, on the other by promoting a security which can prepare the way for aggression. Thus both, without wishing it, compromise the cause of peace at the very time when the human race, crushed under the weight of armaments and in agony at the prospect of fresh and even worse conflicts, shudders at the thought of a future catastrophe. Hence We should like to point out briefly the characteristics of a real Christian will for peace.

## Tranquility of Order

(1) The Christian will for peace comes from God. He is the *God of Peace;* He has created the world to be an abode of peace; He has given His commandment of peace, that *tranquility of order* of which St. Augustine speaks.

The Christian will for peace has its weapons too. But its principal arms are those of prayer and love; constant prayer to the Father in Heaven, Father of us all; brotherly love among all men and all nations, since all are sons of the same Father Who is in Heaven; love which, with patience, always succeeds in being disposed and ready to achieve understanding and agreement with everyone.

These two arms have their source in God, and when they are lacking, where people only know how to wield material weapons, there can be no real will for peace. For purely material armament necessarily awakens distrust, and creates what amounts to a climate of war. Who, then, can fail to see how important it is for nations to preserve and strengthen the Christian way of life, and how grave is their responsibility in the selection and supervision of those to whom they entrust the immediate control of armaments?

(2) The Christian will for peace is easily identified. Obedient to the Divine precept of peace, it will never turn a question of national prestige or honor into an argument for war or even for a threat of war. It is very careful to avoid recourse to the force of arms in the defense of rights which, however legitimate, do not offset the risk of kindling a blaze with all its tremendous spiritual and material consequences.

Here, likewise, the responsibility of the nations is perfectly clear with respect to the paramount problems of the education of youth and the moulding of public opinion, which modern methods and instruments render so sensitive and changeable today in every department of a nation's life. But this influence must be carefully exerted to support the common interest of all States in the defense of peace. Every violator of the law should be banished in disgrace to solitary confinement by civil society, as a disturber of the peace. May the United Nations Organization become the full and faultless expression of this international solidarity for peace, erasing from its institutions and its statutes every vestige of its origin which was of necessity a solidarity in war.

### Practical and Realistic

(3) The Christian will for peace is practical and realistic. Its immediate aim is to remove, or at least to mitigate the causes of tension which aggravate the danger of war morally and materially. These causes are, among others, chiefly the comparative scantiness of national territory and the want of raw materials. So instead of sending foodstuffs, at enormous expense, to refugee groups, crowded into the best place available, why not facilitate the emigration and immigration of families, directing them to countries where they will find more readily the food they need?

And instead of restricting production, often for no just reason, why not allow the people to produce to the limit of its normal capacity and so gain its daily bread as the reward of its own labor, rather than receive it as a gift? Finally, instead of setting up barriers to prevent one another's access to raw materials, why not make their use and exchange free of all unnecessary restrictions, especially of those which created a harmful situation of economic disparity?

(4) The genuine Christian will for peace means strength, not weakness or weary resignation. It is completely one with the will for peace of Eternal and Almighty God. Every war of aggression against these goods which the Divine plan for peace obliges men unconditionally to respect and guarantee and accordingly to protect and defend, is a sin, a crime, an outrage against the majesty of God, the Creator and Ordainer of the world.

A people threatened with an unjust aggression, or already its victim, may not remain passively indifferent, if it would think and act as befits Christians. All the more does the solidarity of the family of nations forbid others to behave as mere spectators, in an attitude of apathetic neutrality. Who will ever measure the harm already caused in the past by such indifference to war of aggression, which is quite alien to the Christian instinct? How much more keenly has it brought home to the "great" and specially to the "small," the sense of their insecurity? Has it brought any advantage in recompense? On the contrary; it has only reassured and encouraged the authors and fomentors of aggression, while it obliges the several peoples, left to themselves, to increase their armaments indefinitely.

Resting for support on God and on the order He established, the Christian will for peace is thus as strong as steel. Its temper is quite different from mere humanitarian sentiment, too often little more than a matter of pure impression, which detests war only because of its horrors and atrocities, its destruction and its aftermath, but not for the added reason of its injustice. Such a sentiment, under a hedonistic and utilitarian disguise, and materialistic in its source, lacks the solid foundation of a strict and unqualified obligation. It creates conditions which encourage the deception resulting from sterile compromise, the attempt to save oneself at the expense of others, and *the success in every case of the aggressor.*

This is so true that neither the sole consideration of the sorrows and evils resulting from war, nor the careful weighing of the act against the advantage, avail to determine finally, whether it is morally licit, or even in certain concrete circumstances obligatory (provided always there be solid probability of success) to repel an aggressor by force of arms.

## Peace Is an Obligation

One thing, however, is certain: the commandment of peace is a matter of Divine law. Its purpose is the protection of the goods of humanity, inasmuch as they are gifts of the Creator. Among these goods some are of such importance for society, that it is perfectly lawful to defend them against unjust aggression. Their defense is even an obligation for the nations as a whole who have a duty not to abandon a nation that is attacked.

The certainty that this duty will not go unfulfilled will serve to discourage the aggressor and thus war will be avoided or, if the worst should come, its sufferings will at least be lessened.

In this way, a better meaning is given to the dictum; *si vic pacem pare bellum*, as also to the phrase "peace at all costs." What really matters is the sincere and Christian will for peace. We are compelled to it surely by the following considerations: The spectacle of the ruins of the last war, the silent reproach which rises from the great cemeteries where the tombs of the victims of war are marshalled in endless ranks, the still unsatisfied longing of prisoners and refugees to return home, the anguish and dereliction of many political captives, worry of unjust persecution. But we ought to find a still greater incentive in the potent word of the Divine commandment of peace —the gently penetrating glance of the Divine Child in the manger.

Listen to the admirable words of the Apostle of the Gentiles ringing out in the night like the bells of Christmas—he too was once a slave to petty prejudices of national and racial pride, laid low with him on the road to Damascus: *He (Christ Jesus) is our peace: He has made the two nations one . . . killing all enmities in His own person . . . coming, He announced the good tidings of peace to you who were afar off, and of peace to those who were near.*

Hence at the present hour, with all the power at Our command, We exhort you, beloved sons and daughters of the entire world: work for a peace that is in accordance with the heart of the Redeemer.

Together with all upright men, who, even though not fighting in your ranks, are united with you in the community of this ideal, work strenuously for the propagation and triumph of the Christian will for peace.

# Barriers to Peace*

(*Christmas Message Broadcast to the Whole World, December 23, 1950*)

EVERY attentive observer who knows how to consider and evaluate the present situation in its concrete reality must be struck by the serious obstacles which oppose the Apostolate of the Church. Like a mass of molten lava, which gradually flows down the side of a volcano, the destructive tide of the spirit of this world advances threateningly and spreads into every sphere of life and into every class of society.

Its progress and its intensity, as well as its effects, vary from country to country, ranging from a more or less conscious disregard of the social influence of the Church, to a systematic distrust, which under some types of government takes the form of open hostility and downright persecution.

We have full confidence that Our beloved sons and daughters will have the clarity of vision and the courage to face and to fulfill with resolution the responsibilities arising from such a situation. Without harshness, but also without weakness, they will endeavor to dissipate the prejudices and suspicions of not a few who have been deceived, but who are still open to a peaceful argument based on facts, they will convince them that, far from there being any conflict between loyalty to the Church and devotion to the interests and well-being of the people and the State, between these two kinds of duties, which

---

* Translation from National Catholic Welfare Conference pamphlet.

a true Christian must ever keep in mind, there exists an intimate union and perfect harmony.

Here We deliberately pass over in silence some recent discord that has arisen between Catholics and those belonging to other religious groups and which has regrettably found an echo in political discussions. We should like to believe that beyond these no less unpleasant than harmful controversies there are to be found in all non-Catholic groups men and women of good will who, fully realizing the dangers threatening the sacred heritage of the Christian Faith, cherish in their hearts thoughts other than those of fraternal dissension and discord.

## A Notable Absence

If any one should be tempted to lose sight of this need and duty, let him turn his gaze—as far as this is possible—towards what is happening in some countries that are encircled about, as it were, with a wall of iron, and see to what state they are reduced as regards their spiritual and religious life.

He would there see millions of his Catholic brethren, men and women, linked together by ancient and sacred traditions of fidelity to Christ and of filial union with this Apostolic See; he would see nations whose heroic actions in preserving and defending the Faith are written indelibly in the annals of the Church's history. He would see them, We say, frequently deprived of civil rights and of their personal liberty and security, cut off from every vital, safe and sure means of communicating with the center of Christianity, even in the most intimate matters of conscience; and all the while there weighs on them the anxiety of feeling alone and at times of believing that they are abandoned!

Underneath Michelangelo's dome, where the voice of pilgrims from every free country resounded as they sang in most varied tongues the same expressions of faith and the same hymns of joy, their place was empty. What a void it was and what a sorrow for the heart of the Common Father and for the hearts of all the faithful united together in the very same belief and in one and the same love. But they, though absent, were, in fact, all the more present when in those countless throngs, conscious of their Catholic faith, there seemed to be but one heart and one soul thus forming a mysterious but very real unity.

To all these confessors of Christ, who are unjustly bound either by visible or invisible fetters, who are suffering contumely for the name of Jesus at the end of this Holy Year, We gratefully send from Our heart Our paternal greeting. May it reach them notwithstanding the walls of their prisons, and the barbed wire of their concentration and forced labor camps, out there in those far off regions which are shut off from the gaze of free men and over which a veil of silence is drawn, but which will not, however, escape the final judgment of God nor the impartial verdict of history.

In the most sweet Name of Jesus, We exhort them to support generously their sufferings and humiliations with which they make a contribution of inestimable value to the great crusade of prayer and penance which will begin with the extension of the Holy Year to the whole world.

With a magnanimous outpouring of charity in keeping with the example of Christ, the Apostles and the true followers of the Redeemer, may their prayers and Ours include even those who are today amid the ranks of the persecutors.

### Peace Within Nations

Now, if we look towards the future, the first urgent problem that presents itself is peace within every country. Unfortunately the struggle for life, the concern to earn a living, divides into opposing groups even those who inhabit the same country and are sons of the same fatherland. Those on either side want, and rightly so, to be considered and treated in social life not as mere chattels but as persons with human dignity, especially in matters regarding the State and the national economy.

For this reason We have repeatedly and with ever greater insistence proclaimed the fight against unemployment and the striving after a sound social security as an indispensable condition if all members of a nation, both high and low, are to be united in a single corporate body.

But he who selfishly sees today in the groups that oppose his own personal interests, the source of every difficulty and an obstacle to recovery and progress—how could he dare to flatter himself that he is serving the cause of peace in his country?

Certain organizations, in order to protect the interests of their own members, no longer appeal to the laws of justice and the common good but depend on the organized members of their followers and the weakness of their opponents, who do not happen to be so well organized, or who always strive to subordinate the use of force to the laws of justice and the common good. How can such organizations dare to flatter themselves that they are promoting the cause of civil peace?

A nation cannot expect to enjoy peace within its own boundaries except on certain conditions. Governors and governed, leaders and followers, must not defend their own social interests and their particular opinions with obstinacy and short-sightedness, but should learn to take a more comprehensive view of things and make their aim the good of all. If it is regretted in some countries that there is a deplorable lack of participation in public life on the part of the younger generation, perhaps the reason is that the younger generation sees too little or too seldom the shining and attractive example of men such as we have described here.

## The Deepest Source of Human Misery

Beneath the surface, then, of unquestionable difficulties in the political and economic sphere, there is hidden a more serious evil of a spiritual and moral character. It is evidenced by the number of men with narrow minds and mean spirits, of egoists and "go-getters," of those who follow fortune's favorites, who let themselves be swayed, whether from illusion or cowardice, by the spectacle of huge mobs, the shouting of opinions, and the intoxication of excitement. Left to themselves, these would not take one step forward, would not, as is the duty of true Christians, advance unwaveringly towards the light of the eternal principles, under the guidance of the Spirit of God and with unshakable faith in His Divine Providence. Herein is to be found the true and deepest source of human misery.

Like a termite in the woodwork of a house, this evil gnaws away at the heart of nations and before it makes its presence known exteriorly, it renders them unfit for their mission in life. Thus the foundations of the industrial and capitalistic system have undergone essential changes, that after a long period of preparation, have been accelerated by the war. Peoples that have known subjection for centuries are winning their way to independence, others who till now have been in a privileged position strive by new means and old to maintain it. The thirst for social security, that is ever growing in intensity and extent, is but a symptom of the present state of society in the various countries, where many things that once seemed traditionally solid have become unreliable and uncertain.

Why, then, does not this common uncertainty and doubt, arising from present circumstances, create a certain solidarity among the peoples in different countries? Is not the interest of employer and employed in this respect identical? Is it not true in every country that industrial and agricultural production are now more than ever linked together on account of the reciprocal influence they exert one upon the other? And you, you who remain insensible to the hardships suffered by the wandering and homeless refugees, should you not have a fellow-feeling for him whose unhappy lot today may well be yours tomorrow?

Why should not this solidarity among all those peoples who are restless and in danger become for all the secure way leading to safety? Why should not this spirit of solidarity be the basis of the natural social order in its three essentials—the family, property and the State—and make these elements collaborate in one organic whole that is adapted to present conditions? These present conditions are, after all, despite all their inherent difficulties, a gift of God. Why should they not contribute to strengthening the Christian spirit?

### Danger to International Peace

The real danger to international, as well as national, peace is the presence of men who are bereft of this Christian sense. Some have been deceived by the past, others are fanatically bent on attaining some Utopia of the future. In every case, they are dissatisfied with the present.

We do not wish to speak here of a foreign aggressor who is proud of his power and scorns every duty of justice and charity. He finds, however, in national crises and the lack of unity within nations as regards spiritual and moral matters, a powerful weapon and, as it were, an auxiliary force inside the country itself.

It is necessary, then, that nations should not be led by motives of prestige or antiquated ideas, and so create political and economic difficulties against the strengthening of the national forces of other countries, while they ignore or take no thought for the common peril.

It is necessary that they should understand that their natural and most faithful allies are to be found among those countries where Christian thought, or at least faith in God, have an influence even in public life. They should not make their only consideration some supposed national or political interest that neglects or overlooks profound differences in fundamental concepts of the world and of life.

The reason why We utter these warnings is the ambiguous and irresolute attitude which We see adopted by some true lovers of peace in face of such a grave peril. And because We have at heart the good of all nations, We believe that the close union of all peoples who are masters of their own destiny and who are united by sentiments of reciprocal trust and mutual assistance is the sole means for the defense of peace and the best guarantee of its re-establishment.

Unfortunately, in these past weeks the cleavage which in the external world divides the entire international community into opposite camps grows constantly deeper, placing in jeopardy the peace of the world. Never has the history of mankind known a dissension of greater magnitude. It reaches to the very ends of the earth. If a regrettable conflict should occur today, weapons would prove so destructive as to make the earth *void and empty*, a desolate chaos, like to a desert over which the sun is not rising, but setting. All nations would be convulsed, and among the citizens of the same country, the conflict would have manifold repercussions. It would place in extreme peril all its civil institutions and spiritual values, seeing that the conflict now embraces all the most difficult problems which normally would be discussed separately. The grim and threatening danger imperiously demands, by reason of its gravity, that we make the most of every opportune circumstance to bring about the triumph of wisdom and justice under the standard of concord and peace. Let it be used to revive sentiments of goodness and compassion towards all peoples whose one sincere aspiration is to live in peace and tranquility. Let mutual trust, which presupposes sincere intentions and honest discussions, return to rule over international organizations. Away with the barriers! Break down the barbed wire fences! Let each people be free to know the life of other peoples, let that segregation of some countries from the rest of the civilized world, so dangerous to the cause of peace, be abolished.

# World Federal Government*

(*Address to Fourth Annual Congress of the World Movement for World Federal Government, April 6, 1951*)

WITH a deep appreciation of your sincere and deferential approach, We extend to you, members of the Congress of the World Movement for World Federal Government, Our cordial welcome.

Our keen interest in the cause of peace for humanity, so harshly tormented, is well known to you. We have given frequent evidence of it. It is, moreover, inherent in Our mission. The maintenance or re-establishment of peace has always been and is, more and more, the object of Our constant solicitude. And if, too often, results have been far from corresponding with Our efforts and Our actions, lack of success will never discourage Us, so long as peace does not reign on earth. Faithful to the spirit of Christ, the Church strives for it and works for it with all its might; it does so by its precepts and by its exhortations, by its unceasing action, by its incessant prayer.

The Church is, in fact, a power for peace, at least wherever its independence and its mission from God are respected and appreciated at their true worth; wherever there is no attempt

* Translation from National Catholic Welfare Conference News.

to make it the docile servant of political self-interests; wherever it is not treated as an enemy. It wants peace; it makes peace its task; its heart is with all those who, as itself, desire peace and devote themselves to it; it knows, as is its duty, how to distinguish between the true and the false friends of peace.

The Church desires peace, and therefore, labors to promote everything which, within the framework of the Divine order, natural and supernatural, contributes to assuring peace. Your movement, gentlemen, dedicates itself to realizing an effective political organization of the world. Nothing is more in conformity with the traditional doctrine of the Church, nor better adapted to its teaching concerning legitimate or illegitimate war, especially in the present emergency. Such an organization should be fostered, if for no other reason than to end the armaments race, in which for decades people have been ruining and exhausting themselves through sheer waste.

You are of the opinion that a world political organization must have a federal form in order to be effective. If by that you mean that it must be free from enmeshment in a mechanical unitarism, here again you are in accord with the principles of social and political life firmly established and upheld by the Church. In fact, no world organization would be practical if it were not in harmony with the whole of natural relations, with the normal and organic order that rules the individual relations between men and between different peoples. Without this, whatever its structure, it would be impossible for it to maintain itself and endure.

### *First Concern: Fundamental Principles*

That is why We are convinced that the first concern must be the solid establishment or restoration of these fundamental principles in all fields: national and constitutional, economic and social, cultural and moral.

In the national and constitutional field: Everywhere today the life of nations is disintegrated by the blind worship of numerical values. The citizen is a voter. But as such he is really nothing more than one of the units whose total constitutes a majority or a minority, which the shift of a few votes, or even of one, is sufficient to reverse. As far as parties are concerned, he counts only for his electoral value, for the contribution of his vote; there is no concern for his place and for his function in his family and occupational group.

In the economic and social field: There is no natural organic unity among producers from the moment when quantitative utilitarianism, the consideration of cost of production, becomes the sole norm determining places of production and the distribution of work, from the moment when it is "class" which artificially divides men in society, and no longer cooperation in the community of the occupational group.

In the cultural and moral field: Individual liberty, freed from all ties, from all rules, from all objective and social values, is in reality nothing but deadly anarchy, especially in the education of youth.

Insofar as the world political organization is not consolidated on this indispensable base, the risk is run of inoculating it with the deadly germ of mechanical unitarism. We should like to invite reflection on this point, precisely from the point of view of federalism, on the part of those who are thinking of applying it, for example, to a world parliament. Otherwise they will play the game of the disintegrating forces from which the political and social order has already suffered too much; they would merely succeed in adding one more legal automatism to so many others which threaten to suffocate nations and reduce man to no more than an inert instrument.

If, therefore, in the spirit of federalism, the future world political organization cannot under any pretext allow itself to become involved in the play of a unitary mechanism, it will enjoy effective authority only insofar as it will safeguard and favor everywhere the life that is proper to a healthy human community, to a society in which all members join together for the good of humanity as a whole.

What a measure of moral steadfastness, intelligent foresight and capacity for adjustment will have to be possessed by this authority, more necessary than ever in critical moments when, in the face of malevolence, men of good will need to rely on that authority! After all the trials of the past and present would one dare to consider today's resources and methods of government and politics as sufficient? In reality it is impossible to solve the problem of world political organization without being ready to depart at times from the beaten track, without appealing to the experience of history, to a sane social philosophy and also to creative imagination.

There, gentlemen, is a vast field of work, study and action: you have understood it and looked it squarely in the face; you have the courage to spend yourselves in it; We congratulate you; We express Our hopes for your success; with all Our heart We ask for you and your work God's light and aid.

# Contribution of the Church to Peace*

(*Christmas Message Broadcast to the Whole World, December 24, 1951*)

I. WHAT THE CONTRIBUTION OF THE CHURCH TO PEACE CANNOT BE

THE present state of affairs demands from Us a frank and sincere judgment upon events. But these events have reached such a critical stage that We are forced to recognize that the world is split into two opposing camps and that all men are divided into two clearly separated groups, which consequently are very loath to concede to anyone any sort of liberty to maintain a position of political neutrality.

Now those who wrongly consider the Church as a kind of earthly power, or a sort of world empire, are easily induced to demand also from her, as from others, the renunciation of her neutrality and a definite election in favor of one or the other side. However, there can be no question of the Church renouncing her political neutrality for the simple reason that she cannot serve purely political interests.

Let it not be thought that this is a mere play on words or concepts. It suffices to have an elementary notion of the foundation upon which the Church as a society is based, in order to understand Our meaning without need of further explanations. The Divine Redeemer founded the Church in order to communicate to all men through her mediation His truth and His grace unto the end of time. The Church is His

---

* Translation from *The Catholic Mind.*

"mystical body." She belongs entirely to Christ, as Christ belongs to God.

Statesmen, and at times even churchmen, who want to make the Spouse of Christ their ally or the instrument of their political alliances, either national or international, would do injury to the very essence of the Church and would inflict damage on the life which is proper to her; in a word, they would bring her down to the same level on which conflicting temporal interests are locked in struggle. And this is and remains true even where there is question of ends and interests legitimate in themselves.

## The Church's Decisions Cannot Be Political

Whoever then would wish to detach the Church from her supposed neutrality, or bring pressure to bear on her in the question of peace, or diminish her right freely to determine whether, when, or how she may wish to come to a decision in the various conflicts, such a one would not make the Church's cooperation in the work of peace easier. For any decision on the Church's part, even in political questions, can never be purely political, but must always be "*sub specie aeternitatis,*" in the light of the divine law, of its order, its values, its standards.

It is not rare to see purely temporal powers and institutions abandon their neutrality and align themselves today in one camp, tomorrow perhaps in another. It is a game of alliances which can be explained by the constant shifting of temporal interests. But the Church keeps herself aloof from such unstable alliances. If she passes judgment, that does not mean that she is thereby abandoning a neutrality hitherto observed; for God is never neutral toward human events, in the course of history, and so neither can His Church be. If she speaks and judges on the problems of the day, it is with the clear consciousness of anticipating in the power of the Holy Spirit the sentence which at the end of time her Lord and Head, Judge of the universe, will confirm and sanction.

Such is the proper and super-human function of the Church regarding political questions. What then is the meaning of that empty phrase about a neutrality which the Church should abandon?

The Church does not judge according to purely political norms.

Others, on the contrary, in the interests of peace, demand the neutrality of the Church. But neither have these a correct idea of the place of the Church in the midst of the world's great events.

She cannot come down from the lofty supernatural sphere where political neutrality has no meaning, in the sense in which this concept is applied to earthly powers. This does not exclude, but rather increases her share in the toils and sufferings of her divided members in either camp, and intensifies her grief at the clash of opinions and desires in her own ranks.

The Church cannot consent to judge according to exclusively political norms. She cannot tie the interests of religion to particular policies of a purely earthly scope. She cannot run the risk of giving any reason for doubting about her religious character. She cannot forget for an instant that her role of representative of God on earth does not permit her to remain indifferent, even for a single moment, between "good" and "evil" in human affairs. If that were asked of her, she would have to refuse, and the faithful on both sides would, in virtue of their supernatural faith and hope, have to understand and respect her stand.

II. WHAT CONTRIBUTION SHOULD THE CHURCH MAKE TO PEACE

Since this contribution cannot be purely political, and since the normal place and essential mission of the Church is not in the area where nations, friendly, antagonistic, or neutral, continually meet, bringing with them their ideas and concrete political tendencies, what then should be her contribution to the peace? What is the legal right, what the peculiar nature of this contribution?

The legal right? Behold! Nowhere will you find it so clear and almost palpable as at the crib of Bethlehem. The Infant lying there is the eternal Son of God made man, and His name is *"Princeps Pacis,"* Prince of Peace. Prince and founder of peace, such is the character of the Saviour and Redeemer of the whole human race. His sublime divine mission is to establish peace between each man and God, between men themselves and between peoples.

183

This mission, however, and this desire for peace are not born of timidity and weakness, which can meet evil and the wicked only with resignation and patience. Everything in the frailty of the Babe of Bethlehem is hidden majesty and contained force, which only love restrains, in order to make the hearts of men capable of begetting and nurturing peace, and give them the strength to overcome and scatter all the forces that might compromise its life.

But the Divine Saviour is also the invisible head of the Church; and for that reason His mission of peace lives on and is active in the Church. Every year with the renewed memory of Christ's birth is renewed in her deep consciousness of her title to contribute to the work of peace, a unique title which transcends every earthly thing and stems immediately from God, an essential element of her nature and of her religious power.

This year once more the Church kneels before the crib and receives her mission from the Divine Infant, the Prince of Peace. At His side she sees revealed true human nature, true in the fullest sense of the word, for it is the very human nature of God, her Creator, her Redeemer, her Restorer. With eyes tenderly fixed on the face of the infinitely lovable Prince of Peace, she listens to the heartbeats which tell of a love embracing all mankind, and is inflamed with ardent zeal for this mission of her Lord and Chief, which is also her own, the mission of a peacemaker.

### A Spiritual Brotherhood

Consciousness of this mission has always been keen and effectively active in the Church, especially in her supreme leaders, the Roman Pontiffs. Justly then, Our great predecessor, Leo XIII, recalled to the world the peace-making activity of the Popes when he said in 1899, on the eve of the first conference for peace: "And what inspired them [the Bishops of Rome] was the consciousness of a very lofty mission, the prompting of a spiritual fatherhood which makes men brothers and saves them" (Allocution to the College of Cardinals, April 11, 1899.) And today, as We have said, the same is true.

But when the Church and her Supreme Pastor pass from this

sweet intimacy of the Babe of Bethlehem, so peaceful and heart-warming, into a world that is far from Christ, it is like stepping out into a gust of freezing air. That world talks nothing but peace; but it has no peace. It claims for itself all possible and impossible legal titles to establish peace, yet does not know or does not recognize the mission of peacemaker that comes directly from God, the mission of peace deriving from the religious authority of the Church.

Poor short-sighted men, whose little field of vision does not go beyond the possibilities of the present hour, beyond statistics of military and economic potential. How can they form the slightest idea of the worth and importance of religion's authority for the solution of the peace problem? Superficial minds, unable to see in all their reality and fullness the value and the creative power of Christianity, how can they help being skeptical and disdainful of the power of the Church for peace? But others, and please God they are the majority, will see with more or less awareness that denying to the religious authority of the Church her competence in effective action for peace has but made more desperate the tragic condition of the troubled modern world.

The defection of many from Christian belief has hastened this extreme and almost intolerable state of affairs. And one would say that God has answered this rejection of Christ by the plague of a permanent menace to peace and the frightening specter of war.

Just as the Church's right to work for peace is unique, so is the worth of her contribution to the same cause.

### Relations of the Church with States

The Church is not a political, but a religious society. That, however, does not prevent her from assuming not merely external but internal and vital relations with States. The Church has in fact been founded by Christ as a society that is visible, and as such meets States in the same territory, embraces in her solicitude the same people, and in many ways and under different aspects makes use of the same means and the same institutions.

And since the Church and the States live together, besides these external and what might be called natural relations, there are others, too, interior and vital relations, which have their principle and origin in the person of Jesus Christ as Head of the Church. For the Son of God by becoming man, and truly man, has by that very fact entered into a new relationship, a truly vital relationship, with human society, with human nature. And this is true whether we consider human nature as a single unit implying equal personal dignity in all men, or human nature as found in multiple particular societies, especially those societies which, within the fundamental unity of human nature, are necessary to effect or at least perfect external order and sound organization.

## Union of States Demanded by Nature

And here we have in mind primarily the family and the State, as well as the society of States, since the common good, the essential purpose of every State, cannot be attained or even imagined without this intrinsic relation of the States to the human race as a whole. Under this aspect the indissoluble union of States is demanded by nature. It is a fact which is imposed upon them. And in consent to it, although sometimes hesitantly, they answer the voice of nature. This natural union they strive to embody in an external stable framework, an organization.

As human experience teaches them, the state and the society of states with its external organization, in spite of all their defects, are naturally, given the social nature of man, forms of union and order among men; they are necessary for human life; they contribute to its perfection. Their very concept involves the tranquillity of order, that *"tranquillitas ordinis"* which St. Augustine gives as a definition of peace. These societies of their very essence exist for peace.

With them, as societies which exist for maintaining peace, Jesus Christ, the Prince of Peace—and with Him the Church in whom He continues to live—has entered into a new and intimate relationship which elevates and strengthens society. This is the basis for the singular contribution which the Church by her very nature makes to the cause of peace, that is, when her life and her action among men occupy the place that is their due.

And how will all this come about except through the continuous, enlightening and strengthening action of the grace of Christ on the minds and hearts of citizens and statesmen, so that in all human relationships they recognize and pursue the purposes of the Creator, so that they strive to enlist the collaboration of individuals and nations for effecting these purposes, so that within as well as among nations they practice social justice and charity?

If men, obeying the Divine Will, will use that sure way of salvation, a perfect Christian order in the world, they will soon see the possibility of even a just war practically disappear. For there will be no reason for such a war, once the activity of the society of states, as a genuine organization for peace, is made secure.

III. THE PRACTICAL CONTRIBUTION OF THE CHURCH TO PEACE

What We have just said shows clearly Our thought in this regard. At the crib of the Divine Prince of Peace, We have to say again today what We have said before: The world is, indeed, far removed from that order willed by God in Christ, the order which guarantees a genuine and lasting peace. Perhaps it will be said that in this case it was no use to trace out the bold outlines of this order, and to set in relief the fundamental contribution of the Church to the cause of peace. It will be objected that if We say that peace cannot be defended but by a return to the eternal values of the individual person and of mankind, We thus only encourage the cynicism of skeptics and deepen the discouragement of the friends of peace. Finally, We will be reproached with admitting that those are right who see in an "armed peace" the definitive and last word on the subject, a solution that would deplete the economic forces and exhaust the nerves of the nations of the world.

*The Christian Order—Foundation and Guarantee of Peace*

Nevertheless, for a practical as well as a theoretical estimate of the contribution each one can make to the cause of peace, especially the Church, even in unfavorable circumstances and in spite of the skeptics and pessimists, We think it absolutely necessary to fix our view on the Christian order, today lost sight of by so many, in order to see the crux of the problem now before us.

187

In the first place, such a survey will convince any impartial observer that the heart of the problem of peace is now of the spiritual order: The problem is a spiritual lack, a spiritual deficiency. Too rare in the world today is the deeply Christian sense of values; too few are the true and perfect Christians. In this way men themselves set obstacles in the way of actuating the order willed by God.

Everyone must be convinced of this spiritual element inherent in the danger of war. To awaken that conviction is in the first place the duty of the Church, and her primary contribution to peace today.

We too—and more than anyone else—deplore the monstrous cruelty of modern weapons. We deplore them and do not cease to pray that they may never be employed. But, on the other hand, is it not perhaps a kind of practical materialism and superficial sentimentality to make the existence and threat of these weapons the sole and principal consideration in the question of peace, while no attention is paid to the absence of that Christian order which is the true guarantee of peace?

Hence, among other reasons, the differences of opinion, and also the inexactitudes, concerning the licitness or illicitness of modern warfare; hence likewise the illusion of statesmen, who count too much on the existence or disappearance of those weapons. The terror they inspire in the long run begins to lose its effect, just like any other cause of terror; or at least it would not suffice, if the occasion should arise, to prevent the outbreak of a war; especially in those countries where the voice of the citizens has not sufficient influence in the decisions of their governments.

### Military Disarmament Not Enough

On the other hand, disarmament, or rather the simultaneous and reciprocal reduction of armaments, which we have always desired and begged for, is an unstable guarantee of lasting peace, if it is not accompanied by the abolition of the weapons of hate, cupidity and of overweening lust for prestige. In other words, whoever connects too closely the question of material weapons with that of peace is guilty of neglecting the primary and spiritual element in every danger of war. He does not look beyond figures, and besides his calculations are necessarily limited to the moment in which the conflict threatens to break out. A friend of peace, he will always arrive too late to save it.

If the desire to prevent war is to be truly efficacious, above all a remedy must be sought for the spiritual anemia of nations, for the ignorance of individual responsibility before God and man, and for the want of a Christian order which alone is able to guarantee peace. To this goal the resources of the Church are now directed.

### *The Christian Order is an Order of Liberty*

But here the Church meets with a particular difficulty which is due to the state of present social conditions: Her exhortation in favor of the Christian order, as the principal factor in securing peace, is at the same time an incentive to form a correct idea of true liberty. The ultimate reason is that the Christian order, since its purpose is peace, is essentially an order of liberty. It is the cooperative effort of free men and peoples toward the progressive realization in all spheres of life of the ends which God has assigned to humanity. It is, however, a pathetic fact that today true liberty is not esteemed, or it is no longer possessed. In these circumstances harmonious cooperation, as the proper condition of peace, is internally enervated and anemic, while externally it is exposed to perils of every moment.

How, for example, can those who in economic or social life want to make everything depend upon society, even the direction and security of their own existence, or those who today look for their sole daily spiritual nourishment less and less from themselves—that is to say, from their personal convictions and knowledge—and more and more from the diet prepared in advance by the press, radio, movies and television, how can they conceive true liberty, how can they esteem and desire it, if it no longer has a place in their lives?

Why, they are no more than mere cogs in the various social organizations: they are no longer free men capable of assuming and accepting a responsible role in public affairs. Therefore, if today they cry "no more war," what trust can be put in them? It is not their voice, but the anonymous voice of the social group to which they happen to belong.

This is the sad state of affairs which also impedes the Church in her efforts to obtain peace and in her plans for the realization of true human liberty which, from the Christian viewpoint, is the indispensable element of the social order, considered as the organism of peace. In vain would she multiply her invitations to men devoid of that realization, and still more uselessly would she direct her pleas to a society which has been reduced to sheer automatism.

Such, however, is the widespread weakness of a world which loves emphatically to call itself "the free world." It deceives itself, or else it does not understand itself. Its strength is not based upon true freedom. This is a new danger which threatens the peace, and which in the light of Christian social order We must deprecate. Whence originates among not a few highly placed persons in what is called "the free world" an aversion to the Church, that importunate preacher of something which others pretend to have, but have not, and which, by a strange inversion of ideas, they unjustly say that the Church has not: We mean respect and esteem for genuine freedom.

But the invitation of the Church meets even colder welcome from the opposite camp. Here, indeed, it is claimed, true freedom reigns, because social life does not depend on that uncertain figment of the imagination, the autonomous individual, nor does it make public order as indifferent as possible to values that are absolute, but everything is strictly bound up with and directed toward the existence and development of a defined collectivity.

The results, however, of the system We are now speaking of have not been happy, nor has the activity of the Church become easier, for here the true concept of freedom and personal responsibility is defended still less. How could it be otherwise when God is not sovereign, when social life and activity do not gravitate around Him, nor have their center in Him? Society is nothing but a gigantic machine whose order is only apparent, because there no longer exists the order of life, of the spirit, of freedom, of peace. Like a machine, its activity is material, destructive of human dignity and freedom.

In such a society, the contribution of the Church to peace and her counsels of genuine order in real freedom are given under very difficult circumstances. However, the alleged absolute social values are capable of inspiring enthusiasm in youth at a critical age, while not rarely the youth of the opposing side, prematurely disillusioned by bitter experience, have become weary, skeptical, incapable of taking any interest in public and social life.

## The Holy See and the Peaceful Solution of Conflicts

Peace, as we have said, cannot be assured unless God reigns in the ordered universe. He has established, in the duly organized society of nations, in which each nation effects peace internally among free men and their families, and externally with other nations, an order guaranteed by the Church according to her office and in her own field of action. Such has always been the aim of great and wise men even outside the Church, as also in modern times on the occasion of the Vatican Council.

Meanwhile, the Church works for peace by awakening and stimulating a practical understanding of the spiritual heart of the problem. Faithful to the spirit of her Divine Founder and to her mission of love, she endeavors to the best of her power to offer her good offices wherever she sees the threat of a conflict between nations. Above all else, this Apostolic See has never shirked such a duty and never shall.

As We well know and deplore with a heart deeply grieved, throughout vast regions of the world, this invitation of Ours to peace does not reach, except in mutilated form, the "church of silence." Millions cannot profess openly their responsibility before God for peace. In their very homes and churches even the ancient tradition of the manger, so dear and familiar, has been abolished by the despotic will of those in power. Millions are in no position to exercise their Christian influence for moral freedom and for peace, because these words, freedom and peace, have become the stolen monopoly of professional trouble-makers and worshippers of force.

Nevertheless, even with bound arms and closed lips, the "church of silence" nobly responds to Our invitation. With a look she points to the still fresh graves of her martyrs, to the chains of her confessors, confident that her silent holocaust and her sufferings are a most potent contribution to the cause of peace because they are a most noble invocation and a most compelling title to win from the divine Prince of Peace grace and mercy for the fulfillment of her mission. *Grant peace, O Lord, in our days.*

# "Blessed Be the Peacemaker"*

*(Letter of Msgr. Giovanni Montini, Vatican Pro-Secretary of State, in the Name of the Holy Father, to the Meeting of* SEMAINES SOCIALES, *Pau, France, July, 1953)*

EXAMINATION of the problems of peace by men of faith, thought, and action is most timely today, when men's souls are more troubled than ever before. Never in human history has greater discord been known. This worldwide dissension invades the daily lives of the people. It feeds and maintains social conflict. Its origins are of an ideological as much as of an economic nature. It eats into the very hearts of families and institutions. Its psychological effects sap will-power and cloud judgment. Even the flag of peace, unfurled for partisan ends, frequently divides mankind.

How can one be surprised, under such circumstances, if many noble minds, some of which are Catholic, allow themselves to be led astray and seduced by the mirage of peace propaganda? But the greater the danger, the more urgent the duty to combat it.

In our restless age, when peace is profaned by the hypocritical pretensions of those who would like to divert that noble ideal of all peoples to their own profit and to the detriment of others, let all the sons of the Church merit the Beatitude of the Gospel: *Beati pacifici!* Blessed are the peacemakers. Such is the hope of the Holy Father, which it is my mission to send you on the eve of the Social Week at Pau.

To be a peace-maker a Christian must first know and spread all the teachings of the Church on peace. Since the first World

---

* Translation from *The Catholic Mind.*

War, in particular, the teachings of the Sovereign Pontiffs have increased. Head of the Church in these tragic times, Pius XII himself has not ceased to warn, instruct and exhort the faithful and all men of good-will. He has not been afraid to point out the paths to peace to them even in the midst of battle, clearly defining the bases of an international community while the rival forces were still confronting one another. Actions, within the limits of his means, accompanied his words and gave evidence, in spite of the most distressing lies, of the Holy See's indestructible desire for peace.

## Deaf to Warnings

Now, in spite of the hard lesson of events, too many Christians still remain deaf to the warnings of the Papacy. How many, for example, continue to shut themselves up within the narrow confines of a chauvinistic nationalism, incompatible with the courageous effort to start a world community demanded by recent Popes? But undoubtedly even more numerous are those who have not renounced their strange inertia despite the frequently repeated appeals of the Holy Father for "action against every inaction and desertion in the great spiritual combat where the stakes are the construction, nay, the very soul, of the society of tomorrow" (Christmas Message, 1942).

The Church's teaching on peace is well known to the Social Week's leaders and they will know how to exploit its riches. But, in view of the dramatic division of the world, the appeal of the Holy Father is more urgent than ever.

Have faith in the Church, he has told all his sons, when she asks you to work for the community of nations. "For her East and West do not represent opposite ideals, but share a common heritage to which both have generously contributed and to which both are called to contribute in the future also" (Christmas Message, 1950).

Her maternal voice, moreover, will never fail to remind responsible statesmen that even today's political and economic difficulties can be solved amicably if good-will is shown by all the parties concerned.

Listen to the Church when, hoping to restore to nations a sense of their human fraternity, she points out to them the paths of justice and truth, self-denial and charity, whose source is Jesus Christ and without which there can be no lasting peace.

Do not doubt the task to which the Church calls you. It is an eminently positive and constructive task, based on the sacred rights of the natural and divine law. It is a realistic task, too, for experience ought to teach everyone that "the policy guided by eternal truths and the laws of God is the most real and tangible of policies. Realistic politicians who think otherwise pile up only ruins" (Christmas Message, 1945).

Faithful to these teachings, which guarantee the integrity of his free initiative, the Christian owes it to himself to go still further in his efforts for peace, even into the depth of his innermost thoughts. Let us listen to what the Holy Father wrote in his first encyclical:

No, Venerable Brethren, safety does not come to peoples from exterior means, from the sword, which can impose conditions of peace but does not create peace. Forces that are to renew the face of the earth should proceed from within, from the soul.

And His Holiness went even further:

For true though it is that evils from which mankind suffers today come in part from economic instability and from the struggle of interests regarding a more equal distribution of the goods which God has given man as a means of sustenance and progress [and was that not the theme of your last Social Week?] it is not less true that their root is deeper and more intrinsic, belonging to the sphere of religious belief and moral convictions (*Summi Pontificatus*).

Peace is one, in fact, and whoever denies it through sin in his personal, family, or social life can never hope to establish it effectively either in a city or in the concert of nations. Peace cannot be built on a lie.

## Asks Examination of Conscience

The Holy Father, therefore, asks us to examine our consciences. We readily agree that world tension today affects the private lives of each one of us. By what fatal lack of logic do we refuse to first seek the remedy in our inner selves? The Christian who overcomes within himself the obstacles to an understanding of others and to brotherly cooperation with them has already made an effective contribution to peace. And what are these inner obstacles but a partisan and sectarian spirit incapable of a disinterested search for truth, an emotionalism open to all divisive propaganda and insensible to the commands of justice, and a self-righteous attitude ever ready to see faults in others, but blind to its own prejudices and unbending towards those who are victims of the error it is fighting? The man who gives in to such tendencies aggravates, in himself and in others, the wound from which suffering humanity is bleeding.

Let all followers of Christ, on the contrary, cast peaceful and Catholic eyes upon the world. Mindful of the commandments of the Master, let them investigate more deeply the demands of charity; let them meditate upon His words and His examples of love for His enemies; and let them bear in mind His great lesson of forgiving injuries.

In view of the broad scope and the difficulties of the task, the peacemaker must have, according to the words of the well-known prayer, "a great and indomitable heart, which hushes all disillusion, for which no trial is too great, which heeds no indifference." He must, following the example of Father de Foucauld, see in all men the soul of a "universal brother."

Such is the indispensable mission that Christians must fulfill in our times. At peace with themselves, at peace with others, their peaceful hosts can batter down the walls of suspicion and injustice which are so sadly dividing the international community.

Let them, moreover, be without illusions, for the powers of darkness are always at work in history, seeking to seduce even the most noble. Let them also be without fear, these sons of light, for the Church, whose good servants they are, speaks the language of eternal life.

It is therefore towards the Church that they will want to turn with confidence in difficult times. Mother of all nations, she can never, without denying herself, remain deaf to the anguished cries of her children of all races and classes. Quite the contrary, she never ceases to extend to all mankind the Easter greeting of Jesus, *Peace be with you.*

The bearer of God's peace, the Church proclaims to the world the basic and inviolable rules on which depends, in the final analysis, the stability of every national and international order. Messenger of peace among men, she brings them with the grace of God the promise of true brotherhood. She brings peace to souls, to cities and to the great human family. Such is the Church in the society of nations. The Kingdom she preaches is not of this world, but she remains in the world as an unchangeable force for peace, as the divinely assisted bride of Christ, the Prince of Peace.

# International Penal Law*

*(Address to Sixth International Congress of Penal Law, October 3, 1953)*

A PEACEFUL and ordered social life, whether within a national community or in the society of nations, is only possible if the juridical norms which regulate the living and working to-gether of the members of the society are observed. But there are always to be found people who will not keep to these norms and who violate the law. Against them society must protect itself. Hence derives penal law, which punishes the transgression and, by inflicting punishment, leads the trans-gressor back to the observance of the law violated.

States and peoples have each their own penal law; these laws are made up of a multitude of parts; between them there always remains a greater or less diversity. But since in our times people easily change their place of residence and fre-quently pass from one state to another, it is desirable that at least the most serious crimes should have a sanction every-where and, if possible, of an equal severity, so that the culprits may nowhere be able to escape or be shielded from the punishment of their crimes. It is an agreement and reciprocal support of this kind between nations that international penal law strives to realize.

If what We have just said holds good in normal times, its urgency is particularly evident in time of war or of violent political disturbances, when civil strife breaks out within a state. The offender in political matters upsets the order of social life just as much as the offender in common law: to

---

* Translation from *The Catholic Mind*.

neither must be allowed assurance of impunity in his crime.

To protect individuals and peoples against injustice and violations of the law, by formulating an international penal code, is a lofty aim to the attaining of which We wish to contribute by addressing a few words to you.

## *Importance of the Law*

We will speak first of all of the importance of international penal law, as brought out by the experience of the last decades.

This experience covers two world wars with their repercussions. During these changes, both within countries and between one country and another, and when totalitarian political regimes were developing without check, deeds were done governed only by the law of violence and success. We were witnesses then of a cynical attitude, which would be unthinkable in normal times, in attaining the end proposed and in neutralizing the enemy, who was in general hardly considered as a human being. It was not blind natural forces but men who, now in savage passion, now in cold reflection, brought unspeakable sufferings, misery and extermination to individuals, communities and to whole nations.

Those who acted thus felt secure, or tried to procure for themselves the assurance that no one could ever or in any place call them to account. If fortune turned against them, it would be always possible for them to flee to a foreign country. Such was the attitude of soul of those who acted as criminals themselves, or, presuming on their power, commanded and forced others to act, or let them commit evil, even though they could and were obliged to restrain them from it.

All this created among those involved the impression that no law existed, of a lack of protection, of being the playthings of an arbitrary will and of brute force. But a demand also made itself felt: that all the culprits of which We have just spoken, without consideration of persons, should be obliged to render account, to suffer the penalty, and that nothing should be allowed to save them from the chastisement of their acts, neither success nor even the excuse of an "order received from a higher authority."

It is the spontaneous human sense of justice that demands a sanction, and which perceives that the threat of a universally applicable penalty is a guarantee, not to be neglected even though not infallible, against such wrongdoing. This sense of justice has, on the whole, found for what concerns offenses of common law a sufficient expression in the penal code of States; to a lesser degree, in the case of political violence within States; and hardly at all, up to the present, for acts of war between States and peoples.

But a balanced sense of justice is no less clear and imperious in its demand for sanctions in the last-mentioned case than in the others, and if it is satisfied, it will be equally strong in its restraining force. The certitude, confirmed by treaties, that one must render an account—even if the criminal act succeeds, even if the offense is committed abroad, even if, after having committed it, one flees to a foreign country—this certitude is a guarantee not to be underestimated. The consideration of these circumstances is calculated to make one understand, even at first sight, the importance of an international code of penal law. For, in fact, we are not dealing here with the simple demands of human nature and of moral duty, but with working out clearly defined coercive juridical norms which, in virtue of formal treaties, may become obligatory for the contracting states.

### Crimes

In the second place We shall speak of the categories of crimes which will concern international penal law.

If already the common penal law must apply the principle that it cannot take as its object all acts against morality but those only which seriously threaten good order in the life of the community, this same principle deserves very particular attention in the construction of an international system of penal law (cf. St. Thomas, *Summ. Theol.* 1. 2ae., q. 96, a1 and 2). It would be an undertaking doomed beforehand to failure to try to set up international agreements covering all violations of law, however slight. In this matter, attention must be directed only to crimes that are particularly serious, even only, We might say, to those which are extremely serious. It is only for such crimes that it is possible to establish a uniform penal code between states.

Besides, the choice and definition of the crimes to be punished must be based on objective criteria: namely, on the serious nature of certain crimes, and on the necessity to take measures precisely against them. In the light of these two considerations it is of paramount importance to consider the following points:

1. The value of the good attacked; it should be something of the highest importance.
2. The force of the inclination to violate the good.
3. The intensity of the evil will which is normally exercised when these crimes are committed.
4. The gravity of the perversion of juridic order, considering the person who commits the crime; for example, in the case where those who should maintain law, themselves break it.
5. The seriousness of the threat to the juridic order because of extraordinary circumstances which, on the one hand, increase the danger of criminal acts being attempted and, on the other, make them much more formidable in their effects. Consider, for example, extraordinary situations, such as war or siege.

With these criteria as a base, a number of cases can be mentioned for which international law ought to establish a sanction.

In the first place, there is the crime of making a modern war which is not required by absolute necessity of self-defense, and which brings with it, as We can assert without hesitation, unthinkable ruin, suffering and horrors. The community of nations must reckon with unprincipled criminals who, in order to realize their ambitious plans, are not afraid to unleash total war. This is the reason why other countries, if they wish to preserve their very existence and their most precious possessions, and unless they are prepared to accord free action to international criminals, have no alternative but to get ready for the day when they must defend themselves. This right to be prepared for self-defense cannot be denied, even in these days, to any state. That, however, does not in any way alter the fact that unjust war is to be accounted as one of the very gravest crimes which international penal law must proscribe, must punish with the heaviest penalties, and the authors of which are in every case guilty and liable to the punishment that has been agreed upon.

The world wars through which humanity has lived and the events which have taken place in the totalitarian states have given rise to many other evils, at times even more serious, which a code of international penal law should render impossible, or from which it ought to free the community of nations.

Also, even in a just and necessary war, the ways of acting which would lead to victory are not all defensible in the eyes of those who have an exact and reasonable concept of justice. The mass shooting of innocent people in reprisal for the fault of an individual is not an act of justice, but an injustice, sanctioned indeed by authority. One does not acquire the right to execute innocent hostages just because it is looked on as a necessity of war. In these last decades we have seen massacres out of racial hatred; the horrors and cruelties of concentration camps have been revealed to the whole world; we have heard of the "liquidation" by hundreds of thousands of "beings not fit to live"; pitiless mass deportations in which the victims were delivered up to destitution, often along with their wives and children; force used against great numbers of defenseless young girls and women; manhunts organized among civilians in order to procure workers, or rather slaves for work.

The administration of justice has in places degenerated into an unlimited arbitrariness, whether in the methods of examination, or in the sentence, or in the carrying out of the sentence. In order to be revenged on one whose actions were perhaps morally irreproachable, they have not at times been ashamed to take action against the members of his family.

These few examples—you know that many others exist—can suffice to show what class of crimes ought to constitute the object of international agreements, which could secure effective protection, and which would indicate clearly the crimes to be proscribed and fix their characteristics with juridic precision.

### Penalties

The third point which calls for at least a brief mention concerns the penalties to be demanded by international penal law, about which a remark of a general nature will suffice.

It is possible to punish in a way that would hold the penal law up to ridicule; but it is also possible to punish in a way that surpasses all reasonable measure. In the case where human life is made the object of a criminal gamble, where hundreds and thousands are reduced to extreme want and driven to distress, a mere privation of civil rights would be an insult to justice. When, on the contrary, the violation of a police regulation, a thoughtless word against authority, are punished by the firing squad or by forced labor for life, the sense of justice revolts. The fixing of the penalties in penal law and their adaptation to the individual case should correspond to the gravity of the crimes.

As a rule the penal law of the various states enumerates the sanctions and defines the norms which determine them, or else it leaves this to the judge to do. But it will be necessary to try and secure, by international agreements, a settlement of these penalties, in such wise that the crimes mentioned in the agreements may not be at an advantage anywhere; that is to say, that their punishment be not less formidable in one country than in another, nor that there be hope of a more lenient judgment before one tribunal than before another. It would be impossible to impose such a settlement on States by force, but an objective exchange of views would, nevertheless, give the hope of attaining agreement bit by bit on essentials. There would be no invincible obstacle, except from a political system built, itself, on the aforementioned injustices which the international agreement is to prosecute. Whoever lives by injustice cannot contribute to the formulation of law, and he who knows himself to be guilty will not propose a law which establishes his guilt and hands him over to justice. This circumstance explains in some degree what happened when recognition was sought for "The Rights of Man," although there are other difficulties which proceed from entirely different causes.

## Juridical Guarantees

We will speak, in the fourth place, of juridical guarantees, of which there is question on several occasions in the program of your Congress.

The function of law, its dignity and the sentiment of equity natural to man all demand that from first to last punitive action should be based, not on arbitrary will and passion, but on clear and firm juridical rules. That means, first of all, that there is a judicial trial—at least summary, if there is danger in delay—and that the trial be not by-passed, in reaction against the offense, and justice thus presented with an accomplished fact. To avenge a bomb thrown by an unknown hand by machine-gunning the passers-by who happen to be in the road is not a legal way of acting.

The very first step in the punitive action, the arrest, must not be done wantonly, but must respect juridical norms. It is not admissible that even the most irreproachable citizen might be able to be arrested arbitrarily and disappear without a word into prison. To send someone into a concentration camp and keep him there, without any regular trial, is a mockery of the law.

The judicial investigation must exclude physical and psychic torture and narcoanalysis; first of all, because these methods violate a natural right, even if the accused is really guilty, and, secondly, because they too often give erroneous results. It is not unusual for them to end in the precise confessions desired by the court, and in the ruin of the accused, not because the latter is guilty in fact, but because his physical and psychic energy is exhausted, and he is ready to make all the declarations required. "Rather prison and death than such physical and psychic torture!" We find abundant proof of this state of things in the spectacular trials well known to all of us, with their confessions, self-accusations and demands for pitiless chastisement.

It is about 1100 years since the great Pope Nicolas I, in the year 866, replied in the following manner to the question of a nation which had just come into contact with Christianity (*Nicolai primi responsa ad consulta Bulgarorum, cap.* LXXXVI, 13 Nov., 866—*Mon. Germ. hist.*, Epp. tom. VI, p. 595):

If a thief or a bandit is caught, and denies what is imputed to him, you say among you that the judge should beat him on the head with blows and pierce his sides with iron spikes, until he speaks the truth. That, neither divine nor human law admits: the confession must not be forced, but spontaneous; it must not be extorted, but voluntary; lastly, if it happens that, after having inflicted these sufferings, you discover absolutely nothing concerning that with which you have charged the accused, are you not ashamed then at least, and do you not recognize how impious your judgment was? Likewise, if the accused, unable to bear such tortures, admits to crimes which he has not committed, who, I ask you, has the responsibility for such an impiety? Is it not he who forced him to such a deceitful confession? Furthermore, if some one utters with his lips what is not in his mind, it is well known that he is not confessing, he is merely speaking. Put away these things, then, and hate from the bottom of your heart what heretofore you have had the folly to practice; in truth, what fruit did you then draw from that of which you are now ashamed?

Who would not wish that, during the long interval passed since then, justice had never departed from this rule! That it should be necessary today to recall this warning, given 1100 years ago, is a sad sign of the aberrations of judicial practice in the twentieth century.

### Freedom for the Defense

Among the safeguards of the judicial action is also reckoned the freedom of the accused to defend himself, truly, and not just for form. Both he and his counsel must be permitted to submit to the court all that speaks in his favor. It cannot be allowed that the defense may only put forward what is acceptable to the court and to a biased justice.

An essential factor of the safeguards of the law is the impartial composition of the court of justice. The judge may not be biased, either personally or for the state. A judge who has a true sense of justice will himself renounce the exercise of his jurisdiction in a case in which he would consider himself to be an interested party. The "popular tribunals" which, in the totalitarian states, were composed entirely of members of the party offered no juridical guarantee.

The impartiality of the college of judges should also be assured, and especially when international relations are involved in the penal process. In such a case it may be necessary to have recourse to an international tribunal, or at least to be able to appeal from a national to an international one. One who is outside the quarrel feels there is something wrong when, at the end of hostilities, he sees the conqueror judge the conquered for crimes of war, when the conqueror himself has been guilty of similar deeds towards the conquered.

The conquered may undoubtedly be guilty; their judges may have a clear sense of justice and the desire to be entirely objective; nevertheless, in such a case, the interest of the law, the confidence which the sentence is to command, will often require that neutral judges be added to the tribunal, and that the decisive majority depends on them. The neutral judge should not then consider that it is his duty to acquit the accused; he should apply law as it exists and regulate his actions according to it.

But the aforementioned addition of neutral judges gives the parties immediately concerned the disinterested third party and world opinion a greater certitude that "right" will prevail in the decision. It undoubtedly constitutes a certain limitation of private sovereignty, but this limitation is more than compensated for by the increase in prestige of, and by the added regard and confidence for, the judicial decisions of the state which acts thus.

### Deciding Culpability

Among the safeguards demanded by the law there is none, perhaps, more important or more difficult to secure than deciding culpability. It should be an unassailable principle of penal law that the "penalty" in the juridical sense always presupposes a "fault." The simple relation of cause to effect does not merit to be considered as a juridical principle, sufficient in itself. This assertion does not in any way undermine the law. In the crime committed with an evil intention, the principle of causality is fully verified; the result—the *"effectu secuto"* of Canon Law—may, in fact, be required in order to be sure that a crime was really committed. But in penal law, causality and the resultant effect are only imputable if accompanied by culpability.

Here the judge meets with difficulties, even with great difficulties, to resolve which a conscientious examination of the subjective element is necessary. Did the author of the offense sufficiently know the illegality of his action? Was his decision to do it substantially free? In answering these questions one will be helped by the presumptions allowed for by the law. If it is impossible to establish the guilt with moral certitude, one will abide by the principle that "in doubt the presumption is in favor of the accused."

All this is already to be found in the simple criminal case. But the numerous trials of the war, and after the war up to our own day, have given the question a particular character. The judge had, and still has to study the case of those who have commanded others to commit a crime, or who have not prevented it when they could and should have done so. More often still there arises the question of the guilt of those who have only acted on the orders of their leaders, or were even forced to act under the threat of the direst punishments and even death. Very often, in these trials, the accused have pleaded the circumstance that they were only acting on "orders from above."

Would it be possible to secure by international agreements that leaders, on the one hand, be rendered juridically incapable of ordering crimes, and punishable before the law if they do so; on the other, that subordinates be dispensed from executing such orders, and punishable in the law if they obey them? Would it be possible to suppress by international agreements the juridical contradiction by which an inferior's property and life are threatened if he does not obey, and by which, if he obeys, he has to fear that at the end of hostilities the injured party, if he gains the victory, will hand him over to justice as a "war criminal"?

The moral principle in such cases is absolutely clear: no higher authority can validly command an immoral act; there exists no right, no obligation, no permission to accomplish an act, evil in itself, even if it is ordered, and even if the refusal to do the action involves the worst personal damages. This moral principle is not under discussion here. We are interested for the moment in putting an end to the juridical contradiction which We have mentioned by establishing, through international agreements, positive juridical rules, well defined and recognized by the contracting states as binding.

The same need for an international settlement exists for the principle of collective guilt, so often used and applied during recent decades, about which the judge had often to decide when determining the culpability of the accused, and which

205

more often has served to justify administrative measures. States and tribunals which found in collective guilt a justification for their pretensions and maneuvers invoked the theory and applied it as a rule of action. Their opponents questioned its validity and even considered it unacceptable in any order of things established by man alone, as tainted with contradiction in itself and from the juridical point of view.

But here again, the ethical and philosophical problem of purely collective guilt is not at stake for the moment. We are concerned rather with finding and fixing a practical juridical formula to be adopted in case of conflict, and especially of international conflict, when collective guilt can be of decisive importance for determining culpability, and has been more than once. The safeguard of a regular juridical trial demands that in this conjuncture the action of governments and of courts should be secured against arbitrariness and purely personal opinion, and be solidly founded in clear juridical rules: a foundation which corresponds to sane reason and to the universal sentiment of justice, and at the service of which the contracting governments may be able to put their authority and their power of coercion.

### Foundations of Penal Law

To conclude We wish to say a word concerning some of the foundations of penal law:

1. The establishment of any positive law presupposes a series of fundamental needs existing in the nature of things.
2. The penal law must be built on man, considered as a personal, free being.
3. Only a person who is guilty and responsible to a higher authority may be punished.
4. The penalty and its application are in the last analysis postulates of the juridic order.

### Juridical Positivism

1. The law is ultimately founded on the stable and immutable nature of things. Wherever there are men and nations gathered in communities with laws, are they not precisely human beings with a nature which is essentially the same? The needs which derive from that nature are the guide-rules of law. However different the formulation given to these needs

in positive law, according to various times and places or varying degrees of development and culture, their central kernel is always the same, because it is the expression of man's nature. Those needs are, as it were, the dead point of a pendulum. Positive law swings beyond the dead point, now on one side, now on the other; but whether it likes it or not, the pendulum always returns to the dead point fixed by nature. It is of little consequence whether these needs of nature are called "law," "ethical norms," or "postulates of nature." The fact is that they exist; that they have not been invented by man's caprice; that they are really rooted in the nature which man himself did not fashion; that they are therefore to be found everywhere; and, consequently, all public law and all law of nations find in our common human nature a clear, solid and durable foundation.

It follows from this that any kind of extreme juridical positivism cannot be justified in reason. This positivism is expressed in the principle: "The law is whatever is established as such by the legislative power in the national or international community, and nothing but that, quite independently of any fundamental need of reason or nature." If one urges that principle, there is nothing to prevent a logical or moral contradiction; that unbridled passion, the whim and brutal violence of a tyrant and criminal might become the law of what is right. History, unfortunately, furnishes many examples of this possibility become reality. If, on the contrary, juridical positivism is so understood that, while recognizing fully those fundamental needs of nature, the term "law" is only used for laws formulated by the legislature, then many may consider this use of the word inexact; but, nevertheless, it offers a common basis for the construction of an international law founded on the ontological order.

## Man, A Personal Being

2. There is an essential difference between the juridical and the physical order of things. In the physical order, nature works automatically; not so in the juridical order, where man's personal decision must intervene, in conforming his conduct to the order established by law. "Man is the arbiter of each of his personal acts" is a phrase that expresses an ineradi-

207

cable human conviction. Men will never admit that what is called the autonomy of the will is only a tissue of internal and external forces.

There is much talk today of security measures destined to replace the punishment for the crime or to accompany it, of heredity, of natural dispositions, of education, of the extensive influence of the instincts at work in the depths of the unconscious or subconscious. Although such considerations may lead to useful conclusions, let us not gloss over the plain fact that man is a personal being, endowed with intelligence and free will, who decides finally himself what he will do or not do. This does not mean that he is free from every internal or external influence, from every inclination and attraction; nor does it mean that he has not to struggle to keep the right path, daily to fight a difficult battle against instinctive, and perhaps unhealthy, urges. But it does mean that, despite all the obstacles, the normal man can and must assert his will; and it is the normal man who must serve as the rule for society and law.

Penal law would have no sense if it did not take into consideration this aspect of man, but penal law makes complete sense because this aspect is true. And since this aspect of man, personal and free, is a conviction of humanity, the effort to establish a uniform penal code has a solid basis.

### Guilt

3. A third presupposition of penal justice is the factor of guilt. It is this which ultimately distinguishes justice properly so called from administrative measures of security. By it the penal juridical order is guaranteed against all arbitrariness, and safeguards for the accused are defined and assured.

Penal law is a reaction of the juridical order against the delinquent; it presupposes a causal relationship between the latter and the former. But this causal relationship must be established by a delinquent who is culpable.

The importance of culpability, of its presuppositions and its effects in law, demands, especially on the part of the judge, a profound knowledge of the psychological and juridical process at its origin. Only on this condition will the judge be spared the painful incertitude which weighs on the doctor, who is obliged to take a decision, but who can make no certain diagnosis according to the symptoms of the sickness because he does not perceive their internal connection.

At the moment of the crime, the delinquent has before his eyes the prohibition imposed by juridical order. He is conscious of it and of the obligation it imposes. But, nevertheless, he decides against his conscience, and to carry out his decision commits the external crime. That is the outline of a culpable violation of the law. By reason of this psychological process the action is attributed to its author as its cause. He is guilty of it because his decision was conscious; the order is violated and its guardian, the state, demands an account of him; he falls under the penalties fixed by the law and imposed by the judge. The many influences exercised on the acts of intelligence and will, that is to say, on the two factors which are the essential constitutive elements of culpability, do not fundamentally alter this process, however great their importance in determining the gravity of the guilt.

The outline sketched above is always valid, because it is taken from the nature of man, and from the nature of a culpable decision. It provides a common basis for international discussions, and may be of use in the formulation of juridical rules to be incorporated in an international agreement.

The deep knowledge of these difficult questions also prevents the science of penal law from digressing into mere casuistry, and, on the other hand, it directs it in the use of that casuistry necessary in practice, and thus justifiable.

If, however, men refuse to base penal law on culpability as an essential element, it will be difficult to create a true penal law and to reach an agreement in international discussions.

### Punishment

4. It remains to say a word about the ultimate meaning of punishment. Most modern theories of penal law explain punishment and justify it in the last resort as a protective measure, that is, a defense of the community against crimes being attempted and, at the same time, as an effort to lead the culprit back to observance of the law. In these theories, punishment may indeed include sanctions in the form of a diminution of certain advantages guaranteed by the law, in order to teach

the culprit to live honestly; but they fail to consider expiation of the crime committed, which itself is a sanction on the violation of the law, as the most important function of the punishment.

It may be permitted to a theory, to a juridical school, to national or international penal legislation to define punishment philosophically in the way in which they understand it, in conformity with their juridical system, provided that they respect the considerations developed above concerning the nature of man and the essence of guilt.

But from another point of view, and indeed a higher one, one may ask if the modern conception is fully adequate to explain punishment. The protection of the community against crimes and criminals must be ensured, but the final purpose of punishment must be sought on a higher plane.

The essence of the culpable act is the free opposition to a law recognized as binding. It is the rupture and deliberate violation of just order. Once done, it is impossible to recall. Nevertheless, in so far as it is possible to make satisfaction for the order violated, that should be done. For this is a fundamental exigency of "justice," whose role in morality is to maintain the existing equilibrium, if it is just, and to restore the balance, when upset. It demands that by punishment the person responsible be forcibly brought to order. And the fulfillment of this demand proclaims the absolute supremacy of good over evil; right triumphs sovereignly over wrong.

Let us take the last step: In the metaphysical order, the punishment is a consequence of our dependence on the Supreme Will, a dependence which is inscribed indelibly on our created nature. If it is ever necessary to repress the revolt of a free being and reestablish the broken order, then it is surely here when the supreme Judge and His justice demand it. The victim of an injustice may freely renounce his claim to reparation, but as far as justice is concerned it is always assured to him.

This more profound understanding of punishment gives no less importance to the function of protection, stressed today, but it goes more to the heart of the matter. For it is concerned, not immediately with protecting the goods insured by the law, but the very law itself. There is nothing more necessary for the national or international community than respect for the majesty of the law and the salutary thought that the law is also sacred and protected, so that whoever breaks it is punishable and will be punished.

These reflections help to a better appreciation of another age, which some regard as outmoded, which distinguished between medicinal punishment—*poenae medicinales*—and vindicative punishment—*poenae vindicativae*. In vindicative punishment the function of expiation is to the fore; the function of protection is comprised in both types of punishment. Canon Law, as you know, still maintains the distinction, which attitude is founded on the convictions already detailed. Only it gives full meaning to the well known word of the Apostle in the Epistle to the Romans: *Non enim sine causa gladium portat; . . . vindex in iram ei qui malum agit.* (*It is not for nothing that he bears the Sword: he is God's minister still, to inflict punishment on the wrong-doer.*) Here it is expiation which is brought out.

Finally, it is only the expiatory function which gives the key to the last Judgment of the Creator Himself, Who *renders to everyone according to his works*, as both Testaments often repeat. The function of protection disappears completely in the afterlife. The Omnipotent and All-Knowing Creator can always prevent the repetition of a crime by the interior moral conversion of the delinquent. But the supreme Judge, in His last judgment, applies uniquely the principle of retribution. This, then, must be of great importance.

Whether or not, as We have said, one leaves to theory and practice the duty of defining the role of punishment in the narrower modern sense, or in the other broader one, it is possible for collaboration in either case, and one can look forward to the creation of an international penal code. But do not refuse to consider this ultimate reason for punishment merely because it does not seem likely to produce immediate practical results.

Our elucidations have followed the line of contact between law and its metaphysical foundations. We will be happy if thereby We have contributed something at least to the labors of your Congress for the protection and defense of man against crime and the ravages of injustice.

We will conclude by wishing all success on your efforts to construct a sane international penal code for the advantage of society, of the Church, and of the community of nations.

# The International Community*

*(Address to Fifth Annual Congress of the Union of Italian Catholic Jurists, December 6, 1953)*

. . . YOUR convention is rather national in character, but the subject it is treating, "The Nation and the International Community," touches again the relations between peoples and sovereign states.

It is not by chance that congresses are multiplying for the study of international questions, be they scientific, economic or political. The clear fact that relations between individuals of various nations and between nations themselves are growing in multiplicity and intensity makes daily more urgent a right ordering of international relations, both private and public; all the more so since this mutual drawing together is caused not only by vastly improved technological progress and by free choice but also by the more profound action of an intrinsic law of development.

This movement, then, is not to be repressed but fostered and promoted.

In this work of expansion, communities of States and peoples, whether already existing or only a goal to be achieved, have naturally a special importance. They are communities in which sovereign States, that is to say, States which are subordinate to no other State, are united into a juridical community to attain definite juridical ends.

It would give a false idea of these juridical communities to compare them to world empires of the past or of the present, in which different racial stocks, peoples and states become fused, whether they want it or not, into a single conglomeration of states.

---

* Translation from *The Pope Speaks*.

In the present instance, however, States, remaining sovereign, freely unite into a juridical community.

## Urge to World Community

In this connection, the history of the world, which shows a continuous succession of struggles for power, no doubt might make the establishment of a juridical community of free States seem almost utopian.

The conflicts of the past have too often been motivated by a desire to subjugate other nations and to extend the range of one's own power, or by the necessity of defending one's liberty and one's own independent existence.

This time, on the contrary, it is precisely the will to prevent threatening conflicts that urges men toward a supranational juridical community. Utilitarian considerations, which certainly carry considerable weight, point toward the working out of peace.

And finally, perhaps, it is precisely because of technological progress that this mingling of men of different nations has awakened the faith, implanted in the hearts and souls of individuals, in a higher community of men, willed by the Creator and rooted in the unity of their common origin, nature, and final destiny.

These and other similar considerations show that advance toward establishing a community of peoples does not look, as to a unique and ultimate norm, to the will of the States, but rather to nature, to the Creator.

The right to existence, the right to respect from others and to one's good name, the right to one's own culture and national character, the right to develop oneself, the right to demand observance of international treaties, and other like rights, are exigencies of the law of nations, dictated by nature itself.

The positive law of different peoples, also indispensable in the community of States, has the office of defining more exactly the rights derived from nature and of adapting them to concrete circumstances; also of making other provisions, directed, of course, toward the common good, on the basis of a positive agreement which, once freely entered into, has binding force.

In this community of nations, then, every State becomes a part of the system of international law, and hence of natural law, which is both foundation and crown of the whole. Thus the individual nation no longer is—nor in fact was it ever—"sovereign," in the sense of being entirely without restrictions.

## True Meaning of Sovereignty

"Sovereignty" in the true sense means self-rule and exclusive competence concerning what has to be done and how it is to be done in regard to the affairs of a definite territory, always within the framework of international law, without, however, becoming dependent on the juridical system of any other State.

Every State is immediately subject to international law. States which would lack this fullness of power, or whose independence of the power of any other State would not be guaranteed by international law, would not be sovereign.

But no State could complain about a limitation of its sovereignty if it were denied the power of acting arbitrarily and without regard for other States. Sovereignty is not a divinization of the State, or omnipotence of the State in the Hegelian sense, or after the manner of absolute juridical positivism.

## Difficulties to be Faced

There is no need to explain to you students of law how the setting up, maintenance and operation of a real community of States, especially one that would embrace all peoples, give rise to many duties and problems, some of them extremely difficult and complicated, which cannot be solved by a simple yes-or-no answer.

Such would be the question of race and origin, with their biological, psychological and social consequences; the question of language; the question of family life, with its relations, varying according to nation, between husband and wife, parents, the larger family group; the question of the equality or equivalence of rights in what regards goods, contracts and persons for the citizens of one sovereign State who either live for a short time in a foreign State or, retaining their own nationality, establish permanent residence there; the question of the right of immigration or of emigration, and other like questions.

The jurist, the statesman, the individual State, as well as the community of States should here take account of all the inborn inclinations of individuals and communities in their contracts and reciprocal relations: such as the tendency to adapt or to assimilate, often pushed even to an attempt to absorb; or contrariwise, the tendency to exclude and to destroy anything that appears incapable of assimilation; the tendency to expand, to embrace what is new, as on the contrary, the tendency to retreat and to segregate oneself; the tendency to give oneself entirely, forgetful of self, and its opposite, attachment to oneself, excluding any service of others; the lust for power, the yearning to keep others in subjection, and so on.

All these instincts, either of self-aggrandizement or of self-defense, have their roots in the natural dispositions of individuals, peoples, races, and communities, and in their restrictions and limitations. One never finds in them everything that is good and just. God alone, the origin of all things, possesses within Himself, by reason of His infinity, all that is good.

From what We have said, it is easy to deduce the fundamental theoretical principle for dealing with these difficulties and tendencies: within the limits of the possible and lawful, to promote everything that facilitates union and makes it more effective; to remove everything that disturbs it; to tolerate at times that which it is impossible to correct but which, on the other hand, must not be permitted to make shipwreck of the community from which a higher good is hoped for.

The difficulty rests in the application of this principle.

### Problem of Coexistence

In this connection, We wish to treat with you who are happy to profess yourselves Catholic jurists, concerning one of the questions which arise in a community of peoples: that is, the practical coexistence (*convivenza*) of Catholic with non-Catholic states.

Depending upon the religious belief of the great majority of citizens, or by reason of an explicit declaration of law, peoples and member states of the international community will be divided into those that are Christian, non-Christian, indifferent to religion or consciously without it, or even professedly atheist.

The interests of religion and morality will require for the whole extent of the international community a well-defined rule, which will hold for all the territory of the individual sovereign member-States of the international community. According to probability and depending on circumstances, it can be foreseen that this ruling of positive law will be thus enunciated:

Within its own territory and for its own citizens, each State will regulate religious and moral affairs by its own laws. Nevertheless, throughout the whole territory of the international community of States, the citizens, of every member-State will be allowed the exercise of their own beliefs and ethical and religious practices, in so far as these do not contravene the penal laws of the State in which they are residing.

### Can Catholics Consent?

For the jurist, the statesman, and the Catholic State arises here the question: can they give their consent to such a ruling when there is question of entering and remaining in an international community?

Now, with regard to religious and moral interests, a twofold question arises. The first deals with the objective truth and the obligation of conscience toward what is objectively true and good.

The second deals with the practical attitude of the international community toward the individual sovereign State and the attitude of the individual State toward the international community in what regards religion and morality.

The first question can hardly be a matter for discussion and legal ruling between the individual States and the international community, especially in the case of a plurality of different religious beliefs within the international community. On the other hand, the second question can be of extreme importance and urgency.

Now to give the right answer to the second question. Above all, it must be clearly stated that no human authority, no State, no community of States, whatever be their religious character, can give a positive command or positive authorization to teach or to do that which would be contrary to religious truth or moral good.

Such a command or such an authorization would have no obligatory power and would remain without effect. No authority may give such a command, because it is contrary to nature to oblige the spirit and the will of man to error and evil, or to consider one or the other as indifferent.

Not even God could give such a positive command or positive authorization, because it would be in contradiction to His absolute truth and sanctity.

### Norm of Tolerance

Another question, essentially different, is this: could the norm be established in a community of states—at least in certain circumstances—that the free exercise of a belief and of a religious or moral practice, which possesses validity in one of the member states, be not hindered throughout the entire territory of the community of nations by State laws or coercive measures?

In other words, the question is raised whether in these circumstances *non impedire* or toleration is permissible, and whether, consequently, positive repression is not always a duty.

We have just adduced the authority of God. Could God, although it would be possible and easy for Him to repress error and moral deviation, in some cases choose the *non impedire* without contradicting His infinite perfection?

Could it be that in certain circumstances He would not give men any mandate, would not impose any duty, and would not even communicate the right to impede or to repress what is erroneous and false? A look at things as they are gives an affirmative answer.

### No Absolute Duty to Suppress

Reality shows that error and sin are in the world in great measure. God reprobates them, but He permits them to exist. Hence the affirmation that religious and moral error must always be impeded when it is possible, because toleration of them is in itself immoral, is not valid *absolutely and unconditionally*.

217

Moreover, God has not given even to human authority such an absolute and universal command in matters of faith and morality. Such a command is unknown to the common convictions of mankind, to Christian conscience, to the sources of revelation, and to the practice of the Church.

To omit here other scriptural texts which are adduced in support of this argument, Christ in the parable of The Cockle gives the following advice: *let the cockle grow in the field of the world together with the good seed in view of the harvest.*

The duty of repressing moral and religious error cannot therefore be an ultimate norm of action. It must be subordinate to *higher and more general* norms, which *in some circumstances* permit, and even perhaps seem to indicate as the better policy toleration of error in order to promote *a greater good.*

## Two Principles for Statesmen

Thus the two principles are clarified to which recourse must be had in concrete cases for the answer to the serious question concerning the attitude which the jurist, the statesman and the sovereign Catholic State is to adopt in consideration of the community of nations with regard to a formula of religious and moral toleration as described above.

First: that which does not correspond to truth or to the norm of morality objectively has no right to exist, to be spread or to be activated. Secondly: failure to impede this with civil laws and coercive measures can nevertheless be justified in the interests of a higher and more general good.

Before all else the Catholic statesman must judge if this condition is verified in the concrete—this is the "question of fact."

In his decision he will permit himself to be guided by weighing the dangerous consequences that stem from toleration against those from which the community of nations will be spared if the formula of toleration be accepted.

Moreover, he will be guided by the good which, according to a wise prognosis, can be derived from toleration for the international community as such, and indirectly for the member State. In that which concerns religion and morality he will also ask for the judgment of the Church.

For her, only he to whom Christ has entrusted the guidance of His whole Church is competent to speak in the last instance on such vital questions touching international life: that is, the Roman Pontiff.

### *International Institutions Compared*

The institution of a community of nations, which today has been partly realized but which is striving to be established and consolidated upon a higher and more perfect level, is an ascent from the lower to the higher, that is, from a plurality of sovereign States to the greatest possible unity.

The Church of Christ has, in virtue of a mandate from her Divine Founder, a similar universal mission. She must draw to herself and bind together in religious unity the men of all races and of all times. But here the process is in a certain sense the contrary: she descends from the higher to the lower.

In the former case, the superior juridical unity of nations was and still is to be created. In the latter, the juridical community with its universal end, its constitution, its powers and those in whom these powers are invested, are already established from the beginning, by the will and decree of Christ Himself. The duty of this universal community from the outset is to incorporate all men and all races and thereby to bring them to the full truth and the grace of Jesus Christ.

The Church, in the fulfilment of this her mission, has always been faced and is still faced in large measure by the same problems which the functioning of a community of sovereign States must overcome; only she feels them more acutely, for she is obligated to the purpose of her mission, determined by her Founder Himself, which penetrates to the very depths of the spirit and heart of man.

In this state of affairs conflicts are inevitable, and history shows that there have always been conflicts. There still are, and according to the words of the Lord, there will be till the end of time.

For the Church with her mission has been, and is, confronted with men and nations of marvelous culture, with others of almost incredible lack of civilization, and with all possible intermediate degrees: diversity of extraction, of language, of philosophy, of religious belief, of national aspirations and characteristics; free peoples and enslaved peoples; peoples that have never belonged to the Church and peoples that have been separated from her communion.

## Church Cannot Ignore Reality

The Church must live among them and with them; she can never declare before anyone that she is "not interested." The mandate imposed upon her by her Divine Founder renders it impossible for her to follow a policy of non-interference or *laissez faire*. She has the duty of teaching and educating in all the inflexibility of truth and goodness, and with this absolute obligation she must remain and work among men and nations that in mental outlook are completely different from each other.

Let Us return now, however, to the two propositions mentioned above: and in the first place to the one which denies unconditionally everything that is religiously false and morally wrong. With regard to this point there never has been, and there is not now, in the Church any vacillation or any compromise, either in theory or in practice. Her deportment has not changed in the course of history, nor can it change whenever or wherever, under the most diversified forms, she is confronted with the choice: either incense to idols or blood for Christ.

The place where you are now present, Eternal Rome, with the remains of a greatness that was and with the glorious memories of its martyrs, is the most eloquent witness to the answer of the Church. Incense was not burned before the idols, and Christian blood flowed and consecrated the ground.

But the temples of the gods lie in the cold devastation of ruins howsoever majestic; while at the tombs of the martyrs the faithful of all nations and all tongues fervently repeat the ancient Creed of the Apostles.

## Tradition of Tolerance

Concerning the second proposition, that is to say, concerning tolerance in determined circumstances, toleration even in cases in which one could proceed to repression, the Church— out of regard for those who in good conscience (though erroneous, but invincibly so) are of a different opinion—has been led to act and has acted with that tolerance, after she became the state Church under Constantine the Great and the other Christian emperors, always for higher and more cogent motives.

So she acts today, and also in the future she will be faced with the same necessity. In such individual cases the attitude of the Church is determined by what is demanded for safeguarding and considering the *bonum commune* on the one hand—the common good of the Church and the State in individual states; and on the other, the common good of the universal Church, the reign of God over the whole world.

In considering the "pro" and "con" for the solution of a "question of fact," as well as what concerns the final and supreme judge in these matters, no other norms are valid for the Church except the norms which We have just indicated for the Catholic jurist and statesman.

The ideas We have set forth may also be useful for the Catholic jurist and statesman when, in their studies or in the exercise of their profession, they come in contact with the agreements (concordats, treaties, agreements, *modus vivendi*, etc.) which the Church (that is to say, for a long time now, the Apostolic See) has concluded and still concludes with sovereign states.

### Purpose of Concordats

The concordats are for her an expression of the collaboration between the Church and the State. In principle, that is, in theory, she cannot approve complete separation of the two powers. The concordats, therefore, must assure to the Church a stable condition in right and in fact in the State with which they are concluded, and must guarantee to her full independence in the fulfilment of her divine mission.

It is possible that the Church and the State proclaim in a concordat their common religious conviction; but it may also happen that a concordat have, together with other purposes, that of forestalling disputes with regard to questions of principle and of removing from the very beginning possible matters of conflict.

When the Church has set her signature to a concordat, it holds for everything contained therein. But, with the mutual acknowledgment of both high contracting parties, it may not hold in the same way for everything.

It may signify and express approval, but it may also mean a simple tolerance, according to those two principles which are the norm for the co-existence (*convivenza*) of the Church and her faithful with the civil powers and with men of another belief.

This, beloved sons, is what We intended to treat of with you rather fully.

For the rest, We are confident that the international community can banish every danger of war and establish the peace, and, as far as the Church is concerned, can guarantee to her freedom of action everywhere, so that she may be able to establish in the spirit and the heart, in the thoughts and the actions of men, the Kingdom of Him Who is the Redeemer, the Lawgiver, the Judge, the Lord of the world, Jesus Christ, Who rules as God over all things, blessed forever.

# Modern Technology and Peace*

*(Christmas Message Broadcast to the Whole World, December 24, 1953)*

. . . AROUND the radiant cradle of the Redeemer . . . there remain zones of darkness, and men go around with their eyes closed to the heavenly light, not because God Incarnate, even in His mystery, has not light to enlighten everyone that comes into His world, but because many are dazzled by the ephemeral splendor of human ideals and achievements, and limit their gaze to the confines of the created world, incapable of raising it to the Creator, the beginning, the harmony and the final end of all existent things.

### Technological Progress

It is to these men whose spirit is in darkness that We wish to point out "the great light" radiating from the manger,

* Translation from *The Pope Speaks.*

asking them above all else to realize the cause which in our time is making them blind and insensible to the Divine. It is the excessive, and sometimes exclusive, esteem for what is called "progress in technology." This dream was first cherished as the omnipotent myth and dispenser of happiness, then pushed forward by every device to the most daring conquests; and it has finally imposed itself on the minds of men as the final end of man and of life, substituting itself therefore for every kind of religious and spiritual ideal.

But now it is becoming ever more clear that its undue exaltation has so blinded men's intelligence that they exemplify in themselves what the Book of Wisdom castigated in the men of its time. They are incapable of learning from the visible world of Him Who is, of discovering the worker from His work; still more today, the supernatural world and the work of redemption, which is above all natural things and was accomplished by Jesus Christ, remain wrapped in total obscurity for those men who walk in darkness.

### It Comes from God and of Itself Leads to God

Nevertheless, the aforementioned erroneous consequence does not follow necessarily, nor are our present criticisms to be understood as a condemnation of technological progress in itself. The Church loves and favors human progress. It is undeniable that technological progress comes from God, and so it can and ought to lead to God. In point of fact, while the believer admires the conquests of science and makes use of them to penetrate more deeply into the knowledge of creation and of the forces of nature, that by means of machines he may better master them for the service of mankind and the enrichment of human life, it most often happens that he feels himself drawn to adore the Giver of those good things which he admires and uses, knowing full well that the eternal Son of God is the *firstborn of every creature. For in Him were created all things in the heavens and on the earth, things visible and things invisible.*

Very far, then, from any thought of disavowing the marvels of technology and its lawful use, the believer may find himself more eager to bow his knee before the celestial Babe of the manger, more conscious of his debt of gratitude to Him

Who gives all things and the intelligence to understand them, more disposed to find a place for those same works of technology with the chorus of angels in the hymn of Bethlehem: *Glory to God in the highest.* He will even find it natural to place beside the gold, frankincense and myrrh, offered by the Magi to the Infant God, also the modern conquests of technology: machines and numbers, laboratories and inventions, power and resources.

Furthermore, such an offering is like presenting Him with the work which He Himself once commanded and which is now being effected, though it has not yet reached its term. *Fill the earth and subdue it* said God to man as He handed creation over to him in temporary heritage. What a long and hard road from then to the present day, when men can at last say that they have in some measure fulfilled the divine command!

### Modern Technology Fruitful

Technology has, in fact, brought man's domination of the material world to a pitch of perfection never known before. The modern machine allows a mode of production that substitutes for, and multiplies a hundredfold, human energy for work, that is entirely independent of the contribution of organic forces and which ensures a maximum of extensive and intensive potential and at the same time of precision. As we embrace with a glance the results of this development, nature itself seems to give an assent of satisfaction to what has been done in it, and to incite to further investigation and use of its extraordinary possibilities. Now it is clear that all search for and discovery of the forces of nature, which technology effectuates, is at once a search for and discovery of the greatness, the wisdom, and the harmony of God. Looked at in this way, there is nothing to disapprove of or condemn in technology.

### Danger of Grave Spiritual Harm

Nevertheless, it can hardly be denied that this technology which in our century has reached the height of its splendor and fruitfulness, is, through certain circumstances, changed into a grave spiritual danger. For it seems to give modern man, prostrate at its altar, a sense of self-sufficiency and satisfaction of his boundless thirst for knowledge and power. In its many varied uses, in the absolute confidence which it awakens, in the extraordinary possibilities that it promises, modern technology displays before man so vast a vision as to be confounded by many with the Infinite itself.

In consequence, it is allowed an inadmissible autonomy which, in turn, is translated, in the thoughts of some, into a false conception of life and of the world, known as the "technological spirit." In what exactly does it consist? In this, that what is most highly prized in human life is the advantage that can be drawn from the forces and elements of nature; whatever is technically possible in mechanical production takes precedence over all other forms of human activity, and the perfection of earthly culture and happiness is seen in it.

### Restricts Man's Gaze to Material Goods

There is a fundamental falsehood in this distorted vision of the world offered by the technological spirit. The seemingly boundless panorama unfolded before the eyes of modern man, however extensive it may be, remains but a partial projection of life in reality, only expressing its relations with matter. Accordingly, it is a deceitful panorama, that finishes by shutting up as in a prison those who are too credulous with regard to the omnipotence and immensity of technology, a prison which is vast indeed, but nevertheless circumscribed, and hence in the long run insupportable to their true spirit. Their glance, far from reaching out over infinite reality as they thought (for reality does not consist only of matter), will feel chafed by the barriers which matter of necessity opposes. From this results the deep anguish of contemporary man, made blind for having wilfully surrounded himself with darkness.

### Makes It Blind to Religious Truth

Much more serious is the damage in the realm of specifically religious truths and of his relations with the supernatural to the man who is intoxicated with the "technological spirit." This, too, is the darkness to which the Evangelist St. John alludes, that prevents the spiritual understanding of the mysteries of God, darkness which the Incarnate Word of God is come to dispel.

Not that technology in itself requires as a logical conclusion the denial of religious values—on the contrary, as We have said, logic leads to their acknowledgment—but it is that "technological spirit" that puts man into a state of mind that is unfavorable for seeking, finding, accepting truths and goods of a supernatural order. The mind which has let itself be led astray by a concept of life outlined by the "technological spirit" remains uncomprehending, uninterested, and hence unseeing in the presence of those works of God, the mysteries of the Christian faith, totally different from technology.

The very remedy for this defect, which would consist in a redoubled effort to extend one's vision beyond the barrier of darkness and to stimulate in the soul an interest in supernatural truths, is made ineffective right from the beginning by the "technological spirit" itself.

For this way of looking at life deprives men of their sense of judgment on the remarkable unrest and superficiality of our time, a defect which even those who truly and sincerely approve technological progress must unfortunately recognize as one of its consequences.

Those who are imbued with the "technological spirit" find with difficulty the calm, the serenity, the inwardness essential for discovering the way that leads to the Son of God made man. They will even go so far as to belittle the Creator and His work, pronouncing human nature a defective product, when the necessary limitations of the human brain and other organs stand in the way of the fulfillment of technological plans and projects. Still less are they fit to understand and rightly esteem those very deep mysteries of life and of the divine economy, such as for example the mystery of Christmas, in which the union of the Eternal Word with human nature brings into play realities and marvels quite other than those of technology. Their thought is along different lines and follows other patterns, under the one-sided influence of that "technological spirit" which only recognizes and reckons real what can be expressed in mathematical formulas and utilitarian calculations.

They think that thus they are breaking up reality into its elements, but their knowledge remains on the surface and deals with but one aspect. It is evident that whoever adopts the method of technology as the sole way of seeking truth must give up any idea of penetrating the profound realities of organic life, and even more so those of the spiritual life, the living realities of the individual person and of human society, because these cannot be analyzed into quantitative relationships.

How can one ask of a mind so formed assent and wonder before the awe-inspiring reality to which we have been elevated by Jesus Christ through His Incarnation and Redemption, His Revelation and His Grace? Even leaving aside the religious blindness which comes from this "technological spirit," a man who is possessed by it is arrested in his intellectual life, and yet it is precisely in that life that man is created to the image of God. God's intellect is infinitely comprehensive, whereas the "technological spirit" makes every effort to restrict in man the free expansion of his intelligence.

The technologist, whether master or pupil, who would free himself from this limitation needs not only an education of mind that aims at depth of knowledge, but above all he needs a religious formation which, despite what is sometimes asserted, is the kind most apt to safeguard his thought from one-sided influences. Then the narrowness of his knowledge will be broken through; then creation will appear before him illumined in all its dimensions, especially when before the crib he will make an effort to comprehend *in all its breadth and length and height and depth the love of Christ.* Otherwise, this era of technological progress will achieve its monstrous masterpiece, making man into a giant of the physical world, at the expense of his soul, reduced to a pygmy in the realm of the supernatural and eternal.

### Influence of Technological Spirit

But this is not the only harm done by technological progress when it is accepted in the thinking of men as something autonomous and an end in itself. No one can fail to see the danger of a "technological concept of life," that is, considering life exclusively for its technological values, as an element and factor in technology. It has its repercussions both on the way modern men live and on their mutual relations.

Look for a moment at this spirit already at work among the

people, and reflect especially how it has changed the human and Christian concept of work, and what influence it exercises on legislation and administration. The people have welcomed, and rightly so, technological progress, because it eases the burden of toil and increases production. But also it must be admitted that if such a way of thinking is not kept within right bounds, the human and Christian concept of work necessarily becomes distorted. Likewise from this distorted concept of life, and hence of work, men come to consider leisure time as an end in itself, instead of looking upon it and using it as reasonable rest and recreation, bound up essentially with the rhythm of an ordered life, in which rest and toil alternate in a single pattern and are integrated into a single harmony.

More evident still is the influence of the "technological spirit" applied to work, when Sunday loses its unique dignity as the day devoted to the worship of God and to physical and spiritual rest for the individual and the family, and becomes instead merely one of the free days in the course of the week, which can even be different for each member of the family, according to the greater profit one hopes to derive from such a mechanical distribution of material and human energy, or when professional work becomes so dependent on, and subordinate to the "efficiency" of the machine and of the tools of labor that the worker is rapidly exhausted, as though one year of working at his trade were to use up the energy required in two or more years of normal life.

## Personal Dignity

We refrain from showing more at length how this system, inspired exclusively by technological considerations, contrary to what was expected of it, causes a waste of material resources, no less than of the principal sources of energy— among which certainly man himself must be included—and how in consequence it must in the long run prove a costly burden on the world economy. We cannot, however, omit calling attention to the new form of materialism which the "technological spirit" introduces into life. It will be sufficient to indicate that it empties life of its meaning, since technology affects the combined spiritual and material values connected with his nature and personal dignity. Wherever technology reigns supreme, there human society will be transformed into a colorless mass, into something impersonal and without substance, and this contrary to the clear designs of nature and of the Creator.

## Threat to the Family

Undoubtedly, large portions of humanity have not yet been touched by such a "technological concept of life"; but it is to be feared that wherever technological progress penetrates without safeguards, there the danger of the aberrations censured above will not be long in showing itself. And with particular anxiety We consider the danger threatening the family, which is the strongest principle of order in society. For the family is capable of inspiring in its members innumerable daily acts of service, binds them to the home and hearth with the bonds of affection, and awakes in each of them a love of the family traditions in the production and conservation of useful goods. Wherever on the contrary the technological concept of life penetrates, the family loses its personal bond of unity, is deprived of its warmth and stability. It remains united only to the extent that is demanded by the exigencies of mass production, which is being pursued with more and more insistence. No longer is the family a work of love and a haven for souls; it is rather a desolate depot, according to the circumstances, either of manpower for mass production, or of consumers of the material goods produced.

## Technological Conception of Life

The "technological concept of life" is therefore nothing else than a particular form of materialism insofar as it offers a mathematical formula and utilitarian calculations as the ultimate answer to the question of existence. Because of this, modern technological development, as if conscious of being lost in darkness, is showing uneasiness and anxiety, experienced especially by those who engage in the feverish search for industrial methods ever more complicated, ever more hazardous. A world guided in this way cannot be said to be illumined by that light, nor animated by that life which the Word, the splendor of God's glory, by becoming man, has come to communicate to men.

## Gravity of the Present Hour

As Our eyes constantly scan the horizon in anxious search of some enduring signs of brightening (if not of that full light of which the Prophet spoke), We see instead the grey vision of a still unsettled Europe, where the materialism of which We have spoken, instead of solving, only aggravates its fundamental problems. These problems are intimately connected with peace and order in the whole world.

In truth, materialism does not threaten this Continent more seriously than other regions of the world. On the contrary We think that countries which have been overtaken late and unexpectedly by the rapid progress of technology are more exposed to the dangers alluded to, and more vitally disturbed in their moral and psychological equilibrium—for the reason that imported development, not flowing with a constant motion but proceeding by discontinuous jumps, does not meet with any strong walls of resistance, of counterpoise, of adjustment, either in the maturity of individuals or in the culture of tradition.

Nevertheless, Our grave fears for Europe are stirred by the repeated disappointments which the sincere desire for peace and a relaxation of tension cherished by these nations has for years met with; this is also due to a material approach to the problem of peace. We are thinking particularly of those who judge that the question of peace is technological, and consider the life of individuals and nations from a technico-economical standpoint. The materialistic idea of life threatens to become the rule of conduct of certain busy peace agents and the mainspring of their pacifist policy. They think that the secret of the solution lies in bringing material prosperity to all nations through constant increase in productivity and in the standard of living. A hundred years ago, another similar formula aroused the absolute confidence of statesmen: with free trade, lasting peace.

## The Right Road Toward True Peace

But no materialism was ever an apt means to establish peace. For peace is above all an attitude of the mind, and only secondarily an harmonious equilibrium of external forces. So it is an error of principle to entrust peace to a modern materialism that corrupts the essence of man and stifles his personal and spiritual life. Experience induces the same distrust, for it proves that the costly distribution of technical and economical forces more or less equally between two parties causes reciprocal intimidation, from which would result a peace based on fear, not that peace which is security for the future.

We must repeat it again and again, and persuade those who are easily deceived by the mirage of a peace consisting in an abundance of temporal goods, that secure and lasting peace is above all a question of spiritual unity and of moral dispositions. This peace demands, under pain of further catastrophes for mankind, that there be discarded that false autonomy of material forces which today are hardly different from war materials. The present state of affairs will not improve, unless all nations recognize the common spiritual and moral ends of humanity; unless they help each other to attain them, and, as a consequence, unless they mutually agree to oppose the cause of division reigning among them in the discrepancy of the standard of living and of productivity.

## The Union of the Countries of Europe

This can and should be done in Europe, by forming the continental union of its peoples, different indeed, but geographically and historically bound together. A strong encouragement to such a union is the manifest failure of the contrary policy, and the fact that the ordinary people in these countries expect it and consider it necessary and possible. The time, then, seems mature for the idea to become reality. Hence, We exhort to action first and foremost Christian statesmen, deeming it sufficient to recall to them that Christianity always considered it its task to promote every sort of peaceful union between nations. Why continue to hesitate? The end is clear; the needs of nations are obvious to all. If any one asks in advance for an absolute guarantee of success, the answer is that there is a risk, but a necessary one; a risk in keeping with present possibilities—a reasonable risk. One must proceed certainly with caution, advance with well-calculated steps; but why distrust at this point the high degree of skill attained by political science and practice? They are sufficiently capable of foreseeing the obstacles and preparing the remedies. The supreme incitement to action is the gravity of the moment through which Europe is struggling; there is no security for her without risk. To demand absolute certainty is to fail in good will toward Europe.

## Genuine Christian Social Action

With this end ever in view, We also exhort Christian statesmen to action within their own nations. If order does not reign in the internal life of nations, it is vain to expect European union and the security of peace in the world. In times like ours, when mistakes easily become catastrophes, a Christian statesman cannot—today less than ever—aggravate social tensions in his own country by dramatically emphasizing them, neglecting a positive approach to problems, and allowing himself to lose sight of a just estimate of what is reasonably possible. He must have tenacity in putting into practice Christian social doctrine, tenacity and faith in his own principles more than the adversaries show in their false tenets. If, during the past hundred years or more, Christian social doctrine has developed and borne fruit in the practical policies of many nations—unfortunately not all—those who have come on the scene very late have no reason today to complain that Christianity leaves something to be desired in the social field, which, according to them, must be supplied by a so-called revolution in Christian consciences. The failure is not in Christianity, but in the minds of her accusers.

Thus, the Christian statesman does not serve the cause of national or international peace when he abandons the solid basis of objective experience and clear-cut principles and transforms himself, as it were, into a divinely inspired herald of a new social world, helping to confuse even more minds already uncertain. He is guilty of this fault who thinks he can experiment with the social order, and especially he who is not resolved to make the legitimate authority of the state and observance of the just laws prevail among all classes of society. Is it, perhaps, necessary to demonstrate that weakness in authority, more than any other weakness, undermines the strength of a nation, and that the weakness of one nation brings with it the weakness of Europe and imperils the general peace?

## The Authority of the State

One must, then, react against the false opinion according to which the reasonable power of authority and of law necessarily opens the road to tyranny. We Ourselves some years ago at Christmas time (December 24, 1944), speaking of democracy, noted that in a democratic state, no less than in any other well-ordered state, authority should be real and effective. Of course, democracy aims at putting into practice the ideal of liberty; but the ideal liberty is only that liberty which is far removed from license, that liberty which joins to the consciousness of one's own rights respect for the liberty, dignity and rights of others, and is conscious of one's own responsibility toward the common good. Naturally, this true democracy cannot exist and thrive except in an atmosphere of respect for God and observance of His Commandments, as well as of the Christian solidarity or brotherhood.

## Conclusion

In this way, beloved sons and daughters, the work of establishing the peace, promised to men in the splendor of Bethlehem's night, will be accomplished in the end by the good will of everyone individually, but it begins in the fulness of Truth Incarnate Who dispels darkness from the mind. Just as in creation *in the beginning was the Word*, and not created material things, not their laws nor their power and abundance, so in the execution of the mysterious task entrusted to men by the Creator, they must put at the beginning this same Word, His truth, His charity and His grace. This hierarchy of values is what We wished to explain to you, and We urge you to safeguard it firmly. In this history supports Us, and you know she is a good teacher. Nevertheless, it would seem that in the face of her lessons, those who do not listen to her and are hence prone to attempt new adventures, are more numerous than the victims of their folly. We have spoken in the name of these victims who still weep over near and distant tombs, and, indeed, have to fear that yet others are being made ready; those who are still living amid ruins, and at the same time see new destruction approaching, those who still are waiting for the return of prisoners and dispersed loved ones, and yet are living in fear for their own freedom. The danger is so great that from the cradle of the eternal Prince of Peace We have had to utter very grave words, even at the risk of provoking still keener fears. But one may always hope that, with the Grace of God, it will be a salutary and efficacious fear, that will lead to the union of nations and thus strengthen the peace.

# The Threat of ABC Warfare*

*(Address to the Peoples Assembled in St. Peter's Square, April 18, 1954)*

IF everything is peace and joy in heaven, on earth the cold hard facts are quite otherwise. Here, in place of the serene joy, whose secret Christ has revealed, anxiety and the alarm of people increases from year to year because of the fear of a third world conflict—the fear of a tomorrow of horror in which they might find themselves abandoned to the mercies of new, destructive armaments, unheard of in their capacity of violence.

Of such weapons We have already spoken; of such We have expressed Our fear as early as February, 1943. For they are of a type that could bring about "a dangerous catastrophe for our entire planet" (*Acta Apostolicae Sedis*, 1943, page 75). They could cause the total extermination of all life, animal and vegetable, and of all the works of man over ever-widening regions. And now, these new weapons, because of artificial radio-active isotopes of extended average life, are capable of infecting for a long period of time even the very atmosphere, the world's surface, the ocean itself—and all this even in areas far from the places directly hit by the nuclear explosives. As a consequence there now rises before the eyes of a terrified world the vision of destruction on a gigantic scale—the vision of vast territories rendered uninhabitable and useless to mankind.

And there is the possibility of further biological consequences that can be brought about by these weapons, either

---

* Translation from *The Pope Speaks.*

234

by the mutations effected in micro-organisms and cells, or by reason of the uncertain outcome which a prolonged radioactive stimulus could have on major organisms, not excluding man and his descendants. In this connection We must not omit highlighting the danger to future generations that could result from these possible mutations—either such biological changes as are already possible or could be brought about in the future by some new processes and which could completely twist all those things which go to make up man's hereditary constitution. We call attention to the fact that among these deviations there probably are or will be pathogenic factors which are the causes of transmissible diseases or even of monstrous deformities.

For Our part, We will tirelessly endeavor to bring about, by means of international agreements—always recognizing the principle of legitimate self-defense (cf., *Acta Apostolicae Sedis,* 1953, pages 748–49)—the effective proscription and banishment of atomic, biological and chemical warfare (*ibidem,* page 749). At the same time we ask: how long will men continue to withdraw themselves from the saving light of the Resurrection and persist in expecting security from the death-dealing explosions of new tools for war? How long will they oppose their designs of hatred and death to the precepts of love and to the promises of life offered by the Divine Saviour? When will the rulers of nations understand that peace does not exist in an exasperating and costly relationship of mutual terror? Rather does peace lie in that greatest of Christian virtues—universal charity. And especially is it found in the virtue of justice—a justice voluntarily observed rather than extorted by force—and in confidence which is truly inspired rather than a mere pretence!

When will the world's scientists turn their wonderful discoveries of the great forces found in matter exclusively to peaceful purposes? When will they use those forces to give to human efforts, at slight cost, powers which will alleviate scarcities and correct unequal geographic distribution of the sources of goods and of work? When will they use those discovered powers for offering new possibilities to the medical sciences, to agriculture, and give to people new sources of prosperity and well-being?

# War and Peace*

*(Address to Delegates to the Eighth Congress of the
World Medical Association, in Rome, September 30, 1954)*

THAT the doctor has a role during war, and a privileged role,
is obvious. At no other time are there so many to be cared for
and cured among soldiers and civilians and friends and enemies. It is necessary to concede to the doctor, without restrictions, the natural right to intervene where his help is needed
and also to guarantee this to him by means of international
conventions. It would be an aberration of the judgment and
the heart to want to deny medical aid to the enemy and let
him die.

Has not the doctor also a role to play in producing, perfecting and increasing the methods of modern warfare, in
particular the methods of ABC warfare? One cannot answer
this question without having first resolved this other one: Is
modern "total war," especially ABC warfare, permissible in
principle? There can be no doubt, particularly in view of the
horrors and immense sufferings caused by modern warfare,
that to unleash it without a just cause (that is to say, without
its being forced upon one by an obvious, extremely serious
and otherwise unavoidable injustice) constitutes a "crime"
worthy of the most severe national and international sanctions.

One cannot even in principle pose the question of the lawfulness of atomic, bacteriological and chemical warfare except
in the case where it must be judged as indispensable in order
to defend oneself under the circumstances pointed out above.
Even then, however, one must strive to avoid it by all possible means through international understandings or to impose limits on its use that are so clear and rigorous that its
effects remain restricted to the strict demands of defense.
When, moreover, putting this method to use involves such an
extension of the evil that it entirely escapes from the control
of man, its use must be rejected as immoral. Here there
would no longer be a question of "defense" against injustice
or a necessary "safeguarding" of legitimate possessions, but

---

* Translation from National Catholic Welfare Conference News.

the pure and simple annihilation of all human life within the radius of action. This is not permitted for any reason whatsoever.

## ABC Warfare Contrary to Basic Duty

Let us return to the doctor. If ever, within the compass of the limits already indicated, a modern ABC war can be justified, the question of the morally lawful collaboration of the doctor can then be raised. But you will be in agreement with Us: one prefers not to see the doctor occupied with a task of this sort. It is in too great a contrast to his basic duty: to give aid and cure, not to do injury or kill.

. . . The doctor is the enemy of war and the promoter of peace. As he is ready to heal the wounds of war, once they already exist, so should he do all he can to prevent them.

Mutual good will always allows states to avoid war as the final means of settling differences between themselves. Several days ago We again expressed Our desire that any war be punished at the international level if is not absolutely necessary for the self-defense of a community seriously threatened by an injustice that cannot be prevented in any other way. Even such a war, however, must be waged at the risk of giving a free hand in international affairs to brute violence and lack of conscience. It is not enough, therefore, to have to defend oneself against just any injustice in order to justify resorting to the violent means of war. When the damages caused by war are not comparable to those of "tolerated injustice," one may have a duty to "suffer the injustice."

What We have just discussed applies especially to ABC warfare—atomic, biological and chemical. As to the question of knowing whether it (ABC warfare) can become clearly necessary in *self-defense* against ABC warfare, let it suffice for Us to have posed it here. The answer can be deduced from the same principles which are today decisive for permitting war in general. In any case, another question arises first, is it not possible through international understandings to proscribe and avert ABC warfare?

After the horrors of two world conflicts We do not have to remind you that any apotheosis of war is to be condemned as an aberration of mind and heart. Certainly spiritual strength and bravery, even to the point of giving one's life when duty demands it, are great virtues; but to want to start a war because it is the school of great virtues and the occasion for practicing them must be characterized as a crime and madness.

## Doctor Cannot Support Injustice

What We have said shows the direction in which one will find the answer to that other question: may the doctor put his knowledge and activity at the service of ABC warfare? "Injustice he can never support, even in the service of his own country, and when that type of war constitutes an injustice, the doctor may not take part in it" (Address to delegates to 16th International Congress on Military Medicine, October 19, 1953). . . . Is there any moral limit to the "medical interests of the community" in content or extension? Are there "full powers" over the living man in every serious medical case? Does it raise barriers that are still valid in the interests of science or of the individual? Or, stated differently, can public authority, on which rests responsibility for the common good, give the doctor the power to experiment on the individual in the interests of science and the community in order to discover and try out new methods and procedures when these experiments transgress the right of the individual to dispose of himself? In the interests of the community can public authority really limit or even suppress the right of the individual over his body and life, his bodily and psychic integrity?

To forestall an objection We assume that it is a question of serious research, of honest efforts to promote the theory and practice of medicine, not of a maneuver serving as a scientific pretext to mask other ends and achieve them with impunity.

In regard to these questions many people have been of the opinion, and are still of the opinion today, that the answer must be in the affirmative. To give weight to their contention they cite the fact that the individual is subordinated to the community, that the good of the individual must give way to the common good and be sacrificed to it. They add that the sacrifice of an individual for the purposes of research and scientific investigation profits the individual in the long run.

## Horrors in Name of Science

The great postwar trials brought to light a terrifying number of documents testifying to the sacrifice of the individual in the "medical interests of the community." In the minutes of these trials one finds testimony and reports showing how, with the consent, and at times even under the formal order, of public authority, certain research centers systematically demanded to be furnished with persons from concentration camps for their medical experiments. One finds how they were delivered to such centers, so many men, so many women, so many for one experiment, so many for another. There are reports on the conduct and the results of such experiments, of the subjective and objective symptoms observed during the different phases of the experiments. One cannot read these reports without feeling a profound compassion for the victims, many of whom went to their deaths, and without being frightened by such an aberration of the human mind and heart. But We can also add that those responsible for these atrocious deeds did no more than to reply in the affirmative to the question We have asked and to accept the practical consequences of their affirmation.

At this point is the interest of the individual subordinated to the community's medical interests, or is there here a transgression, perhaps in good faith, against the most elementary demands of the natural law, a transgression that permits no medical research?

One would have to shut one's eyes to reality to believe that at the present time one could find no one in the medical world to hold and defend the ideas that gave rise to the facts We have cited. It is enough to follow for a short time the reports on medical efforts and experiments to convince oneself of the contrary. Involuntarily one asks oneself what has authorized, and what could ever authorize, any doctor's daring to try such an experiment. The experiment is described in all its stages and effects with calm objectivity. What is verified and what is not is noted. But there is not a word on its moral legality. Nevertheless, this question exists, and one cannot suppress it by passing it over in silence.

In the above-mentioned cases, insofar as the moral justification of the experiments rests on the mandate of public authority, and therefore on the subordination of the individual to the community, of the individual's welfare to the common welfare, it is based on an erroneous explanation of this principle. It must be noted that, in his personal being, man is not finally ordered to usefulness to society. On the contrary, the community exists for man.


# Co-Existence: Its Meaning and Its Future*

(*Christmas Message Broadcast to the Whole World, December 24, 1954*)

. . . ACCORDING to many reports, the cold war has slowly been replaced by a period of decreased tension between the opposing parties, as if they were giving each other a longer breathing space; and not without some irony, this decreased tension has been given the name "cold peace.". . .

In fact, in the political world, what is meant by "cold peace" if not the mere co-existence of various peoples based on fear of each other and on mutual disillusionment? Now it is clear that simple co-existence does not deserve the name of peace, to which Christian tradition, formed in the school of the lofty intellects of Augustine and Thomas Aquinas, has come to apply the definition: *"the tranquility of order."* Cold peace is only a provisional calm, whose duration is conditional upon the changeable sensation of fear and upon the variable calculation of present strength; while it has about it nothing of true "order," which presupposes a series of relationships converging towards a common purpose that is right and just. Besides, by excluding all bonds of a spiritual nature between people so fragmentarily co-existing, cold peace falls far short of that which was preached and desired by the Divine Master; for His peace is founded on a union of souls in the same truth

---

* Translation from *The Pope Speaks.*

and in charity. It is defined by Saint Paul as the *peace of God* which binds in the first place men's minds and hearts, and it is put into practice by acts of harmonious collaboration in every field of life, not excluding the political, social, and economic fields. . . .

## Co-Existence in Fear

It is a common impression, derived from the simple observation of facts, that the principal foundation on which the present state of relative calm rests, is fear. Each of the groups, into which the human family is divided, tolerates the existence of the other, because it does not wish itself to perish. By thus avoiding a fatal risk, the two groups do not live together; they co-exist. It is not a state of war, but neither is it peace: it is a cold calm. Each of the two groups smarts under the fear of the other's military and economic power. In both of them there is a grave apprehension of the catastrophic effect of the latest weapons.

Each follows with anxious attention the technical development of the other's armaments and the productive capacity of its economy, while it entrusts to its own propaganda the task of turning the other's fear to its advantage by strengthening and extending its meaning. It seems that in the field of concrete politics reliance is no longer placed on other rational or moral principles, for these, after so many delusions, have been swept away by an extreme collapse into skepticism.

The most obvious absurdity of the situation resultant from such a wretched state of affairs is this: current political practice, while dreading war as the greatest of catastrophes, at the same time puts all its trust in war, as if it were the only expedient for subsistence and the only means of regulating international relations. This is, in a certain sense, placing trust in that which is loathed above all other things.

## A New Approach

On the other hand, the above-mentioned political practice has led many, even those responsible for government, to revise the entire problem of peace and war and has induced them to ask themselves sincerely if deliverance from war and the ensuring of peace ought not to be sought on higher and more humane levels than on that dominated exclusively by terror. Thus it is that there has been an increase in the numbers of those who rebel against the idea of having to be satisfied with mere co-existence, of renouncing relationships of a more vital nature with the other group, and against being forced to live all the days of their lives in an atmosphere of enervating fear. Hence they have come back to consider the problem of peace and war as a fact involving a higher and Christian responsibility before God and the moral law.

Undoubtedly in this changed manner of approach to the problem there is an element of "fear" as a restraint against war and a stimulus to peace; but here the fear is that salutary fear of God—Guarantor and Vindicator of the moral law—and, therefore, as the psalmist teaches, it is the beginning of wisdom.

Once the problem is elevated to this higher plane, which alone is worthy of rational creatures, there again clearly appears the absurdity of that doctrine which held sway in the political schools of the last few decades: namely, that war is one of many admissible forms of political action, the necessary, and as it were the natural, outcome of irreconcilable disputes between two countries; that war, therefore, is a fact bearing no relation to any kind of moral responsibility. It is likewise apparent how absurd and inadmissible is the principle—also so long accepted—according to which a ruler, who declares war, would only be guilty of having made a political error, should the war be lost. But he could in no case be accused of moral guilt and of crime for not having conserved the peace when he had the power to do so.

It was precisely this absurd and immoral concept of war which rendered vain Our efforts to uphold in both parties the will to continue negotiations in the fatal weeks of 1939. War was then thought of as a die, to be cast with greater or less caution and skill, and not as a moral fact involving obligation in conscience and higher responsibilities. It required tombs and ruins without number to reveal the true nature of war: namely, that it was not a luckier or less lucky gamble between conflicting interests but a tragedy, spiritual more than material, for millions of men; that it was not a risking of some possessions, but a loss of all: a fact of enormous gravity.

## First Steps to Truth

How is it possible—many at that time asked with the simplicity and truth of common sense—that, while every individual feels within himself an urgent sense of moral responsibility for his own most ordinary acts, the dreadful fact of war, which is also the fruit of the free act of somebody's will, can evade the dominion of conscience, and that there be no judge to whom its innocent victims may have recourse? In the atmosphere of that time, when people were beginning to return to common sense, widespread approval was given Our cry "war against war," with which in 1944, We declared Our opposition to the pure formalism of political action and to doctrines of war which take no account of God or of His commandments. That salutary return to common sense, instead of being weakened, became more profound and more widespread in the years of the cold war, perhaps because prolonged experience made more clearly evident the absurdity of a life lived under the incubus of fear. Thus the cold peace, with all its incoherences and uneasiness, shows signs of taking the first steps towards an authentic moral order and towards a recognition of the elevated doctrine of the Church regarding just and unjust war, and the licitness and illicitness of recourse to arms.

This goal will assuredly be attained if, on one side and the other, men will once again sincerely, almost religiously, come to consider war as an object of the moral order, whose violation constitutes in fact a culpability which will not go unpunished. In the concrete this goal will be attained if statesmen, before weighing the advantages and risks of their decisions, will recognize that they are personally subject to eternal moral laws, and will treat the problem of war as a question of conscience before God.

In the conditions of our times, there is no other way to liberate the world from its agonizing incubus except by a return to the fear of God, which in no way debases the man who willingly submits to it; rather, it saves him from the infamy of that awful crime—unnecessary war. And who can express astonishment if peace and war thus prove to be closely connected with religious truth? Everything that is, is of God:

the root of all evil consists precisely in separating things from their beginning and their end.

Hence also it becomes clear that pacifist efforts or propaganda originating from those who deny all belief in God—if indeed not undertaken as an artful expedient to obtain the tactical effect of creating excitement and confusion—is always very dubious and incapable of lessening or of eliminating the anguished sense of fear.

## Two Possible Prospects

The present co-existence in fear has thus only two possible prospects before it: either it will raise itself to a co-existence in fear of God, and thence to a truly peaceful living-together, inspired and protected by the Divine moral order; or else it will shrivel more and more into a frozen paralysis of international life, the grave dangers of which are even now foreseeable.

In fact, prolonged restraint of the natural expansion of the life of peoples can ultimately lead them to that same desperate outlet that it is desired to avoid: war. No people, furthermore, could support indefinitely a race of armaments without disastrous repercussions being felt in its normal economic development. The very agreements directed to imposing a limitation on armaments would be in vain. Without the moral foundation of fear of God, they would become, if ever reached, a source of renewed mutual distrust.

There remains, therefore, the auspicious and lightsome other way which, based upon the fear of God and aided by Him, leads to true peace, which is sincerity, warmth and life, and is thus worthy of Him Who has been given to us that men might have life in Him and have it more abundantly.

Although the "cold war"—and the same is true of the "cold peace"—keeps the world in a harmful state of division, yet it does not, up to the present, prevent an intense rhythm of life from pulsing therein. It is true that this is a life developing almost exclusively in the economic field. It is, however, undeniable that economics, taking advantage of the pressing progress of modern techniques, has by feverish activity attained surprising results, of such a nature as to foreshadow a profound transformation in the lives of all peoples, even those heretofore considered rather backward. Admiration unquestionably cannot be withheld for what it has done and what it promises to do.

### Exaggerated Trust in Economics

Nevertheless, economics, with its apparently unlimited ability to produce goods without number, and with the multiplicity of its relationships, exercises over many of our contemporaries a fascination superior to its potentiality, and extends to fields extraneous to economics. The error of placing such trust in modern economics is again shared in common by the two camps into which the world is today divided. In one of these, it is taught that, since man has given proof of such great power as to create the marvellous technico-economical composite of which he boasts today, he will also be able to organize the liberation of human life from all the privations and evils from which it suffers, and in this way effect a kind of self-redemption. On the other hand, the conception gains ground in the opposing camp that the solution of the problem of peace must be sought in economics, and particularly in a specific form thereof, that of free exchange.

We have already had occasion at other times to expose the baselessness of such teachings. About a hundred years ago followers of the free commerce system expected wonderful things from it, attributing to it an almost magical power. One of its most ardent converts did not hesitate to compare the principle of free exchange, insofar as its effects in the moral world are concerned, with the principle of gravity which rules the physical world, and he attributed to it, as its proper effect, the drawing of men closer together, the elimination of antagonism based on race, faith, or language, and the unity of all human beings in unalterable peace. (Cf. Richard Cobden, *Speeches on Questions of Public Policy*, London, Macmillan and Co., 1870: Vol. 1, pp. 362–366.)

### Primacy of Moral World

The course of events has shown how deceitful is the illusion of entrusting peace to free exchange alone. Nor would the result be otherwise in the future if there were to persist that blind faith which confers on economics an imaginary mystic force. At present, moreover, there are lacking those foundations of fact which could in any way warrant the over-rosy hopes nourished today, as in the past, by followers of this teaching. As a matter of fact, while, in one of the camps which co-exist in cold peace, this highly vaunted economic freedom does not in reality yet exist, it is, in the other, completely rejected as an absurd principle. There is, between the two, a diametrical opposition in their ways of conceiving the very fundamentals of life—an opposition which cannot be reconciled by purely economic forces. Nay more, if there are—as there actually are—relations of cause and effect between the moral world and the economic world, they must be so ordered that primacy be assigned to the former, that is, the moral world which must authoritatively permeate with its spirit the social economy. Once this scale of values has been established and its actual exercise permitted, economics will, insofar as it is able, consolidate the moral world and confirm the spiritual postulates and forces of peace.

On the other hand, the economic factor might place serious obstacles in the way of peace—particularly of a cold peace, in the sense of an equilibrium between groups—if, employing erroneous systems, it were to weaken one of the groups. This could occur if, among other eventualities, individual people of one group were to engage, without consideration or regard for others, in a ceaseless increase of production, and a constant raising of their own living standard. In such a case, an upsurge of resentment and rivalry on the part of neighboring peoples would be inevitable, and consequently also the weakening of the entire group.

Prescinding from this particular consideration, however, one must be convinced that economic relationships between nations will be factors of peace insofar as they will obey the norms of natural law, will be inspired by love, will have due regard for other peoples and will be sources of help. Let it be held for certain that in relations between men, even merely economic relations, nothing is produced spontaneously—as does occur in nature which is subject to necessary laws—but everything depends substantially on the spirit. Only the spirit, the image of God and the executor of His designs, can establish order and harmony on earth, and it will succeed in doing so to the same extent that it becomes the faithful interpreter and docile instrument of the only Saviour Jesus Christ, Who is Himself Peace.

## False Principles of Unity

Moreover, in another matter even more delicate than that of economics, error is shared by the two camps co-existing in the cold peace: an error, namely, regarding the principles which animate their respective unity. One of the camps bases its strong internal cohesion on a false idea, an idea, moreover, violating primary human and Divine rights, yet at the same time efficacious; while the other, forgetful that it already possesses an idea that is true and has been successfully tested in the past, seems instead to be tending towards political principles which are evidently destructive of unity.

## The Nationalistic State

During this last decade since the war, a great yearning for spiritual renovation urged souls: to unite Europe strongly, the impetus coming from the natural living conditions of her peoples, with the purpose of putting an end to the traditional rivalries between one and another, and of assuring a united protection for their independence and their peaceful development. This noble idea did not present motives for complaints or diffidence to the world outside of Europe, in the measure that this outside world was favorably disposed to Europe. It was also believed that Europe would have easily found within herself the animating idea for her unity. But the succeeding events and recent accords which, as is believed, have opened the way to a cold peace, no longer have for a basis the ideal of a more extensive European unification. Many, in fact, believe that the governing policy is for a return to a kind of nationalistic state, closed within itself, centralizing therein its forces, unsettled in its choice of alliances and, consequently, no less perilous than that which had its time of highest development during the last century.

Too soon have been forgotten the enormous mass of lives sacrificed and of goods extorted by this type of state, and the crushing economic and spiritual burdens imposed by it. But the real error consists in confusing national life in its proper

247

sense with nationalistic politics: the first, the right and prized possession of a people, may and should be promoted; the second, as a germ infinitely harmful, will never be sufficiently repelled. National life is, in itself, that operative composite of all the values of civilization, which are proper and characteristic of a particular group, for whose spiritual unity they constitute, as it were, its bond. At the same time, it enriches, as its own contribution, the culture of all humanity.

In essence, therefore, national life is something not political; and this is confirmed by the fact that, as history and practice demonstrate, it can develop alongside of others, within the same state, just as it can also extend itself beyond the political frontiers of the same state. National life became a principle of dissolution within the community of peoples only when it began to be exploited as a means for political purposes; when, that is to say, the controlling and centralizing state made of nationality the basis of its force of expansion. Behold then the nationalistic state, the seed of rivalries and the fomenter of discord.

It is clear that, if the European community were to move forward on this road, its cohesion would become, as a result, quite weakened in comparison with that of the opposing group. Its weakness would certainly be revealed on that day of future peace destined to regulate with foresight and justice the question still in abeyance. Nor should it be said that, in new circumstances, the dynamism of the nationalistic state no longer represents a danger for other peoples being deprived, in the majority of cases, of effective economic and military power. For even when the dynamism of an imaginary nationalistic power is expressed in sentiment rather than exercised with actions, it is equally offensive to the mind; it feeds on distrust and breeds suspicion within alliances, impedes reciprocal understanding and thereby loyal collaboration and mutual help, to the same extent as it would if it had at its command effective force.

### The Natural Law: True Bond of Unity

What would become, then, in such circumstances, of the common bond which is supposed to bind individual states in unity? What kind of a great and efficacious idea would that be which would render them strong in defense and effective in a common program for civilization?

Some would like to see it as agreement in the rejection of that way of life destructive of liberty, proper to the other group. Without a doubt, aversion to slavery is worthy of note, but it is of negative value, and does not possess the force to stimulate the human spirit to action with the same efficacy as does a positive and absolute idea.

Such an idea, instead, could be a love of the liberty willed by God and in accord with the needs of the common good, or else the ideal of natural law, as the foundation of an organization of the state and of states.

Only these, and like spiritual ideas, acquired now for many long centuries as part of the tradition of a Christian Europe, can sustain comparison—and moreover emerge victorious in it, to the extent that these ideas are really lived—with the false idea, though concrete and effective, which apparently holds together in cohesion, not without the aid of violence, the other group—the idea, namely, of an earthly paradise to be attained as soon as a determined form of social organization would be realized. Though illusory, this idea has succeeded in creating, at least outwardly, a compact and hardy unity, and is being accepted by the uninformed masses; it knows how to inspire its members to action and voluntarily to make sacrifices. The same idea, within the political framework which expresses it, gives to its directors a strong capacity for seduction, and to the adept the audacity to penetrate as a vanguard even into the ranks of the other side.

Europe, on the other hand, still awaits the reawakening of her own consciousness. Meanwhile, in what she stands for—such as the wisdom and organization of associated living and as an influence of culture—she seems to be losing ground in not a few regions of the earth.

Verily, such a retreat concerns the promoters of a nationalistic policy, who are forced to fall back before adversaries who have taken over the same methods and made them their own. Especially among some peoples until now considered colonial, the process of organic maturation towards an autonomous polity, which Europe should have guided with perception and care, was rapidly turned into nationalistic out-breaks, greedy for power. It must be confessed that even these unforeseen eruptions, damaging to the prestige and interests of Europe, are, at least in part, the fruit of her own bad example.

Does this mean only that Europe has momentarily lost her way? In any case, that which must remain, and without doubt will remain, is the genuine Europe, that is, that composite of all the spiritual and civil values which the West has accumulated, drawing from the riches of individual nations to dispense them to the whole world. Europe, conforming to the dispositions of Divine Providence, will again be able to be the nursery and dispenser of those values, if she will know how to resume wisely her proper spiritual character and to repudiate the divinization of power.

Just as in the past the well-springs of her strength and of her culture were eminently Christian, so now too will she have to impose on herself a return to God and to Christian ideals, if she is to find again the basis and bond of her unity and true greatness. And if these well-springs seem to be in part dried up, if this bond is threatened with rupture and the foundation of her unity is crumbling, the historical and present responsibility falls back upon each of the two groups who find themselves now facing each other in anguish and mutual fear.

The motives ought to be enough for men of good will, in one and the other camp, to desire, to pray, and to act, in order that humanity may be liberated from the intoxication of power and of pre-eminence, and in order that the Spirit of God may be the Sovereign Ruler of the world, where once Almighty God chose no other means for saving those whom He loved than that of becoming a weak Babe in a poor manger. *A child is born to us, and a son is given to us, and the government is upon his shoulder.*

### Co-Existence in Truth

Although it is a sad thing to note that the present rupture of the human race took place, in the beginning, between men who knew and adored the same Saviour, Jesus Christ, still there appears to Us to be a well founded hope that, in His name too, a bridge of peace may yet be built between opposing shores, and the common bond, so sadly broken, be re-established.

There is, in fact, some hope that today's co-existence may bring mankind closer to peace. In order, however, that this expectation be justified, such co-existence must in some way be co-existence in truth. Now a bridge cannot be built in truth between these two separate worlds unless it be founded on the human beings living in one and the other of these worlds, and not on their governmental or social systems. This is so because, while one of the two parties still strives in large measure, whether consciously or unconsciously, to preserve the natural law, the system prevailing in the other has completely abandoned this basis.

A one-sided supernaturalism might refuse entirely to take such an attitude into consideration, alleging the reason that we live in a redeemed world and are therefore withdrawn from the natural order; or some might say that the collectivist character of that system ought to be recognized as a "historical truth," in the sense that it too corresponds to the will of God —but these are errors to which a Catholic can by no means submit. The right road is quite different.

In both camps, there are millions in whom the imprint of Christ is preserved in a more or less active degree; they too, no less than faithful and fervent believers, should be called upon to collaborate towards a renewed basis of unity for the human race. It is true that, in one of the two camps, the voice of those who stand resolutely for truth, for love and for the spirit, is forcibly suffocated by the public authorities, while in the other people suffer from excessive timidity in proclaiming aloud their worthy desires. It is, however, the duty of a policy of unification to encourage the former and to make heard the sentiments of the latter.

Particularly in that camp where it is not a crime to oppose error, statesmen should have greater confidence in themselves; they should give proof to others of a more firm courage in foiling the maneuvers of the obscure forces which are still trying to establish power hegemonies, and they should also show more active wisdom in preserving and swelling the ranks of men of good will, especially of believers in God, who everywhere adhere in great numbers to the cause of peace.

It would certainly be an erroneous unification policy—if not actually treachery—to sacrifice in favor of nationalistic interests the racial minorities who are without strength to defend their supreme possessions, their faith, and their Christian culture. Whoever were to do this would not be worthy of confidence, nor would they be acting honorably if later, in cases where their own interests demanded it, they were to invoke religious values and respect for law.

### No Base in Materialism or Relativism

There are many who volunteer to lay the foundations of human unity. Since, however, these foundations, this bridge, must be of a spiritual nature, those sceptics and cynics are certainly not qualified for the task who, in accordance with doctrines of a more or less disguised materialism, reduce even the loftiest truths and the highest spiritual values to the level of physical reactions or consider them mere ideologies.

Nor are those apt for the task who do not recognize absolute truths nor admit moral obligations in the sphere of social life. These latter have already in the past—often unknowingly, by their abuse of freedom and by their destructive and unreasonable criticism—prepared an atmosphere favorable to dictatorship and oppression; now they push forward still more to obstruct the work of social and political pacification initiated under Christian inspiration.

In some places it happens not rarely that they raise their voices against those who, conscientiously, as Christians, take a rightful active interest in political problems and in public life in general. . . .

We would exhort primarily the Christians of nations where the Divine gift of peace is still enjoyed to do everything possible to hasten the hour of its universal reestablishment.

Let these convince themselves, above all, that the possession of truth, if it were to remain closed within themselves, would not be of service to the cause of peace; the truth must be lived, communicated, and applied to all phases of life.

# International Reconciliation*

*(Address to the Italian Study Center for International Reconciliation, October 13, 1955)*

. . . THE Conference of Geneva of last July, which at its beginning aroused so many hopes in the world, has brought to light the depths of the dissension among nations, and the difficulty which often exists in finding a way towards its healing.

It is essential to turn attention to the ever more extensive and deeper aspects of the psychology and character of nations, on the internal motives and differences which they reveal, and, at the same time, on the conflicts to which they can, and in fact too often do, lead. It is obvious that the preliminary study of these problems is fundamental to the work for peace, just as there are very important advantages to be gained by observing the changes of thought and sentiment to which nations are subject.

Now it is certain that the face of the world has been profoundly altered in many of its features in the course of the first half of this century—at national, economic, social, cultural, and ideological levels.

The international factor of the increased mutual interdependence among nations has reached an ever greater prominence. At the same time, however, national sentiment has been reawakened, in some places to the intensity of a first flame of fire, overcoming checks and obstacles.

In other places, it is the economic element which is the determining factor; and, in close connection with this, the sociological, both of these building on fixed theories and ideologies which have been developed side by side, though it still often remains difficult to discover whether the prevailing ideology is forming life, or vice versa.

On the other hand, since the economics, sociology, ideology and life of one people frequently differ from those of another, the very difference often produces sharp tensions between them, driving them sometimes to seek a solution in open warfare.

---

* Translation from *The Pope Speaks*.

## Lessons of History

In past ages international relations, whether conducing to or threatening peace, did not then have the extent and influence they have today.

A life, strictly limited and self-contained, was possible for individual peoples or small groups of peoples. In their contact with other peoples, in addition to the incipient movements and differences, there was lacking the free disposal of their own energies; consequently all remained more restricted both in place and in time.

The world empires prior to the Christian era, the Roman Empire itself, if measured by present day knowledge of the extent of the earth and of the human race, would be found more limited than those of the world today. Those world-States were certainly abounding in warlike activity, with the mutual relations which follow, and which in universal history, after the same fashion, are wont to be substantially repeated: "victors and vanquished," "the conquerors and the conquered."

The harshness of these relations varied, and the result endured for a longer or shorter time, but afterwards most commonly they lead to a more or less tolerable *modus vivendi*, especially when new generations, without personal experience of the sufferings of the preceding wars, took up the place of their elders and, above all, when the fact of living and working together had brought "victors and vanquished" step by step to a social, or even a family, intermingling.

This progressive decline and extinguishing of psychic tensions seems to be one of the laws of the psychology of nations, though there should certainly also be foreseen the possibility of the rise of new differences.

But, alas, this is not the sole aftermath of the wars of the past. History does not lack examples in which no reconciliation or relaxation of tension was arrived at; but the conflict, sometimes renewed more than once, reached its conclusion only with the annihilation or reduction to slavery, or the absolute impotence of the enemy.

## Community of Nations

In Our address to the 6th International Congress on penal law, on October 3, 1953 and to the Fifth National Congress of Italian Catholic Jurists on December 6, 1953, We touched on these and similar problems, while recognising that it is not possible to solve them with a simple Yes or No, we set out some directive principles for their interpretation and solution.

We then noted at that time as a fact, the tendency to form a Community of nations.

We observed that this should not ultimately derive from the enormous development of the means of communication and exchange, but from that inner impulse arising from the unity of origin, nature, and end, which manifestly has to contribute to the full development, willed by the Creator, of individuals, of nations, of the whole human family, by means of an ever-increasing collaboration, while all the time paying respect to the moral and cultural heritage of individual groups.

We then pointed out the manifold obstacles which stand in the way of an international community of nations, obstacles which increase with the number of the nations.

Such obstacles are the tendencies, innate or acquired, diverse and often contradictory—tendencies of nature predominantly spiritual, or of character predominantly physical—which operate in all fields of judgment, affection, and action. And equally, the questions of blood and race, of locality and climate, of education and custom, of language, history, and culture—all, in fine, that surrounds and moulds the individual man or nation.

In like manner, there are conditions of ownership and possession, of economic freedom and dependence, in which a nation lives or is forced to live, which, though they may not be the sole determining cause, nevertheless exercise a wide influence in all its thought, desire and action.

Add to these, those numerous natural inclinations or passions which play so large a part in the daily life of individuals. Though they incline to ends in themselves lawful, they do not possess any intrinsic standard of moderation and judgment. Lacking that, they have to draw on a higher control of the man himself, to avoid being changed into disrupting forces.

Such inclinations are self-attachment, the lust for power, the tendency to expand, to assimilate, to absorb.

## Religion and Fanaticism

Among the elements which the Community of States ought to hold in consideration, there is also religion. It can have, on the relations between States, an action deeply conciliatory and pacifying, but also, sometimes, divisive, and provocative. Religious wars have left their own stamp on history. Impulses of deep religious feeling and genuine enthusiasm could evoke heroic sacrifices; but the religious goal is not always maintained in its purity: often enough, somewhat earthly ambitions have been intermingled.

If, subsequently, under the pretext of religion, some wars were stirred up by hatred, they surpassed the other wars in horrors, cruelty, and destruction. Fanaticism, not religion, was then the real compelling force.

In bringing this first section of Our statement to an end, We can say this: notwithstanding the natural and ever more extensive and eager effort for the attainment of comprehensive international relations and legislation, with their obligations and lofty aims, there rise from the hearts of men and nations, from their rights—but not seldom desires and sentiments also perverse—from their secret objectives, from the world about them, from conditions without, from the often deep divergence of interests, there arise, We say, differences, tensions, clashes, finally actual warfare with its inevitable consequences for both belligerents.

It is this state of affairs which, in the course of history, has been repeated up to the present. It appears, therefore, that the time may have come in which educated humanity has to face sincerely the question whether it must resign itself to what, during the past, has seemed an inflexible law of history, or, on the contrary, try new ways and expend generous efforts in every sphere of life, to free the human race from the recurring burden of warfare.

This, then, ought to be the active interest of responsible governments. In this, the Church is ready to do her part, to apply her energies in accordance with the very command of her Divine Founder, with her maternal solicitude for all, towards everything that may bring about among nations the harmony that leads to peace.

## THE CHURCH'S PRINCIPLES OF CONCILIATION FOR THE PREVENTION OF DISPUTES

Of these principles We have spoken time after time in previous Addresses, particularly in the third point of Our last Christmas message. Today, then, We shall restrict Ourselves to mention two: the natural law and the teaching of Christ.

### The Natural Law

The first postulate of every action towards peace is the recognition of the existence of a natural law, common to all men and to all nations, from which flow the guiding principles of existence, of action, and of obligation, the observance of which facilitates and guarantees men's living and working side by side for mutual advantage.

For those who reject this truth, relations between peoples will remain a puzzle, both in theory and in practice. And if the refusal should become common teaching, the course of human history would also be an unending voyage on a storm-tossed sea without any port of arrival.

Instead, in the light of this principle, it is easy for each one, at least in the general outlines, to distinguish justice from injustice, right from wrong; to point out the principles needed to solve disputes; to understand the genuine teaching of history concerning relations between peoples; to become aware of the formation and the binding force of international law.

In a word, the natural law is the solid foundation of every right and duty, the universal language necessary for every understanding between peoples. It is the supreme court of appeal humanity has ever yearned for to put an end to recurring disputes.

But whence and why these disputes? How can they ever come about while there exists a natural law, common to all and recognizable by every man?

In confronting the conditions of life, men and peoples receive from nature a great abundance of qualities and energies through which they can mould individual and social life. Such gifts and impulses of nature show the aims, the directions and the means, the quasimaster lines of the Creator's orderly design. But the manner, the time and place of their actuation, the choice of one end in preference to another, the choice of means, all this nature leaves to the free and intelligent choice of individuals or groups.

Life in common, no less than the private conduct of the individual, is not therefore automatically regulated, as is, for example, that of bees, governed as they are by their instinct. Rather it is ultimately set by the conscious will of the people themselves, or rather by the individuals who make up the group.

## Influences on Will

Now such a will may be influenced by two distinct and contrary forces: either reason and calm judgment, or blind instinct and unbridled passion. The activity of nations, if it is conformed to reason, can find in the natural law the means needed to smooth out difficulties and to transform into so many causes of collaboration and harmony the varieties of their natural tendencies, of their external conditions, even of their own interests—which are not in themselves inevitable sources of violent conflict. If, however, free will is led by passion, these same differences will produce unbearable tension, whose solution will be entrusted to the force of arms.

But how can peoples and individuals recognize with certitude the direction their activity must take if it is to be in conformity with nature's designs? In such an undertaking one must be on guard against mere supposition and conjecture. The general outlines are given by a clear awareness, a consideration of human nature and of the nature of things, and also of the relations and exigencies deriving therefrom.

On this point it is useful to learn from documents and legislative texts of past centuries, even thousands of years ago. These show how the exigencies of co-habitation between peoples have, in the main, been always the same, for human nature is, subtantially, unchanging. They show, moreover, that the same acts of justice and injustice are always repeated, in private as well as in public life; in the internal life of nations as well as in the relations between states.

Nor is it less instructive to see how generally recognized is the need to fix, through treaties and international agreements, that which was not absolutely clear through natural law, and to complete what nature did not reveal. Again the study of history and of the development of law from remotest times shows that, on the one hand, a change of economic and social (and sometimes even political) conditions demands also new expressions of those postulates of natural rights to which previously dominant systems no longer cling. On the other hand, however, in these same changes the basic needs of nature always recur, and are passed on from one generation to the next with a greater or lesser urgency.

Here an attentive observer finds the recognition, which always appears in some guise, of human personality with its basic rights concerning things, be they material or immaterial, and the ineradicable refusal of the person to be absorbed by the community and have his personal activity abolished.

Yet, contrariwise, one also finds the rejection of an exaggerated affirmation of the individual man or individual nation, who must not only not withdraw from the necessary service of the community but are obliged to offer that service in a positive way.

### Right Must Prevail over Might

One finds, moreover, the fundamental principle that force and success do not legitimize aggression, nor of themselves do they constitute a right; that right must prevail over might; that those who violate justice in the community of nations should be regarded as criminals, and as such be called to account for their deeds. (Of this matter We have already spoken in the discourse to the International Congress of Penal Law, Oct. 3, 1953).

Of some of the requirements of natural law which today prevail in international relations, We have spoken in the Allocution to the Fifth National Congress of Catholic Jurists on December 6, 1953, which had as its theme "The Nation and International Community."

Above all We stressed that the prevailing norms cannot be derived merely from the caprice of peoples, because their union must rise from a need, an impulse of nature itself. Consequently the fundamental elements for regulating such a union take on the character of a moral necessity, flowing from nature itself. We also indicated some of these requirements in particular: the right to existence; the right to use the goods of this earth to conserve life; the right of a nation to respect and good name; the right to give a personal stamp to the character of a people; their right to develop and expand; the right of having international treaties and similar agreements observed.

And even if the matter of such agreements is merely of positive law, yet the duty to fulfill them (as long as they hold nothing contrary to sound morality) flows from nature and natural law. Thus natural law covers and crowns all norms of merely positive law that are in force among men and peoples.

If, then, the above mentioned norms of natural law regulate international relations, will not the points of conflict be notably reduced? And when strife and tension are thus lessened, will not understanding be easier, if we sincerely study nature and its true demands?

Experience teaches that long training is not necessary to convince individuals and peoples that the requirements of nature are just. The teacher has, so to speak, his strongest ally in human nature itself and in the healthy intuition of his listener. Proof of this is the fact that when individuals and peoples disregard in practice those requirements, and in their place substitute something diametrically opposite, yet they do not refuse to keep its literal expression. Thus they call servitude freedom, caprice right, forced execution self-determination.

Which shows that it is difficult, indeed, to snuff out entirely the profound aspirations of nature. To make her cry heard, understood and complied with, is an important step toward the establishment of peace.

Hence it has ever been a constant care of the Church to arouse, keep alert and make efficacious, the knowledge and awareness of natural law. Not of a false and obscure law, but of a clear, well-determined law of nature, such as We have tried to describe. And by clearly and boldly stating this law, the Church has striven to open for the nations a path towards understanding and peace, notwithstanding conflicts of interest, which unfortunately it is extremely difficult to banish from the earth.

## Message of Christ

The second principle is the Message of Christ. To preach the message of Christ to men is the Church's *raison d'etre*, her prime duty, which she could not neglect without denying herself, and deluding those who, beset by the trials of life on earth, turn to her.

Hence the Church has ever lived and will live to fulfill this mission. Now the Message of Christ, luminous as the heaven from which it comes, universal as the Church to which it is sent, is in substance nothing else than the divine call to reconciliation, first between man and God, then between man and man. In a word, it is the message of loftiest peace.

Hence it is now necessary to investigate how the Church, as proclaimer of Christ's message, promotes the actual reconciliation of peoples by spreading and perpetuating the echo of that message.

There is a double message of Christ: that of word and doctrine, and that of deed and life.

That the *Message of word* and *doctrine* can reunite men and nations needs no particular explanation. It is, in fact, the announcement of the one and only origin and the one and only last end of all men and peoples; of the one God and Father of all; of the one and unifying command that we love God and our neighbor; of the only Redeemer and the Church He established for all, so that there be but one Shepherd and one flock.

Such a message, which in its origin, its means, and its end is inspired by the thought of the oneness of all men in one God, obviously effects peace and union.

The *Message of deed* and *of life* is the bringing about of the former, as varied as can be the deeds and life of an idea that dominates everything.

It is first of all Christian charity, i.e., the active and living charity of Christ, Who regards as done to Himself what is done for our neighbor out of love for Christ.

It is the charity of Christ in all its forms: hospitals, sanatoriums, homes for the aged, nurseries for infants, asylums for the abandoned, for the wayward, for minors, for the insane.

It is the charity of Christ which does not wait for misfortune to approach, but seeks it out, in foreign lands as well as at home. Charity, which in war makes no distinction between friend and enemy; which in Christ's name moves nurses and doctors to care for the wounded, friend or enemy, with fraternal solicitude. Charity, which is equally ready to serve in the rich man's palace, or in the poor man's hovel.

## The World Apart from the Church

It is true that in the world apart from the Church a vast work of such assistance is flourishing today, excellent in its technique. No doubt, but it was not always so, and it does not prove that the interior motivation of secular assistance is ruled by the same spirit of ardour, of self-denial and of heroism, often prolonged for an entire lifetime.

And yet in some places men have gone so far as to exclude Christian charity, and even to forbid it. A deplorable but useless undertaking. For even if the external forms of charity are suppressed, men can still practice it by personal zeal in their love for Christ, and thus fulfill the Divine message.

Just how does this charity become an efficacious instrument for peace among peoples? It does so most of all in virtue of the accumulated weight of uncounted good deeds, which on the moral scale, as it were, outweigh the dead weight of selfish acts, or at least prevent these from prevailing, to the common harm. When among individuals of various nations thousands upon thousands of good deeds are performed, bonds of mutual understanding are woven, and the renunciation of every hostile quarrel is prepared.

Yet with all that, the full pressure of Christian charity is not completely revealed.

This lies in the fact that the Catholic Church educates conscience to regard as one's neighbor not only this or that individual, but an entire people. And not only a people, but the individuals of every nation as brothers and sisters, who profess the same faith in Christ and share the same Eucharist. And not only the brethren of the Common Mother, the Church, but all men of the entire world, who, according to the command of our only Redeemer, deserve respect, compassion, and love.

This love, in thought and deed, without which the true Christian is not even conceivable, is a great force against every nationalistic selfishness, and a promoter of world peace.

It was present even in the last two world wars, and did much to lessen the evils and horrors of conflict, though it could not stem the tide of events.

Once the engines of war were set in motion, they alone could determine its development and outcome.

### Peace and the Power of Love

The power of love must therefore be put to work in time of peace, to assure its solidity and extension. It must today be alive and alert in every Catholic from his earliest youth. In all its forms it must be aroused and nourished in the family, in school, in education, popular singing, in books, in films.

Catholics from all nations and continents should unite in a common effort for peace, as they have done these past years with notable success. The Church does not have peace simply in her hand, but being a mighty force she cannot and must not remain inactive. And Christ, the Head of the Church, will with His blessings help her to attain so lofty a goal.

It is charity, also, that must animate the activities of the Church, in the fields of teaching and science, in the elementary schools, secondary schools, and the universities. If, prescinding from the contents, We consider only the formal aspect of teaching and scientific work, We must then indicate as the characteristic element, the service of truth.

Those who teach and work in scientific fields want before all else to lead men to a knowledge and acknowledgment of truth. Thus students and those who attend classes must be able to see reflected and almost as it were personified in the teacher this appreciation and ardent desire always to speak and teach the truth, so that they too will feel in their hearts the same love for truth.

It is essential that we search and plumb the depths of truth and teach it, whether one finds it pleasant or unpleasant, accepts it or rejects it. Such a spiritual attitude is evidently opposed to that apathy and indifference towards truth which today deforms the thinking of not a few men and which the skeptical Pilate once expressed in his ironical question: "What is truth?"

## Truth is Above All Else

On the contrary the noble characteristic of the example of Christ was that truth for Him was above everything else. To truth He rendered testimony and concerning truth He made this great promise: *the truth will make you free.*

But this devotedness to truth, promoted by the Church with her tremendous apostolate of teaching, renders a service of inestimable value for the reconciliation and the mutual understanding of men and nations, and for the exchange of thoughts and collaboration of man with man, nation with nation.

If all nations really and sincerely wish and seek, welcome and acknowledge only the truth, then they are truly on the way which leads by its very nature to mutual understanding and union. Since truth is only one (whatever meaning it may have in each individual case), universal desire for truth can only be one. Error on the other hand (since it is opposed to truth and reality) by its very nature means division; it separates, tears apart and scatters, even where many meet in the exact same error; their meeting is by chance, not a result of a solid unifying principle.

There is besides a whole series of other ways of realizing the message of Christ in the interests of promoting harmony and understanding among nations. They have this in common, that they realize in act the life and aim of Christ's message. We shall mention here only one of these: the work of the Church to explain and solve the social problem.

There exists, as We have noted, a Christian social doctrine whose fundamental principles have been determined in the official documents of the Pontiffs. Now it is also well known what a tremendous influence social conditions exercised and exercise today in moulding the lives of the people and their mutual relations, how much discord has arisen from these social conditions time and again between nations, and is continuously breaking out, extending even to international fields. To collaborate then for a solution and a cure of these miseries and social conditions is an outstanding contribution for peace and reconciliation among nations. . . .

# Food, Agriculture, and Human Society*

*(Address to Delegates of the Conference of the United
Nations Food and Agricultural Organization, November 10, 1955)*

. . . It was on October 16, 1945, that the representatives of 20
states were invited to sign the constitution of the Food and
Agriculture Organization of the United Nations. By the end of
the first session of the conference, 42 countries had given their
official adherence to the new institution.

Since then the number of member states has grown constantly to the present 71. In bidding you welcome, it gives Us
particular pleasure to congratulate you on the progress made
during these ten years.

### Aims of FAO

The aims that you set before you were, and still are, of
paramount importance: to raise the levels of nutrition and
standards of living of peoples, to improve efficiency of production and distribution of all food and agricultural products
and to contribute towards an expanding world economy.

The Holy See could not hold aloof from so beneficial and
necessary an undertaking. As far back as 1948 it had its observer at the regional meetings in Rome and the following year
at a session of the council. In 1950 a decision of the Washington Conference admitted it as permanent observer, a status
which it alone has up to the present.

You know, gentlemen, with what interest We have followed
the various phases of your activities since the day FAO was
founded. It was at that time a matter of facing a terrible fact:
over half the population of the world was underfed.

To meet the needs of mankind, food production had to be
doubled. FAO set to work energetically. It formed the International Emergency Food Committee, undertook a world cen-
sus of agriculture and proposed the establishment of a World
Food Council. It took charge of the work begun in nine war-
ravaged countries in order to restore their agriculture.

---

* Translation from *The Pope Speaks*.

To confine Ourselves to a few of the main achievements, We recall that in 1947 the European Forestry Commission was set up. In 1948 the first regional conference on nutrition problems was held, and since 1949 a joint committee of experts of nutrition has been meeting annually at various points of the globe.

Since increasing the productivity and raising the standard of living of rural populations are bound up with the social conditions under which the farmers work, FAO has since 1951 tackled the problems of reforming the agrarian structure and the related question of agricultural credit. At the same time numerous meetings in various continents are supporting the agricultural cooperative movement.

It certainly required boldness to envisage activities of so varied a nature and of such broad scope. But these efforts have not been in vain. Your report on the state of food and agriculture published in 1955 points out that in 1954 world agricultural production had increased by 25 per cent over that of 1946. During these years the underdeveloped countries have rapidly developed their land and water resources. Thanks to technical assistance they have applied to animal and plant production the new methods worked out and perfected in more advanced regions. But besides these positive results it is also necessary to mention the present shortages and difficulties, in order to draw the attention of all responsible men and to guide their endeavors. You have pointed out, among other things, the rigidity of the production patterns and the difficulty of adequately meeting demand, the stagnation of world trade in agricultural products and the insufficient level of agricultural incomes in relation to other industries.

In vast areas of the world men have not yet been given the means to buy all the food they need. It need hardly be said that this fact is still your main incentive to continue your endeavors.

*Soil Conservation and Improvement*

Among the special studies to which your experts have devoted themselves, We should like to mention a few that are particularly stimulative of thought, especially those that relate to the very basis of agriculture, the soil.

In the past the use, conservation, and improvement of the soil were left to the practical good sense of farmers. Experience gained at the cost of prolonged labor and not without disappointments taught them how to work so as not to ruin the land from which they earned their living. We know that while some farmers spared no pains to protect their land, others, moved by the lure of easy profits or the victims of their own inadequacies, inflicted damage on the soil that could not be quickly remedied. To counteract the effects of such errors and to prevent their recurrence as well as to make fullest use of soil potentialities, it was essential to acquire a sound knowledge of the various soils, their structure and properties, and to map their geographical distribution.

Thus it became possible to specify what kind of crop was suitable to a particular area and what improvements were necessary, whether by drainage or the application of fertilizers. In particular, it was impossible to neglect the control of erosion, which is essentially caused by the natural elements but in many cases facilitated and accelerated by the intervention of man, who, to make sloping land tillable, strips it of all protective vegetation. It was ascertained that in the United States the losses in phosphates due to erosion were greater than the depletion brought about by growing crops. The publications devoted to this question, such as, for example, the soil erosion survey of Latin America containing maps, will greatly help to prevent further damage.

### Social and Economic Factors

But soil conservation does not depend on the control of erosion alone. At present it is believed best to consider the subject in a broader framework, taking into account modern methods for improving fertility and the social and economic factors likely to increase the well-being of rural populations, by helping in the settlement of uncultivated lands, by checking the exodus from the countryside and the depopulation of mountain regions by migration to the cities.

The impoverishment of the land may be the result of a poor land ownership system, the concentration of land in the hands of a few, the excessive fragmentation of holdings or too low prices for agricultural products. Living conditions that are too

harsh dishearten the farmer and drive him to seek his livelihood elsewhere. You have not overlooked this aspect of
things since, as We pointed out just now, you have envisaged
action in regard to agrarian reform, as well as in the field of
credit and agricultural cooperatives.

Because of the essential role they play in regulating the flow
of surface and underground water, serious attention should be
paid to forests. They check the run-off of water, facilitate its
seepage in depth and the feeding of springs. They retain the
snow and, even though they cannot prevent exceptional
floods, they regulate the flow of rivers. It is therefore to the
interest of public authorities, who are anxious to develop agriculture, to keep a watch on the way in which forests are
logged.

## The Problem of Hunger

We also mention, among many other points, the research
work on the possibility of utilizing seaweed for human food.
So far, however, the utilization of these resources still seems
to be difficult to achieve.

These brief considerations show fairly well that the initial
program prepared by the Hot Springs Conference and formulated in the Constitution is well on the way to being carried
out. Whereas formerly the problem of hunger seemed insoluble, it is now possible to face up to it and to rely on the collaboration of governments in solving it.

Your soil studies have drawn attention to the physical unity
of the various regions, which makes the plain and the mountain interdependent. The man who wishes to safeguard the
fertility of his land must concern himself with what is taking
place far beyond its boundaries.

This truth takes on symbolic meaning here, it seems to Us.
For peoples favored by nature or the progress of civilization
are in danger of being rudely awakened one day, if they do
not take the trouble henceforth to secure for the less fortunate
the means to live in accordance with human dignity and to
develop on their own account.

To awaken further among a great number of individuals and
nations this feeling of collective responsibility, and above all
to bring about thereby enlightened and generous interventions

is a lofty and noble task. In these times of suspicion, division, and revolt, the moral implications of such a result go far beyond its material consequences.

We take pleasure above all in recognizing in this worldwide activity, intended to effect not a privileged class, but the often powerless and defenceless multitude, an authentic aspect of the charity which Christ illustrated by His life and death and which He wished to make the distinctive sign of His disciples. This universal, unselfish charity, that even demands sacrifice, can only be rooted in the love that God Himself has for mankind. It is its visible manifestation and its strongest proof.

# Nuclear Weapons and Armament Control*

*(Christmas Message Broadcast to the Whole World, December 24, 1955)*

In the Christmas radio message of last year, We set forth the mind of the Church on this topic and We now intend once again to ratify it. We reject Communism as a social system by virtue of Christ's doctrine, and We have a particular obligation to proclaim the fundamental principles of the natural law. For the same reason We also reject the opinion that the Christian ought today to see Communism as a phenomenon or stage in the passage of history, one of the necessary "moments," as it were, of its evolution, and consequently to accept it as if decreed by Divine Providence.

### Warnings to Christians

But at the same time, We again warn Christians of the industrial age, in the spirit of Our immediate predecessors in the supreme pastoral and teaching office, against being satisfied with an anti-communism founded on the slogan and the defense of liberty which is devoid of content; rather We

---

* Translation from *The Pope Speaks.*

urge them to build up a society in which man's security rests on that moral order of which We have very often set forth the need and the consequences, which has regard for true human nature. . . .

It is precisely against him, the religious and Christian man, that the charge will be brought by some of being an obstacle to peace, of opposing the peaceful co-existence of men, of nations, of different systems, because he does not keep his religious convictions unspoken in the privacy of his conscience, but makes them effective even in traditional and powerful organizations, in all the activities of life both public and private. It is asserted that this kind of Christianity makes a man overbearing, biased, oversure and satisfied with himself; that it leads him to defend positions which no longer have any significance, instead of being open to everything and everybody, with confidence that, in a general co-existence, the interior living faith, like "spirit and love" at least in the Cross and the Sacrifice, would furnish a definite contribution to the common cause. In this false idea of a religion and Christianity have we not once more before us that erroneous worship of the human subject and of his positive life-force carried over to the supernatural plane? Man, face to face with opinions and systems opposed to the true religion, is, of course, always bound by the limits established by God in the natural and supernatural order. In obedience to this principle, our peace program cannot approve of an indiscriminate co-existence at all costs with everybody; certainly not at the cost of truth and justice. These irremovable boundary marks, in effect, demand complete observance. Where this is true, including today the question of peace, religion is protected in a sure manner against abuse from the political quarter; whereas when it has been restricted to purely interior life, religion itself is more exposed to that danger.

### Nuclear Arms and Armament Control

This thought of its own accord leads Us on to the ever acute question of peace which constitutes an object of solicitude always present to Our heart, and at this moment one of its partial problems begs for special consideration. We propose to direct Our attention to a recent proposal which aims at putting a check on experiments in nuclear weapons by means of an international agreement. There has been talk also of taking further steps toward conventions through which the use of those weapons would be renounced and all states subjected to effective arms control. Thus there would be a question of three steps: renunciation of experimentation with atomic weapons, renunciation of the use of such, and general control of armaments.

The supreme importance of these proposals is tragically illustrated if one stops to consider what science thinks it can predict about such actions, and which We think it useful to sum up briefly here.

As for the *experiments* of atomic explosions, the opinion of those who fear the effects produced if they are multiplied would seem to be finding greater acceptance. Too many such explosions would in time cause an increased density of radioactive products in the atmosphere, whose diffusion depends on elements not under man's control; thus would be generated conditions very dangerous for many living beings.

Concerning the *use:* in a nuclear explosion an enormous amount of energy equivalent to several thousand million kilowatts is developed in an exceedingly short time; this energy is composed of electromagnetic radiations of very great density distributed within a vast gamut of wave lengths to the most penetrating, and of tiny bodies produced by nuclear disintegration which are hurled at nearly the speed of light. This energy is transferred to the atmosphere and within thousandths of a second increases the temperature of surrounding air masses by hundreds of degrees; their displacement is violent, propagated at the speed of sound. On the earth's surface, in an area of many square kilometres, reactions of unimaginable violence take place, materials volatilized and utterly destroyed by direct radiation, by heat, by mechanical action, while an enormous amount of radioactive materials of varying life-span completes and continues the destruction through their activity.

### There Will Be No Song of Victory

This is the spectacle offered to the terrified gaze as the result of such use; entire cities, even the largest and richest in art and history, wiped out; a pall of death over pulverized ruins, covering countless victims with limbs burnt, twisted and scattered while others groan in their death agony. Meanwhile the specter of a radioactive cloud hinders survivors from giving any help and inexorably advances to snuff out any remaining life. There will be no song of victory, only the inconsolable weeping of humanity, which in desolation will gaze upon the catastrophe brought on by its own folly.

Concerning *control:* Inspection by properly equipped planes has been suggested for the purpose of watching over any atomic activities in large territories. Others might perhaps think of the possibility of a worldwide network of observation posts, each one staffed by experts of different countries and protected by solemn international pacts. Such centers would have to be equipped with delicate and precise meteorological and seismic instruments, with equipment for chemical analysis, with vast spectrographs and such like; they would render possible the real control of many, unfortunately not of all, of the activities which antecedently would be outlawed in the field of atomic experimentation.

We do not hesitate to declare, as We have in previous allocutions, that the sum total of those three precautions as an object of international agreement is an obligation in conscience of nations and of their leaders. We said, sum total of those precautions, because the reason they are morally binding is also that equal security be established for all. If, however, only the first point, concerning experimentation, were put into effect, the result would be that that condition would not be verified, the more so that there would be given sufficient reason to doubt a sincere desire to put into effect the other two conventions. We speak so frankly because the danger of insufficient proposals concerning peace depends in large part on the mutual suspicions that often trouble the dealings of the powers concerned, each accusing the other in varying degrees of mere tactics, even of the lack of sincerity in a matter basic to the fate of the whole human race.

## Preventive Pacification

For the rest, efforts toward peace must consist not only in measures aimed at restricting the possibility of waging war, but even more in preventing, eliminating or lessening with time the quarrels between nations which might lead to war.

To this kind of preventive pacification statesmen must devote themselves with great vigilance, imbued with a spirit of impartial justice and also generosity, within the limits of the course of a healthy realism. In last year's Christmas message We indicated the points of dispute noted in relations between Europeans and those non-Europeans who aspire to full political independence. Can those disputes be allowed to run their course, so to speak—a procedure which might easily increase their gravity, sow hatred in men's souls and create so-called traditional enmities? And might not a third party come to profit from such enmities, a third party which neither of the others really wants, and cannot want? At any rate, let not those peoples be denied a fair and progressive political freedom nor hindered in its pursuit. To Europe, however, they will give credit for their advancement; to that Europe without whose influence, extended to all fields, they might be drawn by a blind nationalism to plunge into chaos or slavery.

On the other hand, the Western peoples, especially those of Europe, should not, in the face of such problems, remain passive in futile regret over the past or in mutual recrimination over colonialism. Rather they should set themselves constructively to work to extend where it has not yet been done those true values of Europe and the West which have produced so many good fruits in other continents. The more Europeans strive for this the more help will they be to the just freedom of young nations which in turn will be saved from the pitfalls of false nationalism. This, in truth, is their real enemy, which would pit them one day against each other, to the advantage of third parties. Such a forecast, not unfounded, cannot be neglected or forgotten by those who handle their problems of peace at congresses where, unfortunately, there gleams the splendor of a unity that is external and predominantly negative. We think that in such considerations and in such modes of procedure there is a valuable assurance of peace, in some respects even more important than an immediate prevention of war.

# No Peace in Materialism*

*(Address to Members of the Vatican Diplomatic Corps, March 4, 1956)*

. . . PEACE! Who can estimate its worth and benefits? Would that we could arouse a more fervent desire for it throughout the world, so that individuals and groups would henceforth consent to make the greatest and most personal sacrifices in order to protect, preserve, and strengthen it. How We wish men and nations would prefer it to the satisfactions of egotism and selfishness. How We hope that the pressure of world opinion will curb resistance and foolish stubbornness, make it necessary everywhere to settle even the sharpest divisions amicably and force the acceptance of arbitration and compromise, through which many irreparable evils can be avoided.

We often hear the present age characterized—not without a trace of complacency—as the era of the "second technical revolution." In spite of the prospect of a better future, which this characterization seems to imply, it is necessary to emphasize the permanency of suffering and of political and economic insecurity among the most fortunate peoples as well as in underdeveloped areas.

### Dangers of the Materialistic Spirit

The bitter experiences of the past century should be enough to explain this. Were not promises of a technically and economically perfect world made then as they are now? Did they not lead to cruel disillusion? The social upheavals brought about by the application of science in a spirit that was too often materialistic ruined the existing order without replacing it with a better or stronger one.

The Church, on the other hand, has never lost sight of man's real needs and has dedicated herself to the mission of preserving the true stability of his existence. She knows that man's temporal destiny finds its sanction and fulfillment only in eternity. Without in any way denying the achievements of science and technology, she keeps them in their proper place and gives

* Translation from *The Pope Speaks*.

them their true meaning. They must serve man without upsetting the balance of all the relationships which make up the plan of his life—family, property, profession, community, and State.

To base the security and stability of human life only on an increasing quantity of material goods is to forget that man is primarily a spirit created in God's image. He is a being responsible for his actions and his destiny and capable of ruling himself. He finds in these facts his highest dignity. It is right to defend this freedom against outside restraints, against the threat of social systems which paralyze it and make it illusory.

### Hierarchy of Values

But the very person who wages this battle must realize that economics and technology are useful and even necessary forces so long as they are subservient to higher spiritual needs. They become harmful and dangerous only when they are given undue predominance and the dignity, so to speak, of ends in themselves. It is the task of the Church to assure respect for this system of values and to subordinate the elements of material progress to truly spiritual goals.

Governments which follow a policy inspired by these principles will maintain an internal strength against which militant materialism will shatter itself. Materialism will strive in vain to dazzle these governments with the lure of a false peace. The road to such a peace, it will be claimed, lies in the establishment of economic relations or the exchange of technical experiences. May the peoples who set out on this road go forth with prudence and a reserve inspired by a keen desire to safeguard spiritual values. May they always remember that they are being guided in a direction that does not and cannot lead by itself to true peace.

Slogans like "national unity" and "social progress" should not deceive us. For militant materialism, "peacetime" means only a truce, a precarious truce during which it awaits the social and economic collapse of other peoples.

That is why We are appealing to all who want peace and unity for mankind. With the help of God, such generous souls are becoming more numerous every day. They victoriously oppose their ideal of light and love to error and evil. Convinced that nothing solid can be built on sand, they rely on eternal truths that cannot be shaken by even the most categoric denials. For what human reason has long groped for, God in His goodness has shown to men in the person of His beloved Son. *For He Himself is our peace.*

# Faith, Peace, and the Atom*

*(Easter Message Broadcast to the Whole World, April 1, 1956)*

A FIRM trust is the indispensable condition for the triumph of peace. Its cause is certainly not helped by those who are easily shaken by the wind of a pessimism which is spread so artfully and finds expression in the cheap phrase: "What's the use?" Nor is it aided by those who close their eyes to the many achievements in the field of social and economic reform and to the gains which they themselves are enjoying, advantages which have often been bought with back-breaking labor and in the face of almost insurmountable obstacles. They have eyes only for what is missing, for what has not yet been fully achieved, and they lend a ready ear to the suggestions of those who sow discontent.

A true friend of peace must know how to react to this kind of instigation. He must realize that it is these weak points of man—pessimism, avarice, envy, and a frenzy of unfounded criticism—which the enemies of peace use to plant the seeds of discord in souls. They use now one, now another of these passions, stirring them up, first threatening, then flattering, arguing here, striking a blow there. Today they glorify their own myths, tomorrow they condemn them. Today they stamp away in anger, tomorrow they return peacefully. One day they announce a new system, the next day they are back to the old.

On the other hand, dear children, it is important to note that

---

* Translation from *The Pope Speaks.*

276

real peace is not a kind of silence which resembles death, but rather a power and a vital dynamism. As a result, the higher the being which is involved and the more intense his activity, the deeper must be the harmony of peace; it is in no way opposed to any conquest in the realm of thought nor to any development of production and technical activities; instead it creates conditions which are best suited to progress in every kind of artistic, economic, political, and scientific activity.

## Nuclear Energy

Everyone knows that sometimes rapid and powerful successes in the field of human conquest can actually create anxieties and fears in men since they put their individual and social lives in serious danger. Just think of what is going on right now in the field of applied nuclear energy, which is such a constant subject of discussion, study, hope, and fear.

The peace-time use of this tremendous energy has been the subject of long and detailed studies, which win Our blessing, along with the applause and approval of every honest soul and every civilized people. Its use for transportation that will bring about a much easier and more rapid exchange of raw materials for distribution to all the members of the great human family; the application of radioactive isotopes to the study of biological facts, to the curing of serious illnesses, to the improvement of certain industrial processes; the production of energy in atomic centers—all are opening new and wonderful vistas in the history of mankind.

Still, everyone is aware that other uses more suited to destruction and death are being sought and found. And what a death! Every day there is another sad step along this tragic road, another rush to arrive there alone, first, best. And the human race almost loses hope of the possibility of stopping this homicidal and suicidal madness. Terror and fear have grown with the coming of modern guided missiles which can travel enormous distances, carrying atomic arms, to bring about the total destruction of men and things.

## A Prayer for Peace

In the hope that all peoples may stop this race toward the abyss, once again We raise Our voice and call down the light and strength of the risen Jesus on those who rule over the destinies of nations. May this Easter be a message of faith and a message of peace to all men for whose temporal and eternal salvation Christ offered His life. May this twofold message reach all souls, bring them comfort and renew their hopes. May they quickly bloom, like flowers opening out in the warmth of Jesus, the Sun of Justice, and bring forth the substantial fruit of full justice and fraternal agreement!

# An Appeal for Peace*

*(Radio Address to all the Peoples of the Earth and their Rulers, November 10, 1956, on the Plight of Hungary)*

OUR heart, the heart of a Father, is sorely distressed by the consummate iniquity involved in the overthrow of Our beloved Hungarian people, who are guilty only of having desired respect for the fundamental rights of mankind. To this distress is added Our anxiety for the recent threats to world peace and Our sorrow when We see a weakening of the forces of those upon whose authority, unity, and good will it seemed that one could rely for the gradual reestablishment of concord among nations in justice and true freedom.

Who can deny that the problems of peace and just freedom have had a deplorable set back, drawing with them into the shadows those hopes that have been reawakened with much effort and confirmed by manifold evidences of sincerity?

## The World is Shocked

So much blood has been unjustly spilled! So much suffering and destruction unexpectedly renewed! The slender cord of mutual confidence that had begun to reunite the nations and to sustain their faltering spirits seems now to be broken; mutual suspicion and want of confidence have uncovered a deeper abyss of separation. The whole world is justly shocked by the hasty recourse to violence, which everyone has a

* Translation from *The Pope Speaks*.

thousand times denounced as a means of settling disputes and assuring the victory of right.

There can be no doubt that the world at large has been confused by the paroxysms of these days of violence and has lost its confidence, since it has been a witness of the rebirth of a policy that, in a different manner, sets arbitration aside and elevates economic interest above human lives and moral values.

In the face of such an attack upon justice and brotherly love, in the face of a creeping skepticism among men with regard to the future, in the face of the grievous disunity of the minds of men, We who have a special mandate from God to promote the welfare of all nations and who firmly believe that peace is not an empty dream but a duty that can be realized by all, with the intention of making a contribution to the salvaging of peace both in itself and in the factors upon which it is based, desire to direct a heartfelt plea to the peoples of the earth: let us restore the ways of peace; let us strengthen the unity of all who long for it; let us bring back confidence to those who have lost it!

### Let Your Rulers Know

Accordingly We address Ourselves above all to you, beloved peoples, men and women, intellectuals, workers, artisans, and farmers, of every race and country. Let your rulers know your inmost sentiments and your genuine aspirations. Recent events have confirmed the belief that nations, families, individuals prefer the tranquillity of labor and of family life to any other form of wealth that men covet. They are quick to reject the latter if its price is to be tyranny or the risk of war with all its terrible consequences—ruined cities, suffering, imprisonment, and death. In the name of religion, of civilization, and of right human feeling, let us have done with unlawful and brutal oppression, with threats of war, with struggles for preeminence among the great powers, all of which transmute life on earth into an abyss of anxiety and terror, deaden the spirit of man, and destroy all the fruits of labor and progress.

This is the voice of Nature herself and it ought to be proclaimed aloud inside and outside every nation; it ought to be heard and accepted by those to whom the peoples have entrusted power. If the public authority, insofar as lies within its ability, does not tend to secure, at the least, life, liberty, and tranquillity for its citizens, it has failed essentially to perform its duty, whatever else it may succeed in accomplishing.

But the significance of the sorrowful plight of the Hungarian people outweighs every other nightmare in the hearts of men. The universal and spontaneous emotion aroused throughout the world, which has not been diminished by the attention given to other grave events, proves how essential and urgent it is to restore freedom to all the peoples who have been deprived of it. Can the world possibly lose interest in these their brothers, and abandon them to a degrading servitude? Surely the conscience of Christendom cannot shake off the moral obligation of trying every lawful means of reasserting their human dignity and of restoring their freedom.

We are not unaware of the present intricate relations among nations and among the continental groups which embrace them. But one must listen to the voice of conscience, of civilization, of brotherhood; one must listen to the voice of God Himself, the Creator and Father of all, postponing, even at the cost of great sacrifice, the solution of every other problem and every particular interest in order to solve the elementary and fundamental problem of millions of human lives reduced to slavery.

## A Union of Peace-Loving Nations

Let men turn their attention as quickly as possible to reforming their ranks and binding by a firm and public agreement all those—both governments and peoples—who desire that the world should walk in the path of honor and of the dignity of the sons of God: an agreement capable, likewise, of defending effectively its members from every unjust attack upon their rights and their independence. It will not be the fault of honorable men if there remains only the wilderness of isolation for him who willfully abandons this path.

Perhaps it will come to pass—and this We desire with all Our heart—that the solid ranks of the nations that sincerely love peace and liberty will suffice to bring to a more merciful frame of mind those who withdraw themselves from the most elementary laws of human intercourse and for this reason deprive themselves of all right to speak in the name of humanity, of justice, and of peace. Their own peoples will be the first to find it impossible to remain oblivious of the need for returning to form a part of the human family, in order to enjoy its honor and its privileges. Then all of you will be united in liberty and in peace, beloved peoples of the East and of the West, as members of a common human family.

Peace and liberty! Nowadays these tremendous words leave no room for an ambiguous position. They have returned to their original and luminous meaning, as they have always been understood by Us, being derived, that is to say, from the principles of nature and the manifest will of the Creator. May your rulers be faithful interpreters of your true sentiments, of your true aspirations. God will assist you; God will be your strength!

God! God! God!

May this ineffable name, the source of all right, justice, and freedom, resound in the parliaments and the public squares, in the homes and the factories, on the lips of intellectuals and of laborers, in the press and on the radio. The name of God, which is synonymous with peace and liberty, must be the banner of men of good will, the bond between peoples and nations, the sign that identifies those who are brothers and co-workers in the task of insuring mutual safety.

May God arouse you from your lethargy, keep you free from all complicity with tyrants and warmongers, enlighten your consciences, and strengthen your wills in the work of reconstruction.

Above all, may His name re-echo in the churches and in the hearts of men, as the highest invocation to the Lord, in order that by His infinite power He may assist in bringing to completion that which our weak human strength is struggling so hard to accomplish.

With this prayer which We hasten to raise to His throne of mercy, We bid you farewell, beloved sons, confident that a clear sky will reappear to shine upon the world and upon downcast countenances, and that after having been tried by such grievous tests, a more serene, more enduring, more just peace will abide.

# The Contradiction of Our Age*

*(Christmas Message Broadcast to the Whole World, December 23, 1956)*

. . . IF unpleasant realities force Us to set forth the terms of the struggle in clear language, no one can properly accuse Us of favoring the stiffening of opposing blocks, and still less of having in some fashion abandoned that mission of peace which flows from Our Apostolic Office. Rather, if We kept silence We would have to fear the judgement of God. We remain closely allied to the cause of peace, and God alone knows how much We yearn to be able to announce it in full and happy tones with the angels of Christmas. But precisely in order to protect it from the present threats, must We point out where the danger lies, the tactics of its enemies and what marks them as such. Not otherwise did the new-born Son of God, Himself infinite goodness, unhesitatingly draw clear lines of demarcation, and face death on behalf of the truth.

We are convinced that today, too, in face of an ememy determined to impose on all peoples, in one way or another, a special and intolerable way of life, only the unanimous and courageous behaviour of all who love the truth and the good can preserve peace and will preserve it. It would be a fatal error to repeat what, in similar circumstances, happened during the years preceding the Second World War; when all the threatened nations, and not merely the smallest, sought their safety at the expense of others, using them as shields, so to speak, and even seeking very questionable economic and political advantages from their neighbor's suffering. In the end all together were overwhelmed in the holocaust.

### Solidarity of Europe One of the Means for World Peace

Hence, a definite need of this period,—a means of ensuring the whole world's peace and a fruitful share of its goods, a force which embraces, too, the peoples of Asia, Africa, the Near East, Palestine with its Holy Places,—is the restoration

---

* Translation from National Catholic Welfare Conference Pamphlet.

282

of European solidarity. But this unity is not assured until all the associated nations realize that the political and economic defeats of one can nowhere, in the long run, result in true gains for the others. It is not strong, as far as the formation of public opinion is concerned, if in the hour of common peril, criticism, even though justified, of one nation's actions is expressed by the others with such onesidedness as to cause doubt that any bond of union at all remains. A good course of action can never be had by mere sentiment; much less can a true political course for today be maintained with the sentiments of yesterday and the day before. Under such influence it would be impossible to judge correctly certain important questions, such as military service, weapons, war.

Present day conditions, which find no counterparts in the past, should be clear to everyone. There is no longer room for doubt concerning the aims and methods which rely on tanks, when these latter noisily crash over borders, sowing death in order to force civilian peoples into a pattern of life they explicitly detest; when destroying, as it were, the stages of possible negotiation and mediation, the threat is made of using atomic weapons to gain certain demands, be they justified or not. It is clear that in the present circumstances there can be verified in a Nation a situation, wherein, when every effort to avoid war has been expended in vain, war—for effective self-defence and with the hope of a favourable outcome against unjust attack—could not be considered unlawful.

If, therefore, a body representative of the people and a Government—both having been chosen by free elections—in a moment of extreme danger decide, by legitimate instruments of internal and external policy, on defensive precautions, and carry out the plans which they consider necessary, they do not act immorally; so that a Catholic citizen cannot invoke his own conscience in order to refuse to serve and fulfill those duties the law imposes. On this matter We feel that We are in perfect harmony with Our Predecessors Leo XIII and Benedict XV, who never denied that obligation, but lamented the headlong armaments race and the moral dangers accompanying barrack life, and urged, as We do likewise, general disarmament as an effective remedy.

283

*Moral Laws and the Dictates of Conscience*

There are then occasions and times in the life of nations in which only recourse to higher principles can establish clearly the boundaries between right and wrong, between what is lawful and what is immoral, and bring peace to consciences faced with grave decisions. It is therefore consoling that in some countries, amid today's debates, men are talking about conscience and its demands. They show that they have not forgotten that social life is saved from chaos only in so far as it permits itself to be supported by absolute norms and an absolute end; they implicitly condemn those who believe that they can resolve the questions of human co-existence on the bases of good external appearances and with a practical view, and seek to act where interest and power may be found in individual cases.

Although the program at the foundation of the United Nations aims at the realization of absolute values in the co-existence of peoples, the recent past has, however, shown that a false realism is prevailing in not a few of its members, even when it is a question of restoring respect for these same values of human society, openly trampled upon. This unilateral view, which tends to work according to the personal interest and power of each State, treats in a different manner each accusation that the peace is being threatened; thus the gravity of each threat, which should be judged individually in the light of absolute values, is completely perverted.

*The Authority of the United Nations*

No one expects or demands the impossible, not even from the United Nations; but one should have a right to expect that their authority should have had its weight, at least through observers, in the places in which the essential values of man are in extreme danger. Although the United Nations' condemnation of the grave violations of the rights of men and of entire nations is worthy of recognition, one can nevertheless wish that, in similar cases, the exercise of their rights, as members of this Organization, be denied to States which refuse even the admission of observers—thus showing that their concept of State sovereignty threatens the very foundations of the

United Nations. This organization ought also to have the right and the power of forestalling all military intervention of one State in another, whatever be the pretext under which it is effected, and also the right and power of assuming, by means of a sufficient police force, the safeguarding of order in the State which is threatened.

If We allude to these defects, it is because We desire to see strengthened the authority of the U.N. especially for effecting general disarmament which We have so much at heart, and on which We have already spoken in other discourses. In fact only in the ambit of an institution like the United Nations can the promise of individual nations to reduce armament, especially to abandon production and use of certain arms, be mutually exchanged under the strict obligation of international law. Likewise only the United Nations is at present in a position to exact the observance of this obligation by assuming effective control of the armaments of all nations without exception. Its exercise of aerial observation will assure certain and effective knowledge of the production and military preparedness for war with relative ease, while avoiding the disadvantages which the presence of foreign troops in a country can give rise to. It indeed approaches almost the miraculous what technical science has been able to attain in this field.

In fact by the use of an adequate wide-angle lens and sufficient light, it is possible now to photograph from a height of several kilometers and in sufficiently great detail, objects which are on the earth's surface. Scientific progress, modern techniques, both mechanical and photographical, have succeeded in constructing cameras which have reached extraordinary perfection in all aspects; film of high sensitivity with very little grain makes it possible to enlarge pictures to hundreds of times their original size. Such cameras, mounted on airplanes which go at a speed very close to that of sound, are able to automatically take thousands of pictures, so that hundreds of thousands of square kilometers can be explored in a relatively short time.

The experiments conducted in this field have given exceptionally important results permitting one to produce concrete evidence of machines, individual persons, and objects existing on the ground, and even at least indirectly in subterranean places. Researches thus far made have shown how very difficult it would be to camouflage movement of troops or artillery, vast stores of arms, industrial centres important for war production. If these surveys could be permanent and systematic, it would be possible to bring out the minutest details, and thus give a solid guarantee against eventual surprises.

The acceptance of the control is the point crucial for victory, where every nation will show its sincere desire for peace.


# The Peaceful Use of Nuclear Energy*

(*Diplomatic Note to Masatoshi Matushita, Special Envoy of Japanese Premier, Nobosuke Kishi, April 14, 1957*)


MAN's increasing mastery over the terrifying forces of nature has given rise to new and urgent grounds for anxiety. For the destructive power of nuclear weapons has become unlimited, being no longer checked by the critical mass which once set a natural limit to the already terrible power of the first atomic weapons.

This unlimited power is now used as a challenge which is tossed from one camp to the other and becomes more and more catastrophic, as each side tries to outdo the other in the increasing and unfortunately real terrors which the power inspires.

Where natural catastrophes are concerned, one can only bow before events that happen through the Almighty's will. But should a catastrophe occur through man's perverse wish to dominate—with all the retaliations that would follow—how could such an act not be reprobated and condemned by every upright soul?

Therefore, instead of the useless waste of scientific activity, of labor, and of material means which the preparation of this catastrophe represents—and, apart from the enormous immediate damage, no one can foretell with certainty what the ulti-

---

* Translation from *The Pope Speaks*.

mate biological effects, especially the hereditary ones, could be on living beings—instead of this exhausting and costly race to death, scientists of all nations and all beliefs must feel a grave obligation to pursue the noble end of mastering these energies for the service of man. Scientific, economic, industrial, and even political organizations should support with all their power efforts aiming at the use of these energies on a scale adaptable to human needs.

# The Christian and the World Community*

*(Address to the Eleventh Plenary Assembly of the International Movement of Catholic Intellectuals, April 25, 1957)*

FOR some years now men and women have witnessed, in wonder and even anguish, the accelerated development of international organizations. They are delighted by the wonderful progress of human relations in material, intellectual, and social fields. At the same time they cannot help but fear that the unification toward which the world is rapidly moving may be accomplished with violence. They fear that the more powerful may attempt to impose their leadership and their concept of the universe on all humanity. This apprehension is all the greater because, in the event of a world conflict, modern armaments are capable of causing a frightful disaster. Some wonder whether the precipitate evolution of the world is not leading the entire human family toward catastrophe or tyranny. There are others who, like you, perceive by faith the great eternal tragedy of the salvation of souls. They feel a deeper need for light and certitude.

How could the Vicar of Christ fail to heed this appeal and

---

* Translation from *The Catholic Mind*.

bring again the comfort of Catholic truth to an anxious world?

In this matter of defining the role that certain persons are called upon to play in the developing world community, we must first remind ourselves of the highest goal—the one to which all others are subordinated. For a Christian the will of Christ is the ultimate reason for his choices and his decisions. The Saviour was made man and gave His life *to gather into one the children of God who were scattered abroad.* He wished *to be lifted up from the earth* on the cross in order *to draw all men to Him* and to unite them under His leadership in *one fold and one shepherd.*

### The Christian and the World

The Christian therefore cannot remain indifferent to the evolution of the world. If he sees now in rough outline a development, under the pressure of events, of a constantly narrowing international community, he knows that this unification, willed by the Creator, ought to culminate in a union of minds and hearts which is held together by a common faith and a common love. Not only can he, but he must, work for the achievement of this community still in the process of formation. The example and the plan of the Divine Master are, for him, a beacon and an incomparable source of strength. All men are his brothers, not only in virtue of their common origin and their participation in the same nature but also, in a more pressing way, in virtue of their common calling to the supernatural life. Sustained by this certitude, the Christian is in a position to gauge to what extent God *wishes all men to be saved and to come to the knowledge of the truth; for there is one God and one Mediator between God and men, Himself man, Christ Jesus, who gave Himself a ransom for all.*

The revealed truth involved in this scriptural text has been confided to the infallible teaching power of the Church. But it also forms the patrimony of the Christian community which takes its nourishment from it and also lives by it. It furnishes to each of the faithful an attitude of thought. It gives him a norm by which he can judge men and events. This Catholic point of view is yours, Dear Sons. You should make it your business to penetrate it still more, to plumb its grandeur and its beauty in order to appreciate its value and its depth. May it truly be a light to your intellects, a source of strength for your actions and a comfort for your souls.

But you are not isolated seekers after truth. You are not autonomous thinkers. You are Catholic intellectuals. This means you are charged with a universal social responsibility toward everything which concerns the spread of Christian truth. Your culture and the competence you have acquired in your profession have conferred upon you an authority which, in your milieu, constitutes for you both a question and an answer. By the grace of your vocation you are a light which attracts and which cannot be rejected by anyone without implicitly condemning himself, provided the light you bear is truly the light of Christ. Nevertheless, this rejection, which human imperfection always justifies under some pretext or other, limits the responsibility of Catholic intellectuals in the confusion of a society in which the essential questions are often left aside, whether they concern current affairs or decisions of universal import involving the political, social, and cultural orientation of countries or continents.

### Catholic Cooperation in the World Community

Does this mean that one cannot collaborate in the service of the world community with those institutions where God is not expressly recognized as the author and legislator of the universe? It is important to distinguish here the different levels of cooperation. Without ever forgetting that his ultimate goal is to contribute to the eternal salvation of his brothers, the Christian will be mindful that the coming of the Kingdom of God in hearts and institutions most often requires a minimum of human enlightenment, a simple appeal to reason with which every man normally concurs, even if he has not the grace of faith.

The Christian will therefore be ready to work for the relief of all material miseries, for the universal development of a basic training in social attitudes—in a word, toward all enterprises which have as their purpose the better lot of the poor and the disenfranchised. In that way the Christian will fulfill his obligation of collective charity. He will pave the way for a greater number of men to enter into a personal life worthy of the name. He will promote the spontaneous cooperation of men in all efforts which lead them to a better state of life. For thus are men permitted to look higher, to receive the light, and to adhere to the sole truth which makes men free.

Those who are constantly in the public eye and, for that reason, able to influence public opinion, should feel themselves charged with a more serious task. Truth does not tolerate in itself either admixture or impurity. Their participation in doubtful enterprises could seem to put the stamp of approval on political or social systems which are inadmissible. Nevertheless, even here a vast area exists in which minds free of prejudice and passion can act in harmony and cooperate for a genuine and worthwhile common good. Sound reason is enough to establish the basis for human rights, to recognize the inviolable character of the individual, the dignity of the family, and the prerogatives and limits of public authority.

For this reason the cooperation of Catholics is desirable in all institutions which, in theory and practice, respect the provisions of the natural law. They will seek to maintain them in their essential purity and, by their active participation in them, play the beneficent role which the Divine Master compared to that of the salt and the leaven. They will find in these organizations, which propose for themselves a universal and humanitarian goal, generous souls and superior minds susceptible of rising above material preoccupations. They will find men capable of understanding that the truly collective destiny of humanity presupposes the absolute value of each of the individuals who constitute it; of recognizing the establishment outside of time of the true society of which the earthly community can only be a reflection and a rough outline.

## The Need for Mutual Sacrifice

Let us develop one essential component of this developing social mentality—greater abnegation. Some Christians will not be surprised to hear Us make this statement. Besides it is a fact of experience and a logical necessity that a real community impose mutual sacrifices on its members. You recall how the Son of God made man, He who *did not come to be served but to serve and to give His life as a ransom for many*, taught men the conditions of unity. By these words He Himself wished to illustrate the necessity and fruitfulness of sacrifice in achieving a kind of superior life to which all men are called by virtue of a supernatural vocation—to form the union of the Sons of God.

In conclusion, need I invoke the joy and victory of Easter? Yes, truly, Dear Sons, you have a beautiful mission to fulfill. Amid a restless world may you bring hope and the peace of fraternal devotion on a universal scale. Be the salt without which everything risks degeneration and corruption. Be the leaven which raises the stolid mass. Make out of the shapeless dough the loaf of human solidarity. May everyone understand, thanks to you, that *it is better to give than to receive*, more noble to serve than to be served, more joyful to give one's life for his brothers than to keep it for oneself.

# European Union*

### (*Address to the "Congress of Europe," June 14, 1957*)

. . . IT has been your wish that your work help strengthen the spirit of cooperation between organizations and political forces in order that European unity might be established more quickly.

You have some idea how closely We have followed the progress of the European idea and how We have watched the concrete efforts being put forth to make the idea penetrate more deeply into men's minds and, under the proper circumstances, to bring about its realization. Despite some wavering between success and regression, this plan has made some headway during the past few years. Not long ago, when this plan first took shape for application to autonomous and independent governmental institutions, people thought that it was an ideal which, albeit desirable, was nonetheless unattainable.

### European Union Today

But in 1952 the legislative bodies of six western European nations approved the formation of the European Coal and Steel

---

* Translation from *The Pope Speaks*.

Community, and the social and economic advantages of the move have been encouraging. On the other hand, the European Defense Community, which was supposed to unify efforts toward defense on a military and political basis, met with such strong resistance that it failed. At the present time, many people are of the opinion that it will be a long while before the initial enthusiasm for unification is revived.

In any case, it is not yet time to consider unity on a supranational basis, and we should fall back upon the formula of the Union of Western Europe which, aside from military aid, is intended to stimulate social, cultural, and economic cooperation. But We still cannot consider this a sufficiently strong basis for a European community, since the majority decisions of the Council of Ministers are under strong limitations and the Assembly is unable to impose its will or use parliamentary control.

From the spring of 1955, when it was touched off, the so-called European revival grew until, on March 25, 1957, it climaxed in the signing of treaties for Euratom and the Common Market. Granted that this community is under some restrictions in the economic area, it is nevertheless able, by extending its field of activity, to make the member-states aware of their mutual interests. This awareness, naturally, will exist at first only in the material order, but, if the attempt is successful, it will extend itself to those areas where moral and spiritual values are concerned.

Your congress has kept a sharp eye on the future, and you have, before anything else, examined the decisive point upon which depends the formation of any community worthy of the name: the formation of a European political authority which will have sufficient responsibility to be felt. From this point of view, the European Economic Community is less successful than the Coal and Steel Community, whose High Authority has powers which are relatively broad and which, except in certain determined cases, do not depend upon any Council of Ministers.

Among the tasks facing you now, the first one is the ratification by interested parliaments, of the treaties We mentioned above, which were signed at Rome on March 25. As a second step, you will have to examine means of reenforcing the powers of the executive branches of the already existing communities, in order to come, finally, to some idea of the constitution demanded by this political unity.

## Political Union

You have already looked into the question of an external political community and you have learned that, for such a situation to be successful and produce results, it does not necessarily presuppose an already existing economic integration. A single external political community in Europe, though it will allow for the differences arising from varying interests, will also base itself on the common economic, spiritual, and cultural interests of its members. Such a community is becoming more and more indispensable in a world which, more and more, is splitting up into small groups.

Fortunately, interests overlap on enough points to permit such a plan for unity to be put into action among the already existing European institutions, but an instrumentality is needed which will effectively refine and apply such a plan.

## Europe and Africa

Finally, you have considered the problems connected with an association between Europe and Africa, which was given special mention in the March agreements. It seems to Us that Europe must keep her influence in Africa insofar as education and formation are concerned and wherever, more basically, she gives a great deal of material aid which helps to raise the standard of living of the people of Africa and enhances the value of the continent's natural resources.

In this way Europe will prove that her desire to form a community of States does not spring from selfish motivation. She will show that she is not, after all, interested simply in a defensive arrangement which will protect her from external threats to her interests. She will prove that, more than anything else, she is working from constructive and disinterested motives.

Right now, it is abundantly clear that there is real need for union and that such a union must be built upon foundations strong enough to support it. Whether it be a painful process or a happy one, the construction of the union is going forward and, despite some unsuccessful tries, it is going forward with courage. You have already ventured to pass beyond the realities of the present and are beginning to select the stones necessary for tomorrow's building. We are happy to see such a spirit, persuaded that it comes from generous and upright motives. Your aim is to secure for Europe, which has so often been torn asunder and bloodstained, a lasting unity which will enable her to continue her mission in history.

## The Christian Message

If it is true that for Europe the message of Christianity was like the leaven in dough, always working and causing the whole mass to rise, it is no less true that this same message remains, today as yesterday, the most valuable of the treasures with which she has been charged. With the concept and exercise of the fundamental liberties of the human person, this message can maintain the vigor and integrity of the operations of family and national society and, in a supra-national community, can guarantee respect for cultural differences and a spirit of conciliation and cooperation, along with an acceptance of the sacrifices which it will entail and the dedication which it will demand.

No undertaking in the temporal order comes to a conclusion without giving rise to another, without generating, in its accomplishment, a whole series of other obligations, needs, and objectives. Human society always depends on the future; it is always in search of a better organization, and cultures often survive only by dying and giving birth to richer and more brilliant cultures which in their turn yield to others.

Christianity brings an element of growth and stability to each of these cultures. Above all, it directs their forward march toward a clearly defined goal, and gives them an unchanging assurance of a homeland which is not of this world and which only knows perfect union, because it originates in the strength and light of God Himself.

It is Our most earnest wish that this ideal will always guide your work and give you strength to bear without discouragement the fatigue, bitterness, and disillusionment inherent in all such undertakings. May you be able to construct for the men of our age an earthly home which bears some resemblance to the Kingdom of God, the Kingdom of truth, love, and peace, to which they aspire from the depths of their beings.

# The Problem of Peace*

*(Christmas Message Broadcast to the Whole World, December 22, 1957)*

. . . To a person pondering and forming a judgment on the actual state of affairs—and always allowing for the right of self-defense—the present-day competition between nations in demonstrating their individual progress in war equipment assuredly offers new "signs in the skies." But even more it offers signs of pride, of that pride which produces on earth wide differences between souls, nourishes hatreds, and prepares the way for conflict. Let those who observe today's competition, therefore, know how to reduce the facts to their true proportions and, while not rejecting approaches aiming at peace agreements which are always desirable, let them not permit themselves to be misled by records, often of very short duration, nor be too much influenced by fears skillfully evoked to win the interest and support of others who may be glad to be connected with a class of men among whom the *homo faber* takes precedence over the *homo sapiens*. May the advantage then go to the Christian man who, making use of the liberty of spirit which is derived from a truly broad understanding of things, recovers in the objective consideration of events that peace and stability of soul which has its source in the Divine Spirit Who, by His constant presence, holds the world in His care.

## The Problem of Peace

But finally, that to which the supporters of divine harmony in the world have been invited to direct their best efforts, is the problem of peace. To all of you who know Our thoughts,

---

* Translation from *The Pope Speaks*.

it will be enough for Us on this occasion—and rather to satisfy Our own mind, which is untiringly devoted to the cause of peace—to recall the immediate ends which the nations ought to aim at and bring to realization. We do this with a father's heart and as interpreting the tender cries of the Divine Infant of Bethlehem, source and pledge of all peace on earth and in the heavens.

The divine law of harmony in the world strictly imposes on all rulers of nations the obligation to prevent war by means of suitable international organizations, to reduce armaments under a system of effective inspection, and to deter whoever should aim at disturbing the nations which sincerely desire it. We are sure that, at the first sign of danger, the tightening of that bond to a greater degree would not be wanting, as has been clearly attested and revealed on several occasions, even recently.

But at the moment, it is a question not so much of hastening to the defense as of preventing the overthrow of order and of giving a deserved breathing space to the world, which has already experienced too much suffering. We have endeavored more than once in times of crisis, with warnings and counsel, to strengthen that mutual dependence, and We regard it as a special task imposed by God on Our Pontificate to forge between nations the bonds of true brotherhood. We renew Our appeal so that among the true friends of peace all possible rivalry may come to an end and so that every reason for lack of trust may be removed. Peace is a good so precious, so productive, so desirable, and so desired that every effort in its defense, even with reciprocal sacrifices of legitimate individual ambitions, is well spent. We are sure that the peoples of the world are wholeheartedly in agreement with Us, and that they expect a like sentiment from their rulers.

# John XXIII

## Plight of the Refugees*

(*Radio Broadcast*, NOUS APPRENONS, *June 28, 1959*)

WE LEARN with deep satisfaction that the United Nations plans a world-wide Refugee Year, to begin June, 1959, and to end June, 1960. We wholeheartedly lend the moral support of Our encouragement to this noble effort.

The lot of those who live in exile far from their fatherland has always attracted the maternal solicitude of the Catholic Church in a very special way, for she cannot forget the words of Christ, her divine founder: *I was a stranger and you took me in; naked and you covered me . . . I was in prison and you came to me.*

As everyone knows, hundreds of thousands of refugees are, for various reasons, victims of the turmoil of recent years, and are still detained in camps, housed in huts, humbled in their dignity as men, and exposed at times to circumstances provocative of severe temptations of discouragement and despair.

What generous man can remain indifferent to the spectacle of so many men, women, and even children being deprived of some of their most basic human rights, through no fault of their own; of families disbanded against their will, husbands separated from their wives, and children kept far from their parents . . . What a pitiful anomaly for modern society, so proud of its technical and social progress! Every individual is duty bound to become aware of this situation and to do what he can to abolish it.

* Translation from *The Pope Speaks*.

What is there that was not done for the refugees of World War I by Benedict XV, whose generous heart was so keenly sensitive to human distress? Then, in his turn, what is there that Our immediate Predecessor, Pius XII, did not do for refugees during the last war? For he too was extremely compassionate toward human suffering and sensitive to every breach of natural law! How many times did not the Holy See intervene on an international plane! What efforts did not the Holy See make and what assistance of all kinds came from Vatican City during those tragic years! We Ourselves were a deeply moved witness and an instrument for some of this work, which achieved such a variety of good results.

### An Exhortation to Catholics

Called to inherit this precious legacy of charity and of defense of the poor, which is one of the most beautiful jewels of the Catholic Church, We, in Our turn, raise Our voice in behalf of refugees and paternally exhort Our sons in every corner of the world to work generously and diligently for the success of this world-wide Refugee Year. It is a Year which is inspired by noble and disinterested intentions, and We are pleased to render homage to it.

Let all then strive, according to their ability, to improve the lot of their unfortunate brothers, mindful of the fact that their attachment to the Church and to Christ has in many a case not been unrelated to their present trials. And should one or the other—which God forbid—be tempted to close his heart to this appeal, let him remember the grave warning of Our Predecessor: "Ought not you who remain indifferent to the anguishes of the refugee, who is wandering about without a roof over his head, consider yourselves responsible for him; for his miserable lot today may well be yours tomorrow?" (Pius XII, 1950 Christmas Message).

We especially exhort pastors of souls to call the attention of their faithful to this invitation by divine Providence to manifest their sentiments of Christian charity.

### Need for State Aid

Since private initiative is powerless of itself to resolve problems of this amplitude, We are confident that public authority will, during this year, be interested in further pursuing and intensifying the efforts which have so laudably been begun in this field. Important results, We know, have already been accomplished on an international scale: notably the formulation and adoption by a rather considerable number of States of the Convention of 1951 regarding the Statute of Refugees. May these States, and others following their lead, open their frontiers ever more generously and work with dispatch for the human and social redistribution of so many unfortunate people. May these latter soon enjoy what they so ardently desire, namely, a respectable existence in the country that hospitably adopts them and the peaceful enjoyment of their personal and family rights.

On all those individuals and groups who will hasten the fulfillment of this very desirable goal by working in some way—as We shall do according to Our means—for the success of the world-wide Refugee Year, We lovingly invoke the protection and the special favors of the all powerful and merciful God.

# At the Chair of Peter*

(*Encyclical Letter*, AD PETRI CATHEDRAM, *June 29, 1959*)

. . . GOD created men not as enemies but as brothers; He gave them the earth to be cultivated by their toil and energy, so that each single one might take from it its fruits and whatever should be necessary for his sustenance and general needs in life. But the various nations are nothing else save groups of men, that is, of brothers. These, linked by that fraternal bond, ought to strive each after his proper end, and also after the common prosperity of the whole human race.

In addition, the journey through this mortal life is not something to be considered only in itself and grasped for the sake of the pleasure it gives; it leads not only to the death of human flesh, but also to immortal life, to the home-land which endures for ever.

If this teaching, if this hope full of consolation, is taken

---

* Translation from National Catholic Welfare Conference News.

away from men's minds, the whole reason for life collapses. Greed, dissensions, disputes necessarily break out in our minds, incapable of any firm control. The olive branch of peace is no guiding light in our minds, but the fires of discord are set ablaze. Our condition is almost on a par with that of beasts, devoid of reason. Nay, it is worse, since, though we are endowed with the power of reasoning, by abusing it, we can produce, and fall into, worse states—as, alas, not seldom has happened. Like Cain, we are capable of staining the earth by the grave crime of shedding a brother's blood.

Before all else, therefore, it is necessary to recall to minds and hearts the right principles, if we wish, as we ought, our actions to be brought back to the path of justice.

For if we are brothers in name and in fact, if we are made partners of a common destiny in this life and in the next, why, We say, are we capable of acting as opponents, private and public enemies, of others? Why envy others, stir up hate against them, prepare death-dealing weapons against our brethren? Already there has been enough strife among men. Already far too many thousands of young men, in the flower of their age, have poured out their blood. Already too many cemeteries of those fallen in war cover the earth's surface and solemnly warn that all should be, at long last, brought back to harmony, unity, and a just peace.

## Men Eager for Peace

Let all, then, direct their energies not at the things which cause men to keep separate from each other, but rather at those by which they can be united in a fair and mutual esteem for their respective goods and interests.

Only if men are eager for peace, as they ought to be, and not for war, only if there is a genuine common desire for the fraternal harmony of nations, will it be possible for state affairs and interests to be rightly acknowledged and, in consequence, happily reconciled.

Likewise, it will be possible, through the union of mutual understanding, for those principles to be sought and established which lead the whole human family to that most desired unity, in the enjoyment of which each nation sees its own rights of freedom not as beholden to others but as completely guaranteed. Those who oppress others, who deprive them of rightful liberty, undoubtedly can contribute nothing to this unity. We are in entire agreement with the opinion expressed by Our wise predecessor, Leo XIII: "To check ambition, grasping greed, and rivalry, which are the chief causes of war, nothing is better adapted than Christian virtue, especially justice."

For the rest, if nations do not aim at this fraternal unity which must rest on the precepts of justice and be nourished by charity, conditions of gravest crisis remain. As a result, all prudent men complain and grieve that it seems to be uncertain whether the same events are moving towards the establishing of a solid, true, and genuine peace or are slipping in complete blindness towards a new and frightful warlike conflagration. We say in complete blindness; for if—which God prevent—a new war breaks out, nothing else will await or confront all peoples (such are the dreadful armaments which our age brings into play) but appalling destruction and ruin; and this, whether they are victor or vanquished.

We therefore ask all, and statesmen in particular, that they ponder these matters prudently and earnestly before God the Judge and, as a result, with genuine good will be ready to try every approach which may lead to essential unity. This harmony and unity, by which alone, We say, the joint prosperity of nations will undoubtedly be increased, will be able to be restored only when minds are at peace and the rights of all recognized, and due freedom shines forth for the Church, for peoples, and for the individual citizen.

# Peace on Earth*

### (*Christmas Message, December 23, 1959*)

. . . No peace will have solid foundations unless hearts nourish the sentiment of brotherhood which ought to exist among all who have a common origin and are called to the same destiny. The knowledge that they belong to the same family

---

* Translation from National Catholic Welfare Conference News.

extinguishes lust, greed, pride, and the instinct to dominate others which are the roots of dissensions and wars. It binds all in a single bond of higher and more fruitful solidarity.

The basis of international peace is, above all, truth. For in international relations, too, the Christian saying is valid: *The truth shall make you free.*

It is necessary, then, to overcome certain erroneous ideas: the myths of force, nationalism or other ideas that have prevented the integrated life of nations. And it is necessary to impose a peaceful living-together on moral principles, according to the teaching of right reason and of Christian doctrine.

Along with this, enlightened by truth, must come justice, which removes the causes of quarrels and wars, solves the disputes, fixes the tasks, defines the duties, and gives the answer to the claims of each party.

Justice in its turn ought to be integrated and sustained by Christian charity: that is, love for one's neighbor and one's own people ought not to be concentrated on one's self in an exclusive egotism which is suspicious of another's good. But it ought to expand and reach out spontaneously toward the community of interests, to embrace all peoples, and to interweave common human relations. Thus it will be possible to speak of living together, and not of mere coexistence which, precisely because it is deprived of this inspiration of mutual dependence, raises barriers behind which nestle mutual suspicion, fear, and terror.

### Errors of Man in His Search for Peace

Peace is a gift of God beyond compare. Likewise, it is the object of man's highest desire. It is moreover indivisible. None of the lineaments which make up its unmistakable appearance can be ignored or excluded.

In addition, since the men of our time have not completely carried into effect the conditions of peace, the result has been that God's paths toward peace have no meeting point with those of man. Hence the abnormal situation of this postwar period has created, as it were, two blocs with all their uneasy conditions. There is not a state of war, but neither is there peace, the thing which the nations ardently desire.

At all times, because true peace is indivisible in its various aspects, it will not succeed in establishing itself on the social and international planes unless it is also, and in the first place, an interior fact. This requires then before all else—it is necessary to repeat—*men of good will.* These are precisely those to whom the angels of Bethlehem announced peace: *Peace among men of good will.* Indeed they alone can give reality to the conditions contained in the definition of peace given by St. Thomas, "The ordered harmony of citizens" and therefore order and harmony.

But how will true peace be able to put forth the two-fold blossom of order and concord if the persons who hold positions of public responsibility, before selecting the advantages and risks of their decisions, fail to recognize themselves as persons subject to the eternal moral laws?

It will be necessary again and again to remove from the path the obstacles placed by the malice of man. And the presence of these obstacles is noted in the propaganda of immorality, in social injustice, in forced unemployment, in poverty contrasted with the luxury of those who can indulge in dissipation, in the dreadful lack of proportion between the technical and moral progress of nations, and in the unchecked armaments race, where there has yet to be a glimpse of a serious possibility of solving the problem of disarmament.

### The Work of the Church

The most recent events have created an atmosphere of so-called disengagement which has caused hopes to blossom anew in many minds, after life has been lived for so long in a state of fictitious peace, a situation of great instability that more than once has been threatened with a complete rupture.

All that makes obvious how rooted in the souls of all is the craving for peace.

In order that this common desire may be promptly fulfilled the Church prays confidently to Him who rules the destinies of nations and can direct the hearts of rulers to good. No daughter of the world, but living and working in the world, the Church, as it has from the dawn of Christianity—as St. Paul wrote to Timothy—offers *prayers, intercessions and thanksgivings . . . for all men, for kings, and for all in high positions, that we may live a quiet and peaceful life in all piety*

303

*and worthy behavior.* So also today the Church accompanies with prayer the peaceful solution of controversies, the establishment of relations between nations and their mutual collaboration, just as it helps peaceful discussions in international relations.

Besides prayer, the Church makes available its maternal offices, points to the incomparable treasure of its doctrine, and urges its children to lend their active cooperation for peace by recalling St. Augustine's famous invitation: *It is more glorious to slay war with words than men with steel; and it is true glory to secure peace by peaceful means* (St. Augustine, Epistle 129, II).

It is a function and office proper to the Church that it should devote itself to peace. And the Church is aware of having omitted nothing that was within its capacities to obtain peace for nations and individuals. The Church looks with favor on every initiative which can help to spare humanity new conflicts, new massacres, and incalculable new destruction.

Unfortunately, the causes which have disturbed, and now disturb, international order have not yet been removed. It is therefore necessary to dry up the sources of evil. Otherwise the dangers to peace will remain a constant threat.

The causes of international sickness were clearly proclaimed by Our predecessor, Pius XII of immortal memory, especially in his Christmas messages of 1942 and 1943. It is well to repeat them.

These causes are: the violation of the rights and dignity of the human person and the overruling of the rights of the family and of labor; the overthrow of the juridical order and of the healthy idea of the state in keeping with the Christian spirit; impairment of the liberty, integrity, and security of other nations to whatever extent; the systematic oppression of the cultural and lingual characteristics of national minorities; the egotistical calculations of all who strive to seize control of the economic sources of the materials of common use to the detriment of other peoples; and, in particular, the persecution of religion and of the Church.

It needs still to be noted that the peace which the Church prays for cannot possibly be achieved if it is mistaken for a yielding or relaxation of its firmness in the face of ideologies and systems of life which are in open and irreconcilable opposition to Catholic teaching. Nor does peace denote indifference to the laments which come to Us even now from the unhappy lands where the rights of man are ignored and falsehood is adopted as a system.

Still less can one forget the sorrowful calvary of the Church of Silence, where the confessors of the Faith, rivaling the early Christian martyrs, are endlessly exposed to sufferings and torments for the cause of Christ. These established facts put one on guard against excessive optimism. But they render all the more earnest Our prayers for a truly universal return to respect for human and Christian liberty.

# The Campaign Against Hunger*

*(To the Tenth International Conference Sponsored by the United Nations Food and Agriculture Organization, May 3, 1960)*

You have come to seek the benediction of the Pope for the immense project which today is the object of your efforts and interests: the organization, on a world scale, of the "Campaign Against Hunger," launched recently through the initiative of the Director General of the United Nations Food and Agriculture Organization. Be indeed welcome, for your interests in this area are united with those of the Church, and the task to which you are giving your attention seems to Us eminently worthy of Our approval and encouragement. What indeed is the Church doing in this world? It is continuing Christ's work, of whom it is written that *He went about doing good and healing . . . qui pertransit benefaciendo et sanando . . .* So she recommends very warmly to her children the practice of the spiritual and corporal works of mercy, and among these last the one that heads the list states precisely this: *to feed those who are hungry.*

Certainly, *not in bread alone doth man live,* Holy Scripture teaches us and experience confirms for us. However,

---

* Translation from *The Pope Speaks.*

it is by the multiplication of this essential material food that Christ wished twice during His mortal life to manifest His power to the crowds that followed Him. And if He made use of a miracle then to turn minds toward spiritual realities, no less did He wish to satisfy bodily hunger. The Gospel, which brings us these episodes in detail, even specifies the deeply moving sentiments that then animated the divine miracle worker: *Misereor super turbam.* He said, *I have compassion on the crowd, for behold, they have now been with me three days, and have nothing to eat; and if I send them away to their homes fasting, they will faint on the way.*

Is not your activity, gentlemen, inspired by similar sentiments? You are animated, certainly, by the love of justice, by the desire to assure a more equitable distribution of the goods of this world among all men; but also, after the example of Christ, you are experiencing deep compassion at the thought of this innumerable multitude of under-nourished people— more than half the human race!—who are awaiting a gesture of mercy from their more favored brothers. To draw them out of their wretched state and to make accessible to them an intellectual life and a moral life more worthy of man, more conformable to the will of God, an enormous collective effort is necessary. You have understood this, and you are preparing to collaborate with the United Nations Food and Agriculture Organization, with the aim of assuring the success of this vast undertaking.

### Much Remains to Be Done

We do not have to say again here all the good that We think of that organization. Not so long ago We received the delegates who were participating in its recent biannual conference. We said to them:

The Church is vitally interested in the FAO. What a great and beautiful sight you are indeed putting before her maternal eyes, with your technicians at work in the whole world to organize the 'struggle against hunger,' to labor for the betterment of soils, of plantations, of animal species, of dairy farming, of the exploitation of forests . . . and all that in order at last to help the most unfortunate of our brethren, the most abandoned, those who are suffering, those who are hungry! A great and wonderful sight indeed, that inspires admiration, edification, trust in the future. [Address to the Delegates of the FAO, November 10, 1959].

306

That is what We said to the delegates of the FAO last No-vember. But it would be pointless to take pleasure in what has already been done, if one did not find it a stimulus for what remains to be done.

What remains to be done—in truth, an immense task! It is first of all to draw the attention of the whole world, if pos-sible, to the sad problem of hunger and undernourishment. And that is the first goal of the campaign to which your or-ganizations are going to contribute their thinking and their action.

Millions of human beings in the world are suffering from hunger; others, while not actually hungry, do not get enough of the foods that they need. There are the facts. It is necessary to know them, to preach them from the housetops, according to the word of the Gospel. *Praedicate super tecta!* It is necessary to awaken consciences to the meaning of the responsibility that weighs on all and on each, especially on the most favored. No one today, in a world where distance no longer counts, can give the excuse that the needs of his far-away brother are not known to him, nor can one say that the task of helping this far-away brother is not his concern. We all have a solid responsibility toward undernourished popula-tions. It is this conviction that your organizations are going to help instill in the mind of the public, which, once enlightened, will demand appropriate measures and support their fulfill-ment.

The second goal of the "Campaign Against Hunger" is to institute those measures, that is, to take direct action for raising the levels of production and consumption in undernourished areas. World production of food commodities does not an-swer the needs of all men, especially in view of the anticipated increase in population in the years to come; besides, the avail-able foods are not equally distributed. It is therefore necessary to cultivate new lands and to increase food production in areas already being utilized. There again your organization—in ac-cordance with the objectives and traits proper to each one of them—will have to suggest projects for action and research, to cooperate in their execution, and to collect from their ad-herents the contributions which will allow them to arrive at concrete results without excessive delay. It is enough to men-

tion the importance of the collaboration that is asked of you.
We are experiencing a lively joy at the thought of the immense possibilities of this campaign, which will have, We are
sure, the support of all sympathetic men, and of all institutions,
private and public, truly concerned about the welfare of humanity. So We have confidence, in giving you Our most
hearty encouragement, that the echo of Our voice will reach
beyond those who are now listening to all men of good will, as
an urgent invitation to share in this great outburst of generosity, in this enormous "work of mercy," which the "Campaign Against Hunger" is going to be.

# Self-Determination*

*(Statement to Secret Consistory, January 16, 1961)*

WE would like to hope—and We prayerfully ask this favor
from God—that, once the legitimate aspirations of people for
liberty and independence have been satisfied, the richer will
aid the poorer, the stronger support the weaker, the more advanced reach out a helping hand to the less developed, and, in
the end, that all will feel themselves brothers, for all are sons
of the same loving Father Who is in heaven. . . .

# New Aspects on Modern
# International Crises*

*(Encyclical Letter, MATER ET MAGISTRA, May 15, 1961)*

. . . THE world situation, which has changed during the period mentioned by Pius XII in his radio message of June 1, 1941,
has undergone in these past two decades profound transformation both in the internal structure of each political community
and in their mutual relations:

---

* Translation from National Catholic Welfare Conference.

In the areas of science, technology, and economics: the discovery of nuclear energy, first employed for the ends of war, but now increasingly applied to peaceful purposes; unlimited possibilities presented by chemistry in synthetic products; the growth of automation in the branches of industry and services; a modernization of agriculture; the virtual elimination of distances by means of communications, particularly brought about through radio and television; an increased speed in transportation; the initial conquests of interplanetary space.

## Standards of Justice and Equity

Our heart is filled with a deep sadness in contemplating the immeasurably sorrowful spectacle of vast numbers of workers in many lands and entire continents who are paid wages which condemn them and their families to subhuman conditions of life. This is doubtless due, among other reasons, to the fact that for these countries and continents the process of industrialization is merely beginning or still insufficiently developed.

In some of these countries however, there stands in harsh and offensive contrast to the wants of the great majority the abundance and unbridled luxury for the privileged few. In still other countries the present generation is compelled to undergo inhuman privations in order to increase the output of the national economy at a rate of acceleration which exceeds the limits permitted by justice and humanity, while in other countries a notable percentage of income is absorbed in building up and furthering an ill-conceived national prestige or vast sums are spent on armaments.

## The Underdeveloped Regions

. . . Among citizens of the same political community there is often a marked economic and social inequality due for the most part to the fact that some live and work in areas that are economically more developed, while others live and work in areas that are economically underdeveloped. When this situation exists, justice and equity demand that the public authorities should seek to eliminate or reduce such inequality. To this end public authorities should see to it that in the underdeveloped areas essential public services exist. These should be of the kind and extent suggested or required by the surroundings and correspond to the average standard of life in the national communities. Furthermore, it is necessary to develop a suitable economic and social policy regarding the supply of labor and the dislocation of population, wages, taxes, interest, and investments, with special attention to expanding industries. In short, there should be a policy capable of promoting complete employment of the labor force, of stimulating enterprising initiative, and of exploiting the natural resources of the place.

But governmental action along these lines must always be justified by the demands of the common good, which requires that all three areas of production—agriculture, industry, and public services—be developed gradually, simultaneously, and harmoniously in order to obtain unity on the national level. Special effort must be made that the citizens of the less developed regions take an active part, insofar as circumstances allow, in their economic betterment.

Finally, it is necessary to remember that even private enterprise must contribute to effecting an economic and social balance among the different zones of the same country. And indeed public authorities, in accordance with the principle of subsidiarity, must encourage and help private enterprise, entrusting to it, as far as efficiently possible, the continuation of economic development.

## Unbalance between Land and Population

It is not out of place to remark here that there are not a few countries where a gross disproportion between land and population exists. In some countries there is a scarcity of population and abundance of tillable land. In others, on the other hand, the population is large, while arable land is scarce.

Furthermore, there are some countries where, in spite of rich natural resources, not enough food is produced to feed the population because of primitive methods of agriculture. On the other hand, in some countries, on account of modern methods of agriculture, food surpluses have become an economic problem.

The solidarity of the human race and Christian brotherhood demand an active and manifold cooperation among the peoples of the world. They demand a cooperation which permits and encourages the movement of goods, capital, and men with a view to eliminating or reducing unbalance. Later on, We shall treat this point in more detail.

Here, however, We should like to express Our sincere appreciation for the highly beneficial work which the United Nations Food and Agricultural Organization (F.A.O.) is undertaking to establish fruitful accord among nations, to promote the modernization of agriculture, especially in countries in the process of development, and to alleviate the suffering of hunger-stricken peoples.

### Demands of Justice in Relationships between Nations

Probably the most difficult problem of the modern world concerns the relationship between political communities that are economically advanced and those in the process of development. The standard of living is high in the former, while in the latter countries poverty, and in some cases extreme poverty, exists. The solidarity which binds all men and makes them members of the same family requires that political communities enjoying an abundance of material goods not remain indifferent to political communities whose citizens suffer from poverty, misery, and hunger and who lack even the elementary rights of the human person. This is particularly true since, given the growing interdependence among the peoples of the earth, it is not possible to preserve lasting peace if glaring economic and social inequality among them persists.

Mindful of Our role of Universal Father, We feel obliged to stress solemnly what We have stated in another connection: "We are all equally responsible for the undernourished peoples . . . Therefore, it is necessary to educate one's conscience to the sense of responsibility which weighs upon each and everyone, especially upon those who are more blessed with this world's goods."

It is obvious that the obligation to help those in want and misery, which the Church has always taught, should be felt more strongly by Catholics, who find a most notable motive in the fact that we are all members of Christ's Mystical Body. John, the Apostle, said: *In this we have known the charity of God, because He hath laid down His life for us: and we ought to lay down our lives for the brethren. He that hath the substance of this world, and shall see his brother in need, and shall shut up his bowels from him: How doth the charity of God abide in him?*

We therefore see with satisfaction that those political communities enjoying high economic standards are providing assistance to political communities in the process of economic development in order that they may succeed in raising their standards of living.

## Scientific, Technical and Financial Cooperation

There are countries which produce consumer goods, especially farm products, in excess, while in other countries large segments of the population suffer from misery and hunger. Justice and Humanity demand that the former come to the aid of the latter. To destroy or squander goods that other people need in order to live is to offend against justice and humanity.

While it is true that to produce goods, especially agricultural products, in excess of the needs of the political community can cause economic harm to a certain portion of the population, this is not a motive for exoneration from the obligation of extending emergency aid to the indigent and hungry. Rather, all ingenuity should be used to contain the negative effects deriving from surplus goods, or at least to make the entire population equally share the burden.

Emergency aid, although a duty imposed by humanity and justice, is not enough to eliminate or even to reduce the causes which in not a few political communities bring about a permanent state of want, misery and hunger. These causes flow, for the most part, from the primitiveness or backwardness of their economic systems. And this cannot be remedied except by means of varied forms of cooperation directed to making these citizens acquire new outlooks, professional qualifications, scientific and technical competence. This cooperation must also consist of putting at their disposal the necessary capital to start and to speed up their economic development with the help of modern methods.

We are well aware that in recent years the realization has grown and matured that efforts should be made to favor the economic development and social progress in the countries which face the greatest difficulties.

World and regional organizations, individual states, foundations, and private societies offer to the above mentioned countries, in an increasing degree, their own technical cooperation in all productive spheres. They multiply facilities for thousands of young people to study in the universities of the more developed countries and to acquire an up-to-date scientific, technical and professional formation. Meanwhile world banking institutes, individual nations and private persons furnish capital and give life, or help to give life, to an ever richer network of economic enterprises in the countries in the process of development. We are happy to profit by the present occasion to express Our sincere appreciation of such richly, fruitful works. But We cannot excuse Ourselves from pointing out that the scientific, technical, and economic cooperation between economically developed political communities and those just beginning or on the way to development needs to be increased beyond the present level. And it is Our hope that such a development will characterize their dealings during the next decades.

On this matter We consider some reflections and warnings opportune.

## Avoiding the Errors of the Past

Wisdom demands that the political communities which are themselves in the initial stage or a little advanced in their economic development keep before their eyes the actual experiences of the already developed political communities.

More and better production corresponds to a rational need and is also an absolute necessity. However, it is no less necessary and in conformity to justice that the riches produced be equally distributed among all members of the political community. Hence an effort should be made to see that social progress proceeds at the same pace as economic development. This means that it be actuated, as far as possible, gradually and harmoniously in all productive sectors of agriculture, industry, and services.

Political communities on the way toward economic development generally present their own unmistakable individuality, due either to their resources and the specific character of their own natural environment, or to their traditions, frequently abounding in human values, or to a quality typical of their own members.

The economically developed political communities, when lending their help, must recognize and respect this individuality and overcome the temptation to impose themselves by means of these works upon the community in the course of economic development.

A bigger temptation with which the economically developed political communities have to struggle is the temptation to profit from technical and financial cooperation so as to influence the political situation of the less developed countries to bring about plans of world domination.

It must be explicitly declared that such would be a new form of colonialism which, however cleverly disguised, would not for all that be less blameworthy than that from which many peoples have recently escaped and harm international goodwill by constituting a menace and danger to world peace.

It is, therefore, indispensable and closely related to the needs of justice that technical and financial aid be given in sincere political disinterestedness, for the purpose of putting communities on the way to economic development and in a position to realize their own proper economic and social growth.

In such a way a precious contribution to the formation of a world community would be made, a community in which all members are subjects conscious of their own duties and rights, working on a basis of equality to bring about the universal common good.

### Respect for the Hierarchy of Values

Scientific and technical progress, economic development, and the betterment of living conditions are certainly positive elements in a civilization. But we must remember that they are not nor can they be considered the supreme values. They are essentially instrumental in character.

It is with sadness that We point out that in the economically developed countries there are not a few persons in whom the consciousness of the hierarchy of values is weakened, dead, or confused. That is, there are not a few persons in whom spiritual values are neglected, forgotten, and denied, while the progress of the sciences and technology, economic development, and material well-being are often fostered and proposed as preeminent, even elevated to the unique, purpose of life. This constitutes an insidious poison, one of the most dangerous, to the work which the economically developed peoples give to those on the way to development, those in whom ancient tradition has quite often preserved a living and operating consciousness of some of the most important human values.

To undermine this consciousness is essentially immoral. One must respect it and, where possible, clarify and develop it so that it will remain what it is: a foundation for true civilization.

## The Contribution of the Church

The Church, as is known, is universal by divine right. And she is universal historically from the fact that she is present, or strives to be so, among all peoples.

The entrance of the Church among a people has always brought positive reactions in the social and economic fields, as history and experience show. People on becoming Christian cannot but feel obliged to improve the institutions and the environment in the temporal order, whether to prevent harm to the dignity of man or to eliminate or reduce obstacles to the good and to multiply the incentives and invitations to virtue.

Moreover, the Church, entering the life of the people, is not nor does she consider herself to be an institution which is imposed from outside. This is due to the fact that her presence is brought about by the rebirth or resurrection of each person in Christ. And he who is reborn or rises again in Christ never feels himself constrained from without. Indeed, he feels himself liberated in the deepest part of his being and thus open towards God. And whatever in him is of worth, whatever be its nature, is reaffirmed and ennobled.

As Our predecessor, Pius XII, wisely observed:

The Church of Jesus Christ is the respository of His wisdom; she is certainly too wise to discourage or belittle those peculiarities and differences which mark out one nation from another. It is quite legitimate for nations to treat those differences as a sacred inheritance and guard them at all costs. The Church aims at unity, a unity determined and kept alive by the supernatural love which should be actuating everybody. She does not aim at a uniformity which would only be external in its effects and would cramp the natural tendencies of the nations concerned. Every nation has its own genius, its own qualities, springing from the hidden roots of its being. The wise development, the encouragement within limits, of that genius, those qualities, does no harm. And if a nation cares to take precautions, to lay down rules, for that end, it has the Church's approval. She is mother enough to befriend such projects with her prayers. We notice with profound satisfaction how today also, the Catholic citizens of the countries moving towards economic development are not, as a rule, second to any in taking their part in the effort which their own countries are making to develop and raise themselves in the economic and social fields.

Furthermore, Catholic citizens of the economically developed countries are multiplying their efforts to help and make more fruitful work being done for the communities still developing economically. Worthy of special consideration is the varied assistance that they increasingly give to students from the countries of Africa and Asia who are scattered throughout the universities of Europe and America, and the preparation of persons trained to go to the less developed countries in order to engage in technical and professional activity.

To these, Our beloved sons, who in every continent show forth the perennial vitality of the Church in promoting genuine progress and in giving life to civilization, We wish to join Our kind and paternal word of appreciation and encouragement.

### Population Increase and Economic Development

In recent years the problem concerning the relationship between population increase, economic development and the availability of the means of sustenance, whether on a world plane or as it confronts economically developing political communities, is very much to the fore again.

On a worldwide scale, some observe that according to sufficiently reliable statistics, in a few decades the human family will reach a very high figure, while economic development will proceed slower. From this they deduce that, if nothing is done in time to check the population flow, the lack of balance between the population and the food supply in the not too distant future will make itself felt acutely.

Insofar as this affects the political communities which are developing economically (still relying on statistical data), it is clear that the rapid spread of hygienic measures and of appropriate medical remedies will greatly reduce the death rate, especially among infants, while the birth rate, which in such countries is usually high, tends to remain more or less constant, at least for a considerable period of time. Therefore, the excess

316

of births over deaths will notably increase, while the productive efficiency of the respective economic systems will not increase proportionately. Accordingly, an improvement in the standards of living in these developing political communities is impossible. Indeed it is inevitable that things will get worse. Hence, to avoid a situation which will result in extreme hardship, there are those who would have recourse to drastic measures of birth control or prevention.

## The Terms of the Problem

The fact is that, considered on a world scale, the relationship between population increase on the one hand and economic development and availability of food supplies on the other, does not seem—at least for the moment and in the near future—to create a difficulty. In every case the elements from which one can draw sure conclusions are too uncertain and changeable.

Besides, God in His goodness and wisdom has diffused in nature inexhaustible resources and has given to man the intelligence and genius to create fit instruments to master and satisfy the needs and demands of life. Hence, the real solution of the problem is not to be found in expedients that offend the moral order established by God which injure the very origin of human life, but in a renewed scientific and technical effort on the part of man to deepen and extend his dominion over nature. The progress of science and technology, already realized, opens up in this direction limitless horizons.

We realize that, in certain areas and political communities with developing economies, really serious problems and difficulties can and do present themselves, due to a deficient economic and social organization which does not offer living conditions proportionate to the rate of population increase as well as to the fact that solidarity among peoples is not operative to a sufficient degree.

But even in such a hypothesis, We must immediately and clearly state that these problems must not be confronted and these difficulties overcome by having recourse to methods and means which are unworthy of man which find their explanation only in an utterly materialistic concept of man himself and of his life.

The true solution is found only in economic development

and social progress which respects and promotes true human values, individual and social. It is to be found only in economic development and social progress brought about in a moral atmosphere, conformable to the dignity of man and to the immense value of the life of a single human being, and in cooperation on a world scale that permits and favors an ordered and fruitful interchange of useful knowledge, capital and manpower.

## Respect for the Laws of Life

We must solemnly proclaim that human life is transmitted by means of the family, the family founded on marriage, one and indissoluble, raised for Christians to the dignity of a sacrament. The transmission of human life is entrusted by nature to a person in conscious activity and, as such, is subject to the all wise laws of God, inviolable and immutable which are to be recognized and observed. Therefore, it is not permissible to use means and follow methods that may be licit for the transmission of plant or lower forms of animal life.

Human life is sacred, and from its very inception, the creative action of God is directly operative. By violating His laws, the Divine Majesty is offended, the individuals themselves and humanity degraded and, likewise, the community of which they are members is enfeebled.

It is of the greatest importance that the new generations be brought up with an adequate cultural as well as religious formation. It is the duty and right of parents to obtain this formation which leads to a profound sense of responsibility in all the expressions of life and, therefore, in regard to the forming of a family and the procreation and education of children. These ought to be formed in a life of Faith and great trust in Divine Providence in order to be ready to undergo fatigue and sacrifices in the fulfilment of a mission, so noble and often so arduous as the cooperation with God in the transmission of human life and the education of offspring. For such education no institution provides so many efficacious resources as the Church which, even for this reason, has the right to full liberty to fulfill her mission.

Genesis relates how God imposed on the first human beings two commands: that of transmitting life—*Increase and multi-*

318

*ply*—and that of dominating nature—*Fill the earth and sub-due it.* These commands complement each other.

Certainly the Divine command to dominate nature is not aimed at destructive purposes. Instead it is for the service of life.

We point out with sadness one of the most disturbing contradictions by which Our epoch is tormented and by which it is being consumed, namely that, while on the one hand in strong relief situations of want, the spectre of misery and hunger haunts us; on the other hand scientific discoveries, technical inventions and economic resources are being used, often extensively, to provide terrible instruments of ruin and death.

A provident God grants sufficient means to the human race to solve in dignified fashion the many and delicate problems attendant upon the transmission of life. But these problems become difficult of solution or insoluble because man, led astray in mind or perverted in will, turns to such means as are opposed to reason and hence he seeks ends that do not answer man's social nature or the plans of Providence.

### Cooperation on a World Scale

The progress of science and technology in all aspects of life multiply and increase the relationships between political communities and hence render their interdependence ever more profound and vital.

As a result, it can be said that problems of any importance, whatever their content may be—scientific, technical, economic, social, political or cultural—present today supranational and worldwide dimensions.

Hence, the different political communities can no longer adequately solve their major problems in their own surroundings and with their own forces, even though they be communities which are notable for the high level and extent of their culture, for the number and industriousness of their citizens, for the efficiency of their economic systems and the vastness and the richness of their territories. Political communities react on each other. It may be said that each succeeds in developing itself by contributing to the development of the other. Hence, understanding and cooperation are necessary.

One can thus understand how in the minds of individual human beings and different peoples the conviction of the urgent necessity of mutual understanding and cooperation is becoming ever more widespread. But at the same time, it seems that men, especially those entrusted with greater responsibility, show themselves unable to understand one another. The root of such inability is not to be sought in scientific, technical or economic reasons but in the absence of mutual trust. Men, and consequently States, fear each other. Each fears that the other harbors plans of conquest and is waiting for the favorable moment to put these plans into effect. Hence, each organizes its own defenses and arms itself not for attacking, so it is said, but to deter the potential aggressor against any effective invasion.

As a consequence, vast human energies and gigantic resources are employed for nonconstructive purposes. Meanwhile, in the minds of individual human beings and among peoples there arises and grows a sense of uneasiness and reluctance which lessens the spirit of initiative for works on a broad scale.

## Failure to Acknowledge the Moral Order

The lack of reciprocal trust finds its explanation in the fact that men, especially the more responsible ones, are inspired in the unfolding of their activity by different or radically opposed concepts of life. Unfortunately, in some of these concepts the existence of the moral order—transcendent, universal, absolute, equal and binding on all—is not recognized. Thus, they fail to meet and understand each other fully and openly in the light of one and the same law of justice, admitted and adhered to by all. It is true that the term justice and the phrase "demands of justice" are uttered by the lips of all. However, these utterances take on different and opposite meanings.

Wherefore, the repeated and impassioned appeals to justice and the demands of justice, rather than offering a possibility of meeting or of understanding, increase the confusion, sharpen the contrasts, and keep disputes inflamed. In consequence, the belief is spread that to enforce one's rights and pursue one's own interests, no other means are left than recourse to violence in the face of the most serious evils.

Mutual trust among men and among states cannot begin or increase except by the recognition of and respect for the moral order.

The moral order does not hold except in God. Cut off from God, it disintegrates. Man, in fact, is not only a material organism but is also a spirit endowed with thought and freedom. He demands, therefore, a moral and religious order which bears more than any material value on the directions and solutions it can give to the problems of individual and group life within the national communities and the relationships among them.

It has been claimed that in an era of scientific and technical triumphs, men can construct their civilization without God. But the truth is that these same scientific and technical advances present human problems of a worldwide scope which can be solved only in the light of a sincere and active faith in God, the beginning and end of man in the world.

These truths are confirmed by the realization that the same limitless horizons which are opened up by scientific research add to and develop the conviction that mathematical and scientific notions point out but do not gather, much less express entirely, the more profound aspects of reality. The tragic experience that the gigantic forces placed at the disposal of technology can be used for purposes both constructive and destructive makes evident the pressing importance of spiritual values so that scientific and technical progress may preserve its essentially instrumental character with reference to civilization.

Further, the sense of increasing dissatisfaction which spreads among human beings in national communities with a high standard of living destroys the illusion of a hoped for paradise on earth. But at the same time, the consciousness of inviolable and universal rights becomes ever clearer, and ever more forceful the aspiration for more just and more human relations. These motives contribute toward making human beings more conscious of their own limitations and toward creating in them a striving for spiritual values. And this cannot but be a happy symbol of sincere understanding and profitable cooperation.

## The House of the Lord

Whatever the technical and economic progress, there will neither be justice nor peace in this world until men return to the sense of their dignity as creatures and sons of God, the just and final reason of the being of all reality created by Him. Man separated from God becomes inhuman to himself and to those of his kind, because the orderly relation of society pre-supposes the orderly relation of one's conscience with God, font of truth, justice, and love.

It is true that the persecution of so many of Our dearly be-loved brothers and sons, which has been raging for decades in many countries, even those of an ancient Christian civiliza-tion, makes ever clearer to Us the dignified superiority of the persecuted and the refined barbarity of the persecutors, so that, if it does not give visible signs of repentance, it induces many to think.

But it is always true that the most perniciously typical aspect of the modern era consists in the absurd attempt to reconstruct a solid and fruitful temporal order, prescinding from God, the only foundation on which it can endure, and to want to celebrate the greatness of man by drying up the font from which that greatness springs and from which it is nourished, hence restraining and, if possible, extinguishing man's sighing for God. Everyday experience continues to witness to the fact, amidst the most bitter delusions and not rarely in terms of blood, that, as stated in the inspired book: *Unless the Lord build the house, they labor in vain that build it.*

# All Is Lost by War*

(*Address to World Leaders, September 10, 1961*)

THE Apostle Peter, in his speech to those who were come to-gether in the house of the Roman centurion Cornelius, de-clared that all the nations of the earth without distinction are henceforth invited to consider the universal Fatherhood of God. He sums up this heavenly doctrine in the message of peace: *Preaching peace through Jesus Christ.*

This same message is the very pulsation of Our heart, the heart of a father and of a bishop of the Holy Church. It comes more eagerly to Our lips whenever the clouds seem to gather darkly on the horizon.

---

* Translation from National Catholic Welfare Conference.

We have before Us the memory of the popes who most closely preceded Us, whose outspoken manifestations of solicitude and anxious appeals have passed into history. From the exhortation of Pius X when the first European conflagration was imminent—a few days before his saintly death—to the encyclical of Benedict XV *Pacem, Dei Munus Pulcherrimum* ("Peace, the Most Beautiful Gift of God"), which looked to true peace "not as written into treaties but rather as sealed in the hearts of men," to that fervent, last-minute appeal of Pius XII on August 24, 1939: "It is by the power of sound reason, not by force of arms, that justice makes its way." We have a whole series of pleadings—sometimes deeply sorrowful and moving but always paternal—calling upon the whole world to guard against the danger while there is yet time, and assuring the nations that whereas everything is lost, and lost to everyone, through war, nothing will be lost through peace.

We make this appeal Our own, extending it once more to those who bear on their consciences the gravest weight of public and acknowledged responsibilities. The Church by her very nature cannot remain indifferent to human suffering, even were it no more than anxiety and anguish. And this is the reason why We call upon the rulers of nations to face squarely the tremendous responsibilities they bear before the tribunal of history, and what is more before the judgment seat of God, and We entreat them not to fall victims to false and deceiving provocations.

It is truly upon wise men that the issue depends: that force shall not prevail, but right; through free and sincere negotiations that truth and justice shall be vindicated by safeguarding the essential liberties and the insuppressible values of every nation and of every human person.

## Call to Believers and Unbelievers

Though We are far from exaggerating the importance of what has, up to now, only the appearance—but we must say the too irresponsible and tragically deplorable appearance—of a threat of war, as reported in the sources of daily public information, it is quite natural that We should make Our own the anxious solicitude of Our predecessors and present it as a sacred warning to all Our children, as We feel it Our right and Our duty to call them, to all who believe in God and in His Christ, and even to unbelievers, since all men belong to God and to Christ by right of origin and of redemption.

Those two pillars of the Church, SS. Peter and Paul, give us the warning.

The former does this in his affirmation, several times repeated, of peace in Christ the Son of God and the latter, the Doctor of the Gentiles, in a very detailed indication of counsels and instructions which are for that matter timely and appropriate for all who hold or will hold any post of responsibility in the course of human generation.

*I have no more to say, brethren, except this: Draw your strength from the Lord, from that mastery which His power supplies . . . it is not against flesh and blood that we enter the lists. We have to do with principalities and power, with those who have mastery of the world in these dark days, with evil influences in an order higher than ours.*

Possessing the wisdom and the fulness of fatherhood as the humble successor of St. Peter and custodian of the deposit of Faith—which remains always the great Divine Book open to all men of all nations—and consequently also the keeper of Christ's Gospel, We deem it opportune to offer some personal, concrete reflections on the present world situation insofar as it gives rise to uncertainty and fear.

Following the counsel of St. Paul in regard to the attitude to be taken towards the evil spirits in an order higher than ours, We should note the interesting description he makes of the good fighter poised to meet the assault of his adversary: *Stand fast, your loins girt with truth, the breastplate of justice fitted on, and your feet shod in readiness to publish the gospel of peace, the* evangelium pacis. *With all this, take up the shield of Faith, with which you will be able to quench all the fire-tipped arrows of your wicked enemy. Make the helmet of salvation your own, and the sword of the spirit, God's word.*

All these are spiritual weapons described in figures of speech by means of which, beloved brethren and children, you can discern indications of what can be and what ought to be the attitude of a good Christian in the face of any event, at any time and under any circumstances. That which comes from the evil one and from unbridled natural inclinations is a war of the spirit, a continuous warfare—and always the hideous fire that can penetrate and destroy everything.

Therefore, it is through the guidance of the Apostle of the Gentiles that we are led to the clearest and most solid foundation upon which must be based the attitude of the Christian spirit in the face of whatever Providence may dispose or permit. Between two words, war or peace, are entwined the anguish and the hopes of the world, the anxieties and the joy of individual and social life.

### Frightful Effect of New Weapons

He who cannot forget the history of the more or less distant past, years filled with afflictions and now recorded in old books, and who still has a vivid recollection of the blood-stained half century between 1914 and the present, and remembers the sufferings of our peoples and our lands—even if there were peaceful interludes between one tribulation and the next—trembles at the thought of what could happen to each one of us and to the whole world. Every war brings upheaval and destruction to persons, regions and the entire world. What could happen especially now with the frightful effects of new weapons of destruction and ruin which human ingenuity continues to multiply to everyone's loss?

In Our youth We were always deeply moved by that ancient cry of despair which, when the army of Charlemagne first appeared on the Alps, Desiderius, the King of the Lombards, gave out while rending his hair: "The sword, alas, the sword!" What should be said of the modern implements of war derived from the secrets of nature and capable of unleashing unheard of energy to wreak havoc and destruction?

By the mercy of God, We are persuaded that up until the present time there is no serious threat of either immediate or remote war. In making this reference of Our own to a subject that the press of all nations is discussing, We mean nothing more than to take still another opportunity of appealing with confidence to the serene and sure wisdom of all men who guide the nations of the world.

While it is true that at the end of his letter to the Ephesians, written in a prison in Rome where he was chained to a Roman soldier guarding him, the Apostle Paul was inspired by military weapons to teach Christians the arms necessary to defend themselves against, and to gain victory over, spiritual enemies, still it is not surprising that at the end of the list of weapons, he stresses prayer as the most effective of them all.

Listen to his words: *Galeam salutis adsumite et gladium spiritus, quod est verbum Dei per omnem orationem et obsecrationem orantes omni tempore in spiritu et in ipso vigilantes in omini instantia et obsecratione pro omnibus sanctis—Use every kind of prayer and supplication, pray at all times in the Holy Spirit: Keep awake to that end with all perseverance: Offer your supplication for all the saints.*

With this earnest invitation the Doctor of the Gentiles brings us to the particular purpose of our being united here today in spirit in a gathering that a mere hint has been sufficient to bring about and which has resulted in a great uplifting of spirit towards order and peace. The children of the Catholic Church well know this aspiration and this invocation.

In days of sorrow the worldwide prayer to Almighty God, Creator of the universe, to His Son Jesus Christ, made man for man's salvation, and to the Holy Spirit, Lord and lifegiver, has received from heaven and upon earth wonderful answers, which are recorded as happy and glorious pages in the history of mankind and of individual nations. We must open our hearts and empty them of the malice with which at times the spirit of error and evil seeks to infect them, and thus purified, we must lift them up confident of receiving heaven's blessing as well as prosperity in the things of earth.

### Prayer for Peace of Christ

Venerable brothers and beloved children, our simple and spontaneous meeting together in spirit today could well be— who knows?—the first of a series of assemblies of peace, not marred by pointless clamoring. But We are gladdened by a heartfelt sentiment of elevation and peace, an assurance of the tranquility and nobility of life in the happiness of Christian society, which is, in Christ, divine brotherhood and a foretaste of the joys of heaven.

Reflect that the Catholic Church scattered throughout the world, today, alas, troubled and divided, is preparing for a universal gathering—the ecumenical council—which is aimed at the promotion of that true brotherhood of the nations which exalts Christ Jesus, the glorious and immortal King of Ages and of peoples, *light of the world, and way, truth and life.*

This afternoon, during the Holy Sacrifice of the Mass, the blood of Jesus Christ has come down upon us, upon our lives, upon our souls. By it we are sanctified and redeemed and lifted up with joy.

We have prayed together and in so doing we have felt great joy in our hearts. Let us continue to pray in this way, as St. Paul invites us to do at the end of his touching letter. Let us pray with one another and for one another, and for all the scattered creatures of God who make up the Holy Church and the human family, which is also all His own.

We would extend our most urgent invitation to prayer to priests, to consecrated souls, to the innocent and to the suffering. Let us all together beg the Father of Light and of Grace to enlighten the minds and move the wills of those who hold the chief responsibility for the life or death of the peoples. Let us pray for the peoples themselves that they may not allow themselves to be dazzled by exacerbated nationalism and destructive rivalry, and that, as We so earnestly exhorted in Our encyclical *Mater et Magistra,* the relationships in the life of human society may be reintegrated in truth, in justice and in love. Let us all pray that, by means of the penetration of the Christian spirit, morality may grow strong: the vigorous strength of Christian families, the source of noble power and dignity and of blessed and joyful prosperity.

Ever and always let us pray for the peace of Christ here below, between all men of good will: *that all the families of the nations, rent asunder by the wound of sin, may be subjected to the most gentle rule of Christ.*

And finally We turn to you, O Blessed Virgin Mary, mother of Jesus and our mother also. How can we, with trembling hearts, apply ourselves to this greatest problem of life or death, which overshadows all mankind, without confiding ourselves to your intercession to preserve us from every evil?

This is your hour, O Mary. Blessed Jesus entrusted us to you in the supreme moment of His bloody sacrifice. We are certain of your intervention.

On September 8, the Church celebrated the anniversary of your most happy birth, saluting you as the beginning of the salvation of the world and the heavenly promise of an increase of peace.

Yes, yes, for this We supplicate you, O our most sweet mother, O Queen of the World. Of victorious war or of a conquered people it has no need, but of a renewed and more robust health, of fruitful and serene peace. Of this it has need, and for this it cries with a great voice: the beginning of salvation and increase of peace. Amen.

# Statements by the Bishops of the United States of America

## The Crisis of Christianity*

*(November 14, 1941)*

CHRISTIANITY faces today its most serious crisis since the Church came out of the catacombs.

We, the members of the Administrative Board of the National Catholic Welfare Conference, deputed in the annual meeting of the Bishops of the United States to express their mind on the crisis of Christianity, declare, as shepherds of souls, that our concern is the supreme interest of religion. Our thoughts, therefore, turn to the two greatest evils of today, which would destroy all spiritual values. We find two subversive forces, both in control of powerful governments, both bent on world dominance. They are Nazism and Communism.

However plausible their constitutions and their propaganda, the alarming reality is that neither system understands nor permits freedom in its true Christian sense. Both systems usurp arbitrary power over the lives and destinies of men; their dictators assume a power which belongs to God alone.

Our late Holy Father significantly issued his epochal encyclicals on Nazism and atheistic Communism within five days of each other.

---

* From National Catholic Welfare Conference pamphlet.

329

## Systems and Their Victims

His Holiness condemned the aberrations of Nazism, its denial of God in the true Christian sense, its deification of the State, its usurpation of the powers of God, of religion and of parents, its falsification of Christian terminology, its betrayal of the eternal principles of objective morality, and its rejection of the rights and dignity of every human being. Pope Pius XI, with prophetic vision, declared that "its (Nazism) machinations, from the beginning, had no other aim than a war of extermination." He branded the Nazi oppressors of the Church in Germany as "the nullifiers and destroyers of the Christian West."

The late Holy Father, while condemning the Nazi system, expressed his love for the German people in these words:

Before Our eyes stands the countless throng of faithful sons and daughters for whom the suffering of the Church in Germany, and their own suffering, has in no way diminished their devotion to the cause of God . . . nor diminished their cheerful readiness to remain true to what they have believed and have received from their forefathers as a sacred inheritance. From a heart that is deeply moved, We send them Our paternal greeting.

The Holy See has condemned atheistic Communism. Popes Pius IX, Leo XIII, and Pius XI pronounced their solemn condemnations of the system. Exercising their God-given commission, the Roman Pontiffs could take no other course than to condemn the errors, the tactics, the satanic designs of Communism. At no time can there be any possibility of compromising with an ideology that proclaims and acts upon the denial of a personal and omnipotent God, rejects contemptuously the Divine Saviour of the world, all Christian principles and Christian culture, ruthlessly persecutes religion and brutally murders its ministers. The leaders of atheistic Communism have done this nefarious work. Under them only anti-God and anti-Christian propaganda can have liberty of action.

## Pope Pius XI's Condemnation of Communism

Pope Pius XI, who pronounced the most explicit condemnation of atheistic Communism, expressed in the same encyclical his paternal and compassionate benevolence for the people of Russia in these words:

In making these observations it is no part of Our intention to condemn *en masse* the peoples of the Soviet Union. For them We cherish the warmest paternal affection. We are well aware that not a few of them groan beneath the yoke imposed on them by men who, in very large part, are strangers to the real interests of their country. We recognize that many were deceived by fallacious hopes. We blame only the system, with its authors and abettors who considered Russia the best field for experimenting with a plan elaborated decades ago, and who from there continue to spread it from one end of the world to the other.

We, the Bishops, who here express, at this critical hour, our judgment in these matters of gravest import, while enjoying, as we do, a well-ordered liberty in a free country, declare our devotion to His Holiness, Pope Pius XII, and our loyalty to his leadership as the Vicar of Christ and the Common Father of all nations and peoples. We unite with our Holy Father in praying for the attainment of a peace that will be accepted by all right-thinking governments and individuals as permeated by justice and charity. We earnestly ask our priests and people to continue their prayers that the violence of the war tempest may soon be spent, and that a just peace and an ordered prosperity may be restored to a distracted world.

In a Christmas message to the world, His Holiness, Pope Pius XII, on December 4, 1939, laid down five points for a just and honorable peace. In our own statement of April, 1941, we urged the consideration of these conditions proposed by our Holy Father.

Again, in his message delivered on Christmas Eve, 1940, His Holiness reiterated these five indispensable prerequisites for the right kind of a new order in the world. He called them triumphs—the triumph over hate, over mistrust, over the spirit of ruthless selfishness, over the conflict in world economy, over the false principle that might makes right.

### Fundamental Values in World Reconstruction

Observing the fiftieth anniversary of the Magna Charta of labor, the *Rerum Novarum* of Leo XIII, His Holiness, Pope Pius XII, on June 1, 1941, spoke of "three fundamental values"

331

which must be kept in mind for the reconstruction of the world after the present devastating war.

The first of these values has to do with the use of material goods. His Holiness quotes from the letter which he addressed to the American Hierarchy, *Sertum Laetitiae,* on November 1, 1939, in which he stated that "the goods which were created by God for all men should flow equitably to all, according to the principles of justice and charity."

The second fundamental value considered by His Holiness is human labor. He says:

The duty and the corresponding right to work are imposed on, and conceded to, the individual in the first instance by nature and not by society. . . . The duty and the right to organize the labor of the people belong above all to . . . the employers and the workers. It devolves upon the State to intervene in the field of labor and in the division and distribution of work according to the form and measure that the common good, properly understood, demands. Every legitimate and beneficial interference of the State in the field of labor should be such as to safeguard and respect its personal character.

The third "value" emphasizes the importance of the possession of private property by the family. His Holiness insists that, of all goods which can be held as private property, "none is more conformable to nature than the land." The Holy Father lays stress on the social significance of widespread ownership of land in the form of the family homestead. To him, the function of the family as the root of a nation's greatness and power is bound up with family ownership of "the holding on which it lives, and from which it draws all or part of its subsistence." Without that "stability which is rooted in its own holding," the family cannot be the "cell of society" which nature destined it to be.

Domestic progress and peace depend on securing vital space for the rural family, as world progress and peace depend on securing living space for all the nations of the world. Accordingly, an adequate solution of the problems of emigration is of major importance in bringing tranquillity to a confused world.

### Hope for Tomorrow

Our Holy Father, despite the horrors of war, which sadden his paternal heart, and the crushing burdens which his Pon-

tificate has laid upon him, is full of hope. His Holiness is looking, as he tells us, to that tomorrow "when the ruin of this
world hurricane is cleared, and when the onset of a reconstruction of new social order (which is a desire worthy of
God and of man) will infuse new courage and a new wave of
profusion and growth in the garden of human culture."
The words of the Pope of Peace regarding the conditions he
lays down for peace and the triumphs to be achieved in the
reconstruction of a world order in which justice and charity
are to prevail deserve our most careful study.

With apostolic liberty and with fraternal charity we send
our greetings and sympathy to our suffering brother Bishops
and their flocks in all countries where subversive forces are
persecuting religion and denying freedom of conscience.
Our fervent prayers are offered for their liberation, for their
freedom to worship God according to the dictates of their
conscience, for their freedom of education, their freedom of
assembly, their freedom from the slavery of tyranny: the
freedom of the sons of God.

Our sympathy goes out again to the peoples of those countries who have been crushed under the heel of the invader,
and, indeed, to all upon whom war has imposed so heavy a
burden of suffering and sacrifice. We cannot too strongly condemn the inhuman treatment to which the Jewish people have
been subjected in many countries.

In this hour of cruel torture, we are mindful, daily at God's
altar, of all the innocent victims of the war, of the homeless,
the exiled, the imprisoned, and all who are suffering because
of hunger or disease. We ask the faithful to unite with us in
offering daily prayers and sacrifice in their behalf.

## Defense of Our Country

We support wholeheartedly the adequate defense of our
country. Thoughtful statesmen are perplexed, patriotic citizens are divided in their opinions as to the procedure our
country should follow. In these crucial times, when the civil
fabric of every country is threatened and when dictators
would destroy all religion, we herewith restate the position of
the Catholic Church in the language of the immortal Pope
Leo XIII:

333

The Almighty has appointed the charge of the human race between two powers, the ecclesiastical and the civil: the one being set over divine, and the other over human things. Each in its kind is supreme; each has fixed limits within which it is contained, limits which are defined by the nature and special object of the province of each, so that there is, We may say, an orbit within which the action of each is brought into play by its own native right.

But inasmuch as each of these two powers has authority over the same subjects, and as one and the same thing, under different aspects but still remaining identically the same, might chance to fall under the jurisdiction and determination of both powers, God, who foresees all things and is Author alike of these two powers, has marked out the course of each in correlation to the other. *For the powers that are, are ordained of God.* Were this not so, deplorable contentions and conflicts would often arise, and not infrequently men, like travellers at the meeting of two roads, would hesitate in anxiety and doubt, not knowing what course to follow. Two powers would be commanding contrary things, and it would be a dereliction of duty to disobey either of the two.

But to judge thus of the wisdom and goodness of God would be most repugnant. . . . One of the two has for its proximate and chief object the well-being of this mortal life; the other, the joys of heaven. Whatever, therefore, in things human is of a sacred character, whatever belongs, either of its own nature or by reason of the end to which it is referred, to the salvation of souls, or to the worship of God, is subject to the power and judgment of the Church. Whatever is to be under the civil and political order is rightly subject to the civil authority. Jesus Christ has Himself given command that what is Caesar's is to be rendered to Caesar, and that what belongs to God is to be rendered to God.

## Respect for Authority

Pondering this solemn teaching of Pope Leo XIII, we must recognize that all lawful authority is from God. *Let everyone be subject to the higher authorities, for there exists no authority except from God.* Disrespect for authority, both ecclesiastical and civil, must be condemned. In the confusion of the hour, we deplore the presumption of those who, lacking authority, strive to determine the course of action that the Church should take within her clearly defined field. Recognizing the liberty of discussion, and even of criticism, which our democratic form of government guarantees, we urge and commend respect and reverence for the authority of our civil officials which has its source in God.

At the present moment, in varying degrees, in every part of

the world, the peaceful course of events is disturbed. People are called upon to make sacrifices and to suffer. Comparing our conditions in the United States with those of other lands, we must recognize that our country is singularly blessed. But we cannot avoid the repercussions of a world cataclysm. Our faith in a Divine Providence ruling the universe should inspire us to have confidence in the benevolent designs of a loving God who permits suffering to correct evil and to bring forth the fruits of justice and charity and peace.

In this solemn hour when fateful decisions are to be made, it is evident that a spirit of exemplary restraint should characterize our priests and people. In every national crisis and every danger, our priests have been an inspiration. We are confident that their good example of strong faith and courage, founded on the virtue of fortitude, will not be lacking now. As moral teachers, they show that freedom has its limitations. It is limited, first of all, by the rights of God, and next, by the rights of others and by the interests of the common good. . . .

# International Order*

## (*November 16, 1944*)

WE have met the challenge of war. Shall we meet the challenge of peace?

This is the question uppermost in the minds of men everywhere who in suffering and hardship have stood out against ruthless aggression. The men of our armed forces, the masses of our citizens, our leaders, all want to be true to our heroes who have given so much, some even their lives, in this war for freedom. They want to be true, as well, to future generations on whom we have been forced to place a heavy burden as the price for their freedoms. Honestly, earnestly, we want to garner from the sacrifices, hardships, and losses which have gone into this war, the full fruits of victory in a

---

* From National Catholic Welfare Conference pamphlet.

good peace. The foremost problem in post-war planning is how to secure for ourselves and all the world a just and lasting peace.

Recently representatives of the United States, the United Kingdom, the Soviet Union, and China at Dumbarton Oaks formulated and presented to their governments broad tentative proposals for an international organization for "the maintenance of peace and security and the creation of conditions which make for peace." These proposals have been given to the public for full study and discussion by peoples of all countries. Our own Secretary of State has expressed the hope that leaders of our national thought and opinion will discuss them in the spirit of constructive effort.

### Freedom from Hatred, Greed

Public opinion in our country can exert a tremendous influence in making the peace and determining the manner of international collaboration for its maintenance. If public opinion is indifferent or uninformed, we shall run the risk of a bad peace and perhaps return to the tragedy of "power politics," which in the past divided nations and sowed the seeds of war. If public opinion is alert and informed, we can have a lasting peace and security. It is imperative that all our citizens recognize their responsibility in the making and maintenance of the peace. They must inform themselves on the issues and form their judgments in the light of sound reason and our Christian democratic traditions. They must free themselves from hatred, from distrust, from the spirit of mere expediency, from national greed, and from indifference to right in the use of might; they must form their judgments on the basis of stern objective realities.

This war came largely from bad education. It was not brought on by primitives or unlettered peoples. The contemporary philosophy which asserts the right of aggression is the creation of scholars. Discarding moral principles and crowding God out of human life, scholars produced the monstrous philosophies which, embodied in political and social systems, enslave human reason and destroy the consciousness of innate human rights and duties. In these systems the notion of the common good is utterly distorted; it is no longer conceived as the consequence of the common enjoyment of rights and the common discharge of duties, but the creation of the caprice of a dictator or a group or a party. The gilded dreams of a new era, which these systems heralded, have proved to be a hideous nightmare. If we are to have a just and lasting peace, it must be the creation of a sane realism, which has a clear vision of the moral law, a reverent acknowledgement of God its Author, and a recognition of the oneness of the human race underlying all national distinctions.

## Atlantic Charter, Without Equivocations

We have no confidence in a peace which does not carry into effect, without reservations or equivocations, the principles of the Atlantic Charter. We feel, too, that it should provide assistance for prostrate nations in reconstructing their economic, social, and political institutions. If justice is compromised, if unreasonable concessions are made to might, grievances will rankle in the bosom of aggrieved nations to endanger the peace of the world. If prostrate nations are not assisted in giving to their people fair economic opportunities, they will become the arena of civil strife and turmoil. No international organization will be able to maintain a peace which is unfair and unjust.

There is an international community of nations. God Himself has made the nations interdependent for their full life and growth. It is not therefore a question of creating an international community but of organizing it. To do this we must repudiate absolutely the tragic fallacies of "power politics" with its balance of power, spheres of influence in a system of puppet governments, and the resort to war as a means of settling international difficulties.

After the last world war an attempt was made to organize the international community. It failed not because its objective was mistaken, but because of inherent defects in its charter; more especially perhaps because the nations were not disposed to recognize their duty to work together for the common good of the world. International law must govern international relations. Might must be subordinated to law. An international institution, based on the recognition of an objective moral obligation and not on the binding force of covenant alone, is needed for the preservation of a just peace and the promotion

337

of international cooperation for the common good of the international community. The common good of every nation is inseparably connected with the common good of the international community.

The international institution must be universal. It must seek to include, with due regard to basic equality of rights, all the nations, large and small, strong and weak. Its constitution must be democratic. While it is reasonable to set up a Security Council with limited membership, this Council must not be an instrument for imperialistic domination by a few powerful nations. Before it every nation must stand on its rights and not on its power. It must not allow any nation to sit in judgment in its own case. Frankly it must recognize that for nations as well as individuals life is not static. It must therefore provide in its Charter for the revision of treaties in the interest of justice and the common good of international community, as well as for the recognition of a people's coming of age in the family of nations.

### Strong Nations Must Help Weak

The function of the international organization must be the maintenance of international peace and security, the promotion of international cooperation, and the adoption of common policies for the solution of common economic, social, and other humanitarian problems. In the maintenance of peace it is reasonable that the organization have at its disposal resources for coercing outlaw nations even by military measures.

In fostering and promoting international cooperation it must seek to guarantee to the weak and poor nations economic opportunities which are necessary to give their peoples reasonable standards of living, and it must seek to prevent selfish monopolistic control of raw materials which are needed for the economic stability of other nations. Effective international cooperation lays definite duties on favored nations. No nation may view with unconcern conditions that permit millions of workers in any country to be without the opportunity to secure from their labor adequate family support. Nations rich in natural resources must remember that ownership of property never dispenses from the social obligations of stewardship. Nations gifted with inventive and productive genius are obligated to serve the reasonable needs of other nations. Nations should open, under effective guarantees, world lanes of commerce and world avenues of communication to all law-abiding countries. Protective national legislation for legitimate national economic interests must not impede the flow of international commerce and the right social function of international exchange.

## Teeth for World Court

In the international organization there should be a World Court to which justifiable disputes among nations must be submitted. Its authority should not be merely advisory but strictly judicial. A condition for the right functioning of this Court is the proper development and codification of international law. Competent international authority must enact into positive law the principles of the moral law in their international references, and to these will be added positive treaty provisions and the charter and legislation of the international organization.

The World Court should be empowered to render decisions in cases submitted to it either by any party in interest or by the international organization. It must have authority to refer its decisions to the international organization for execution. It would be useless to set up a World Court and either deny it the right to demand the execution of its decisions or make the execution of them subject to the discretion of the international organization. Nations which refuse to submit their international disputes which constitute a threat to the peace or the common good of the international community, should be treated by the international organization as outlaw nations. Moreover obligatory arbitration of international disputes which threaten world peace would mark a signal advance in international relations.

The international organization must never violate the rightful sovereignty of nations. Sovereignty is a right which comes from the juridical personality of a nation and which the international organization must safeguard and defend. However, national sovereignty may not be interpreted as absolving a nation from its obligations in the international community. Moreover even within the state, national sovereignty is limited by the innate rights of men and families. Since civil authority does not confer these God-given rights it may not violate them.

The ideology of a nation in its internal life is a concern of the international community. To reject this principle is tantamount to maintaining that the violation of the innate rights of men in a country by its own government has no relation to world peace. Just at this moment, in the interest of world peace, our nation is exerting itself to root out some ideologies which violate human rights in the countries we are liberating. We hold that if there is to be a genuine and lasting world peace, the international organization should demand as a condition of membership that every nation guarantee in law and respect in fact the innate rights of men, families, and minority groups in their civil and religious life. Surely our generation should know that tyranny in any nation menaces world peace. A nation which refuses to accord to its own people the full enjoyment of innate human rights cannot be relied upon to cooperate in the international community for the maintenance of a peace which is based on the recognition of national freedom. Such a nation will pursue its own selfish international policies, while paying lip service to international cooperation.

### Free Men, Free Nations

We have it within our power to introduce a new era, the era for which peoples have been longing through the centuries, the era in which nations will live together in justice and charity. It is a Christian hope we want to realize, the hope of a world at peace, a world of sovereign states cooperating in assuring all men the full enjoyment of their rights, a world of free men and free nations with their freedom secured under law. War may come, but if our hope is realized it will be a war of punishment meted out to outlaw nations. Through all the sufferings and sacrifices of this war we have remembered and we recall today the words of our Chief Executive, written at its beginning: "We shall win this war and in victory we shall seek not vengeance but the establishment of an international order in which the spirit of Christ shall rule the hearts of men and of nations."

# Organizing World Peace*

## (*April 15, 1945*)

THE organization of the community of nations in an international institution to maintain world peace and achieve world cooperation will test the fullness of our victory. This conviction inspired the statement made by the Catholic Bishops of the United States last November. The trend of events since then prompts us to reaffirm and further interpret the principles of that statement.

A sound world organization is not a utopian dream. With honest good-will in all the victors, it will be realized, and a new era in international relations will begin. If any one of them refuses it full support, or insists on introducing into its charter provisions which radically vitiate it, we shall witness the tragedy, so often recorded in history, of a glorious martial victory largely nullified by sheer political expediency. Experience warns us that unless strong, courageous leaders, with the full support of their peoples, put their hands to this task, there will be no genuine progress in international life. To yield to the fear that this thing cannot be done is defeatism. In nations, as well as in individuals, we must indeed face the fact of human weakness, but we must face it to conquer it; we must not accept it in a spirit of paralyzing fatalism. An opportunity is here, as in every world crisis, to begin a new era of genuine progress in the community of nations.

### Disillusionment Breeds Isolationism

Isolationism, whether expressed in the refusal of a nation to assume its obligations in the international community, or masked in the setting up of a sphere of influence in which a great nation surrounds itself with weak puppet states, or disguised in a balance of power policy is no answer to the world's problems, or indeed to the problems of any nation. There is, however, the danger present at this time, that if in the name of realism an attempt is made to substitute for a juridical world institution what is in effect only an alliance of the Great

---

* From National Catholic Welfare Conference pamphlet.

Powers, many nations will take refuge in isolationism. Disillusionment in our country will express itself in the isolationism of the abstentionist.

The proposals for an international organization which will be presented to the coming San Francisco Conference have been studied by able and experienced men who, in a spirit of constructive criticism, have brought to light some of their outstanding defects. The admittedly tentative character of these proposals suggests that the delegates at San Francisco will be given the opportunity of free, open discussion and action. But the official information on agreements reached by the Three Great Powers—the United States, Russia, and Great Britain—on certain fundamental provisions in the Charter, gives rise to doubt and fear. We fail to see that the voting procedure in the Security Council agreed upon at Yalta is consistent with the sovereign equality of peace-loving nations recognized as basic in the Dumbarton Oaks Proposals. Whatever concessions may, under existing conditions, have to be made to certain nations in view of their power and corresponding responsibility, it seems inequitable and dangerous to give any nation in perpetuity a virtual veto on parity of treatment for all. It is a manifest denial of a prime attribute of a juridical institution to extend the veto to the execution of decisions of the World Court to which, by explicit provision, all justifiable disputes should be referred. And the concession in question is not even limited to cases directly involving the nation to which it is made. This makes the Charter give a preferred status not only to the powerful aggressor, but even to any aggressor with a powerful patron.

While there is reason in setting up a Committee or Council to act in emergencies, in the Proposals the functions of the General Assembly are too restricted, and the functions of the Security Council are too broad. It is hoped, then, that the Security Council will be made more responsible to the General Assembly and, at least in time, will become merely its Executive Committee. It is imperative, too, that there be lodged in the international organization, and ultimately in the World Court, the authority to make changes in the peace settlements and other treaties which, in view of past mistakes or changed conditions, may be required. The Proposals, as they stand, outline not the plan for an organization under law of the international community, but rather the draft of an Alliance between the Great Victorious Powers for the maintenance of world peace and the promotion of international cooperation, in which these Powers definitely refuse to submit themselves in every eventuality to the world authority which they propose to invoke in compelling other nations to maintain world peace.

## Inter-Nation Bill of Rights

Sovereign equality among the nations demands that each nation be free in its internal government, and that its juridical personality be recognized in its international relations. It does not mean, however, that a nation is exempt from its obligations in the international community. Even in internal government, sovereignty does not include the authority to violate the inalienable rights of subjects. In all history, and particularly in modern history, dangers to world peace have come from the unjust treatment of minorities, the denial of civil and religious liberties, and other infringements on the inborn rights of men. To remove these dangers, the nations should adopt an Internation Bill of Rights, in which men and groups everywhere would be guaranteed the full enjoyment of their human rights. That this is definitely a matter of international concern is evident in the problem now confronting the Intergovernmental Committee in regard to displaced persons. If they are reluctant to return to their homelands, it is largely because they cannot look forward to the enjoyment of fundamental human rights under the new tyrannies in control. Active participation in the international organization ought to be conditioned on the acceptance of this Bill of Rights. Will a nation which does not make its own citizens secure in the enjoyment of their human rights work honestly and sincerely for the maintenance of world peace and mutual cooperation in the international community?

The solution of the Polish question agreed upon by the representatives of the Three Great Victorious Powers in the Crimean Conference, was a disappointment to all who had built their hopes on the Atlantic Charter. Poland, which stood against the Nazi aggressor from the very beginning of the

343

war; Poland, which has suffered more than any other nation in the war; Poland, which has fought and is fighting with our armies on every European Front, has been forced by her allies to surrender a very large part of her territory. In apparent exchange, it was guaranteed at Yalta that in the reconstructed world there will be a strong, independent Poland, with a government chosen in a free election by its own people. Pending the action of the people of Poland in a free election, agreements were made to set up a provisional regime which will be recognized by the Three Great Powers. This provisional government must not be the creation of a single foreign power but the choice of all parties to the Yalta Engagements. Our President is pledged to see that in the choice of a permanent Polish government, the people of Poland be guaranteed in their right of free secret ballot. No foreign power must be permitted to influence this election in a way which will determine its results. The peace of the world demands a free, independent, democratic Poland. It must not be that Poland become a puppet state under the domination and control of any foreign power. If Poland is secured in its rights of freedom and independence, it will make great sacrifices and do its full part in the international community. If it is enslaved, and its leadership forced into exile or inhumanly liquidated, the love of freedom will not be crushed in Polish hearts, but the seeds of war will have been sown.

### The Fate of the Baltic States

In reading official reports on current peace discussions, we are struck by the ominous silence of the Three Great Powers on Lithuania, Estonia and Latvia. Contrary to the protests of our government four years ago and to the assurances of Soviet authorities even before that time, the indications are that they will be absorbed without their free and unfettered consent in an alien system of government. The sympathy of all lovers of freedom goes out to them in their disaster. We hope that when the final peace treaty is framed and approved, it will not be recorded that our country condoned the enslavement of these freedom-loving nations.

We hope, too, that our government will discharge its full

responsibility in reestablishing all the liberated nations of Europe under genuine democratic regimes which will accord to all their citizens the full enjoyment of their human rights and open to them an era of prosperity.

In the treatment of the enemy nations, justice must obtain. Justice, indeed, is stern. It is not, however, born of hatred or vengeance, and prevails only when the mind is clear and calm. Moreover, the common good of the whole world must be kept in mind in dealing with these peoples. They must be freed from tyranny and oppression, and they must be given the opportunity to reconstruct their institutions on the foundations of genuine democracy. There are things, too, which charity and a right sense of world cooperation urges us to do for them. Only in the unity of human brotherhood will it be possible for them to do their full part in the community of nations.

People living on the near-starvation level, without the means of beginning the work of reconstruction for themselves, are not clear in their thinking and become easy victims of bad leadership. It is imperative indeed to keep before them the sound principles of genuine democracy, which is a product of our culture and at its base recognizes human rights of individuals and groups. It is equally imperative to keep them fit rightly to appraise sound principles. The work of relief before us is very great, and it must be done quickly and efficiently if there is to be a sound world peace.

### Democracy and Marxism Incompatible

Every day makes more evident the fact that two strong essentially incompatible ways of life will divide the loyalties of men and nations in the political world of tomorrow. They are genuine democracy and Marxian totalitarianism. Democracy is built on respect for the dignity of the human person with its God-given inviolable rights. It achieves unity and strength in the intelligent cooperation of all citizens for the common good under governments chosen and supported by the people. It will advance, expand, and develop our culture. It will maintain continuity with our Christian past. It will give security for our Christian future. Fascism and Nazism, rampant in their might, sought its destruction. Fascism is gone, we hope, forever. And soon Nazism will be only a horrible historical memory.

However, we have to reckon with the active, cleverly organized and directed opposition of Marxian totalitarianism to genuine democracy. This system herds the masses under dictatorial leadership, insults their intelligence with its propaganda and controlled press, and tyrannically violates innate human rights. Against it, genuine democracy must constantly be on guard, quick to detect and penetrate its camouflage. Democracy's bulwark is religion, and justice is its watchword. We entered this war to defend our democracy. It is our solemn responsibility in the reconstruction to use our full influence in safeguarding the freedoms of all peoples. This, we are convinced, is the only way to an enduring peace.

# Between War and Peace*

## (November 18, 1945)

THE war is over but there is no peace in the world. In the Atlantic Charter we were given the broad outline of the peace for which we fought and bled and, at an incalculable price, won a great martial victory. It was that ideal of peace which sustained us through the war, which inspired the heroic defense of liberty by millions driven underground in enslaved countries. It made small oppressed nations confide in us as the trustee of their freedoms. It was the broad outline of a good peace. Are we going to give up this ideal of peace? If, under the pretext of a false realism, we do so, then we shall stand face to face with the awful catastrophe of atomic war.

Since the Moscow Conference of 1943, the United States, Great Britain and Russia have undertaken to shape gradually the peace which they are imposing on the nations. From the conferences of these victorious powers there is emerging slowly their pattern for the peace. It is disappointing in the

---

* From National Catholic Welfare Conference pamphlet.

extreme. Assurances are given us in the announced peace principles of our country, but so far results do not square with these principles. We are in perhaps the greatest crisis of human history. Our country has the power, the right, and the responsibility to demand a genuine peace, based on justice, which will answer the cry in the hearts of men across the world.

We want to work in unity with other nations for the making of a good peace. During the war perhaps, it may have been necessary for strategic reasons to postpone final decisions on many questions mooted at the conferences of the three great powers.

## Russia and Democracy

Now we must face the facts. There are profound differences of thought and policy between Russia and the western democracies. Russia has acted unilaterally on many important settlements. It has sought to establish its sphere of influence in eastern and southeastern Europe, not on the basis of sound regional agreements in which sovereignties and rights are respected, but by the imposition of its sovereignty and by ruthlessly setting up helpless puppet states. Its Asiatic policy, so important for the peace of the world, is an enigma.

The totalitarian dictators promised benefits to the masses through an omnipotent police-state which extends its authority to all human relations and recognizes no innate freedoms. Their theories, moreover, look to the realization of world well-being as ultimately to be secured by the inclusion of all countries in their system. Sometimes Russia uses our vocabulary and talks of democracy and rights, but it attaches distorted meanings to the words. We think in terms of our historic culture. We see God-given, inviolable human rights in every person, and we know democracy as the free collaboration under law of citizens in a free country.

There is a clash of ideologies. The frank recognition of these differences is preliminary to any sincere effort in realistic world cooperation for peace. The basis of this cooperation must be mutual adherence to justice. It would be unjust for us to be an accomplice in violating the rights of nations, groups, and individuals anywhere in the world.

347

A first step towards effective negotiation for peace is to have a plan. A good plan states principles in terms of all the specific questions at issue. Instead, so far we have compromised and sought to make mere piece-meal settlements. Instead of honest, promising discussion even on diverging plans, we are witnessing a return of the tragedy of power politics and the danger of balance of power arrangements which, with the substitution of mere expediency for justice, have begotten war after war. We must indeed aim at collaborating with all of our allies in the making of a good peace. There are, however, concessions which we dare not make because they are immoral and destructive of genuine peace.

## Our Program for Peace

Our peace program envisions a world organization of nations. The Charter which emerged from the San Francisco Conference, while undoubtedly an improvement on the Dumbarton Oaks proposals, does not provide for a sound, institutional organization of the international society. The Security Council provisions make it no more than a virtual alliance of the great powers for the maintenance of peace. These nations are given a status above the law. Nevertheless, our country acted wisely in deciding to participate in this world organization. It is better than world chaos. From the provision in the Charter for calling a Constituent Assembly in the future, there comes the hope that in time the defects may be eliminated and we may have a sound, institutional organization of the international community which will develop, not through mere voluntary concessions of the nations, but from the recognition of the rights and duties of international society.

While peace is in the making, there are urgent issues which we can no longer evade. At Yalta we gave a pledge to the Polish people and assumed responsibility before the world that they would be unhampered in setting up their own independent, democratic government. Are we working to the fulfillment of that pledge in the full measure of our responsibility and our power? What apology can be offered for the failure of the protagonists of democracy to protest the absorption by force and artifice of the Baltic countries* into the

---

* Latvia, Estonia and Lithuania.

Union of Soviet Republics? We are shocked by the news which is leaking out from Slovakia, Croatia, Slovenia and other southeastern European countries. Religious persecution which is both brutal and cunning rages in many lands. No reason of policy justifies our silence. What is happening behind the blackout of eastern and southeastern Europe is a stark contradiction to the high ideals which inspired our fighting to save the world from totalitarian aggression.

No one can fail to see the importance of a reconstructed, revitalized Europe, which is the cradle of western culture. We deplore the tragic indifference to the plight of the Italian people who threw off the chains of a Fascist regime, who fought side by side with us in ardent loyalty. For over two long years of agony the friends of democracy in that country have had to stand by in impotence while we have toyed with the vital problems of relief and rehabilitation and deferred the fulfillment of our own solemn promises.

Our own national interest, as well as the cause of world peace, and the fate of Christian culture are at stake in Italy. Today it is an outpost of western civilization. We are fully confident that the Italian people, if we save them from despair by our helpful interest, will stand fast against the deceitful appeal of alien and subversive ideologies and shape their future in the spirit of their own noble Christian tradition.

### Fate of Vanquished Nations

We cannot be unconcerned about the future of Germany, Austria, and Hungary. Whatever period of probation must be imposed on the vanquished nations, we must help them to take their rightful place in the family of nations. To treat them in a spirit of vengeance is neither right nor politic. Justice demands the punishment of the guilty and reasonable reparations of damage done. But we cannot forget, or allow our representatives to forget, that our traditional system of punitive justice is anchored to the concept of individual responsibility. The inhumanities which now mark the mass transference of populations, the systematized use of slave labor, and the cruel treatment of prisoners of war should have no place in our civilization.

Acute suffering is the daily lot of whole populations in

349

many war-torn lands. Every report indicates that, unless heroic measures are taken at once, millions will die from starvation and exposure during the coming winter. The feeding and clothing and sheltering of these suffering people is not a work which can be left to some future convenient date. Our country, because of our greater resources, must do the major part of this work of relief. In it we have the right and duty to insist on the leadership which corresponds to our sacrifices and contributions. It is imperative that Congress make adequate appropriations for this work from the public treasury.

It is equally imperative that private relief agencies be given a full opportunity to carry on their beneficent work among all suffering peoples. And relief must envision something larger than merely feeding the starving and sheltering the homeless. Help must be given to peoples whose economies are ruined. They have the right to assistance in getting back to normal economic life. Neither the prosperity of the greater nations nor their might will prevent war unless conditions are removed in which poor, helpless peoples are denied the opportunity of a decent living standard. The world is one only insofar as men live together as brothers under God.

Ours is a grave responsibility. The heart and hand of America are called upon in a way that is unique, not only in the history of our country but even in the annals of mankind. We know that democracy is as capable of solving the admittedly difficult problems of peace as it has shown itself in war. We must be true to ourselves. We must hold fast to our own free institutions. We must resolutely oppose the few amongst us who are trying to sabotage them. We may well pity those who in their half-veiled sympathy for totalitarianism are playing with the thought that perhaps in this great emergency its day is at hand. On bended knees let us ask God in His Blessed Providence to help us to be the vigorous champion of democratic freedom and the generous friend of the needy and oppressed throughout the world.

# Man and the Peace*

(*November 17, 1946*)

AT the bottom of all problems of the world today is the problem of man. Unless those who bear the responsibility of world leadership are in basic agreement on what man is, there is no way out of the confusion and conflict which block the road to real peace. Clashes on the question of boundaries, national security, minority safeguards, free movement of trade, easy access to raw materials, progressive disarmament, and the control of the atomic bomb, important as these are, take a second place to the need of unity, in protecting man in the enjoyment of his God-given native rights. The struggle of the small nations for their indisputable rights and the stalemate among the strong nations in a contest of power would admit of bearable, even though hard, compromise if the fate of man, as man, did not hang in the balance.

To be more explicit, it is a question whether national governments are disposed to protect or to hinder the individual in the exercise of rights and in the discharge of duties which are proper to him prior to any action by the State. The words of our own Declaration of Independence express no new doctrine but voice the basic tradition of Christian civilization: "We hold these truths to be self-evident, that all men are created equal, that they are endowed by their Creator with certain unalienable rights, that among these are life, liberty, and the pursuit of happiness." Respect for the rights and duties of man as an individual and as a member of civic and domestic society we hold to be the first obligation of any government to its citizens. The State has a just claim on the cooperation of its citizens for the common good, but not to the point of coercion in violation of their personal political, social, and religious rights. What a government cannot do in the exercise of its own sovereignty, it cannot approve or abet on the part of another government in the settlement of complicated issues, such as confront the nations in making peace and planning for its preservation.

---

* National Catholic Welfare Conference pamphlet.

351

### The Conflict Between Russia and the West

The menace to man as man looms large in the outstanding questions which engage the attention of the victorious allies. It hangs in the background of the conflict between Russia and the West which has so long delayed the making of the peace. Eighteen months have passed since the surrender and occupation of Germany and fifteen months since the capitulation of Japan. There have been continuous negotiations among the three great victors, the United States, Britain, and Russia, for the conclusion of agreements on stable peace and reconstruction. These negotiations have brought out in the clear the tragic lack of unity among the peacemakers on fundamental issues. In some instances agreements which were pointed to the safeguarding of basic human rights, reached in Conferences, have been repudiated unilaterally by the action of one of the victors, and these repudiations have been tolerated by the other nations which were parties to the agreements. In an effort to preserve unity, fatal compromises have been made, either explicitly or by tolerance of shocking aggressions.

In so difficult a task it is understandable that there should be differences and a clash of interests. Some sort of sacrifice of particular national advantages for the common good of the international community, and therefore for the ultimate good of all nations, must be made. But the tragic fact is that the cleavage touches issues on which there can be no compromise. While it is stated that the Western Democracies and Russia with her satellite governments in the countries of Eastern Europe are at a stalemate over questions of security against aggressions, the fact is that underlying these questions there is the question of man, as man.

Throughout the war our battle cry was the defense of native freedoms against Nazi and Fascist totalitarianism. The aftermath of war has revealed victorious Soviet totalitarianism no less aggressive against these freedoms in the countries it has occupied. Totalitarianism does not acknowledge and respect these freedoms. It persecutes the citizen who dares assert his native rights. It imposes on peoples its philosophy of life, in which there is no authority above the State, and in which all values in life are derived from human conventions. The corollary of such philosophy is the police State, which terrorizes its citizens and dominates them in all fields of human behavior.

Before we can hope for a good peace there must come an agreement among the peacemakers on the basic question of man, as man. If this agreement is reached, then secondary, though important, defects in the peace may be tolerable in the hope of their eventual correction. Misrepresentations, deceitful promises, the use of equivocal language, and violation of agreements only widen the cleavage between nations. In the Charter of the United Nations the signatories have contracted to cooperate "in promoting and encouraging respect for human rights and for fundamental freedoms for all without distinction as to race, language or religion." Let the nations in the making of the peace do even more and in solemn covenants actually secure men everywhere in the enjoyment of their native rights. Then there will be the beginnings of peace, and the fear of war will be banished from men's minds.

## Plea for Prisoners of War

Considerations of human dignity are deeply involved in the fate of prisoners of war. The strict observance of international law does not oblige the victorious nations to repatriate prisoners of war until after the conclusion of the peace, but owing to the circumstance of the long delay in making the peace, the contention of our country for the speedy repatriation of these prisoners is admirably humane and almost a dictate of justice. There are millions of them separated from their families and kept from their normal occupations, engaged in forced labor, and in many cases underfed. They are needed at home for the work of reconstruction.

The use of prisoners of war as slave laborers in alien lands should not be any part of reparations levied by the victors. They are men, and they should be treated as men. So large is their number, estimated as high as 7,000,000, that even with every effort put forth for their speedy repatriation, it will take years to transport them back to their own countries in an orderly way. It is the strict obligation of all nations to treat these prisoners as we demanded that our combatants, who fell into the hands of the enemy, be treated. It is unworthy of the victors to revenge injustices by violating human rights and heaping insults on human dignity. As things are now, future generations may well charge the victors with guilt of inhumanities which are reminiscent of Nazism and Fascism.

## Humane Treatment of Displaced Persons

A serious problem which challenges the nations is finding a way rightly to provide for the hundreds of thousands of refugees from persecution and dire danger now in camps in Central Europe. These victims of injustice have the right of refuge—a right that is sacrosanct in our history and culture. To provide for them and to give them an opportunity to begin life anew in useful pursuits without fear is the inescapable responsibility of the nations. All of them, the displaced persons and the persecuted peoples, must be treated humanely without discrimination.

A perfect solution of the problem would be to give them the full guarantee for the enjoyment of their native rights in their countries of origin. Since this solution is not forthcoming, the nations must extend to them the help which their very human rights demand. It is plain that to continue indefinitely to support them in camps is not a solution of the problem and is, in fact, an injury to them. To force them against their will to return to their countries of origin, where, with reason, they fear that grave dangers await them, is stark inhumanity. By agreement among the victors those in the displaced persons camps allegedly guilty of crimes must be returned to their countries of origin. If guilty, they should be punished but they should not be made the victims of political persecution with the cooperation of the authorities of the military occupation. Before honoring demands for the return of these persons to their countries of origin, the military authorities are obligated to give the accused honest juridical preliminary hearings to prevent grave injustice. Tragic indeed was the decision of the United Nations Committee on Refugees that "all measures be taken" to repatriate child refugees to their countries of origin. Nor can we condone with any sense of humanity the alternative of either returning refugees against their will to their countries of origin or throwing them on the economy of an already overcrowded and impoverished Germany.

With justice to all these unfortunate men, women and children, and without discrimination in favor of any group of them, the nations must find a way to resettle them in countries where opportunities to begin life anew await them. It is heartening that the President of the United States has pledged himself publicly to ask our Congress to enact a law which will permit the entry of considerable numbers of them into the United States. If this is done, the generosity of our country will stir other nations to give these unfortunate people a haven and a chance to live in the enjoyment of their God-given rights. The problem is admittedly very difficult, but the difficulty in it should be a challenge to the nations to solve it in a constructive, humane way, in which charity will do even what justice does not compel.

## Ruthless Herding of Uprooted People

Something has been happening in Europe which is new in the annals of recorded history. By agreement among the victors, millions of Germans who for centuries have lived in Eastern Europe are being forced from their homes, without resources, into the heart of Germany. The sufferings of these people in their weary travels, the homelessness of them, and the hopelessness, make a sad story of the inhumanity of their transplantation. Had there prevailed in the councils of the victor nations a right appreciation of the dignity of man, at least arrangements would have been made for transplanting these people in a hummane way. We boast of our democracy, but in this transplantation of peoples we have perhaps unwittingly allowed ourselves to be influenced by the herd theory of heartless totalitarian political philosophy.

The reports of the deportation of thousands in areas of Soviet aggression to remote and inhospitable regions just because they cannot subscribe to Communism tell of a cruel violation of human rights. These men are men and have the rights of men. Our sympathy also goes out to the technicians and skilled workers in enemy countries who have been seized and forced to work for the strengthening of the economy of victorious nations. It is not in this way that peace is made and the nations are united in mutual cooperation. No lasting good can ever come from the violation of the dignity of the human person.

## Continued Relief Imperative

In many lands, men, women, and children are in dire need of the very necessities of life. In some large measure this need is the consequence of the stoppage of that normal interchange of goods between the industrial and agricultural areas of Europe, which for centuries has been at the base of European economy. In some places it is the result of political, racial, and religious persecution. For many millions it is the heavy penalty of war. In our charity we must not be insensible to the misery of our fellow men. Human solidarity, as well as Christian brotherhood, dictates the sharing of our substance with our brothers in distress. We may well be proud of the generosity of the people of the United States in their relief work in war-torn lands. The want, however, is so great that, without continued governmental aid, private charity will be inadequate to relieve it. A way must be found for the nations to continue their work of relief, until the danger of widespread starvation and disease is gone and peoples are able to provide for at least their own basic needs. The winter before us will be a hard, bitter winter for millions, and the charity of individuals and governments must be very large to prevent an awful catastrophe. But charity is not a substitute for justice. The continuance of widespread want is largely due to the delay of the nations in making the peace. Justice demands that they make promptly a peace in which all men can live as men.

## Dignity of Human Person

In the aftermath of war, public opinion tends to overlook the sacredness of human life. We have just been through our first experience with mechanized war, in which the manhood of the world has been in battle on fields of combat and in industry, agriculture, and transportation. Our enemies, with utter disregard for the sacredness of human life, committed brutalities that horrified us and unfortunately we used weapons which brought widespread, unspeakable suffering and destruction. Day after day there were the accounts of the killing and the maiming of thousands. Never before did the human family suffer so large a number of casualties. It was hard always to be mindful of the sacredness of the life of the individual. There was the temptation to think only in terms of mass killings and mass murders. Out of it all, many have failed to interpret in terms of the human sufferings which they connote, the headlines in our daily press which even now tell of race and religious persecution, of the transplantation of millions of people from one area to another, and of the seizure of political control by the liquidation of opposition. How can there be a beginning of even a tolerable peace unless the peacemakers fully realize that human life is sacred and that all men have rights?

### Prayer for Peacemakers

And for us who profess the Christian name, human life is even more precious and sacred, because for every man the Saviour shed His Blood in bitter anguish on Calvary. We know that in His Sacred Blood all men are called to be brothers. We are our brothers' keepers. It is not possible for us to be complacent and inactive while any of our brothers in the human family groan under tyranny and are denied the free exercise of their human rights. In Christian solidarity, with humble hearts, we confess our sins and the sins of our race, and pleadingly beg, through the merits of Christ, merciful forgiveness from our Father Who is in heaven. Mindful of the sacred promise of the Saviour, we pray for light and strength for those who in our country bear the heavy responsibility of making decisions for us in the peace conferences; and, indeed, for all the peacemakers. May the Saviour enlighten and strengthen them to imitate His blessed example and, in sacrifice and unselfishness, in the clear light of reason, secure for all men the enjoyment of their God-given rights, so that they may follow their vocation as sons of God and brothers in Christ.

# Discrimination and the Christian Conscience*

(*November 1958*)

FIFTEEN years ago, when this nation was devoting its energies to a World War designed to maintain human freedom, the Catholic Bishops of the United States issued a prayerful warning to their fellow citizens. We called for the extension of full freedom within the confines of our beloved country. Specifically, we noted the problems faced by Negroes in obtaining the rights that are theirs as Americans. The statement of 1943 said in part:

"In the Providence of God there are among us millions of fellow citizens of the Negro race. We owe to these fellow citizens, who have contributed so largely to the development of our country, and for whose welfare history imposes on us a special obligation of justice, to see that they have in fact the rights which are given them in our Constitution. This means not only political equality, but also fair economic and educational opportunities, a just share in public welfare projects, good housing without exploitation, and a full chance for the social advancement of their race."

## Progress Made

In the intervening years, considerable progress was made in achieving these goals. The Negro race, brought to this country in slavery, continued its quiet but determined march toward the goal of equal rights and equal opportunity. During and after the Second World War, great and even spectacular advances were made in the obtaining of voting rights, good education, better-paying jobs, and adequate housing. Through the efforts of men of good will, of every race and creed and from all parts of the nation, the barriers of prejudice and discrimination were slowly but inevitably eroded.

Because this method of quiet conciliation produced such excellent results, we have preferred the path of action to that

---

\* National Catholic Welfare Conference pamphlet.

of exhortation. Unfortunately, however, it appears that in recent years the issues have become confused and the march toward justice and equality has been slowed if not halted in some areas. The transcendent moral issues involved have become obscured, and possibly forgotten.

Out nation now stands divided by the problem of compulsory segregation of the races and the opposing demand for racial justice. No region of our land is immune from strife and division resulting from this problem. In one area, the key issue may concern the schools. In another it may be conflicts over housing. Job discrimination may be the focal point in still other sectors. But all these issues have one main point in common. They reflect the determination of our Negro people, and we hope the overwhelming majority of our white citizens, to see that our colored citizens obtain their full rights as given to them by God, the Creator of all, and guaranteed by the democratic traditions of our nation.

There are many facets to the problems raised by the quest for racial justice. There are issues of law, of history, of economics, and of sociology. There are questions of procedure and technique. There are conflicts in cultures. Volumes have been written on each of these phases. Their importance we do not deny. But the time has come, in our considered and prayerful judgment, to cut through the maze of secondary or less essential issues and to come to the heart of the problem.

## Question is Moral and Religious

The heart of the race question is moral and religious. It concerns the rights of man and our attitude toward our fellow man. If our attitude is governed by the great Christian law of love of neighbor and respect for his rights, then we can work out harmoniously the techniques for making legal, educational, economic, and social adjustments. But if our hearts are poisoned by hatred, or even by indifference toward the welfare and rights of our fellow men, then our nation faces a grave internal crisis.

No one who bears the name of Christian can deny the universal love of God for all mankind. When Our Lord and Saviour, Jesus Christ, *took on the form of man* and walked among men, He taught as the first two laws of life the love

359

of God and the love of fellow man. *By this shall all men know that you are my disciples, that you have love, one for the other.* He offered His life in sacrifice for all mankind. His parting mandate to His followers was to *teach all nations.*

Our Christian faith is of its nature universal. It knows not the distinctions of race, color, or nationhood. The missionaries of the Church have spread throughout the world, visiting with equal impartiality nations such as China and India, whose ancient cultures antedate the coming of the Saviour, and the primitive tribes of the Americas. The love of Christ, and the love of the Christian, knows no bounds. In the words of Pope Pius XII, addressed to American Negro publishers twelve years ago, "All men are brothered in Jesus Christ; for He, though God, became also man, became a member of the human family, a brother of all." (May 27, 1946)

Even those who do not accept our Christian tradition should at least acknowledge that God has implanted in the souls of all men some knowledge of the natural moral law and a respect for its teachings. Reason alone taught philosophers through the ages respect for the sacred dignity of each human being and the fundamental rights of man. Every man has an equal right to life, to justice before the law, to marry and rear a family under human conditions, and to an equitable opportunity to use the goods of this earth for his needs and those of his family.

From these solemn truths, there follow certain conclusions vital for a proper approach to the problems that trouble us today. First, we must repeat the principle—embodied in our Declaration of Independence—that all men are equal in the sight of God. By equal we mean that they are created by God and redeemed by His Divine Son, that they are bound by His Law, and that God desires them as His friends in the eternity of Heaven. This fact confers upon all men human dignity and human rights.

### Personal Differences Among Men

Men are unequal in talent and achievement. They differ in culture and personal characteristics. Some are saintly, some seem to be evil, most are men of good will, though beset with human frailty. On the basis of personal differences we may distinguish among our fellow men, remembering always the admonition: *Let him who is without sin . . . cast the first stone . . .* But discrimination based on the accidental fact of race or color, and as such injurious to human rights regardless of personal qualities or achievements, cannot be reconciled with the truth that God has created all men with equal rights and equal dignity.

Secondly, we are bound to love our fellow man. The Christian love we bespeak is not a matter of emotional likes or dislikes. It is a firm purpose to do good to all men, to the extent that ability and opportunity permit.

Among all races and national groups, class distinctions are inevitably made on the basis of like-mindedness or a community of interests. Such distinctions are normal and constitute a universal social phenomenon. They are accidental, however, and are subject to change as conditions change. It is unreasonable and injurious to the rights of others that a factor such as race, by and of itself, should be made a cause of discrimination and a basis for unequal treatment in our mutual relations.

### Enforced Segregation

The question then arises: Can enforced segregation be reconciled with the Christian view of our fellow man? In our judgment it cannot, and this for two fundamental reasons:

1) Legal segregation, or any form of compulsory segregation, in itself and by its very nature imposes a stigma of inferiority upon the segregated people. Even if the now obsolete Court doctrine of "separate but equal" had been carried out to the fullest extent, so that all public and semipublic facilities were in fact equal, there is nonetheless the judgment that an entire race, by the sole fact of race and regardless of individual qualities, is not fit to associate on equal terms with members of another race. We cannot reconcile such a judgment with the Christian view of man's nature and rights. Here again it is appropriate to cite the language of Pope Pius XII: "God did not create a human family made up of segregated, dissociated, mutually independent members. No; He would have them all united by the bond of total love of Him and consequent self-dedication to assisting each other to maintain that bond intact." (September 7, 1956)

361

2) It is a matter of historical fact that segregation in our country has led to oppressive conditions and the denial of basic human rights for the Negro. This is evident in the fundamental fields of education, job opportunity, and housing. Flowing from these areas of neglect and discrimination are problems of health and the sordid train of evils so often associated with the consequent slum conditions. Surely Pope Pius XII must have had these conditions in mind when he said just two months ago: "It is only too well known, alas, to what excesses pride of race and racial hate can lead. The Church has always been energetically opposed to attempts of genocide or practices arising from what is called the 'color bar.' " (September 5, 1958)

## Economic and Educational Opportunity

One of the tragedies of racial oppression is that the evils we have cited are being used as excuses to continue the very conditions that so strongly fostered such evils. Today we are told that Negroes, Indians, and also some Spanish-speaking Americans differ too much in culture and achievements to be assimilated in our schools, factories, and neighborhoods. Some decades back the same charge was made against the immigrant, Irish, Jewish, Italian, Polish, Hungarian, German, Russian. In both instances differences were used by some as a basis for discrimination and even for bigoted ill-treatment. The immigrant, fortunately, has achieved his rightful status in the American community. Economic opportunity was wide open and educational equality was not denied to him.

Negro citizens seek these same opportunities. They wish an education that does not carry with it any stigma of inferiority. They wish economic advancement based on merit and skill. They wish their civil rights as American citizens. They wish acceptance based upon proved ability and achievement. No one who truly loves God's children will deny them this opportunity.

To work for this principle amid passions and misunderstandings will not be easy. It will take courage. But quiet and persevering courage has always been the mark of a true follower of Christ.

## Plans Should Be Based On Prudence

We urge that concrete plans in this field be based on prudence. Prudence may be called a virtue that inclines us to view problems in their proper perspective. It aids us to use the proper means to secure our aim.

The problems we inherit today are rooted in decades, even centuries, of custom and cultural patterns. Changes in deep-rooted attitudes are not made overnight. When we are confronted with complex and far-reaching evils, it is not a sign of weakness or timidity to distinguish among remedies and reforms. Some changes are more necessary than others. Some are relatively easy to achieve. Others seem impossible at this time. What may succeed in one area may fail in another.

It is a sign of wisdom, rather than weakness, to study carefully the problems we face, to prepare for advances, and to by-pass the non-essential if it interferes with essential progress. We may well deplore a gradualism that is merely a cloak for inaction. But we equally deplore rash impetuosity that would sacrifice the achievements of decades in ill-timed and ill-considered ventures. In concrete matters we distinguish between prudence and inaction by asking the question: Are we sincerely and earnestly acting to solve these problems? We distinguish between prudence and rashness by seeking the prayerful and considered judgment of experienced counselors who have achieved success in meeting similar problems.

## Vital That We Act Now

For this reason we hope and earnestly pray that responsible and soberminded Americans of all religious faiths, in all areas of our land, will seize the mantle of leadership from the agitator and the racist. It is vital that we act now and act decisively. All must act quietly, courageously, and prayerfully before it is too late.

For the welfare of our nation we call upon all to root out from their hearts bitterness and hatred. The tasks we face are indeed difficult. But hearts inspired by Christian love will surmount these difficulties.

Clearly, then, these problems are vital and urgent. May God give this nation the grace to meet the challenge it faces. For the sake of generations of future Americans, and indeed of all humanity, we cannot fail their short life here.

# Dignity of Man*

(*November 21, 1953*)

EVERY man knows instinctively that he is, somehow, a superior being. He knows he is superior to the land he tills, the machine he operates or the animals which are at his service. Even when unable to define this superiority in terms of "honor and dignity," if a man enjoys the fruits of his nobility, he is content and accepts that status as his due; lacking honor and dignity for any cause, a man is restless, depressed, even rebellious because something proper to him, as a man, is withheld or denied.

The Catholic Church has always taught and defended the natural dignity of every human being. She has preached the burden of individual responsibility. She has insisted upon the importance of personal conscience. She has reminded mankind that there is a great division between "things" and "men." She has never forgotten that "things" were made for men and that "men" were made for God.

In thus holding up a mirror to men that they may see their own greatness and realize their personal dignity, the Catholic Church has taught that man's true honor is from God, has been enhanced spiritually by divine grace and is preserved without degradation only when the honor and dignity of God Himself are first maintained.

Often in times past men have failed to live up to the honor of their state. They have degraded their dignity in many ways. But, always till now, violence and vice, injustice and oppression or any other assaults on human dignity were recognized as abominations and were so abhorred. It has remained for our day to attempt to disregard human personality and to fortify such disregard with the force of legislation or the approbation of custom, as if a man were only a "thing."

* National Catholic Welfare Conference pamphlet.

364

The present has been described as a rationally established inhumanity working with all the expedients of administrative and mechanical techniques. Our Holy Father, Pope Pius XII, in his 1952 Christmas allocution, gave warning of the attempted mechanization of mankind and protested the stripping of personality from men by legal or social devices. The Bishops of the United States, conscious of the growing depersonalization of man, reaffirm man's essential dignity and reassert the rights which flow from it.

### True Roots of Human Dignity

Man's essential worth derives from a threefold source: from the fact of his creation, from the mode of his existence, and from the nobility of his destiny.

The mere fact that any creature exists at all requires the creative and sustaining power of God. When God exercises this power to summon any possible reality into actual existence, that reality is thereby sealed with value from within. Such a dignity man shares with the animal and material world around him.

But his special type of existence confers on man a special claim to honor. Though immersed in a universe of fleeting and random sensations, he is endowed with an intellect able to pierce the flux of passing images and discover beneath them enduring patterns of truth. Though subjected to the pressures of his environment, and a prey to unthinking appetites, he is endowed with a self-determining will capable of choosing wisely within the framework of law.

Intellect and will, then, are man's distinctive adornments. It is their distinctive role to allow a finite creature to grasp truth consciously and to choose goodness freely, and thus to mirror the Infinite Creator Who is conscious Truth and absolute Goodness.

Man's natural honor, however, has been enhanced by grace, conferred at creation, lost through sin, but restored through the Incarnation and Redemption of our Lord and Saviour, Jesus Christ. When the Son of God took human flesh as an instrument of salvation, all human flesh was honored by His association with it. Through His death and resurrection Christ demonstrated the role and destiny, the honor and dignity of every man for whom He lived and suffered. Since those days of Christ on earth, no man lives by his body alone, nor by the natural powers of his soul alone; every man is sanctified, made holy, made more worthy and more honorable by the enjoyment of the special spiritual life which flows from the Cross, or by the possibility that this life will one day be his, to raise him above the limitations of nature, to honor him in unending union with the God Who became man.

Such is the triple fountain of man's dignity. To the extent these truths cease to energize the sense of reverence in every man, assaults upon the majesty of the human person must increase and intensify. Heedless that his nature has God for its origin and destiny, and reason and revelation for its divinely commissioned guide, man will do what no other creature can —he will deny his true nature and will destroy all that is good within himself.

## Man's Dignity and the Body

Such a process of degradation is viciously at work in our own country, where the deification of the flesh continues to enlist new devotees. Through its liturgy of advertisement, entertainment, and literature, this cult bids fair to corrode our national sense of decency.

When reason abdicates its sovereignty over bodily energies, their purpose is destroyed; and, by a sort of instinctive vengeance, they themselves become destroyers. Like wild animals, these energies are hard to tame, and remain dangerous even when tamed. But whatever lawful use an animal may serve, it is not wisdom for man to accept as his master the lion who seeks to devour him.

The Catholic Church, however, has never failed to accord the human body an immense measure of honor. She affirms that it was originally created by God; in one instance actually assumed by Him; in every instance meant to be on earth His special temple, and destined eventually to rejoin the soul in His Beatific Presence.

Whatever is uncompromising in her teaching about the body stems from her realism on two points: the body, though good, is not the highest good; and the undisciplined body is notoriously bad.

366

Other sacrileges against personality flow from errors less crude perhaps, but hardly less injurious. Such are some prevailing misconceptions about society, economics, labor, and education.

## Man's Dignity and Society

The practical social theory of the last century enthroned the individual but not the person. An individual can be a thing: as for instance an individual tree; but in virtue of his rational soul, a person is more than a thing. Yet the depersonalized view of man gained ascendency, and generated a society which was a crisscross of individual egotism, and in which each man sought his own.

Against this error our century has seen a reaction which has sought to overcome the isolation of man from man by imposing upon rebellious individuals a pattern of compulsory and all-embracing state organization, with unlimited power in the hands of civil government. Hence socialism in its various guises has appeared as a forcible organization imposed upon the confusion which resulted from false concepts of human freedom.

The Christian concept of man, however, is that he is both personal and social. As a person he has rights independent of the state; as a member of society he has social obligations. Parents and society contribute to the making of a man; hence man is indebted to the social order. At the same time, since his soul comes not from society but from God, a man has rights which no society may violate.

The State is a creature of man, but man is a creature of God; hence the State exists for man, not man for the State.

## Man's Dignity and Liberty

The Christian view, then, avoids the opposing extremes of individualism and collectivism, both of which are grounded on false concepts of liberty—either the unfettered liberty of individualism, which gives the "individual" the right to ignore society; or the unfettered liberty of dictatorship, which gives the government the right to ignore the person by absorbing him into a race or class, thus destroying his freedom of choice.

The false liberty of individualism wrecks society by defining freedom as individual license; the false liberty of dictatorship wrecks humanity by defining freedom as the right of the dictator to nullify the person—a right which he claims to derive from social necessity.

Concerning the results of such false notions of liberty, Leo XIII issued these warnings:

"The true liberty of human society does not consist in every man doing what he pleases, for this would simply end in turmoil and confusion and bring on the overthrow of the state . . . likewise, liberty does not consist in the power of those in authority to lay unreasonable and capricious demands upon their subjects, a course which would be equally criminal and would lead to the ruin of the commonwealth."

Liberty in political life may be described as the condition in which the individual finds himself unhampered in the discharge of his duties and in the exercise of his rights.

Liberty, however, is something more than a political phenomenon as some disciples of free enterprise maintain. It is something more mature than that dream of rights without responsibilities which historic liberalism envisioned; it is certainly different from that terrorism of responsibilities without rights which Communism imposes.

It is something wiser than free thought, and something freer than dictated thought. For freedom has its roots in man's spiritual nature. It does not arise out of any social organization, or any constitution, or any party, but out of the soul of man.

Hence to the whole tradition of the Western world, liberty does not come essentially from improved conditions of living, either political or economic, but is rather the spring out of which better conditions must flow. A free spirit creates free institutions; a slave spirit permits the creation of tyrannical ones.

## Man's Dignity and Economics

Closely connected with freedom and human dignity is the right of private property. On the question of private property the aforementioned misconceptions of liberty beget two other extremes: first the belief that a man's right to property is absolute, and that he may do with it what he pleases, without regard for the moral law or social justice; and, secondly, the reactionary error of Communism, which denies all personal rights and lodges all property in the hands of the state.

The Christian position maintains that the right to property is personal, while the use of property is also social. Unrestrained capitalism makes its mistake by divorcing property rights from social use; Communism hits wide of the mark by considering social use apart from personal rights.

Much of our economic restlessness, however, is the festering of man's wounded dignity. Karl Marx himself was perceptive enough to see that "Democracy is based on the principle of the sovereign worth of the individual, which, in turn, is based on the dream of Christianity that man has an immortal soul."

Ignoring the testimony of both reason and revelation and believing the "dream" to be only a dream, modern men have tended to concentrate almost exclusively on economic security and to pursue it at times with the fervor of religious devotion.

Often the hope is voiced that man will turn to the cultivation of the spirit after all his economic needs are supplied. We are reminded of the delusion of Jean Jacques Rousseau that man, good in himself, has been corrupted only by society. Marxism, changing the formula, gives the same false primacy to external circumstances—man's goodness will depend upon the economic system under which he lives. But the exclusive dependence on economic security and social reform to right the wrongs of mankind is by no means confined to Marxism. It affects the thought of great masses of men who reject the fundamental tenets of Marxism.

While we have deep sympathy with all people in their craving for economic security and while we acknowledge the evils, individual and spiritual as well as social, which often flourish in a society when many are forced to live in conditions of degrading poverty, yet we cannot refrain from pointing out the fact that man's goodness is from within. It depends upon man's personal convictions and upon his efforts aided by God's grace. Economic and social reform, to be effective, must be preceded by personal reform. The perfection of a society may not be measured by the moral goodness of the individuals who compose it; but the goodness of a society cannot rise above the goodness of its members.

The position of the Church relative to the economic order is based on the principle that the rights man possesses as an individual and the function he fulfills in society are inseparable. Many of the rights of the individual depend upon the function he fulfills in society. Capital and labor from this point of view are related and made inseparable by the common good of society. This is a prime principle of social justice. The right of the capitalist to his business and to his profits and interest, and the right of the laborer to his wages and his union are both conditioned by their service to the common good.

## Man's Dignity and Labor

It is only in the light on the spiritual worth of man that the dignity and importance of labor become evident. Labor is not something detached from the rest of life. Economically, it is bound up with capital as a co-partner in production. Socially, it is bound up with leisure as an avenue to cultural enrichment. Spiritually, it is bound up with the soul's development and with salvation. The worker is not a hand, as individualistic capitalism contends; not a stomach to be fed by commissars, as Communism thinks; but a person who through his labor establishes three relations: with God, with his neighbor, and with the whole natural world.

First of all, work unites us to God not only by its ascetic character and through the discipline it imposes on man by subjugating his lower passions to order and reason, but principally because, through the intention of the worker, the material universe is brought back again to God.

Second, labor is also the bond uniting man to man, a kind of school of social service, a base of human solidarity, a testimonial to man's insufficiency without his neighbor. In working with others, man ratifies his social dependence and performs an act of natural charity, because he helps create utility for others and thus promotes the happiness of his fellow men. The Catholic view, it will be noted, here adds that labor must always be used, not to dissociate ourselves from our neighbor, but to unite us with him. The greater the material advancement of any country, therefore, the more energetic should be its spirit of neighborliness.

Finally, work unites us with nature. It does this by enabling us to share in the creative work of God and by making each of us, in the language of St. Paul, *a helper of God.*

God, the supreme Artist, has communicated artistic causality to men, so that they can now make things and shape events to the image and likeness of their own ideas. The marriage of man's intelligence and will with the material world and the natural forces with which he is surrounded becomes a fruitful union, and from them is generated a culture.

### Man's Dignity and Education

In transmitting culture from generation to generation, it is the purpose of education to safeguard and develop the dignity of man.

At the end of the eighteenth century, our first President spoke of religion and morality as indispensable supports of political prosperity.

At the end of the nineteenth century our highest court declared that "the reasons presented affirm and reaffirm that this is a religious nation."

What is true of our political prosperity and our nation is true as well of our Western culture in general. Yet everywhere modern education is being drained of moral content through the movement which is known as secularism. It has been well said that the education of the soul is the soul of education.

Therefore, when education tries to thrive in a religious and moral vacuum, and does not aspire to impart a set of principles and a heirarchy of values, it degenerates into a dead and deadening juxtaposition of facts.

And even worse. For though it tries to thrive in such a vacuum, education can never really be neutral in practice. It has been truly said that "men must be governed by God or they will be ruled by tyrants."

Similarly, education must inculcate a religious and moral outlook, or it will inculcate a materialistic one. And there is no word for dignity in the vocabulary of materialism.

### Forces Created But Not Controlled

Every day in Holy Mass, Almighty God is addressed as He Who wondrously established the dignity of man and restored it more wondrously still. Only by regaining our reverence for God can we of America in the twentieth century rediscover both our own value and the solid basis on which it rests.

We must at the same time expend every effort to see that this dignity is reflected in our sense of decency, made aware of itself by education, nurtured by society, guarded by the state, stabilized by private ownership and exercised through creative activity.

The alternative is increasing chaos. The words of a contemporary historian of culture may serve to summarize the issues at stake:

"Unless we find a way to restore the contact between the life of society and the life of the spirit, our civilization will be destroyed by forces which it has had the knowledge to create but not the wisdom to control."

# Peter's Chains*

*(November 21, 1953)*

THE heroic constancy of the martyrs and the unwavering witness of the confessors have always been pre-eminent among the signs that distinguish and identify the true Church of Jesus Christ. Look where you will in Europe and in Asia, in every land now shrouded in the gloom of Communism, and you will see the solid phalanx of bishops, priests, religious and faithful, our modern martyrs and confessors, gathered around the Cross of Christ, the Standard of Salvation—the one steady light which still shines in the general darkness. We in the free countries still speak of a cold war; these men and women are enduring the bitterest, the bloodiest persecution in all history.

Shepherds of the flock of Christ are hunted down, imprisoned, debased, tortured, slain. Sick and helpless Sisters are dragged from their convents, condemned to the slow death of forced labor on roads, in forests and in mines, or to the

___
* National Catholic Welfare Conference pamphlet.

quicker death of starvation. Peasants are slaughtered and flung upon the pyres of their burning churches. Innocent children are torn from the arms of their Christian mothers and handed over to atheist debauchers.

## War Against Believers in God

It is a war against all who believe in God and His Christ, against all who dare to claim for man the liberty of the sons of God. It rages from Korea to China and to Indo-China; from Russia to the Baltic lands; from Poland and Lithuania to Yugoslavia; from the Ukraine to Albania; from Czechoslovakia to Hungary, to Roumania and Bulgaria; it rages in the eastern parts of Austria and Germany. And everywhere the Church of God, her sacred ministers and her faithful children are the first targets of the persecution. Millions of them have already died for the Faith. Who shall count the number of those who are now suffering and marked for death?

This is a war against the true religion of Jesus Christ. When will men in the free world come to realize that the crisis of today is first of all a crisis of religion, that the Communist debaser of man is essentially a hater of God, that his long-range and his short-range purpose is the destruction of Christianity. From Marx to Malenkov, the Communist sees Christ as the enemy to be exterminated.

Is it not, then, the strange anomaly of our times that a calculated confusion has been able to hide from so many of our people the primary, the changeless purpose of the enemy? How few there are who understand that the struggle for liberty is a warfare against the fanatical foes of Christ! How few there are who know that millions of Catholics have already died that the rest of us might live!

Here is a story of epic nobility, of unsurpassed human grandeur, of deathless spiritual devotion. Our martyrs and confessors are the glory of the age in which we live. One would have thought that the western world would rise as one man to do them reverence, would write their deeds of valor in letters of enduring gold. Instead, indifference, scant notice or silence. Only in the Catholic press will you find the martyrology which the historians of tomorrow will account the greatest glory of today.

## Nero, Voltaire, Peter and Paul

Who can now recall the chroniclers of Nero's day? But the names of Peter and of Paul have endured throughout the centuries; above their tombs rise the noblest temples of Christendom, and pilgrims come in multitudes unnumbered to remember and to pray.

Nor can history be kind to those men of State who retreated to the refuge of a polite neutralism while the crucial battle of our times was being fought.

History can record only in reprobation that while Nero raged in the East against the true Church of Christ, the Voltaires of the West raised their olden cry *"Ecrasez l'Infame"* and sought to crush these valiant fighters for God and human freedom. Genuine philosophy must list Nero and Voltaire as allies. History will register the fact of that alliance in the Warsaw maneuver which would cut off from help the champions of the authentic liberties.

And what shall we say of those ungenerous men, who in the crisis of our times have been found so sadly wanting—those narrow sectarians who allowed their petty or their imagined grievances to obscure the true greatness of our blessed martyrs and confessors? We shall leave them to God and to the worm of conscience, as we pray *Father, forgive them for they know not what they do.*

The Catholic Bishops of the United States of America, gathered together in their annual assembly at Washington, proclaim to all their faithful priests and people the solemn duty of instant and constant prayer for our suffering brethren of the Church of Silence. When Peter was in prison, the Church prayed without ceasing for him, and the Angel of the Lord touched him and the chains fell off from his hands. Peter is again in chains.

## Let Us Pray and Protest

Let there then be supplication to God and penance that His grace be poured out in superabundant measure to strengthen those who hold the place of honor and of danger in the new warfare launched against the Church. Let us all cherish in our hearts the epic story of our Martyrs and Confessors. Let us tell this story to our children that they may learn the names of Stepinac and Mindszenty and Wyszynski, of Beran, of Cule, of Ford and of Byrne, along with the heroes of the Faith in ages past; that they may understand how great it is to be a Catholic.

And let us raise our voices, in a unison of protest, a protest that will penetrate into the consciences of all decent men, into all the chancelleries of the world, against this new scourge of God and man.

To our brother bishops, to the priests, religious and people of the Church of Silence, we send affectionate greeting and the tribute of our devotion, of our admiration, of our entire solidarity. We salute you; we embrace you; we minister in spirit to your necessities; we bind in prayer the wounds you suffer for justice's sake. For you are blessed when the enemies of Christ persecute and revile you. You are the light of the world, giving to our generation that saving example of fidelity spoken of by St. Paul: *Who shall separate us from the love of Christ? Shall privation or distress, or famine or nakedness, or danger, or persecution or the sword? As it is written: For Thy sake, we are put to death all the day long. We are accounted as sheep for the slaughter.*

*But in all these things we overcome because of Him that hath loved us.*

Indeed your Faith is the victory which overcometh the world. By your stripes will the modern world be healed.

Peter's Successor Who is Pius spoke the deepest sentiments of our own hearts when He said to you: "We embrace you with a special love and we kneel to kiss your chains."

# The Hope of Mankind*

(*November 18, 1956*)

ONCE again in our time the alarm bell is ringing in the night. The world, inured as it is to tragedy, is apprized of a tragedy still more profound. In the events of this hour at which the Bishops of the American hierarchy meet in annual session,

---

\* *The Catholic Mind.*

they and all men concerned with human welfare under God read the threat of catastrophe so dire as to destroy the last bulwarks of civilization.

One voice, urgent and clear, has made itself heard above the tumult of the nations. The Common Father of Christendom, Pope Pius XII, has spoken out with unhesitating forthrightness. To those peoples who have been made the victims of a brutality so gross as to defy historic comparison, he has addressed words of compassion which could only come from a father's heart. To those nations bent upon aggression and which have ignored the sacred rights of humanity and the instruments of justice upon which they rest, he has issued stern warning of their madness.

### Primacy of Law and Order

To all, whether inspired by selfish interest or led astray by rash counsel, who would jeopardize the delicate balance of world peace he has recalled the primacy of law and order in the settlement of human disagreements.

In this crisis we can only add our voice to his. We echo his burning reproof of those who have dared to unleash the hounds of war in a world which has already suffered so long and so bitterly. With him we denounce with all our strength this fresh outbreak of aggression which sets at utter defiance the hard-won concert of the nations for the outlawing of international banditry. With him we plead for a renewal of that basic sanity among men and nations which will establish peace upon its only enduring foundations of justice and charity. With him we urge upon the world not the counsels of despair which would describe the situation as beyond salvation, but the promise of a better hope implicit in the dawning recognition of human solidarity under the universal fatherhood of God.

We share his anguish for those whose unmerited sufferings have again filled the cup of human misery to overflowing. Our eyes follow his as he surveys the ravaged cities, the desolated countrysides, the charred ruins of a thousand homes and shrines. We count with him the ghastly casualties of modern warfare, the broken bodies, the dead in their silent windrows.

Foremost, inevitably, in our thinking are the heroic people

of Hungary. For centuries they have been a bastion of Christendom against the outer perils, and for centuries their blood has been spilled for the ideal of a united Christian society. Now again they have received the full brunt of a calculated fury and have written a matchless chapter in the annals of freedom. To them, in their darkest hour, we offer the sympathy of our common faith and we pledge our unremitting efforts to help them achieve that ultimate liberty for which their sons and daughters have died, surely not in vain.

## War Would Only Annihilate

It is not mere rhetoric to say that at this juncture the world is poised on the brink of disaster; it is grim realism. Yet war in modern terms would be a nightmare of unimaginable horrors. It can only annihilate; it has no power to solve our problems. If, in the ultimate resort, it is the duty of man to resist naked aggression, still it is obvious that every possible means consistent with divine law and human dignity must be employed and exhausted to avoid the final arbitrament of nuclear warfare. It has been the hope of humankind that a means adequate to the necessity might be found in the concert of the United Nations.

This is neither the time nor the place to review its history or to pass judgment on its achievement. If there have been mistakes in its decisions and faltering in its procedures, that is no more than a commentary on our human condition. The fact remains that it offers the only present promise we have for sustained peace in our time; peace with any approximation of justice. The implication of our Holy Father's recent impassioned messages, clearly revealed in their context, is that the nations must employ their unity with such revived strength and purpose as to banish the spectre of war. It is division which tempts the aggressor; it is unity which gives him pause.

## Threat of Disunity

Nothing could be conceived more disheartening for the cause of peace, nothing more discreditable to the honor of nations which have pledged themselves to peace, than the disunity which threatens to disrupt our immediate counsels and dissipates our strength. With the Sovereign Pontiff we recognize the urgency of prompt and effective intervention to

377

silence the guns of war and to enforce the pacific arbitration of conflicting claims. With him, also, we emphasize the paramount need for a heightened concept of the universal validity of law among nations as among men. For unless God and His justice are acknowledged as basic to the very substance of law, there is no foundation upon which men may hope to build a lasting citadel of peace. There, for those who will read it, is the poignant warning of our present tragedy.

It is with genuine satisfaction, amid all this distress, that we as Americans have followed the course set by our own Government for the avoidance of international calamity. Worthy of highest praise are its efforts, rising above considerations of party and politics, to bring the problems before the tribunal of the nations, to restore mutual confidence in all those who seek justice, and to counter the threat of anarchy by marshaling the full strength of those forces of law and order which the world commands. Our President, indeed, has set a pattern of vigorous leadership, and has emphasized many of the points which have been dwelt upon by Pope Pius XII. He too is alert to the overriding need of a developed reverence for international law, clearly mindful, as he stressed in his recent address to the American people, that without law there can be no peace.

"If you wish peace," said the pagan axiom, "prepare for war." Christianity has revised that saying: "If you wish peace, prepare for peace." Though the hour is late indeed, it is not yet too late. There is the Divinity which governs the destinies of this world, and the supreme folly is to leave God out of our reckoning. As the Bishops of the United States we solemnly call upon the faithful throughout the land to pledge themselves to a veritable crusade of prayer. Let it be for the specific ends that international sanity will triumph over war; that justice may be vindicated by the nations united under law; and that our own beloved country, under God, may lead the way to that better hope for all mankind. Nor let us forget those who have suffered and who suffer now; that out of the crucible of their sacrifice may come the minted gold of freedom. We stand with the Vicar of Christ, and our prayer is for peace for our country and all the world—a peace with justice and charity.

# World Refugee Year and Migration*

(*Statement by the Administrative Board, National Catholic Welfare Conference, November, 1959*)

WORLD Refugee Year began last July on a note of high hope for the homeless refugees of the world. His Holiness Pope John XXIII added his voice to the chorus of those earnestly seeking to remind nations of their obligations:

> We raise Our voice on behalf of refugees, and We paternally exhort all Our children in every part of the world to collaborate generously and efficaciously in making a success of this World Refugee Year, an undertaking inspired by aims so noble and disinterested, to which it pleases Us to pay tribute.

The earliest records of history indicate that migration and resettlement are common occurrences in the life of men. People move from their native land for various reasons. Some seek opportunity and adventure. Others flee from the disasters of nature, or of war and the aftermath of war. In many instances the tyranny of rulers, economic and political pressures, or religious and social tensions force countless families to seek new homes in distant lands.

Migration is as much a part of current history as of past history. In the present-day world there are two groups of potential migrants: those forced to flee as refugees and displaced persons, and those who emigrate voluntarily.

Those who are refugees and displaced persons have lost their homes because of war, persecution, or political pressures. Some are refugees from Communist persecution. Others are expelled, or subjected to intolerable pressure, as minority groups in a highly nationalistic society.

The second group of potential migrants comprises those seeking better living conditions or aspiring to a more abundant life.

Even in relatively prosperous nations of Western Europe there are millions who either lack work or who barely subsist on the products of their labor, however diligent. In Asia, Africa and Latin America there are literally millions living in

* National Catholic Welfare Conference pamphlet.

sheer destitution. They do not have even the utter minimum of food, shelter, clothing, and medical care needed for a truly human life.

Any assertion that migration is the ultimate solution for all refugees or for the economically destitute can certainly be challenged. In many instances, vigorous and realistic plans for economic development might more effectively serve the purpose of aid.

The fact remains, however, that great numbers of these people understandably clamor for the chance to seek a new home where they can more adequately meet their needs and those of their families.

Their plea and their plight should be heard and examined in the light of Christian principles.

### A Christian Attitude Toward the Problem

The attitude of the Christian toward his fellow man is based on the second of the two great laws of God, *Thou shalt love thy neighbor as thyself*. Christ Himself insisted on love of neighbor as essential to the life of His followers. He even singled it out as a test for salvation:

*If anyone says, 'I love God,' and hates his brother, he is a liar. For how can he who does not love his brother, whom he sees, love God, whom he does not see? And this commandment we have from Him, that he who loves God should love his brother also.*

Love of neighbor is fundamental and it must transcend nation, race, creed, and status.

From this principle spring the basic moral considerations for formulating national policy on behalf of potential migrants in other countries. True love of neighbor will motivate us to assist these people in attaining the measure of justice that is rightfully theirs and to share with them in charity the temporal abundance God has given us.

Migration is a right due in justice to the individual. Pope Pius XII spoke of the "natural right of the individual to be unhampered in immigration or emigration." It is the right of human beings to have access to the resources of the earth created by God for the good of man. In the present order of things, it is necessary for nations to make laws to insure the use of these resources in a reasonable and orderly fashion, but the tenor of the law should be such as to facilitate, not impede, access to them.

It must be recognized, however, that migration is not the only solution, nor always the best solution for the problem of poverty in overcrowded lands.

True, for many of those who are refugees and displaced persons there is no other hope but migration. Those, however, who are victims of disrupted economic and social conditions may prefer to remain in their homeland if these conditions are improved. A few years ago, for example, the world was deeply concerned about refugees and expellees from East Germany and from German lands now occupied by other powers. Today many of these persons have been absorbed by a prospering West German economy.

### Prosperous Should Aid Less Favored

On the other hand, in some countries such as Italy, Greece, the Netherlands and Japan, there is no apparent prospect in the immediate future for an expansion of the economy sufficient to provide a decent livelihood for all of their people.

Accordingly, the nations of the world, especially those that are prosperous, should unite in effective long-range programs designed to raise productivity and thus make such nations as self-supporting as possible.

Sometimes migration is impossible because of the sheer numbers involved. Also migration is slow and in the meantime many millions are destitute, homeless and hungry. Here the obligation of charity, love for neighbor, strikes directly at the Christian conscience.

The plight of these people cannot be ignored. Each nation, in a manner commensurate with true ability and wealth, must provide needed food, shelter, clothing, and medical care. To neglect these people is to neglect the human family.

In summary, migration is an absolute need for many refugees and displaced peoples. It is a solution for economic and social pressures in some areas where there seems to be little hope for internal economic and social improvement.

But, when migration becomes an impractical solution because of the sheer numbers involved, then heroic measures must be taken to alleviate present misery and to institute long-range reforms, designed to raise the standard of living.

### The United States Is Involved

The moral principles just stated, and the applications outlined above, have special relevance for a nation such as ours which is so lavishly blessed with God's bounty.

Our obligation is fourfold: to share our own abundance; to welcome the immigrant; to promote and cooperate with world policies of resettlement; and to aid underdeveloped nations.

There is no need to restate here completely our record in this regard. Traditionally we have been generous in helping others in need. Until recent decades, we have been relatively liberal in accepting immigrants. In present restrictive immigration laws, we have made exceptions for refugees and displaced persons. Since World War II, our aid to nations and peoples in distress has been extensive indeed.

Even though our record has been good, it is, nevertheless, not inappropriate to conduct a careful examination of the needs of the world to see whether we have done all within our power to aid the homeless and the hungry. The following questions might legitimately be raised:

1) Have we made a sufficiently urgent effort to develop to the fullest extent possible a program for distributing our food surpluses to the hungry? The difficulties involved are formidable, ranging from the political to the purely logistic. But could not these difficulties be overcome, were we determined to do so?

2) Are we meeting, according to our abilities and needs of other nations, the demands for technical assistance, development loans, and stimulation of private investment in newly developing nations? Should we increase our efforts to influence other comparatively wealthy nations to associate with us in international programs of this type?

### Could We Do More for Homeless?

3) Are we doing all within our power, particularly during this World Refugee Year, to help the refugee and displaced person? Could we do more in accepting the homeless within

our own borders, or in helping them to find homes elsewhere in a suitable or desirable environment?

4) Do our own laws tend to discriminate against the "difficult to resettle" and "hardship" cases? Many students of our immigration laws feel they are designed to favor the best educated, the strongest, and the healthiest immigrants. This in effect bleeds a nation troubled with population problems of its best citizens, leaving behind those who can contribute least to national prosperity. Such ungenerous laws seem to bespeak a spirit of selfishness rather than a genuine desire by a privileged people to help those in need.

5) Are our basic laws sufficiently sensitive to problems of compassion, such as reuniting of families or the provision of homes for orphan children?

6) Are we observing the precepts of justice and charity by keeping in our laws prejudicial elements such as token quotas for Orientals or a national-origins clause? Do not these laws in effect favor nations whose people show the least desire for emigration?

7) Have we considered the possibility that some regulations designed to keep out criminals and subversives may affront the human dignity of immigrants not belonging to this category? Could we not find less offensive methods for securing the same purpose?

8) Is the total number of quota immigrants too low, considering the immense economic strength of our nation? It is certainly no kindness to admit immigrants if there are no jobs available, but the ability of our economy to offer jobs has steadily and vigorously risen. Even doubling the present effective quota immigrant level would be an insignificant factor in adding to our work force.

9) Is our effort to help the immigrant adjust adequate to the problem? Could we not display warmer understanding toward him in his struggle with the new and complex difficulties involved in the process of social assimilation?

### Might We Not Sacrifice Comforts?

These questions are raised to stimulate Christian thinking on the concrete problems connected with migration and immigration. They are raised at a time when most Americans are acutely aware of the sacrifices they are making, especially in the form of taxes to meet the costs of national defense and an expanding population.

The burdens we have been carrying are admittedly heavy, especially since they have been prolonged over many years, but sacrifice is essentially comparative. How many of us, even with heavy taxes and extensive programs of aid, are deprived of luxuries and possibly some comforts? There are few employed Americans whose lot is not incomparably better than that of the overwhelming majority of workers in the rest of the world.

When we realize that a great portion of the world's population goes to bed hungry each night and that preventible disease is endemic in whole countries, we know that our sacrifices are relatively minor.

In the light of these problems the thoughtful Christian will read again the words of our Saviour:

> *I was hungry and you gave me to eat;*
> *I was thirsty and you gave me to drink;*
> *I was a stranger and you took me in;*
> *Naked and you covered me;*
> *Sick and you visited me;*
> *I was in prison and you came to me . . .*
> *Amen, I say to you, as long as you did*
> *it for one of these, the least of my brethren, you did it for me.*

# Freedom and Peace*

### (*November, 1959*)

ALL the world craves peace. Without freedom under God for every man and for every nation there can be no peace.

On his recent visit to our country the Communist spokesman took every opportunity to compare unfavorably, Capitalism with Communism in their economic aspects. This is not

---

* National Catholic Welfare Conference pamphlet.

the basic issue. The choice that men and nations must make today is between freedom and coercion.

Such words as "democracy," "republic," "peace," and "friendship" are words to which the Western world is long accustomed. These words have been taken into their current vocabulary by the proponents of Communism. But while we may use the same words, we are not speaking the same language. By "peace" the Communist means submission to his program. By "friendship" he means the acceptance on the part of others of his formula for co-existence.

Freedom is not the product of any political or social system; it is man's natural birthright, and, in the words of Pope Leo XIII, "the highest of man's natural endowments."

This freedom under God permits man to use his faculties for his own just benefit and for the service of his fellow man in accordance with the law of God. Furthermore, to protect the freedom and rights of its citizens, each nation has the right to be free.

## Freedom—The American Ideal

Our country was "conceived in liberty and dedicated to the proposition that all men are created equal." This recognition of the dignity of every citizen, endowed with inalienable rights that are God-given is indelibly woven into the origin and history of the American republic.

Ours is a tradition of freedom under God with justice and charity for all. It seems opportune to emphasize the importance of this heritage of freedom. In it lies the moral strength that makes the contribution of America to the world's rebuilding unique and distinctive.

Above and beyond the material aid that we distribute so generously around the globe to those in need, we should be equally concerned in sharing our ideals of liberty and justice. Proper standards of living and material prosperity are not enough. These are but means to an end and not in themselves the goal we would attain, if world peace is, as it should be, the aim of all our efforts.

Peace, as demonstrated by our nation's experience, rests on disciplined freedom with its attendant virtues. True peace for nations as well as for individuals comes from justice, from charity, from the faithful observance of the moral law. The might of arms can do no more for peace than to discourage aggressors that are belligerent. Pacts and treaties can bring at best an uneasy truce, restraining an open hostility without achieving friendship or understanding. Not even international organizations and international law, essential as they are for order in the world can bring about world peace. Fundamentally, that peace depends on the acceptance by men and nations of a fixed, unchangeable, universal moral law.

There is no need to tell again the noble efforts that have been made in behalf of peace since the dawn of the present century. Nor is there need to retell disappointments that have laid low the hopes of men. The two most destructive wars in history have left their indelible mark on the first half of our century. Now well into the second half, men live under the threat of a third world war that would be immeasurably more destructive than the previous wars.

## Present Obstacles to Peace and Freedom

We would recognize that the chief obstacles to peace are the obstacles to real freedom. First among the main obstacles to peace and freedom in our present world is obviously world communism. Communists do indeed preach peace and freedom and preach it incessantly; their actions, however, belie their word. They stir up hatred and mistrust. They reopen the old wounds of people who had real grievances in the days when they were subject to alien rule. While they themselves enslave whole nations over whom they have no shadow of claim, they seize wherever possible, upon economic and racial injustice to incite class warfare and violent revolution.

Thus the Communist world poses a twofold threat to peace: first, that of military aggression of which the more recent instances continue to exemplify both ruthlessness and perfidy; secondly, the widespread sowing of the seed of hatred within nations and among nations. To meet this constant threat to peace is the free world's greatest problem.

A second obstacle to peace and freedom, personal and national, is the spirit of excessive nationalism. The world-wide movement toward independence is in itself good and laudable, and we rejoice that many nations formerly subjected to external control now guide their own destinies. But all too often a morbid preoccupation with past grievances arouses a spirit of revenge that defrauds certain minorities of freedom and obstructs the clear vision of the constructive and peaceful paths that lead to national greatness.

A third obstacle to freedom and peace is found in the inhuman conditions that prevail among so many millions of the world's population. Poverty, hunger, disease and the bitterness engendered by social injustice is their common lot. Embittered by the contrast between their own wretchedness and the wealth of the rich and powerful in their own lands, and between nations, they are ripe for exploitation by both the Communists and extreme nationalists.

Nor can we be unmindful of the plight of the millions of refugees whose present status is a challenge to all who believe in freedom and peace. Victims of totalitarian tyranny, deprived of family, of homeland, of liberty itself, they pose no threat to the peace and security of any land that may be their haven. But continued apathy to the problem of their resettlement is a reproach to the conscience of the free world.

### Obstacles to Peace—at Home

We must also recognize that conditions at home, which threaten our moral integrity, seriously threaten the cause of freedom and peace.

Our attention is directed to the subversive and evil forces that may undermine the moral strength of the nation. Chief among these currently are racial injustice, laxity in home life and discipline, preoccupation with the sensual, selfishness and self-seeking in economic life, and the excessive desire for wealth and ease.

The forces of religion in this country face no problem more pressing than the restoration within our people of respect for the moral law as God's law, and the inculcation of those virtues on which the soundness of family and civic life depends. Reverence for God's law, the keeping of His commandments, the practice of self-restraint, of justice, and charity will contribute beyond measure to the strength and unity of our country, which are so essential for effective leadership in the cause of freedom and of peace.

Although Communism is the overriding danger to peace and freedom, our preoccupation with Communism should not deter us from seeking to solve other problems that may endanger peace and freedom. The social and economic problems of the world and particularly those of Asia, Africa, and Latin America in some areas pose a twofold challenge that can be met. In the first place, our Christian sense of justice and mercy impels us to do all that we can to help those who suffer from avoidable poverty, ignorance, and disease. Secondly, we know that tensions engendered by these conditions tend to foment both militant nationalism and communist infiltration. Hungry and destitute, desperate people may grasp at short range solutions in the effort to compress within a decade a progress that elsewhere took centuries.

Our people have been generous in responding to the appeals of the afflicted victims of war and famine. But the needs of the world will not be met by charitable aid alone. The greater charity is to help people to help themselves. Programs of education, technical assistance, and developmental aid, now being carried out both by individual governments and by international bodies, can do much to build the foundations for prosperity and peace in nations suffering from poverty and hunger.

### Roads to Peace and Freedom

In the long run, at least, the cause of peace and freedom so intimately connected with the independence of nations would be better served, if we could rely less upon programs of governmental aid and more on private investment and international trade adequately regulated for the good of all nations. In view of such serious problems as the pressure of population in some areas upon resources, the world needs every element of cooperation and good will to step up production and distribution of food and fibers. The potential abundance made possible by modern technology should be made a reality, as a result of programs inspired by our love of our fellow man and the quest for peace and freedom.

In regard to Communism, our goal is nothing less than the conversion of the Communist world. Our moral judgment is absolute: Communism is godless; it is aggressive and belliger-ent; it is unbelievably cruel. Witness the commune system in China! Hungary and Tibet are but the more recent manifesta-tions of its total disregard for human rights and human dig-nity. Nevertheless, conscious of Christ's example and the in-finite power of grace, we pray for the Red persecutors and for the persecuted. We wish no conquest except that of the spirit. We wish those who constructed the Iron Curtain to tear down the barbed wire and the machine gun posts and to join us in the enjoyment of God's freedom and peace.

Even today there are signs that the tyranny of Communism is not the same in every nation under its sway. There are indications that the spirit of man will not stay crushed. We should storm heaven with prayer and penance, knowing that what to man seems impossible, God will grant to those who pray to Him with humble hearts, free of hatred and a spirit of revenge. As the early Christians converted their persecu-tors, we can seek to move those whose hearts seem hardened by blasphemous contempt for God and inhuman disregard for their fellow men.

In this spirit, statesmen of the world must continue their of-ten disheartening quest for peace, reductions in armament, and the introduction of the rule of law into the society of nations. They must be firm in upholding principle and justice, know-ing that appeasement in such matters leads only to the peace of the conquered. It is a delusion to place hope in seeking real understanding when the true problem is a conflict of essential principles, not lack of understanding.

While negotiating unceasingly for better relations with the Communist regimes, we must never forget that their system and ours are as basically different as slavery and freedom. To palliate the difference is to subvert the cause of freedom and peace. Recently the Communists have been cleverly veiling the sharp differences between the systems, as witnessed by the statement of a member of the Russian press group, "Our sys-tems are different but there is not a single obstacle which would deny us peace of friendship or cooperation." In other words, Red slavery is only different, not opposed to our sys-tem of peace and freedom under God.

389

## Materialism, No Answer to Communism

Ultimately the problem of Communism as a threat to peace and freedom will be met only when we exemplify the principles that we proclaim as Christian members of a nation dedicated to God's law. There must be a searching reappraisal of our devotion to the principles we proclaim. We cannot live as materialists and expect to convert others to our system of freedom and peace under God.

Instead of upholding boldly the principles of peace and freedom under God, we have emphasized the material fruits of our freedom, material wealth from industrialization and education. Instead of proclaiming freedom under God as we did in a more robust time in our history, we have so praised a program of supplying the machines and calories and pleasure that these fruits of freedom and peace are made its substitutes. Today throughout the world, too often it is thought that when we speak of our American way of life, we are speaking only of a high standard of living.

We have often acted in our international relations as if the products of industry and methods of production were our only contribution to the welfare of our neighbors. We have given the impression that material progress is our sovereign if not our exclusive concern. In particular we have fostered industrialization and education as the ends and not the means of elevating nations. Insofar as we have done this, we have tacitly accepted the materialistic way and philosophy of Communism as our way of life. We have aimed our efforts at satisfying the body, and, paradoxically, have allowed the Communists to capture the minds of men.

We must convince the world that our industry, our education, our technology are made not only to serve the body, but the free spirit of man, that the grandeur of our heritage and extent of our contribution to the world is not measured in dollars, and in machines, but in the spirit of God's freedom and the dignity of the human person. Our motive in gladly pouring out our resources is not simply a natural pity for the misery of our fellow man or a damper to conflict, but recognition of his dignity as an equal son of God endowed with freedom.

To accomplish this we must be totally dedicated to our beliefs in God, the source of freedom and peace. We must be ready to give our country's principles the same unlimited measure of devotion that led to the birth of our nation. Mankind will follow those who give it a higher cause and leadership of their dedication. It is up to us to give that leadership to mankind in the cause of God's freedom and peace.

# Personal Responsibility*

(*November 19, 1960*)

. . . THIS tendency to delegate excessive responsibility to an organization is discernible also in the realm of international affairs. Some manifest no sense of personal responsibility in the affairs of the international community. On the other hand, many citizens seem to feel that our mere adherence to the United Nations absolves us from further responsibility in the international order and that decisions made by the United Nations, regardless of their objective value, are always to be regarded as morally right. Admitting the undoubted value of a policy of supporting the United Nations and recognizing the genuine contribution it has made in many areas, we must understand clearly that the citizens of this country, and of all countries have a responsibility to judge and to evaluate the United Nation's deliberations and decisions according to objective norms of morality universally binding. This involves also the duty of citizens to make proper representation of such judgment to their respective governments.

---

* National Catholic Welfare Conference News.

# *Appendix*

---

## Pattern For Peace*

### Catholic, Jewish, and Protestant Declaration on World Peace

*The Moral Law Must Govern World Order*

1. The organization of a just peace depends upon practical recognition of the fact that not only individuals but nations, states, and international society are subject to the sovereignty of God and to the moral law which comes from God.

*The Rights of the Individual Must Be Assured*

2. The dignity of the human person as the image of God must be set forth in all its essential implications in an international declaration of rights and be vindicated by the positive action of national governments and international organizations. States as well as individuals must repudiate racial, religious or other discrimination in violation of those rights.

*The Rights of Oppressed, Weak or Colonial Peoples Must Be Protected*

3. The rights of all peoples, large and small, subject to the good of the organized world community, must be safeguarded within the framework of collective security. The progress of undeveloped, colonial, or oppressed peoples toward political responsibility must be the object of international concern.

*The Rights of Minorities Must Be Secured*

4. National governments and international organizations must respect and guarantee the rights of ethnic, religious, and cultural minorities to economic livelihood, to equal opportunity for educational and cultural development, and to political equality.

---

* Catholic Association for International Peace.

## International Institutions to Maintain Peace with Justice Must Be Organized

5. An enduring peace requires the organization of international institutions which will develop a body of international law; guarantee the faithful fulfilment of international obligations, and revise them when necessary; assure collective security by drastic limitation and continuing control of armaments, compulsory arbitration, and adjudication of controversies, and the use when necessary of adequate sanctions to enforce the law.

## International Economic Cooperation Must Be Developed

6. International economic collaboration to assist all states to provide an adequate standard of living for their citizens must replace the present economic monopoly and exploitation of natural resources by privileged groups and states.

## A Just Social Order within Each State Must Be Achieved

7. Since the harmony and well-being of the world community are intimately bound up with the internal equilibrium and social order of the individual states, steps must be taken to provide for the security of the family, the collaboration of all groups and classes in the interest of the common good, a standard of living adequate for self-development and family life, decent conditions of work, and participation by labor in decisions affecting its welfare.

In a world troubled to despair by recurring war, the Protestant churches have been seeking to show how moral and religious convictions should guide the relations of nations. Their conclusions are in many important respects similar to those of men of other faiths. In this we rejoice, for world order cannot be achieved without the cooperation of all men of good will. We appeal to our constituency to give heed to the foregoing proposals enunciated by Protestants, Catholics, and Jews, which must find expression in national policies. Beyond these proposals we hold that the ultimate foundations of peace require spiritual regeneration as emphasized in the Christian Gospel.

Rt. Rev. Henry St. George Tucker, *New York City, President, Federal Council of the Churches of Christ in America and Presiding Bishop, Protestant Episcopal Church*

Bishop William Y. Bell, *Cordele, Ga., President, Board of Evangelism, Colored Methodist Episcopal Church*

Rev. Ferdinand Q. Blanchard, *Cleveland, Ohio, Moderator, General Council of the Congregational Christian Churches*

Rev. P. O. Bersell, *Minneapolis, Minn., President, Lutheran Augustana Synod and National Lutheran Council*

394

*Appendix*

Bishop A. R. Clippinger, *Dayton, Ohio, President, Board of Administration of the Church of the United Brethren in Christ*
Rev. Henry Sloane Coffin, *New York City, Moderator, General Assembly of the Presbyterian Church in the U. S. A.*
Rev. Robert Cummins, *Boston, Mass., General Superintendent, Universalist Church*
Rev. Frederick May Eliot, *Boston, Mass., President, American Unitarian Association*
Rt. Rev. S. H. Gapp, *Bethlehem, Pa., President, Provincial Elders' Conference of the Moravian Church*
Rev. L. W. Goebel, *Chicago, President, General Synod of the Evangelical and Reformed Church*
Rev. C. E. Lemmon, *Columbia, Mo., President, International Convention of the Disciples of Christ*
Bishop G. Bromley Oxnam, *Boston, Mass., Secretary, Council of Bishops of the Methodist Church*
Commissioner Edward J. Parker, *New York City, National Commander of the Salvation Army*
Rev. W. W. Peters, *McPherson, Kan., Moderator, General Conference of the Church of the Brethren*
Rev. Jacob Prins, *Grand Rapids, Mich., President, General Synod of the Reformed Church in America*
Rev. Donald W. Richardson, *Richmond, Va., Moderator, General Assembly of the Presbyterian Church in the U. S.*
Rev. Joseph C. Robbins, *Wollaston, Mass., President, Northern Baptist Convention*
Rev. Albert N. Rogers, *Yonkers, N. Y., President, General Conference of the Seventh Day Baptist Churches*
Bishop John S. Stamm, *Harrisburg, Pa., President, Board of Bishops of the Evangelical Church*
Allen U. Tomlinson, *Whittier, Calif., Presiding Clerk of the Five Years Meeting of the Society of Friends*
Bishop P. A. Wallace, *Brooklyn, N. Y., Senior Bishop, African Methodist Episcopal Zion Church*
Bishop James C. Baker, *Los Angeles, Calif., Chairman, International Missionary Council*
Frank S. Bayley, *Seattle, Wash., President, National Council of Young Men's Christian Associations*
Rev. G. Pitt Beers, *New York City, Chairman, Christian Commission for Camp and Defense Communities*
Mrs. J. D. Bragg, *St Louis, Mo., President, Women's Division of Christian Service of the Methodist Board of Missions*
Dr. Arlo A. Brown, *Madison, N. J., Chairman, International Council of Religious Education*
Rev. Rex S. Clements, *Bryn Mawr, Pa. President, Board of Christian Education, Presbyterian Church in the U. S. A.*
Rev. Charles E. Diehl, *Memphis, Tenn., Chairman, National Commission on Church Related Colleges*

395

Dr. John Foster Dulles, *New York City, Chairman, Federal Council's Commission to Study the Bases of a Just and Durable Peace*

Rev. Robert M. Hopkins, *Indianapolis, Ind., President, United Christian Missionary Society*

Mrs. Henry A. Ingraham, *Brooklyn, N. Y., President, National Board of the Young Women's Christian Associations*

Dr. Rufus M. Jones, *Haverford, Pa., Chairman, American Friends Service Committee*

John T. Manson, *New Haven, Conn., President, American Bible Society*

Bishop Francis J. McConnell, *New York City, Chairman, Christian Conference on War and Peace*

Rev. William P. Merrill, *New York City, President, The Church Peace Union*

Bishop Arthur J. Moore, *Atlanta, Ga., President, Board of Missions of the Methodist Church*

Dr. John R. Mott, *New York City, Honorary Chairman, International Missionary Council*

Rt. Rev. G. Ashton Oldham, *Albany, N. Y., President, American Council, World Alliance for International Friendship through the Churches*

Mrs. Norman Vincent Peale, *New York City, President, Home Missions Council of North America*

Rev. Daniel A. Poling, *Philadelphia, President, International Society of Christian Endeavor*

Rev. Charles P. Proudfit, *Chicago, President, Council of Church Boards of Education*

Dr. Leland Rex Robinson, *Bronxville, N. Y., President, American Committee for Christian Refugees*

Rev. Russell H. Stafford, *Boston, Mass., President, American Board of Commissioners for Foreign Missions*

Charles P. Taft, II, *Cincinnati, Ohio, Chairman, Friends of the World Council of Churches*

Rev. Henry P. Van Dusen, *New York City, President, American Association of Theological Schools*

Rev. A. Livingston Warnshuis, *Bronxville, N. Y., Chairman, Foreign Missions Conference of North America*

Rev. Luther A. Weigle, *New Haven, Conn., Chairman, World's Sunday School Association*

Miss Amy Ogden Welcher, *Hartford, Conn., President, United Council of Church Women*

Rev. Herbert L. Willett, *Wilmette, Ill., President, Association for the Promotion of Christian Unity*

*Representatives of Eastern Orthodox Churches*

Most Rev. Theophilus Pashkovsky, *San Francisco, Calif., Metropolitan of the Russian Orthodox Greek Catholic Church of America*

*Appendix*

Most Rev. Antony Bashir, *Brooklyn, N. Y., Metropolitan of the Syrian Antiochian Orthodox Church*
Right Rev. Bohdan, *New York City, Bishop of the Ukrainian Orthodox Church of America*

The American Synagogue commends to the attention of its own constituency and to all men of faith the foregoing principles as a guide to thought and action in dealing with the grave world problems of our time. These seven principles, while they do not exhaust the teachings of the Jewish tradition on issues of social relationships, have their sanction in Judaism, both Biblical and rabbinic. Judaism's highest goal has ever been "to amend the world through the kingdom of God." The Synagogue therefore calls upon its adherents, both as citizens and as Jews, to seek after the implementation of these principles. They will thereby act in faithful conformity with the moral values of the Jewish religion, and at the same time serve the best interests of country and of mankind.

Dr. Israel Goldstein, *New York City, President, Synagogue Council of America*
Dr. Louis Finkelstein, *New York City, President, Jewish Theological Seminary of America*
Dr. Julian Morgenstern, *Cincinnati, Ohio, President, Hebrew Union College*
Rabbi Saul Silber, *Chicago, Ill., President, Hebrew Theological College*
Dr. Stephen S. Wise, *New York City, President, Jewish Institute of Religion*
Rabbi William Drazin, *Savannah, Ga., President, Rabbinical Council of America*
Rabbi Solomon B. Freehof, *Pittsburgh, Pa., President, Central Conference of American Rabbis*
Rabbi Louis M. Levitsky, *Newark, N. J., President, Rabbinical Assembly of America*
Rabbi Ferdinand M. Isserman, *St. Louis, Mo., Chairman, Commission on Justice and Peace of Central Conference of American Rabbis*
Rabbi Joseph Zeitlin, *New York City, Chairman, Social Justice Commission of Rabbinical Assembly of America*
Louis J. Moss, *Brooklyn, N. Y., President, United Synagogue of America*
Dr. Samuel Nirenstein, *New York City, President, Union of Orthodox Jewish Congregations*
Adolph Rosenberg, *Cincinnati, Ohio, President, Union of American Hebrew Congregations*

397

Mrs. Isidore Freedman, *New York City, President, Women's Branch of Orthodox Jewish Congregations of America*

Mrs. Hugo Hartmann, *Cincinnati, Ohio, President, National Federation of Temple Sisterhoods*

Mrs. Samuel Spiegel, *New York City, President, Women's League of United Synagogue of America*

Rabbi Philip S. Bernstein, *New York City*

Rabbi Barnett R. Brickner, *Cleveland, Ohio*

Rabbi Henry Cohen, *Galveston, Texas*

Rabbi Norman Gerstenfeld, *Washington, D. C.*

Rabbi B. Benedict Glazer, *Detroit, Michigan*

Rabbi Samuel H. Goldenson, *New York City*

Rabbi Solomon Goldman, *Chicago, Ill.*

Rabbi Herbert S. Goldstein, *New York City*

Rabbi Julius Gordon, *University City, Mo.*

Rabbi Simon Greenberg, *Philadelphia, Pa.*

Rabbi James G. Heller, *Cincinnati, Ohio*

Rabbi Leo Jung, *New York City*

Prof. Mordecai M. Kaplan, *New York City*

Rabbi C. E. Hillel Kauvar, *Denver, Colo.*

Rabbi Jacob Kohn, *Los Angeles, Calif.*

Rabbi Isaac Landman, *Brooklyn, N. Y.*

Rabbi B. L. Levinthal, *Philadelphia, Pa.*

Rabbi Israel H. Levinthal, *Brooklyn, N. Y.*

Rabbi Felix A. Levy, *Chicago, Ill.*

Rabbi Morris Goldstein, *San Francisco, Calif.*

Rabbi Joshua Loth Liebman, *Boston, Mass.*

Rabbi Joseph H. Lookstein, *New York City*

Rabbi Edgar Magnin, *Los Angeles, Calif.*

Rabbi Louis L. Mann, *Chicago, Ill.*

Rabbi Abraham A. Neuman, *Philadelphia, Pa.*

Rabbi David De Sola Pool, *New York City*

Rabbi Irving F. Reichert, *San Francisco, Calif.*

Rabbi Herman N. Rubenovitz, *Boston, Mass.*

Rabbi Abba Hillel Silver, *Cleveland, Ohio*

Rabbi Milton Steinberg, *New York City*

Rabbi Jonah B. Wise, *New York City*

We present for the consideration of all men of good will the foregoing postulates of a just peace as embodying principles of the moral law and their prime applications to world problems of our day. To our mind they express the minimum requirements of a peace which Christians can endorse as fair to all men. They are the foundation on which Catholics in a free world can work from deep motives of Christian justice and charity for the building of a better social order.

Appendix

Most Rev. Edward Mooney, *Archbishop of Detroit, Chairman, Administrative Board, National Catholic Welfare Conference*
Most Rev. Samuel Alphonsus Stritch, *Archbishop of Chicago, Vice-Chairman, Administrative Board, N.C.W.C., Chairman, Bishops' Committee on the Pope's Peace Points*
Most Rev. Karl J. Alter, *Bishop of Toledo, Chairman, Social Action Department, N.C.W.C., Honorary President, Catholic Association for International Peace*
Most Rev. Edwin Vincent Byrne, *Archbishop of Santa Fe*
Most Rev. John J. Cantwell, *Archbishop of Los Angeles*
Most Rev. Michael J. Curley, *Archbishop of Baltimore and Washington*
Most Rev. Edward D. Howard, *Archbishop of Portland, Oregon*
Most Rev. Robert E. Lucey, *Archbishop of San Antonio*
Most Rev. John T. McNicholas, O.P., *Archbishop of Cincinnati*
Most Rev. John J. Mitty, *Archbishop of San Francisco*
Most Rev. Joseph F. Rummel, *Archbishop of New Orleans*
Most Rev. Constantine Bohachevsky, *Bishop of Ukrainian Greek Catholic Diocese, Philadelphia*
Most Rev. John A. Duffy, *Bishop of Buffalo, New York*
Most Rev. John M. Gannon, *Bishop of Erie, Pa.*
Most Rev. Richard O. Gerow, *Bishop of Natchez, Miss.*
Most Rev. Charles Hubert Le Blond, *Bishop of St. Joseph, Mo.*
Most Rev. Aloisius J. Muench, *Bishop of Fargo, N. D.*
Most Rev. John F. Noll, *Bishop of Fort Wayne, Indiana*
Most Rev. Edwin V. O'Hara, *Bishop of Kansas City, Mo.*
Most Rev. John B. Peterson, *Bishop of Manchester, N. H.*
Most Rev. James H. Ryan, *Bishop of Omaha, Nebraska*
Most Rev. Basil Takach, *Bishop (Greek Rite), Diocese of Pittsburgh*
Most Rev. Emmet M. Walsh, *Bishop of Charleston, S. C.*
Most Rev. Francis J. Haas, *Bishop-elect of Grand Rapids, Michigan*
Rev. Edward A. Conway, S.J., *Denver, Colo., Regis College*
Rev. John F. Cronin, S.S., *Baltimore, Md., St. Mary's Seminary*
Rev. Hugh A. Donohue, *San Francisco, Calif.*
Rev. Vincent C. Donovan, O.P., *New York City*
Rev. Cyprian Emanuel, O.F.M., *St Louis, Md., Franciscan Monastery*
Rt. Rev. Msgr. Reynold Hillenbrand, *Mundelein, Ill., Rector, Mundelein Seminary*
Rt. Rev. Msgr. George Johnson, *Washington, D. C., Director, Department of Education, N.C.W.C.*
Rev. John La Farge, S.J., *New York City, Executive Editor*, America
Rev. Daniel A. Lord, S.J., *St. Louis, Mo., Editor*, The Queen's Work
Rt. Rev. Msgr. Patrick J. McCormick, *Washington, D. C., Rector, Catholic University*

399

Rev. J. Hugh O'Donnell, C.S.C., *Notre Dame, Ind., President, Notre Dame University*

Rt. Rev. Msgr. John A. Ryan, *Washington, D. C., Director, Social Action Department, N.C.W.C.*

Rt. Rev. Msgr. Fulton J. Sheen, *Washington, D. C., Catholic University*

Rt. Rev. Msgr. Matthew Smith, *Denver, Colo., Editor,* Denver Catholic Register

Rev. Edward V. Stanford, O.S.A., *Villanova, Pa., President, Villanova College*

Rev. Paul F. Tanner, *Washington, D. C., Director, Youth Department, N.C.W.C.*

Mrs. Robert A. Angelo, *York, Pa., President, National Council of Catholic Women*

Frederick P. Kenkel, *St. Louis, Mo., Director, Central Bureau, Catholic Central Verein*

Francis P. Matthews, *Omaha, Nebr., Supreme Knight, Knights of Columbus*

Francis E. McMahon, *Notre Dame, Ind., President, Catholic Association for International Peace*

Charles P. O'Donnell, *Washington, D. C., Chairman, Post-War World Committee, Catholic Association for International Peace*

Wilbert J. O'Neill, *Cleveland, Ohio, President, National Council of Catholic Men*

Harold A. Stevens, *New York City, President, Catholic Inter-racial Council*

OCTOBER 7, 1943

# Index

*Ad Petri cathedram,* 299–301
Africa, problems of association with Europe, 293–94
Aggression, condemnation of wars of, 125–27; problems of neutral nations and, 170–71; as a crime of war, 199–200
Agriculture, and human society, 265–69; *see also* Food, Supply of; Land, Problems of.
Aid to underdeveloped areas. See Economic aid.
*Allorchè fummo,* 9
*Allo strazio,* 278–81
Anti-Communism. *See* Communism.
Anti-Semitism, condemnation of treatment of Jews, 333
Anxiety. *See* Fear.
Apostolate, Lay, collaboration of laity with priesthood, 90–91; and gigantic tasks of era, 89–90; invited to combat Communism, 65–66; obligation of, to study and act on papal teachings, ix–x
Aquinas, Saint Thomas. *See* Thomas Aquinas, Saint.
Arbitration, International, and peace proposal of Benedict XV, 10–11; principle of, approved by Holy See, 4
Armaments, contrast of preparedness and pacifism, 167–68; control of, *see* Disarmament.
Atheism, cause of postwar strife, 25–26; duties of a Christian state against, 68–69; the need for an awakening against, 160–62; as a war against believers in God, 373; and the war, 104–105
Atlantic Charter, and peace, 146;

recommended with praise, 337–38
Atomic energy, and prayer for peace, 277–78; peaceful uses of, 286–87
Atomic tests, and inspection methods, 285–86; and armament control, 270–71
Atomic warfare, and the role of the doctor, 236–40; the threat of, 234–35; without a final victory, 271–72
Atomic weapons, and armament controls, 269–73
Augustine, Saint, on international relations, 18; on peace, 304
Austria, fate of vanquished nations, 349–50
Authority, appeal to, 81; in a democracy, 122–24; respect for civil and religious, 93–94; 334–35; of state, defined, 233; *see also* God, State.

*Benedetto il natale,* 34–35
*Benignitas et humanitas,* 118–30
Biological warfare, and the role of the doctor, 236–40; the threat of, 234–35
Birth control, respect for laws of life, 318–19
Brotherhood of man, loss of spirit of, 158–60; not based on materialism or relativism, 252; and personal differences among men, 360–61; as solidarity of peoples, 176; and the unity of mankind in biblical teaching, 77–78
Brotherly love. *See* Charity, Love of neighbor.

401

Captive nations. *See* Communism, Persecution.

Cardinals, College of, addressed by Benedict XV, 12–13, 19–20; by Leo XIII, 1–2; by Pius XI, 34–35; by Pius XII, 102–103, 131–40, 141–45, 145–53

*Caritate Christi*, 36, 37, 68

Catholic Action, and the gigantic tasks of the age, 89–90; and invitation to combat Communism, 65–66; *see also* Apostolate, Lay.

Catholic Church, compared to other international institutions, 219–20; and concordat with Germany, 132–33; contribution of, to culture, 315–16; efforts of, for peace, 181–92; as guardian of liberty and human dignity, 128–30; magisterium of, ix–x; and the meaning of liberty, 69; the obligation of, to denounce error, 155; as a principle of unity, 92–93; and relations with non-Catholics, 215–18, 262–63; and right to liberty of action, 91–92; role of, in regeneration, 88–89; sphere of authority of, 93–94; work of, 303–304; work of, by the "Church of Silence," 191–92

Catholics, necessity of unity among, in struggle against Communism, 67; cooperation of, in societies promoting peace, 7; obligations of, to know and act upon encyclicals, ix–x; and peace through the power of love, 263; in war time and duties of charity, 10; and the world, 288–90

Catholic workers. *See* Workers, Catholic.

*C'est une vive satisfaction*, 76

Charity, at the chair of Peter, 299–300; and claims of patriotism, 79–80; as foundation of peace, 1–2; and the message of Christ on peace, 261–63; as a necessary premise of a new order, 102–03; necessity of, in fighting Communism, 56–58; and tranquility of order, 168; treaties among

nations useless without, 13; true, if justice is included, 58–59

Chemical warfare, and the role of the doctor, 236–40; threat of, 234–35

Christ. *See* Jesus Christ.

Christianity, and coexistence, 270; crisis of, 329–35

Christian Workers' Syndicates, French, address of Pius XI to, 71–72

Christmas, messages of, John XXIII, 301–305; Pius XI, 34–35; Pius XII, 99–101, 102–103, 104–108, 108–115, 118–31, 141–45, 145–53, 153–63, 167–72, 172–79, 181–92, 222–34, 240–52, 269–73, 282–86, 295–96

Church, The. *See* Catholic Church.

Church and State, Leo XIII on, 333–34; and problems of conscience, 215–18; relationship of, 185–86; tradition of tolerance, 220–21; spheres of authority, 93–94; stress on non-political nature of decisions of Church, 182–83

Cicero, Marcus Tullius, on morality, 43

*Ci riesce*, 212–22, 255

Citizenship, characteristics proper to, in democracy, 120–21

Civilization, and influence of technological spirit, 227–28

Civilization, Western, and conflict with Russia, 352–53; and heritage of Christianity, 165–67

Civil wars, following world war, horror of, 19–20

Clergy, native, and nationalism, 78–79

*Col cuore aperto*, 269–73

Cold War, neither war nor peace, 346–50; and the errors of man, 302–303; and the meaning and future of co-existence, 24–52; and the necessity of honesty, 156–57

Collective guilt, and culpability, 204–06

*Collegio de Propaganda Fide*, address of Pius XI to, 71

*Come desti dallo squillo*, 276–78

Common Good, of nations and

international welfare, 36–37; and pressure groups, 174–75

Communism, Atheistic, condemnation of, by Pius XI, 45–70; and the conflict with the West, 352–53; failure of, in Russia, 50–51; incompatibility of Marxist, and democracy, 345–46; papal denunciation of, 33; and persecution of the Church in Communist countries, 173–74; present obstacle to peace and freedom, 386–87; Russian and democracy, 347–58; weapons necessary to oppose: moral and spiritual, 54–62, prayer and penance, 62, opposition of the Church, 304–305, total conversion, 388–89; see also Cold War.

Communist propaganda. See Propaganda, Communist.

Compulsory military service. See Conscription.

Conciliation, Church's principles, natural law, 257–62

Concordat with Germany (1933), requested by Germans, 132–33; responsibility for breaking, 38–39

Concordats, purpose of, 221–22

Concupiscence, as cause of contentions, 24

"Congress of Europe," address of Pius XII to, 291–94

Conscience, moral laws and dictates of, 284

Con sempre nuova adunanza, 108–15

Conscription, abolition of compulsory military service, 11–12

Conservation, Soil, 266–67

Con vivo piacere, 21

Crime and criminals. See Punishment; War crimes; Collective guilt.


Democracy, problems of, 118–31; and Russia, 347–48

Dès le début, 10–11

Detachment, as weapon against Communism, 55–56

Dialectical materialism. See Materialism.

Disarmament, and abolition of compulsory military service, 11–12; and control of nuclear weapons, 269–73; and inspection of atomic testing, 285–86; and international conferences, 149; military, not sufficient, 188–89; proposed in peace plan of Benedict XV, 10–11; requires rebirth of mutual trust, 107–108

Discrimination, 362

Dishonesty, in international relations, 154–57

Displaced persons, assistance from US and UN for, 354–55; and world refugee year, 379–84

Distribution of goods, and right to private property, 116–18

Diuturni, 13

Divini Redemptoris, 45–70, 329, 330–31

Doctors. See Physicians.

Dumbarton Oaks Conference, and imperatives of the United Nations, 342–43; statement by the Bishops of the United States on, 336–37

D'une nation lointaine, 98

Duthoit, Eugène, letter of Cardinal Pacelli to, 36–37


Easter, message of Pius XII, 73–74

Ecce ego declinabo, 240–52

Economic aid, necessary for underdeveloped areas, 309–310; obligation of wealthy nations to render to poor, 381–82; a road to peace and freedom, 388; with scientific, technical and financial cooperation, 312–15

Economic problems, and the dignity of man, 368–69; and exaggerated trust in economics, 244–46; obstacles to peace and freedom, 387; and peace, 174–75; and postwar extremes of poverty and wealth, 116–18; among refugees, 169–70; and respect for life, 318–19; solutions of, essential to new order, 106–107; and standards of justice, 309–10; and world government, 179–80

Education, and the dignity of man,

371; in Germany, 39; the responsibility of family and state, 82–83; *see also* Religious education.

*E la quinta volta,* 12

Emigration. *See* Immigration.

Encyclicals, papal. *See* Papal encyclicals.

Eppstein, John, letter of Cardinal Gasparri to, 32

Equality, characteristic of a democracy, 120–21

Estonia, and fate of the Baltic states, 344; protest by Bishops of Russian persecution in, 348–49

Europe, and African problems, 293–94; causes of false peace in, 22–23; and the Christian message, 294; and economic recovery, 159–60; and economic unity, 292; foundations of the unity of, 164–67; and gravity of dangers to present peace, 230; as the heritage of Christian civilization, 165–67; moral foundations of, 164–67; nationalism and the unity of, 247–48; and peaceful mission of the Church in medieval times, 2–3, 17–18; plea for peace in, 74–76; progress toward peace in, 248–49; and reparations by occupation, 29–30; requirements for peace in, 100–101; solidarity of, for peace, 282–83; unity of, 231–32

Europe, Congress of, address to, 291–94

Falsehood. *See* Lying.

Family, and Communist control, 47–48; defense of, 110–11; principles of reconstruction of, 332; rights of the, 82–83; threats to, in technological concept of life, 229–30

Famine. *See* Hunger.

Fatherhood of God, 322; and totalitarianism, 80–81

Fear, and coexistence, 241–42; and national tensions, 73–74

Food, and the campaign against hunger, 151–53, 305–309; supply of, 265–69; uneven balance between land and population in raising, 310–311

Force, cult of, against right, 98; recourse to, 4; right must prevail over, 259–60

Foreign aid. *See* Economic assistance.

Forgiveness, and the example of Our Lord, 14

Freedom, and the Church, 128–30; in a democracy, 120–121; and the dignity of man, 367–68; and peace, 280–81, 384–91; of religion, essential to Christian order, 189–91; the right of the Church to, 91–92

Gasparri, Pietro, Cardinal, interprets letter *Quando nel principio,* 30–32; letter to, from Pius XI, 29–30; letters of: to J. Eppstein, 32, to D. Lloyd George, 11

Germany, ability of, to pay reparations, 30–32; concordat of (1933), 38–39; encyclical of Pius XI to the Bishops of, 38–45; letter of Benedict XV to the Bishops of, 13; Nazi, and peace, 131–40; Nazi, and relations with the Church, 38–45; recommendations for occupation of, 345; religion of, and pantheism, 40–41; and the vanquished nations, 349–50; and the victims of Nazism, 330; *see also* Education, Germany; Religious Education, Germany.

God, authority of, 122–24; pagan denial of, 26; *see also* Fatherhood of God.

Good Samaritan, example of, 16

*Gratum vehementer,* 19–20

*Grazie, venerabili fratelli,* 102–03

Guilt, presupposition of penal justice, 208–09

Hartmann, Felix von, Cardinal, letter of Benedict XV to, 10

Hatred, prelude to future wars, 21

Holy See, impartiality of, 34–35; and the League of Nations, 32

Human body, and the dignity of man, 366

Human nature. See Man.

Human rights, 110, 356–57; and the Church, 128–30; pattern for peace in, 393

Human solidarity. See Brotherhood of man.

Hungary, 349–50; Pius XII on the Revolution in, 278–80; Statement by the Bishops of the United States on the Revolution in, 376–77; vanquished nation of, 349–50

Hunger, campaign against hunger, 305–09; papal efforts to relieve famine, 33

Immigration, attitude of the Christian towards, 379–81; need for legal changes, 382–83

Immortale Dei (1885), 81

Independence, fundamental point for peace, 99

Industrialism, Marxist claims of progress in, 46

In questo giorno di santa, 99–101

Insincerity. See Dishonesty.

Intellectuals, Christian in the world, 288–90

International Congress of Penal Law, Sixth, address of Pius XII to, 196–212

International cooperation, and self-determination, 308; a pattern for peace, 394; scientific, technical and financial, 312–15; strong must aid the weak, 338–39; on a world-wide scale, 319–20; in war ravaged areas for recovery, 148–49

International law, demands good faith and trust, 86–87; founded on Christian public law, 2–3; and the international community, 212–22; necessity of, for peace settlements, 100; penal, 196–212; statements of the Bishops of the United States on, 342–43, 377–78; and strong world court, 339–40

International Movement of Catholic Intellectuals, address of Pius XII to Eleventh session of, 287–91

International organizations, and the Atlantic Charter, 337–38; and the Christian community, 287–91; and the international community, 212–22; and the pattern for peace, 394; plea for unity of, 17; unity of states demanded by nature as basis of, 186–87; see also United Nations, World government, League of Nations.

International relations, Christian and world community in, 287–91; a contradiction of our age in, 282–86; and dangers to peace in, 176–78; necessity of new order founded on moral law in, 105–106; obligations of justice in, 311–14; personal responsibility for, 391; plea for peaceful intentions in, 140; position of the Holy See in, 34; reconciliation in, 253–64; and a world peace, 341–46

Iron curtain countries. See Communism.

Irreligion. See Religion.

Isolationism, prohibited for a Christian, 167–68

Israel. See Palestine.

Italian Study Center for International Reconciliation, address of Pius XII to, 253–64

Jesus Christ, and contribution of the Church to peace, 183–84; example of, in forgiveness, 14; message of, on peace, 261–63; and the myth of race and blood, 41; and the path to peace, 26–27

Jews, approval of pattern for peace by leaders of, 397; see also Anti-Semitism.

Jordan. See Palestine.

Joseph, Saint, patron against Communism, 70

Journalists, duties of, 16

Justice, as foundation of peace, 1–2; as a necessary premise of a new order, 102–103; obligations of, to recognize the moral order, 320–21; requires negotiations, not war, 75–76; true charity includes, 58–59

Kindness, example of Our Lord, 15

Labor, dignity and prerogatives of, 111–12; papal teachings opposed to Communism, 53–54; *see also* Work.
*La festivita natalizà*, 153–64
Land, social and economic factors in problems of, 267–68; lack of proportion in population and in, 310–11
Latvia, fate of the Baltic states, 344; protest by Bishops of Russian oppression in, 348–49
Law, necessity of rehabilitation in juridical foundations of, 113; *see also* Natural law, International law, Trial law, Immigration laws, Penal law.
Law of nations. *See* International law.
Law, penal, International, 196–212
Lay apostolate. *See* Apostolate, Lay.
League of Nations, and the Holy See, 32; the peace of the Middle Ages and the, 28
Leger, Nicolas, address of Pius XII to, 98
*Leva Jerusalem*, 295–96
*Levate capite vestra* (1952), 365
Liberty. *See* Freedom.
Liberty of religion. *See* Freedom, of religion.
*L'inesauribile mistero*, 282–86
Lithuania, fate of the Baltic states, 344; protest by the Bishops of the United States against Russian oppression in, 348–49
Lloyd George, David, letter of Cardinal Gasparri to, 11–12
Love. *See* Charity.
Luxury, and Communism, 57
Lying, in international discourses, 154–57

Man, dignity of, 364–72; nature and rights of, 51–52; and peace, 351–57; technology and the dignity of, 228–29; unity of, in biblical teaching, 77–78; *see also* Human rights.
Marriage, and the family under Communism, 47–48
Marxism. *See* Communism.
Mary, Blessed Virgin, prayer to, for peace, 327–28
*Mater et magister*, ix–x, 308–22, 327
Materialism, and the dignity of man, 366; and the gravity of the present hour, 230; and national power as supreme law of, 5; no answer to Communism, 390; no peace in, 274–76; and peace, 35; and relativism, false doctrines of, 252; in theory and in practice, 46–47; and the "technological spirit" as opposed to the dignity of man, 225–27
*Maitrisse croissante La*, 286–87
Matushita, Masatoshi, diplomatic note of Pius XII to, 286–87
Mediation, International, approved by Holy See, 4
Medicine, role of, in ABC warfare, 236–40
Middle Ages, ideal of peace, 28
Might. *See* Force.
Migration. *See* Immigration.
Military Service, Compulsory. *See* Conscription.
Minorities, pattern for peace, 393
*Missioni e il nazionalismo Le*, 71
*Mit brennender Sorge*, 38–45, 134, 329, 330
Monarchy, and democracy, 119
Montini, Giovanni, Cardinal, letter of, to meeting of *Semaines Sociales* (1953), 192–96
Morality, and the cult of might against right, 98; and the failure to acknowledge moral order, 320–21; moral laws and the dictates of conscience in, 284; and the moral order, 42; as a pattern for peace, 393; and present-day neglect of the norms of, 77; right must prevail over might in, 259–60; and war as the object of the moral order, 243

Muraviev, Michael Nikolaievich, Count, notes of Cardinal Rampolla to, 2–3, 4

National character, contributions of the Church to the development of, 315–16; influence of economic and social factors on, 253–64; respect of the Church for, 78–79

Nationalism, and causes of rebellion, 5; evils of excessive, 77–78; exaggerated, and the threat of war, 71–72; and the natural law in European unity, 249–50; present obstacles to peace in, 386–87; selfish, exaggerated, 36

Nations, Bill of Rights for all, 343; characteristics of democratic, 120–21; and the international community, 212–22; national life and the unity of European, 247–48; obstacles to a community of, 255; a pattern for peace among, 393; unity of, demanded by nature, 186–87

National Socialist Movement (Nazism). See Germany.

Native clergy. See Clergy, Native.

Natural law, and juridical positivism, 207–208; a principle of conciliation, 257–60; recognition of, 43–44; as true bond of unity, 249–50

Nazism. See Germany.

Negli ultimi sei anni, 141–45

Negroes, demands of the Christian conscience towards discrimination against, 358–63

Nell'alba, 104–09

Nicholas I, Saint, Pope, Nicolai primi responsa ad consulta Bulgarorum, 202–203

Nieuwenhuys, Adrian, address of Pius XII to, 76

Non altrimenti, 234–35

Nostis errorem, 1–2

Nostis qua praecipue, 33

Nous apprenons, 297–99, 379

Nous croyons que trés, 196–212, 255

Nuclear energy. See Atomic energy.

Nuclear tests. See Atomic tests.

Nuclear weapons. See Atomic weapons.

Occupation, military, as guarantee of reparations, 29–30

Oppression. See Persecution.

ora grave Un', 74–76, 323

Ownership. See Property.

Pacelli, Eugenio, Cardinal, letter of, to Eugène Duthoit, 36–37

Pacem Dei munus pulcherrimum, 13–18, 323

Pacifism, and preparedness, 167–68

Paganism. See German religion.

Palestine, strife in, 159

Papal encyclicals, and the mission of the Church for peace, 184–85; necessity of study and action based upon, ix–x; urgent and clear, 376

Paroles, les, 274–76

Patriotism, and charity, claims of, 79–80; debased by extreme nationalism, 25; see also Nationalism.

Paul, Saint, Apostle, on persecution, 375; on truth and evil, 324–26

Peace, "Blessed be the peacemaker," 192–96; Catholics and organizations for, 7; and the causes of strife, 301–305; at the chair of Peter, 299–300; and the chastisement of the aggressor, 126–27; and Christian law, 2–3; the Christian will for, 167–72; and co-existence, 240–52; and divine law, 295–96; and faith, 276–78; founded on justice and charity, 1–2; and freedom, 384–91; fundamental points for, 99–101; and the future, 87–88; as the hope of mankind, 375–78; "How can there be peace?" 73–74; influences of reason and passion on, 258–59; through materialism or spiritual life, 34–35; and modern technology, 222–24; the nature and conditions of, 124–25; necessity of a just, 147–49; and negotiations, 153–57; obligations of conferences on, 12; organizations for world, 341–46; plea by Pius XII for, 74–76; points for the attainment of, 145–53; and preventive pacification, 272–73; and revisions of treaties, 150; Saint Thomas on, 27–28

Penal law. *See* Law, Penal.

Persecution, tyranny of the totalitarian state, 143–44

———, Communist, 372–75; and the Church of Silence, 191–92; and interference with the work of the Church, 173–74; opposition of the Church to, 304–305; revolution of our times in, 45–46

———, Nazi, attacks upon Church, 133–38; condemnation of Jews, 333; victims of, 330

Perseverance, message from Bethlehem, 150–51

*Pervenuti*, 5

Physicians, and ABC warfare, 238

Poland, letter of Pius X to the Bishops of, 7; solution of the Polish question, 343–44; statement of the Bishops of the United States against Russian oppression in, 348–49

Political problems, and world government, 179–80

Politics, and the Church, 182–83; and religious co-existence, 215–18; *see also* Church and State.

*Poloniae populum*, 7

Poor, pastoral work among, 63–64

*Il popolo, che abitava*, 222–34

Popular government. *See* Democracy.

Population, increase of, and economic development, 316–19; lack of proportion between land and, 310–11; problems of increases in, 317–18;

Positivism, extreme juridical, 206–07

Prayer, of children hastens peace, 97–98; for peace, 327–28; for peacemakers, 357; and penance

as weapons against Communism, 62; the tranquility of order, 168; for the United Nations, 163

Press, and propaganda, 60–61

Pressure groups, ignoring common good, 174–75

Priests, obligations to study and follow papal teaching, ix–x; pastoral activity of, among poor, 63–64; of Poland and the Nazis, 136–37

Prisoners of war, plea for, 353–54; and political prisoners, 144–45

Private property. *See* Property.

Production (economic). *See* Economic problems.

*Programma, Il*, 253–64

Progress, technological, comes from God, 222–24

Propaganda, in peace and war, 142

———, Communist, distrust of, 61–62; explains spread of Communism, 49–50

Property, and the dignity of man, 368–69; and reconstruction, 332; right to private, 116–18

Protestant leaders, approve pattern for peace, 394

Providence. *See* Fatherhood of God.

Punishment, and collective guilt, 204–206; expiatory, 209–11; and juridical guarantees of penalties, 200–202; of war crimes, 128

*Quadragesimo anno*, 37

*Quando nel principio*, 29–30; interpretation of, 30–32

*Quoniam paschalia sollemnia*, 73–74

Racial problems, and characteristics among men, 360–61; the Christian conscience and discrimination based upon race, 358–63

Racism, the myth of race and blood, 41; summary of Nazi hostility in, 135

*Rassemblés*, 287–91

Realism (politics), coexistence in truth, 250–52

Reconstruction, essential conditions for peace in, 104–108; fundamental values in, 331–32; peace hastened by, 95–97

Refugees, appeal for the plight of, 297–99; assistance by the United Nations and the United States to, 354–55; World Refugee Year, 379–84

Religion, and the community of nations, 256; postwar suffering due to lack of, 25–26; and the Christian spirit in the state, 113–14; see also Spiritual Life.

Religious education, and functions of state, 84–85; in Germany, 44–45

Religious freedom. See Freedom, of religion.

Religion and politics. See Politics, Church and State.

Reparations, necessity of justice and charity in, 30–32; problems of, 29–30; proposals of Benedict XV, 10–11

Rerum Novarum (1891), 331

Responsibility, individual, to study papal teaching, ix–x; in the conduct of international affairs and in the United Nations, 391

Revenge, in the punishment of war criminals, 157–59

Rivedere qui oggi (1899), 184

Rulers, world appeal to, for flexibility in peace treaties, 150; appeal to, for a reestablishment of all things in Christ, 92; appeal to, in testing of frightful weapons of war, 325; gratitude to, for relief funds, 130

Russia, papal efforts to relieve famine, no approval of Communism or socialism, 33; see also Communism.

Russia (Foreign relations). See Cold War.

Sacra propediem, 18

Sacrifice, of comforts, 383–84; necessity of, for peace, 19–20

Satellites, Russian. See Communism, Persecution.

Science, horrors in name of, ABC warfare, 239–40; see also Technology.

Segregation, and the conscience of the Christian, 358–63

Semaine Sociale, letter of Cardinal Pacelli (1932), to, 36–37; letter of Cardinal Montini (1953) to, 192–196

Seminarians, obligation to study and action upon papal teaching, ix–x

Sertum laetitiae (1939), 332

Signori, Giosuè, Abp., letter of Pius XI to, 21

Social justice, in economic life, 59–60; in papal teaching as opposed to Communism, 53–54

Social order, and authority in a democracy, 122–24; and national interdependence, 36–37; and new aspects on modern international crises, 308–22; a pattern for peace, 394; and the renovation of society, 114–15

Social problems, and propaganda, 60–61; and security, 175–76; and world government, 179–80

Social reconstruction, fundamental values in, 331–32

Society, and the dignity of man, 367; and the natural law, 43–44; and the teaching of the Church opposed to Communism, 52–54

Solidarity of peoples. See Brotherhood of man.

Sovereignty, meaning of, 214; new order of, 104–106

Spiritual life, and anti-Communism, 55; and foundation of peace, 187–88; and modern technology, 224–27; value of, must be respected, 314–15

State, Absolutism, 124; according to the Christian spirit of the, 113–14; authority of the, redefined, 233; Communist, 48–49; duties of the Christian, 67–68; function of the, in the modern world, 77–98; internal order in the, 108–15; limits and prerogatives of the, 81–82; rights of the, not absolute, 85; social pantheism of the, 71–72

State and church. *See* Church and state.

Subversion, distrust of Communist tactics, 61–62

*Summi pontificatus*, 77–98, 194, 315–16

Supernaturalism (politics), coexistence in truth, 250–52

Technology, beneficial effects of progress in, 308–309; modern, and peace, 222–34; *see also* Science, Materialism.

Terror. *See* Fear.

Third Order of St. Francis, encyclical on seventh centenary of, 18–19

Thomas Aquinas, Saint, peace of Christ, 27

Toleration, norm of, duty to suppress error, 217–18

Torture, Pope Nicholas I on, 202–203

Totalitarianism, destructive effects of, 80–81; tyranny of, 143–44; *see also* Communism, Nazism.

Treaties, anxiety of war in broken, 74; obligations basic in, 86–87; permanence of, depends on peaceful intentions, 18–19; *see also* Peace.

*Trés sensible*, 178–81

Trial law, and freedom for the defense, 203–04

Truth, above all else, 264; coexistence in, 250–52

*Ubi arcano Dei*, 22–28

Unbelief. *See* Atheism.

Underdeveloped areas, achievements of FAO in, 266; demands of justice and charity for, 309–11; needs of technical and financial assistance to, 311–14

Understanding, demands examination of conscience, 194–95

Unemployment, and the peace, 73–74

Union of Italian Catholic Jurists, address of Pius XII to Fifth Congress of, 212–22

United Nations, authority of, 284–85; Bishops of the United States

state imperatives of, 342–43; charter agreements of, 353; concerted action by, 377; hopes for success of, 169; personal responsibility in the affairs of, 391; an appeal for prayer on behalf of, 163–64; *see also* Dumbarton Oaks Conference (1944).

United Nations Food and Agricultural Organization, address of John XXIII to delegates of, 305–308; address of Pius XII to delegates of, 265–269

United States, and the ideal of freedom, 385–86; and obstacles to peace, 387–88; Pius XII expression of gratitude to, 130; and world economic assistance, 382; for Foreign relations of, *see* Cold War.

Vatican Council, Second, reflections on, 326–27

Vatican State. *See* Holy See.

Vengeance. *See* Revenge.

Violence, morality supplants, 138–39; postwar, 23–24; *see also* Force.

*Voilà une audience*, 71–72

War, of aggression condemned, 125–27; all is lost by, 322–28; and the causes of strife, 301–305; concepts of, 242; as a crime, 199–200; as the heritage of hatred, 9; and the hopes of mankind, 375–78; moral aspects of ABC, 236–40; psychic tensions of, 254; and the renovation of society, 114–15; in self-defense, 170–71; *see also* Atomic warfare, Biological warfare, Chemical warfare, Civil war.

War Crimes, necessity of law in punishment of, 197–200; points for evaluation of seriousness of, 198–99; punishment of, 128; 157–59; rules for trials, 142; *see also* Collective guilt.

War recovery, many are still hungry, 151–53; principles of cooperation in, 148–49

War relief, continuance of, necessary, 356; gratitude of Pius XII for, 130

War reparations. *See* Reparations.

West, The. *See* Civilization, Western.

Will, influence of reason and passion on, 258–59

Work, and the dignity of man, 370–71; papal teaching opposed to Communism on, 53–54; reconstruction through, 332; rightful prerogatives of, 111–12; *see also* Labor.

Workers, Catholic, appeal to, for the apostolate, 66

World cooperation. *See* International cooperation.

World court. *See* International law.

World government, 178–81

World Medical Association, address of Pius XII to Eighth Congress of, 236–40

World Refugee Year (1960), 297–99; 379–84

World War (1914–1918), appeal of Benedict XV, 9, 10–11; effects of, 12, 22–23; *see also* Reparations.

World War (1939–1945), causes of, 73–74; conditions essential to lasting peace, 104–108; fundamental points for peace, 99–101; future peace expectations, 115–16; hopes for tomorrow, 332–33; the hour of darkness, 94–95; intellectual origins of, 336–37; necessary premises of new order, 102–103; the peace of, 351–57; plea to belligerents on conduct of, 76; plea for peace, 74–76; the peaceful settlement of, 87–88; punishment of war criminals of, 157–59; recommendations of Bishops for peace in, 335–40; recovery from, 265–69; results of, 131–40, 145–46, 346–50

Writers, duties of, in war reconstruction, 16

Youth, religious education of, 84–85; spiritual and physical heroism of, in Germany, 44–45